IN THE NORTH OF OUR LIVES

In the North of our lives
Here
where distance wears down hearts full
of the mineral tenderness of the
land of stone forests and cold

We
stubborn underground and together
let fly our rough and rocky cries
to the four winds of the possible future.

> —Robert Dickson
> "In the North of Our Lives"

In the North of Our Lives

A Year in the Wilderness of Northern Canada

CHRISTOPHER NORMENT

Down East Books

Lisa Norment 89

Book design by Janet Patterson
Composition by Typeworks, Belfast, Maine
Printed and bound at Hamilton Printing Co., Renssalaer, N.Y.

5   4   3   2   1

Down East Books
P.O. Box 679, Camden, Maine 04843

Grateful acknowledgment is made to quote from the following works:

"In the North of Our Lives," from *Une bonne trentaine*, by Robert Dickson. Translation by the author. Used by permission of Prise de Parole, Sudbury, Ontario.

Winnie-the-Pooh, by A.A. Milne. Copyright 1926 by E.P. Dutton, renewed 1954 by A.A. Milne. Reprinted by permission of the publisher, E.P. Dutton, a division of Penguin Books USA Inc.

Runes of the North by Sigurd Olson, copyright © 1963 by Sigurd Olson, and *Reflections from the North Country* by Sigurd Olson, copyright © 1976 by Sigurd Olson. Reprinted by permission of Alfred Knopf.

Sometimes a Great Notion, by Ken Kesey, copyright © 1963, 1964 by Ken Kesey. All rights reserved. Reprinted by permission of Viking Penguin, Inc.

Chuang Tsu: Mystic, Moralist, and Social Reformer, by Herbert Giles. Reprinted with permission of AMS Press from the edition of 1972.

Lands Forlorn, by George Douglas. Reprinted by permission of Putnam Publishing Group.

"To Great Slave and Great Bear: P.G. Downes' Journal of Travels North from Ille a la Crosse in 1938," edited by R.H. Cockburn, in *Arctic* 38(3), copyright © 1985 by the Arctic Institute of North America.

Sleeping Island by P.G. Downes, Coward-McCann, New York, 1943.

"The Waking," by Theodore Roethke, copyright © 1953 by Theodore Roethke. Reprinted by permission of Doubleday Publishing Company.

A Biological Investigation of the Thelon Game Sanctuary, by C.H.D. Clarke. National Museums of Canada Bulletin No. 96, 1940.

The Legend of John Hornby by George Whalley. Copyright © 1962 by George Whalley. Reprinted by permission of John Murray, London, and Elizabeth Whalley.

The Barren Ground of Northern Canada, by Warburton Pike. MacMillan, London, 1892.

Tundra, by Farley Mowat, copyright © 1973 by Farley Mowat. Reprinted by permission of Farley Mowat.

"The Dead," from *The Collected Poems of Rupert Brooke*. Reprinted by permission of Dodd, Mead and Company.

"Cold Mountain Poems," in *Riprap, & Cold Mountain Poems*, by Gary Snyder, copyright © 1958, 1959, 1965 by Gary Snyder. Reprinted by permission of Gary Snyder.

Unflinching, by Edgar Christian. Reprinted by permission of John Murray, London.

At Play in the Fields of the Lord, by Peter Matthiessen, copyright © 1965 by Peter Matthiessen. Reprinted by permission of Random House, Inc.

"The Blues Got the World . . .," copyright © 1973 Golden Mountain Music Corp. Words and music by Bruce Cockburn. Taken from the album *Night Vision*. Used by permission.

"Moon Festival," in *One Hundred Poems From the Chinese*, by Kenneth Rexroth, copyright © 1971 by Kenneth Rexroth. Reprinted by permission of New Directions Publishing Corporation.

Shoeless Joe, by W.P. Kinsella. Copyright © 1982 by W.P. Kinsella. Reprinted by permission of Houghton Mifflin Company.

Contents

Preface

THIS IS AN ACCOUNT of fourteen months spent in the wilderness of northern Canada—of a canoe trip from the Yukon to Hudson Bay and a winter of isolation deep within the Barren Grounds, 250 miles from the nearest settlement. In the course of this long journey, which lasted from June 1977 to August 1978, my five companions and I paddled over twenty-two hundred miles. We got soaked, frozen, scared (occasionally), and exhausted; we also had some wonderful times along the way, the types of experiences that come only to those who have immersed themselves in a place or an activity for an extended period.

But why write a book about such a journey in this era of expeditionary superlatives, of oxygenless ascents of Everest, solo dogsled trips to the North Pole, and whitewater raft trips down the Zambezi River? I doubt there was enough derring-do, life-threatening drama, or machismo on the tundra to carry the narrative. We pioneered no new routes; all the rivers and lakes had been paddled before, some many times. Probably no one had put the water systems together in the way that we did, and completed a canoe traverse of the Northwest Territories, but this achievement alone seems almost inconsequential. The logbook at Warden's Grove, our winter camp, records the passage of two canoeists who, some years before our arrival, completed a trip from Liard River, British Columbia, to Baker Lake in one season. They were traveling simply and efficiently—"without expedition," and we, too, probably could have completed our entire journey in a single summer, given the favorable September weather that we had.

So where is the all-out struggle against fierce rivers, bitter cold, and voracious insects? Mostly in other books. What's worth the telling lies elsewhere—in part, along the route of an interior journey that paralleled our travels through the vast northern wilderness. There were many aspects to this quest, but three seem most prominent. First, the duration of the expedition gave us the opportunity to become intimately familiar with the land—to learn about its natural history, the cycles of birth and death, the great dance of the seasons—and strip away some of the barriers that Industrial Man (or is it Post-Industrial Man?) erects between himself and the earth. Second, a group of novices inexperienced in the North envisioned a goal, traveled out into the Barrens, and survived in reasonably good style. Third, six people mostly unknown to each other before the journey began spent more than a year in isolation and emerged still on speaking terms. The lessons that we learned (or failed to learn) about cooperation and communication should have a range of applicability that extends beyond the confines of the journey.

And then there was Cosmos 954, the Russian nuclear satellite that came hurtling out of the sky in January 1978. A small piece of it just happened to land ten miles from our winter camp, and two members of our party just happened to find the wreckage—an insignificant tangle of metal lost in thousands of square miles of snow, but one that spawned an absurd sequence of events. Suddenly our journey became much more than a wilderness trip; the satellite altered the character of our winter and forced us to confront much of what we had sought to escape. The intersection of our lives with the trajectory of Cosmos 954 reads like bad fiction, with an artificial contrivance of plot that strains the reader's credibility; but it did happen, and for us there were many painful implications in the satellite's glowing descent.

But beyond all the other aspects of our story, there is the North and its elemental purity—its aching, brittle beauty. This beauty is based primarily on harshness and emptiness, and thus it lies beyond the realm of society's aesthetic. Yet for a small minority of people it has had an intoxicating, irresistible effect, and has drawn them into a world of cold, isolation, and sometimes death. Whatever the source of this beauty, it came to dominate my thoughts and our lives; it was the context for the journey, and it is the context for this book.

This narrative is chronological, tracing the path of our travels through northern Canada; its structure is a physical journey, set in the arctic wilderness. Yet it is not primarily a day-to-day, mile-by-mile account of our collective experiences. Dates, itineraries, and geography are mentioned, especially during descriptions of our summer travels and the satellite incident, but they often provide no more than a framework for the story. Thus, the reader may find it difficult to determine exactly what we did on November 20, or April 10. Time was not the organizing principle for the expedition, particularly during our stay at Warden's Grove. The days were part of a continuum, and the threads of our lives were interwoven with the flow of time in the Barrens—weeks of quiet existence, punctuated by peaks of beauty, strife, or drama. The severity and cycles of the environmental conditions, and our relationships with one another, dictated much of what we could do and what we had to do. Our lives came to revolve around various themes—the search for a connection with the land, the labor of preparing for winter, self-reliance, friendship and conflict, the harsh vagaries of the weather, and the joys of running sled dogs. Discussions of these and other topics form the basis for much of the book.

Albert Camus wrote that a writer must not express himself solely "by reference to an inner context the reader cannot know." I hope that this account extends beyond that "inner context," even while remaining a personal narrative. I do not speak for the rest of the group, nor am I attempting to present an account of our collective adventures. I think that I have been fair to my companions, and that I have not violated their trust. Yet I know that my story will differ from theirs. Ask six people to describe a single incident and you will get six different stories.

Compound this phenomenon over fourteen months and there is the potential for much disparity. I apologize in advance for any frustration that I may cause other members of the expedition.

It has been so long since the trek ended—ten years—that I sometimes wonder whether my recall is accurate, whether I have exaggerated certain aspects of the trip and ignored others. Did I really feel that strongly? Did the North move me in the way that I remember? Or has my experience been transformed by the winnowing effect of memory into something much greater than it actually was? Hard to tell. But when I leaf through the stained and scribbled pages of my journal, I realize that it *was* the way I remember, that there *was* an intensity of emotion and immersion in the journey. Or I glance at a map and mentally retrace our route, following the blue necklace of lakes and rivers back to Warden's Grove. Then I am transported: back to a gentle bend along the Thelon River, to the smell of woodsmoke and the first breath of spring blowing over the tundra, to the calloused miles of paddling, the weary portages, the patient lines of caribou heading south through the drifting snows. . . .

Acknowledgments

WRITING THIS BOOK HAS been a time-consuming, but mostly straightforward task: sift through several thousand journal pages, read background materials, outline chapters, write, consider the suggestions of readers, and rewrite. This process has been enhanced by the contributions of several people. Particular thanks are due John Mordhorst, who supplied important materials and offered, without solicitation, to let me examine his journal of the expedition. His narrative, which I first read six years after the journey ended, offered a valuable alternate view of many incidents. Other volunteers—Mac Bates, Gwen Norment, Melissa Norment, Ann Vileisis, and Paul Willis—have read and commented on various portions of the manuscript, thereby helping this neophyte writer navigate his way through mangled syntax and awkward prose. Gardner Spungin, of Gardner Press, commented on several chapters and made many helpful suggestions about how to get the manuscript published. Great thanks are also due Karin Womer at Down East Books and Kathy Brandes, my copy editor, for their careful readings of the manuscript and efforts to transform my rough work into a published book.

The above people have vastly improved the quality of this account; however, any inaccuracies, or statements about persons or events that may cause offense, are entirely my responsibility. Finally, thanks to Tilde Hungerford for lettering the maps—a tremendous improvement over my own penmanship.

If the writing was mostly a straightforward process, organizing and undertaking the expedition was not. Although our "Traverse of the Northwest" was modest in size and goals, it still required the combined energies, resources, and time of many individuals, companies, and government agencies to make it a success, and this is an appropriate place to belatedly thank those who assisted us.

I am sure that all members of the expedition would join me in offering a special thanks to Ron Catling, formerly officer-in-charge of the Yellowknife weather station. Ron took an active interest in our endeavor and provided invaluable help with advice about the North, transportation, managing our Yellowknife bank account, ordering supplies, collecting our mail, and a thousand other tasks. In many ways, Ron was the seventh man on our expedition. Thanks are also due his son Roger, who rented us his dog team for the winter; without his pooches, our stay on the Thelon River would have been a far poorer one. Great appreciation is also due to Mrs. Dee Mordhorst, who contributed tremendous amounts of time while typing expedition correspondence and newsletters, assembling our funding proposal, and serving as our financial manager back in the States.

Acknowledgments

None of us was wealthy, and personal savings fell far short of meeting our funding needs. Thus I am tremendously appreciative of the generosity of the following individuals and organizations, whose financial support allowed us to undertake the journey without incurring a large debt: Norman Anderson; the Brentwood School of Duncan, British Columbia; Ann Coste; William DeCoster; Frances and Dave Magee; Minnesota Outward Bound School and its former director, Derek Pritchard; Hollis and Dee Mordhorst; Isabella Morrison; the National Geographic Society; Willits Sawyer; Dr. Gary Soldati; William Salomon; Paddy Stewart; Hank Taft; Dr. Ron Watts; and Charles Wilson. Willits Sawyer was particularly helpful in advising us on fund-raising strategies.

Many companies donated specialized equipment, which helped make the expedition a safe, relatively comfortable one. Special thanks go to Old Town Canoe Company, which supplied three canoes, plus paddles, wet suits, storage bags, and spray covers. Old Town's support, offered through Deane Gray, convinced us that we would be able to organize the expedition. Snow Lion Corporation (now defunct) supplied down parkas; Dacron overpants, sleeping bags, mitts, and booties; and tents. Madden Mountaineering custom-manufactured canoe packs and rainsuits. Two three-person tents were donated by Sierra Designs. Powderhorn Mountaineering supplied 60/40 parkas and Dacron vests. Our ski-touring needs were generously met by Haugen Nordic Products, which contributed skis, boots, poles, and bindings, while Tubbs Vermont supplied snowshoes. Phoenix Products loaned us waterproof storage bags and paddling jackets. Bob Schaumberg of Highland Outfitting donated two Optimus 111-B stoves. Two Sleeping Bag Systems,™ each consisting of a vapor-barrier liner, down-filled inner bag, and Dacron-filled outer bag, were supplied by Camp 7. Uptown Sewing of Jackson, Wyoming, manufactured a tarp to our specifications. The National Geographic Society provided film and processing throughout the journey. Other companies that donated supplies included Black and Sons, Mountain Paraphernalia, W.L. Gore and Associates, Alpine Designs, and Wilderness Experience. Finally, Dr. and Mrs. Jack Fickel, and Dr. and Mrs. Dennis Woods donated the supplies for a very extensive first-aid kit. Several companies and individuals also helped to meet our food and drink needs: Canada Starch Company, Foremost Foods, General Mills, Murchie's, Jack Daniel's Distillery, Celestial Seasonings, and Eleanor Onyon of Jackson, Wyoming.

Several Canadian federal and territorial government agencies also played important roles in the expedition. The Northwest Territories Fish and Wildlife Service allowed us to travel and reside in the Thelon Game Sanctuary, while the Land Use Office of the then Department of Indian and Northern Affairs supplied the necessary land-use permit. The expedition contracted with the Atmospheric Environment Service (A.E.S.) to run a weather station at Warden's Grove; the A.E.S. provided the necessary meteorological equipment and funding for rental of a short-wave radio. A special note of appreciation is due the A.E.S. staff of the Reliance weather station—Mike Greenwood, Bert Meeks, Fern Schultz, and Jim Wells—

whose hospitality helped make our Reliance resupply an enjoyable one. During the "satellite incident," the Department of National Defence, Canadian Nuclear Accident Search Team, and American Nuclear Emergency Search Team assisted us in many ways, and we were treated fairly and courteously by their personnel.

The vast distances of the North, and our resupply needs, meant that transportation was crucial to the expedition's success; La Ronge Aviation and Northern Transportation Company met our needs in this area with professional competence. Dave Swedlow provided a very helpful service when he volunteered to return our rented truck to Seattle from Dawson Creek. Thanks are also due to Keith Argo and Chris Brunning, managers of the Hudson's Bay Company posts in Fort Simpson and Chesterfield Inlet, respectively, who helped with our transportation arrangements. Chris was also kind enough to open his house to us at the end of the journey.

Several individuals provided valuable information on the Thelon River prior to our departure for the North: Ernie Kuyt of the Canadian Wildlife Service; Dr. David R. Gray of the National Museums of Canada; Dr. Katherine L. Bell of the University of Nevada, Las Vegas; and Mabel Braathen of Travel Arctic. Other individuals who provided various forms of encouragement and assistance included Quisty and Willard Anderson, Alistair McArthur, Joseph Nold, Bob Pieh, Willi Unsoeld, and Betsy Wainwright.

Our journey would have been far less enjoyable and memorable were it not for the hospitality and generosity of the residents of the Northwest Territories. Wherever we traveled, we found people who were eager to talk and listen, willing to open their homes to us, and ready to help us in any way possible. Rather than risk omitting anyone, I will simply say, "Thanks to you all!"

Back in the States, Tom and Susan Duffield allowed us to invade their Seattle home for two weeks while we prepared to leave for the North. They tolerated a tremendous confusion of people and supplies, and endured everything short of outright eviction with remarkably good humor.

I have left the most important people until the end. Kurt, John, Robert, Gary, and Mike: thanks for you companionship, thanks for sharing your personal journeys with me, and thanks for the effort that you poured into the expedition. I imagine that we all have our regrets about our traverse of the Northwest Territories, and if given the opportunity, we would no doubt choose to do some things differently. But, all things considered, I believe that we did a pretty good job. And Bruce and Owen—thanks for your humor, your help with logistics, your financial contributions, your long hours in the *Yukon Rose*, and for paddling with us from Fort Simpson to Reliance. You were entrusted with important but unglamorous tasks, and you did them well.

Finally, I would like to thank my wife, Melissa, for her support, and for tolerating my erratic schedule and long absences during the writing of this book. This one's for her.

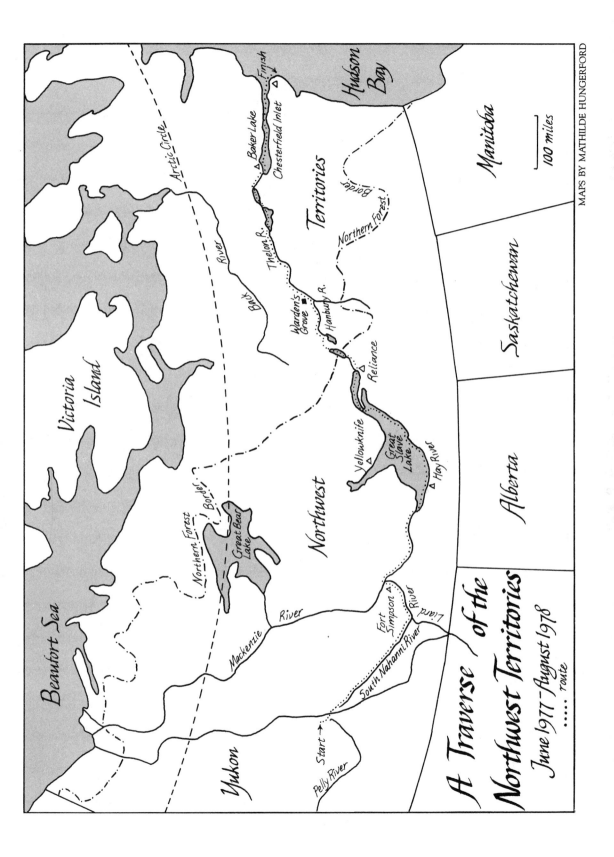

Beaufort Sea

Victoria Island

Arctic Circle

Northern Forest

Border

Great Bear Lake

Back River

Thelon R.

Warden's Grove

Hanbury R.

Baker Lake

Finish

Chesterfield Inlet

Hudson Bay

Manitoba

Territories

Northern Forest

Border

Saskatchewan

Northwest

Yellowknife

Great Slave Lake

Reliance

Hay River

Alberta

Mackenzie River

Fort Simpson

Liard River

South Nahanni River

Pelly River

Start

Yukon

A Traverse of the Northwest Territories
June 1977 – August 1978
...... route

100 miles

MAPS BY MATHILDE HUNGERFORD

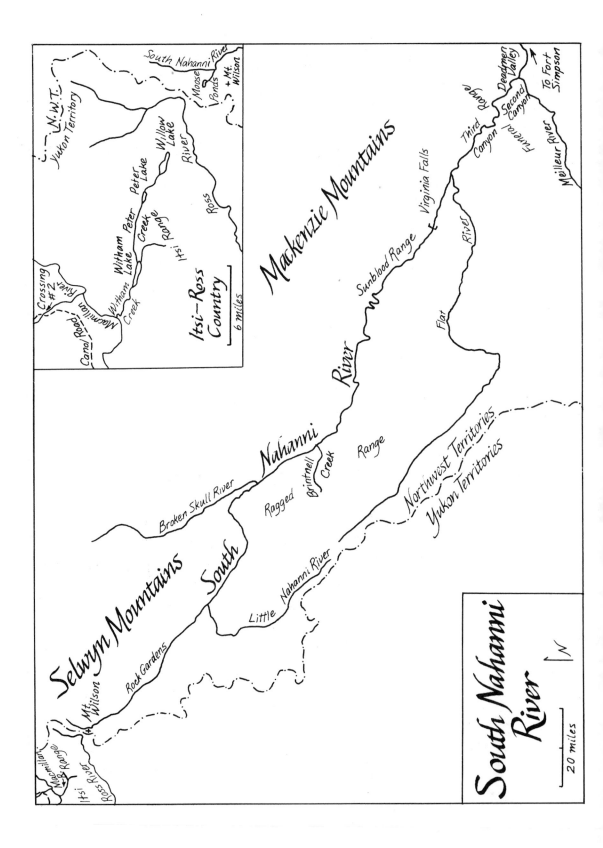

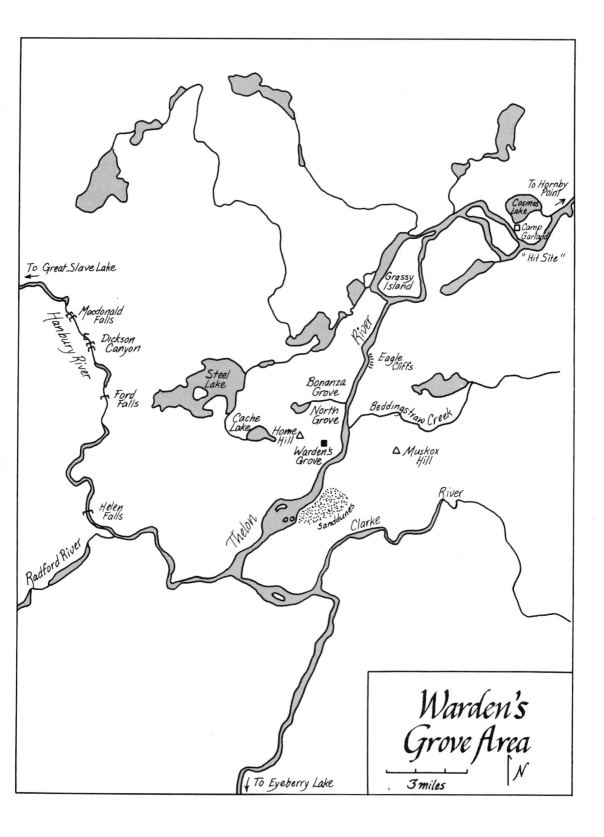

To Hornby Point →

Cosmos Lake

Camp Garland

"Hit Site"

← To Great Slave Lake

Grassy Island

Hanbury River

Macdonald Falls

Dickson Canyon

River

Eagle Cliffs

Ford Falls

Steel Lake

Bonanza Grove

North Grove

Beddingstraw Creek

Cache Lake

Home Hill

Warden's Grove

Muskox Hill

Helen Falls

River

Thelon

Sanddunes

Clarke

Radford River

↓ To Eyeberry Lake

Warden's Grove Area

3 miles

N

CHAPTER ONE
Beginnings

"We are all going on an Expedition," said Christopher Robin, as he got up and brushed himself. "Thank you, Pooh."

"Going on an Expotition?" said Pooh eagerly. "I don't think I've ever been on one of those. Where are we going on this Expotition?"

"Expedition, silly old Bear: It's got an 'x' in it."

"Oh!" said Pooh. "I know." But he didn't really.

"We're going to discover the North Pole."

"Oh!" said Pooh again. "What is the North Pole?" he asked.

"It's just a thing you discover," said Christopher Robin carelessly, not being quite sure himself.

—A.A. Milne, *Winnie-the-Pooh*

OUR JOURNEYS OFTEN BEGIN long before we are aware of movement, long before the first footstep, the first mile of asphalt, the first paddlestroke. What comes before movement is the conscious mental and physical preparation. A decision is made. A route is planned. Equipment is gathered, good-byes are said. These actions, and a thousand more, are part of the journey. What precedes conscious preparation is a subconscious blossoming of desire: "Got to wander, got to cover ground." The soil is tilled, the seedbed laid: You are not happy in a job, school is tedious, a book is read, a relationship turns sour. You are ready, you have already begun to travel, but you are not aware of the motion. And then comes the letter, or the phone call: "We are doing a trip. Can you come?" And your mind is already made up.

And so my journey began, in December 1976, with a letter from Kurt Mitchell, an old friend from college. He told me of an expedition that he had been invited to join—a canoe traverse of the Northwest Territories from the Yukon to Hudson Bay. The journey would involve overwintering in isolation on the Barren

1

Grounds, and would commemorate John Hornby, an Englishman who had wandered over much of the Northwest Territories during the first quarter of the twentieth century and finally starved to death with two companions on the Thelon River in 1927. Then came the question: "Are you interested?" I knew nothing about Hornby, I hadn't met any of the other participants, I had no firsthand knowledge of the North, and fourteen months was a long time to be away. But I was completing a temporary job as a biologist with the National Park Service in Death Valley and was uncomfortable with my decision to start graduate school. I wanted something different, and I'd recently finished reading Vilhjalmur Stefansson's *The Friendly Arctic* and Fred Bruemmer's *The Arctic*. And lodged in my memory was a recollection of a photograph I had found while rummaging through a library. It showed the South Nahanni River in the Northwest Territories, a broad stream winding between massive limestone walls. Some indefinable quality in that photograph haunted me; it drew me toward the North, and toward my decision. So I said that I would go—if Kurt went, and if I was accepted by the expedition.

So I waited for decisions from Kurt and the others. In January 1977 came a phone call from John Mordhorst, one of the trip's organizers: "It looks like there will be room." Kurt committed himself a few weeks later, and suddenly I was contemplating a fourteen-month, two-thousand-mile journey without a clear understanding of why I had become involved. Why should I give myself over to a glorified canoe trip, to the longest and coldest vacation of my life? Why devote the money, time and energy to the North, to the insects, cold, and long, long winter? In order to explain myself to others, I came up with five reasons for my decision: (1) the chance to see the North and experience its beauty; (2) the opportunity to test my mental and physical reserves; (3) the lure of a great adventure; (4) the potential for developing a close relationship with the other members of the expedition through shared experience; (5) and the opportunity to live in the wilderness for an extended period of time. Yet even as I assembled these "reasons," I suspected that most were only rationalizations. For the most part it was a matter of participating in an exciting adventure and casting off into the unknown. Besides, I figured that reasons weren't all that important. What seemed most crucial was that my motives, whatever they were, would be sufficient to see me through to Hudson Bay.

The expedition, christened "A Traverse of the Northwest," originated in the minds of two men: John Mordhorst, an Outward Bound instructor from Illinois, and Robert Common, an Outward Bound instructor and lecturer at Queen's University in Kingston, Ontario. John had heard and read of the Nahanni River and wanted to do a long trip in the North; Robert had become interested in the Thelon River through the story of the Hornby tragedy of 1926–27. From their meetings in the autumn of 1976, John and Robert decided to undertake a year-long canoe trip in the North. The proposed route came from their interests in the Nahanni and Thelon rivers, at opposite ends of the Northwest Territories; the

Mackenzie River and Great Slave Lake provided an obvious link between the two river systems.

The final party consisted of six men: John, Robert, Kurt, Mike Mobley, Gary Anderson, and me—five Americans and one Canadian, all except Gary with extensive wilderness experience. Two Canadians, Bruce Jamieson and Owen Williams, agreed to help with logistics during the first summer and to paddle with us from Fort Simpson on the Mackenzie River to Reliance at the eastern end of Great Slave Lake. John, Robert, Kurt, and Mike were acquainted with each other, at least superficially, through their work at Minnesota Outward Bound. Gary was a friend of John's, while I knew no one except Kurt. We were a group with considerable outdoor skills, but without an interlocking web of friendship.

It would have been preferable if we all had traveled together beforehand in the wilderness. But it was difficult to find six people willing to devote the time and financial resources to the trip, and the composition of the party was in large part contingent upon who was willing to make the commitment. In agreeing to spend fourteen months together in a harsh environment, with little opportunity for privacy, we were risking serious conflict. Many expeditions much shorter than ours have foundered on acrimony, but I had faith that we would be able to live and work together and deal with whatever problems might arise. This conviction was based on my prior wilderness experiences—which had been remarkably free of contention—rather than on an impartial analysis of expeditionary literature, with its many tales of both rational and irrational antagonisms. We could have ended up squabbling over the correct recipe for split-pea soup, or over more serious matters, but I had the rather Panglossian attitude that we would be able to avoid major strife.

Early in the planning, John requested that we assent to his leadership of the expedition. It was a difficult thing to ask of five independent people. I was uncomfortable promising my allegiance to someone I had never met, and my previous wilderness trips had worked well without a leader. Friends would get together for a week or two in the mountains or on a river; we would solve problems and decide issues by consensus. I hoped that this process would work for us, but the seriousness of the trip seemed to demand that someone should assume responsibility for situations requiring an immediate decision. John's role as an initiator and coordinator made him a logical choice, and after working through my misgivings, I agreed. Still, I wondered how John's role would evolve, and whether any of the others were also uneasy with what was apparently a necessary decision.

Thus we began preparations for a June 1977 departure. What needed to be accomplished in six months was overwhelming. Seven-and-one-half man-years of food, specialized clothing and equipment for canoeing and the Barrens winter, funds for transportation, extensive medical supplies, tools, and countless pieces of miscellaneous gear had to be gathered. The permit necessary for overwintering in the Thelon Game Sanctuary had to be obtained from the Canadian federal government, and the five Americans needed visas and medical examinations. The "must-do" list seemed endless. These tasks required hundreds of letters and contacts with individuals, government agencies, and potential donors of supplies and money. The bulk of the organizational tasks fell to John, Kurt, and Robert. John was responsible for much of the equipment procurement and fund-raising, while Robert handled transportation arrangements, liaison with the Canadian government, additional fund-raising, and contact with people who had special expertise in the North. Kurt was responsible for planning and ordering the food and acted as treasurer of our meager funds. I was to help John with equipment and funding, work on medical supplies, and perhaps develop several research projects to be conducted during the trip. Although I had few responsibilities in comparison to John, Robert, and Kurt, the winter days were more than filled by my regular job; writing letters; pursuing leads for equipment, funds, and research; and gathering information about the North.

It was obvious that we would have to embark upon "the selling of an expedition" in order to legitimize our endeavor and convince potential benefactors that we were a worthy charity; we had about fourteen thousand dollars among us, while we estimated total expenditures at forty thousand dollars. Yet I hoped that we would not betray our motives and become enmeshed in the machismo, rhetoric, and self-importance that accompany many adventures to faraway mountains, deserts, rivers, and icebergs. Wilderness-oriented pursuits have become big business and are influenced by the Madison Avenue ethic: "Sure it's good—but will it sell?" In addition, there are now so many expeditions that a plea for support must be exceptional if it is to succeed. Emphasis on the unique aspects of our journey was particularly important when approaching equipment manufacturers. While partially motivated by a sincere desire to assist legitimate expeditions, the "What's in it for us?" attitude was also evident. This concern was understandable; they are in business to make money, and many firms have been disappointed by groups that did not approach them in good faith and fulfill the responsibilities of a sponsor/recipient relationship.

To further our cause, we invested in expedition stationery—complete with calligraphy, a map of our route, and a scene depicting two voyageurs paddling a birch-bark canoe. John also developed a proposal describing our route, the reasons for making the journey, the individuals involved, and projected costs. The proposal was generally well received; here was proof that the Traverse of the Northwest group, whoever they were, had put some thought into their undertaking and might carry through with it.

Armed with the proposal and the stationery, we began contacting potential donors as well as magazines such as *North/Nord*, *The Beaver*, *Canadian Geographic Journal*, and *National Geographic*. We solicited donations from Snow Lion, North Face, Recreational Equipment, Sierra Designs, Camp 7, Woolrich, Eddie Bauer,

Dartmouth Nordic, Tubbs Vermont, and a multitude of other companies. We approached numerous organizations—Outward Bound, the Gates Foundation, Canada Council, the IBM Foundation, and Molson's Foundation—plus private individuals. Out of these efforts came a series of rejections and an occasional affirmative reply—enough successes to revive sagging spirits and maintain our faith that the necessary funds and equipment ultimately would appear.

During this stage, when we had received few donations and little encouragement, communication among the six of us was crucial. John acted as a clearinghouse, writing newsletters and phoning when important developments occurred. These letters and calls helped maintain my enthusiasm. It seemed that whenever my doubts were greatest, optimistic news arrived from somewhere in North America. We gathered strength from the cheerful energy of others; mutual encouragement gave us faith that the necessary money, equipment, food, and transportation eventually would become available, and that early June would find us canoeing in the Northwest Territories.

In mid-April, with our departure only seven weeks away, everything was still in a desperate state of flux. None of the estimated six thousand pounds of food had been ordered; we had not received permission to overwinter in the Thelon Game Sanctuary; and we lacked the funds to meet our anticipated costs. We had no transportation from our Seattle rendezvous site to the Yukon; supplies for the winter and the following summer also had to be transported to Hay River in the Northwest Territories and placed on a barge bound for Reliance, at the eastern end of Great Slave Lake. Not the least, we still had not assembled as a group and would not do so until late May.

On the positive side, most of the necessary equipment had been promised. An early and exceedingly important break came in February, when Old Town Canoe offered us three seventeen-foot Tripper canoes. These high-volume boats were manufactured from ABS plastic, a tough synthetic laminate, and they were ideal for our needs. Old Town also supplied paddles, spray covers, carrying yokes, wet suits, and waterproof storage bags. This donation was a wonderful encouragement. Snow Lion promised Polarguard parkas, pants, sleeping bags, overmitts, and two A-frame mountain tents. Sierra Designs donated two three-person tents, which we planned to use during our summer travels. Haugen Nordic provided cross country ski equipment, while Tubbs Vermont gave us six pairs of snowshoes. Six large-volume canoe packs were designed and manufactured for us by Madden Mountaineering. In addition, we were promised day packs, tarps, cooking gear, stoves, Dacron vests, and wind parkas. All in all, our equipment requests were generously met, and we received enough gear to satisfy the most ardent equipment fanatic.

In early May I traveled to Jackson, Wyoming, to help Kurt organize the food. It was good to see him; we were close friends, and had climbed and hiked together in the Southwest. He was twenty-seven, bearded, and wiry, and his presence on the trip reassured me for several reasons. First, I knew him fairly well and was confident that we would be compatible. Second, he was about my size and I figured that I would be able to keep up with him. I'd heard that John, Robert, and Gary were big, and I didn't want to be the weakest member of the group, the one who always held back the hard-chargers. Kurt was an Outward Bound instructor and carpenter. At the time, he was pondering his occupation and his relationship with a woman in Jackson; the trip seemed an opportunity for him to work out his problems and come to some decision about his future.

The next three weeks were frantic—filled with phone calls, letters, listmaking, arguments about items in our proposed diet, and financial worries. We faced a seemingly overwhelming task—to order and assemble all the expedition's food in Seattle by the end of the month. Kurt had planned the basic diet, yet a great deal remained to be done. We were initially intimidated by the large quantities of food that we confronted: Did we really need 500 pounds of flour, 350 pounds of peanut butter, and 425 pounds of dried fruit? The days became a cluttered string of rolled oats, margarine, lemonade mix, and curry powder; and my life was reduced to a purgatory of complementary proteins, calories, and pounds-per-person.

As we searched for the best deals, we began to learn the rules of the "expedition planning game." First, we discovered that more than three months are needed for dealing with large corporations. Kurt had sent out letters requesting food donations in March. Many of these had been deposited in corporate circular files, while others had generated negative responses after lapses of several months. We finally resorted to the telephone to press our case, and although we were able to establish contacts, we still had trouble getting answers: "No, Mr. Mitchell, we have not received your letter. What organization do you represent? How many pounds of dried kumquats do you need? One hundred and fifty? I'm sorry, you'll have to talk with Mr. Big in consumer relations."

Unfortunately, Mr. Big was always out and wouldn't return until next Tuesday. When he was finally cornered, he would refer us to Ms. Grosbeak in sales, who referred us to Mrs. Hornswaggle. Kurt was once transferred five times while talking to a large fruit-packing firm in San Francisco. An executive eventually transferred him to the distributor in Seattle, who referred Kurt to a wholesale grocery outfit, since the quantity of fruit we needed didn't justify the hassles involved in dealing with us. The wholesaler also refused to help us; he only dealt in large accounts. Back to square one. We were novices, but we persisted, despite numerous rejections. And along the way there were some successes—peanut butter from Canada Starch, instant milk from Foremost Foods, cake mixes from General Mills, tea from Celestial Seasonings, and even a case of Canadian Club whiskey.

A bearded and cheerful John Mordhorst arrived from the Midwest on May 23, 1977, and we prepared to leave for Seattle. He brought with him enthusiasm, fancy equipment, and tales of last-minute funding possibilities. With his arrival the trip took on an air of immediacy. The Old Town canoes sat on top of his car—I could touch those beauties, run a hand over their smooth sides, and dream of the rivers they would run. It was also encouraging to meet John, one of my five companions for the next year. My initial reaction to him was positive; I sensed that we would get along well and that the leadership matter would work itself out.

That evening I got my first look at the maps of our route. We were excited, jabbering about this lake and that river, discussing details gleaned from our readings.

"Remember this from Patterson's book—Hole-in-the-Wall Lake?"

"Here's where Billy Hoare's cabin is, probably the best overwintering spot on the Thelon."

"We'll follow Hornby's route to the Narrows."

As I searched the contours and coordinates, followed lakes and rivers from their sources toward the sea, I wondered what it would be like up there, removed from the warmth of a snug house, wine, the companionship of women, and the comforts that I took for granted. I thought of an immense space, of a winter with minus 50°F temperatures and brutal winds, of insect hordes and ten months' isolation, and the morbid details of Hornby's death. Was I making too much of all this? Not enough? *Ultima Thule*, the Unknown Land. Spread out a map of North America: it's a long way to the headwaters of the Nahanni River, farther still to Hudson Bay. I realized that the context of my life would change drastically, that another world was only weeks away. I was inspired by the approaching journey, yet also intimidated by what we did not understand about the land, each other, and the nature of our quest.

We left Jackson amid flurries of snow, headed north and west through Yellowstone National Park and into the Madison River Valley. It had been almost five years since I had last seen the valley. It was fall then; the river was low, the cottonwoods and aspens had turned to gold. The valley was filled with clouds, the ridges dusted with the first snow of the season—a land blessed by peace, deserted after the departure of hordes of tourists, passing south to Yellowstone. I had been going east to Minnesota, to a canoe trip in the Boundary Waters and an uncertain future. There were four of us then, an uneasy group, and the tensions had built between us as the miles rolled away.

This time around, it was spring. There was the same quiet, pastoral feeling about the valley, and the river was low after a winter of poor snow. Yet a sense of renewed growth was everywhere—in the red-winged blackbirds that sang from atop cattails, in the bright green cottonwoods that traced the path of the Madison and its tributaries. It was spring and I was off on another canoe trip. But this was a quantum leap, a journey of fourteen months, a watershed in my life. Somehow, the future seemed more positive, the initial group feelings less uneasy than during my last trip through the valley. Rain was falling just as before, but I was heading north instead of east, and I knew that a different sort of journey lay before me.

We set up our Seattle headquarters in a four-room house belonging to Tom and Susan Duffield, friends of John's. This was our combination hotel/office/warehouse/staging area. Within several days, 90 percent of our six thousand pounds of food had arrived, and the house resembled a perfect illustration of the second law of thermodynamics: "All systems tend toward maximum disorder." The place was a chaotic jumble of boxes, sacks, tubs, and more boxes. Piles of food and equipment were in the basement, the living room, and one of the bedrooms: hundred-pound sacks of peas, lentils, and whole-wheat flour; five-gallon tubs of margarine and thirty-pound tubs of honey; boxes of Jell-O, cake mixes, dates, and raisins; five-pound bags of dried fruit; 490 pounds of cheese; three hundred pounds of brown sugar; and more. For two weeks we packaged and repackaged, sorted and re-sorted, listed and counted, marked and labeled, weighed and measured, lived, talked, and slept food. During marathon sessions we divided the food into quantities needed for each resupply, and bagged portions for the first summer's meals. And in our spare time we placed last-minute orders, baked granola in a commercial oven, and ran innumerable errands.

By the end of May, most of the group was in Seattle. Robert and Owen drove down from British Columbia in a fourteen-passenger, red-and-white, 1968 GMC bus—our transportation to the Yukon, purchased with meager expedition funds. I was impressed by Robert—an ex-rugby player with dark curly hair and a massive build who showed up looking quite Scottish in a tweed coat, white shorts, and red knee socks. He seemed very cheerful, bursting with impatient energy, and he played a great harmonica. Gary arrived from Illinois, blond and tan after a winter in Florida. He was twenty-nine, six feet four inches tall, and had a weight lifter's build, but he also had back problems and a lack of wilderness experience that made him a question mark in my mind. Mike flew in from St. Louis at three o'clock one morning, the final member of the canoe party to show. I knew less about him than any of the others—just that he had been working with juvenile delinquents in an Outward Bound adaptive program, that he had vacillated about his participation in the trip, and that he had a job commitment for the following fall. Mike planned to fly out from the Barrens in late August rather than spend the winter, and then rejoin us in the spring. I wondered how this arrangement would work, and whether the rest of us would be set apart by our experiences during the long winter.

We had our first group meeting on May 30. It was a grand feeling finally to assemble and discuss the adventures and problems before us. The expedition had become more palpable, transformed from fanciful vision into impending reality: our own vehicle, our own equipment, the food approaching a state of organization, and now everyone except for Bruce Jamieson together for the first time. We were on a roll!

Our initial face-to-face contacts were crucial, for they were the source of first perceptions about individuals and the group's dynamics. In that first session we discussed our reasons for participating in the expedition, in an attempt to understand something about each other's motivations. Mike talked of recharging his spirit, of "experiencing mutual interdependence and common concern," and of interacting with a group of competent peers instead of the juvenile delinquents with whom he had been working. Robert said that, at age thirty-two, it was "now or never," and that he was attracted by the "particular courage of Edgar Christian." Christian was eighteen years old in 1927, when he starved to death with Hornby and Harold Adlard on the Thelon River. He had left a simple but moving diary as a legacy, and Robert saw the trip as a way to commemorate Christian's struggle and death.

It was the thrill of an adventure, a chance to explore the unknown, and the possibilities for group reliance that appealed to John. Kurt was attracted by the length of the journey and the physical challenges that we would undoubtedly find along the way. He talked of his love of the winter environment, the deliberate tasks that would be necessary to survive, and doing away with the extraneous clutter in his life. Gary said only that it would be a magnificent learning experience. I mentioned that I saw the trip as a wonderful adventure, a once-in-a-lifetime shot for someone who had always felt an attraction to Lewis and Clark; the Traverse of the Northwest was as close as I would probably ever come to a vanished way of life.

Once again I wondered about motives. Would these, expressed and unexpressed, be sufficient to see us through? Did it really matter why were were tearing off into the North, visors drawn and lances leveled, charging vague windmill dreams like pale imitations of Don Quixote? At the time I couldn't decide; later events might suggest an answer, but it was still clear that we were driven by our dreams, following our hearts northward in a romantic quest.

While in Seattle we were subjected to a series of psychological tests designed to provide basic personality inventories for each member of the group; these were to be used in a study of relationships and changes within individuals over the course of the trip. Since few studies of this type had been conducted on groups living in stressful, crowded conditions for extended periods, we were a fertile field for investigation. Dr. Frances Parks, a clinical psychologist and friend of Mike's, became interested in the expedition and came up from San Diego to begin a research project.

Although I was skeptical of attempts to quantify human personality traits and somewhat unwilling to have a stranger poking around in the murky depths of my psyche, I put aside my prejudices and submitted to the tests. And we *were* tested. We took the Minnesota Multiphasic Personality Inventory, the California Personality Inventory, the Briggs-Myers Value Test, the Thematic Aperception Test, and the Strong Vocational Test; we penciled in tiny rectangles, looked at Rorschach inkblots, drew pictures, and were interviewed. As prospective adventurers, we commented on statements such as: "I have never had any black, tarry-looking bowel movements." "I am a special agent of God." "Sexual things disgust me." "I used to play hopscotch." "Most of the time I wish I were dead." "People say vulgar and insulting things about me." I was not sure what connection all of this had with the canoe trip, or if our experiences could be expected to change our responses ("I am not, nor have I ever been, a special agent of God."), but I went along with the probing. The most difficult part was the time involved; it wasn't easy to concentrate on batteries of five-hundred-question tests when confronted by a disorganized mass of food and equipment.

During May, some of our earlier requests for assistance finally produced results. Because of inquiries made to the Atmospheric Environment Service about operating a weather station on the Thelon, we came into contact with Ron Catling, officer-in-charge of the Yellowknife weather station. Ron, whom we came to call "Our Man in the North," was invaluable in both the planning and the execution of our journey. Initially cautious and skeptical, he nevertheless gave great amounts of time and energy to our project. He was very familiar with transportation problems in the North and saved us thousands of dollars in air-charter fees by arranging for side charters from flights already scheduled for Reliance. Through his son Roger, a Barren Grounds trapper, he also arranged for us to rent a dog team, which became an important part of our winter.

Our funding shortage was still severe, but money was flowing into our exhausted coffers. A big break came when we were taken under wing by Willits Sawyer, a professional fund-raiser. His efforts helped raise forty-five hundred dollars from private donors. These funds, combined with a fifteen-hundred-dollar gift from Outward Bound USA and $1,000 from the Brentwood College School in British Columbia, where Robert once taught, ensured that we would have enough money to cover all costs through the fall resupply flights into the Thelon. At this point we were basically home free; even though we might be candidates for debtor's prison upon our return, the major financial obstacles had been overcome.

The Atmospheric Environment Service (A.E.S.) agreed to supply the equipment and training necessary so that we could take meteorological observations while overwintering. In return for our services, we would receive compensation equal to the cost of radio rental, which would be necessary to relay our data to Yellowknife. We had hoped simply to record observations and forward them to the A.E.S. at the conclusion of our journey, but the information would have been of little value without daily reports useful for aviation. We were confronted by a dilemma: accept the presence of a radio or forgo a strong connection to the A.E.S. Practically, it seemed wise to have the radio, as it would legitimize Ron Catling's work on our behalf, and it also would provide a safety margin in the event of a medical emergency. Yet most of us felt that a radio would detract from our feelings of isolation and self-sufficiency. We would be able to contact the "Outside," and neither our intended break with civilization nor our commitment to the Barren Grounds and each other would be complete. We would not experience complete isolation, and because we would always know that evacuation was only twenty-four hours away, the character of our winter and our relation to the environment would be drastically altered. Yet in the end, practical considerations won out and we accepted the radio—but not without ambivalent feelings.

During our last few days in Seattle, we had to resolve innumerable last-minute logistical problems. Would Canadian Customs allow us to take the drugs in our medical kit across the border? If not, what Canadian physician would be willing to prescribe them for us? Would promised but yet-undelivered equipment arrive on time? Not yet accounted for were large-volume, internal-frame packs; overpants, parkas, and outer sleeping bags; rainsuits; and tents. Some equipment companies apparently had systems of organization that rivaled ours for confusion. In one case, we were forgotten entirely—a frustrating discovery one week before departure. In several other instances, we were assured that the needed gear would arrive on time, only to find ourselves leaving Seattle without it and hoping that it would catch up to us somewhere in the North.

Then there was *National Geographic*. We were waiting to hear whether the magazine would sponsor us, a decision that rested with an editorial committee scheduled to meet in May. However, the meeting was postponed for one week, and then another. As a result, we were unsure of our film needs and had to spend hundreds of dollars on what later might be supplied without charge.

It was an insane two weeks. We were victims of a self-inflicted adrenalin trip, living on less than six hours of sleep a night and working sixteen hours a day. But in spite of the external pressures, the push to organize and depart, those two weeks were still a contemplative time for me. Many questions came to mind—about my abilities, about my companions, about the North and the length of the journey. I was going to enter an unknown country, and I wondered.

I also felt separate from others. The distance was greatest between me and those who weren't part of the trip. Some people were concerned, envious, and encouraging. Others were disbelieving, uncomprehending, and critical. I greatly appreciated those who were supportive and ignored the others, but in both cases there was a distance born out of the conflicting emotions and sensations I experienced as the journey drew nearer. I even felt removed from my companions; they were going through similar transitions, but they also had their private concerns. I was isolated, yet I also felt a sense of transcendence and excitement. And although I occasionally longed for the company of close friends or a lover, I was not lonely. I'd said my good-byes more than a month before, and any feelings of loss had vanished in the rush of activity. Crowded into a small house with eight people and working long into every evening, I thought a great deal about what lay ahead. I was happy, and I took strength from the distant panoramas of the Cascade

11

and the Olympic ranges rising beyond the tangled mass of freeways, power lines, and houses of suburban Seattle. I cannot explain why, but those mountains gave me encouragement and resolve when I most needed it.

Finally, on the afternoon of June 6, 1977, we stuffed ten thousand pounds of food, canoes, tents, cooking gear, stove parts, and sleeping bags into and onto the bus and a rental truck and prepared for our departure. Four of us would leave that day, Gary would follow with the truck the next day, and John would fly to Watson Lake in the Yukon after tying up loose ends in Seattle. So it was that late on a warm evening, beneath the glare of street lamps, we said good-bye to the Duffields and began the long drive northward. We passed through the sleepy suburbs of the city and climbed toward Stevens Pass, at the crest of the Cascades. As we crossed the divide, I felt as though we were leaving behind the urban world and six months of preparation and dreaming. Dawn found me at the wheel, too excited to sleep and riding a surge of energy through the Okanagan Valley. Robert and I sang as the others slept; morning broke over the mirrored lakes, tiny orchards, and quiet towns. I was euphoric—headed north, moving in the right direction as meadow-larks sang the day into light.

We cleared Canadian Customs without a hitch and stopped at the Canadian Outward Bound School in Keremeos, where we were to meet Bruce, pick up 350 pounds of peanut butter, and finish organizing the food for the first segment of our trip. We soon discovered that the peanut butter had not been sent, and that we were being charged freight on our twenty-five-foot North canoe—an unanticipated four-hundred-dollar expense. After thirty hours without sleep, it was difficult to consider these last-minute problems. The morning's euphoria vanished, replaced by complete exhaustion. Yet we couldn't stop. We needed to start paddling as soon as possible, and there was still much work to be done before we could leave Keremeos. Every hour or so, I stumbled down to the Similkameen River, which ran by the Outward Bound School, and threw myself into the frigid water; fortified, I would return to work, only to wind down again and have to repeat the immersion. I comforted myself with a simple phrase that I repeated again and again, like a mantra: "Only four more hours and I can sleep . . . only four more hours. . . ." The tasks were finally finished in the late afternoon, and Gary arrived with the truck. So we drove on, through exhaustion, toward the Alaska Highway.

We were a small but colorful convoy—a bright yellow truck topped with an orange tarp, followed by a red-and-white bus crowned with red, yellow, and green canoes. As we drove deeper into British Columbia, past the lakes of the Okanagan Valley, along the Fraser River, and up into a plateau country dissected by gentle valleys, I began to sense the immensity of the North. There was a feeling that the spruce, aspen, and water stretched on into the infinite distance. The days seemed endless, too, with our constant motion illumined by eighteen hours of sunlight. It was as if we were entering a vastness of both time and space, and had crossed the boundary that marked our southern lives.

The people we encountered along the way were friendly and helpful. At Seventy Mile House we met a couple who had lived in the area for sixteen years; they had seen the population grow from twenty-five hundred to eighteen thousand. We talked about their attempt to escape the pressures of urban life in a rural environment, only to find that what they sought was dying under the burden of growth and development. They were sad to see the area change but felt there was little they, or anyone else, could do about it. The woman commented wistfully, "You've got to learn to live next to your fellow man. If only people would be kind to one another."

Outside of Chetwynd, British Columbia, the truck suffered two flat tires. It was evening, but we were able to get them repaired by a mechanic who was willing to work an extra hour. He was a dour, lean fellow, efficient and patient with the task: "Doesn't do any good to get mad at your tools." When we left, we gave him a bottle of whiskey from our supplies by way of thanks. He shook his head as he accepted the gift: "The last time I had one of these, I didn't work for a week. . . ."

On through the rain-soaked Peace River Valley, a place of verdant fields and waving cottonwoods. We put most of our food and equipment into storage in Dawson Creek for later shipment to Hay River. The truck then started back to Seattle, and we headed up the Alaska Highway in our bus, now christened the "Yukon Rose." The pavement disappeared about fifty miles out of Dawson Creek, and soon we were saturated with dust kicked up by passing vehicles. Rattling by ramshackle combination gas station/store/cafes with such names as Toad River, Sikanni Chief, and Liard River, we picked up hitchhikers who seemed bemused by our hyperactivity and silliness. In Watson Lake we met John, who brought with him news from *National Geographic*—they had finally agreed to donate one thousand dollars and supply all of our film in return for first refusal rights on our "story." At Watson Lake we left the Alaska Highway and headed toward the start of the Canol Road, our route to the headwaters of the Macmillan River. We spent the night by the Ross River, sorting gear and food once again, packing and repacking, trying to lighten the loads for the upcoming portages. Out came everything that seemed unnecessary, including some rations. I needed help to get one of the "lightened" food packs on my back, and as I staggered around camp, I wondered how we would ever drag the damned things over the trailless divides between us and the South Nahanni River.

In the morning we began the 110-mile drive up the Canol Road, a relic from World War II. It had been constructed during work on a pipeline meant to transport oil from Norman Wells on the Mackenzie River to Whitehorse (Canol is an acronym for Canadian-American National Oil Line). Built at a cost of $134 million, phenomenal for the times, the pipeline carried very little oil before the end of hostilities rendered it obsolete. Along the road were long lines of wheelless, rusted military trucks, reminders of the conflict of the 1940s. Fortunately, the road was in much better condition than the abandoned vehicles, since mining companies operating in the area kept it maintained.

The road took us over a low divide separating the Ross and Macmillan rivers, and close to the Itsi Range. Since we would have to cross the Itsis, we compared our maps to the terrain, looking for the planned route through the mountains. Finally we arrived at Macmillan River crossing number 2, a small bridge close to a cluster of mining-camp tents. Bruce and Owen helped unload the canoes and carry our packs down to the Macmillan, which was not much of a river, even when swollen with rain; its headwaters were low in volume, rocky, and precipitous. For half an hour we fiddled with the canoes, rigging bow and stern lines (painters), working at the most stable arrangements for our loads, and tying them in. Finally we were set. I looked down the valley, a broad, glaciated trough filled with spruce and backed by the ragged peaks of the Itsis. Curtains of rain broke against the mountains, and our canoes bumped against the banks of the infant river. So here we were: ready to paddle, ready to begin our wilderness year. We said good-bye to Bruce and Owen, and then there was only the river—only the river and the great journey that lay before us like some long-imagined and suddenly realized dream, a dream that would take us into the North of our lives.

CHAPTER TWO
Nahanni

There is a certain something in the air at the beginning of a trip. One is perhaps a little more alive and aware than at any other time during an expedition and, because one is aware, somehow everything stands out in sharper forms and seemingly insignificant things are important.

—Sigurd Olson, *Runes of the North*

WE DIDN'T BEGIN THE journey by pushing out onto a calm lake, with a warm sun on our backs and paddles dipping quietly into the water. The river's condition and the collective level of our rusty whitewater skills suggested that it would be better to line (or lower) the canoes along the bank until the gradient eased. So out came the painters and off we went. A few minutes after starting, I glanced back and saw Bruce and Owen watching us from near the road. I gave a final wave and then we were around the corner and gone, starting the first mile of a twenty-two-hundred-mile journey.

Lining is not necessarily a demanding task; much easier and quicker than portaging, it requires only an ability to communicate with your partner and an understanding of how a canoe behaves when lowered through fast water. If the painters are kept at a proper tautness and angle to the canoe, and the canoe's orientation is parallel to the current, it will slide easily downstream without running into shore or drifting into the main current—theoretically, at least. Other factors, such as eddies, rocks, and thick brush, can complicate the maneuver. On the Macmillan, obstructions along the bank and our unfamiliarity with the technique of lining slowed us down and prevented an easy, rhythmic progression. We ended up wading through waist-deep water, thrashing through a tangled mass of willows, and stumbling over slippery rocks as the canoe either nosed into the bank or veered into midchannel—hard going as branches whipped across our faces or grabbed our ankles and the vegetation forced us into the freezing river.

Then, as I was leaning on a streamside snag and passing the painter from hand to hand, the wood splintered and I tumbled into the river. The canoe drifted broadside into the main current, filled with water, and rolled over. A mad dash ensued, over rocks and through pools, as we swam more than ran to retrieve the line and bring the swamped canoe to shore. After rescuing it, we emptied it of packs and water and surveyed the damage. Gone were an extra paddle and our spray cover, formerly attached by Velcro strips and now gifts to the river spirits. Fortunately, everything else had been lashed in as a precaution against such a catastrophe. The lameness of it all—the first day out, and I had already starred in Episode One of *Bozos in the North:* "The Bozos Line a Canoe." A novice could have done as well. Oh, well. It was a good place to pull the canoe out of the water: the river was getting wilder, the lining harder. Why not dry off and try a portage? Naturally, it turned out to be one of the worst ones of the summer—not long, but through head-high thickets and sloppy sphagnum-moss bogs. I was wearing shorts, and my suspicion that bare legs were not a good idea in the Mackenzie Mountains was confirmed by the abrasions and bruises that sprouted on my shins—scratches on scratches, and what looked like a second kneecap growing where I had made contact with a rock. There was nothing to do except wade on, until I toppled backward into some muck with ninety pounds on my back, my arms waving wildly in the air like an inverted turtle. . . .

We camped a short while later, pitching two tents within a few yards of the river. It was a bit demoralizing to look at my bloody legs and remember my anguish as the canoe rolled over into the silty water—and discouraging to be so tired, to have covered so little distance. "Let's see," I said, "at this rate it will take us four hundred days to reach the Thelon." But after donning dry clothes and drinking a cup of scalding tea, my spirits brightened. Across the way, a spur of the Itsi Range burned gold in the evening light, its dark rock contrasting with parallel snow couloirs. At my feet was the river—noisy, a turbid brown, but now heartening. Our journey had begun. We had made the commitment, and already the Canol Road seemed distant. I sensed that things would work out and tried to forget about the rapids and portages. They would come, but for the moment there was the river, and the clean and distant mountains—and they were enough.

The next day was filled with rapids interspersed between sections of fast, easy water and one quiet stretch. The calm water came soon after we broke camp, a quiet meander through spruce bottomlands rich with the songs of warblers and sparrows. To the south were the Itsis, rough and broken in the morning sun, with one prominent snowfield a symmetrical arc of white ending below an unnamed summit. We stripped off layers of clothes and enjoyed the warm, relaxed paddling. Everyone was in good spirits, and I said to Kurt, "This is how it will be: quiet beauty mixed with scattered bursts of adrenalin." Then it was time to don shirts and life jackets, as a familiar sound rose ahead, at first almost subliminal but slowly growing in volume: the sound of rushing water and the vague rumble of a rapid.

The first whitewater was mostly straightforward—a fortunate thing since none of us had ever canoed together before. Since Kurt had more canoeing experience than I did, he took the stern and became director of our river-running operations, which initially were a curious blend of adroit and dismal technique. Both of us were experienced boaters, yet we weren't familiar with each other's paddling styles—how we communicated with our partner, our aggressiveness in rapids, the kinds of strokes we preferred. So our initial efforts were woefully inconsistent. In one rapid, we would time our strokes well, communicate effectively, and make each maneuver with reasonable precision. In the next we would adopt a contrasting posture of incompetence and struggle to finish what can only be described as an "ugly" run—working at cross-purposes, hitting rocks, missing strokes, and improvising an Alphonse-and-Gaston routine as we went. John and Gary were learning, too, perhaps in an even more intense manner: They flipped three times on the Macmillan, and lost a paddle and their spray cover along the way.

This was not an ideal way to begin our journey, for we expected much more severe whitewater on the upper Nahanni, which was rocky and most likely swollen with spring runoff. The Selwyn Mountains were not the best paddling classroom, and I asked myself why we had not taken a few days to practice before heading north. I supposed that we were too caught up in assembling the myriad pieces of the expedition, and too filled with the longing for movement, to take the necessary time. It would have been a sound decision to do so, yet we were confident enough of our skills: except for Gary, we all had extensive paddling experience. What we lacked was not the proper repertoire of paddlestrokes, but the experience of having worked with our partners. But Kurt and I learned a great deal in those first few miles of rapids; hints of eventual competence began to emerge, and I was confident that we would do well enough on the Nahanni.

After twelve miles we came to Witham Creek, a tributary of the Macmillan entering from the east. There we turned upstream toward the South Nahanni River and camped on a small island a short distance up the creek, where it became an impassable torrent. Here we planned to begin a route that we hoped would take us, via creeks, three lakes, and six miles of portages, to a divide separating the Ross and Macmillan rivers. From there a two-mile portage led down to the Ross; we would have to haul the canoes upriver and cross another pass to gain the Moose

Ponds at the head of the Nahanni drainage. Although most parties canoeing the upper Nahanni fly into the Moose Ponds, we felt that the Itsi-Ross portages would be more in keeping with the spirit of the expedition.

We began portaging in the morning, carrying over rising ground on the north side of the creek, far back from the stream. The initial going was easy—through open stands of scrub birch, with good footing on a carpet of dry lichen. We rose slowly above the Macmillan River, its broad valley lush and green in the morning sun, fleecy cumulus floating here and there, and Mounts Sheldon and Riddell standing isolated to the west. The afternoon thundershowers would come, but the morning was pleasant and it was easy to measure our progress as the expanse of land grew. However, the terrain soon steepened, the brush thickened, and our pace slackened dramatically. We had about 850 pounds of food, equipment, and canoes to portage, and two carries per person were needed to get everything from one point to another. Every mile of progress required three miles of walking. At first, paddling partners worried only about their own packs and canoe, but we were soon working to ensure that all of the gear made it to the next drop point without any-one's having to return for a third load. So we slowly leapfrogged uphill, sweating as flabby muscles tightened under forgotten strains. Robert was already doing yeo-man service, and was obviously the strongest member of the party. He attacked each carry with intensity and good humor, crashing barelegged and bare-chested through the underbrush with a fifty-pound equipment pack balanced atop a hundred-pound food pack.

In the afternoon we picked up a distinct game trail, which took us back to Witham Creek, three miles above camp. The stream's gradient had eased, but it was still too swift to paddle; we crossed the creek, made a short carry, and tracked the canoes upstream to Witham Lake. I ended up in waist-deep water, cold and weary as rain showers broke, in a foul mood but resigned to my fate, as it was the easiest way to get the canoe up the creek. Finally, a horizontal plane of water appeared at eye level—the outlet stream from the lake spilling over a cobble of neatly fitted stones. We paddled halfway down the lake and camped on a narrow promontory jutting out into the water. I was done in, glad that I didn't have to cook, wanting only dinner and a chance to fall into an exhausted sleep.

Yet the camp was one of the most beautiful that we would have on the entire trip; the magic of the spot tempered memories of the day's work and revitalized my spirits. The lake was cupped in a broad bowl, surrounded on three sides by the flanks of the Itsis rising several thousand feet above the water. Bands of spruce flowed down tongues of scree, cutting through twisted strata of red, black, and brown rock on their way toward the lake. To the west were unknown peaks, shining in the evening sun. This was good country, with only game trails for paths, empty and wild. We were only twenty miles out, yet I felt more isolated than I ever had in the wilderness "down south." If it hadn't been for my knowledge of a previous party that had traversed our route, it would have been easy to imagine that we were the first people to travel up Witham Creek. How would this land have felt before there was a Canol Road, before mining concerns brought helicopters north in search of ore? It must have been something—unsurveyed, the courses of rivers no more than hypothetical, dotted lines on maps. Much of that wilderness was gone, vanished in the onslaught of aerial mapping and seismic exploration, but I still could be grateful for what had been left behind.

We shared the lake with common loons, Bonaparte's gulls, scaups, northern phalaropes, and arctic terns. In our fatigue, we erected our tents within twenty feet of a tern nest, and the adults resented the intrusion of six suspected nest predators into their territory. Angry and aggressive, they hovered fifteen feet in the air, with forked tail feathers spread and white translucent wings outstretched, calling in raspy, nasal voices and falling in Stuka-like power dives whenever someone approached their nest. We learned to keep low and wear hats, as one attacker drew blood from Gary's bald pate. As Robert stood by a canoe pack, one tern hovered momentarily, then plopped down on his head, as if to say, "Now, dammit, get out!" But when we settled down around the campfire, the female returned to brood her eggs, and she was still there when we arose the next morning.

It took two more days of difficult going to reach the Ross River. After leaving Witham Lake, we made several tough carries to Peter Lake, camped, tracked up the inlet stream to Willow Lake, and the next day reached the divide separating the river systems. A grand feeling, although it wasn't much of a pass—a boggy meadow only a few feet higher than Willow Lake. But behind us was the valley we had ascended, the elevation that we had won with so much exertion. And in the distance was Mount Wilson—the first view of our lodestone rising three thousand feet above the Moose Ponds, a symmetrical cone that marked the headwaters of the Nahanni and the promised land of a downriver run.

Those were brutal days full of eight-foot-high spruce and willow thickets and knee-deep muck that tenaciously held ankles, feet, and calves in a vacuum grip. Wonderful moments: trying to balance the canoe as I swatted mosquitoes and forced my way through stands of whatever shrub was most handy. Branches lashed at exposed skin, neck and shoulder muscles knotted into iron-like lumps as game trails petered out and the forest closed in. "Looks like clear sailing from here," someone said, "but, unfortunately, we're on foot." Route-finding often involved little finesse and became a simple matter of forcing our way through a latticework of vegetation, searching for the weak points but powering through any obstructions. A crash of branches, a grunt, and a curse; either I was through the barrier or I was tightly wedged in a tangle of spruce, filling the air with the aroma of crushed needles. Often I couldn't see more than twenty feet ahead and wondered where I was supposed to go. I sought comfort by exhausting my vocabulary of four-letter words on the environment and the canoe. Hung up in some blasted thicket, I became even more tired, frustrated, and livid as I cursed my immobility. "Does it hurt more in your back or in the Yukon?" I asked. Hard to say, really. Once I tripped on a root and sprawled headfirst, the canoe landing on top of me. I lay under my comfortable carapace of red plastic and laughed: perhaps it would have been better to remain where I was. But no escape was possible; helping hands soon lifted the canoe and it was back to the grind once again.

On the worst portages, my exhaustion induced a mental and physical separation that made my mind into a detached observer of my stumbling body. On these occasions I was susceptible to one of the worst wilderness mental traps possible—personification of the environment, endowing it with mischievousness and antagonism. The branches and bogs were no longer indifferent, impersonal objects; their mission was to frustrate and obstruct me. Mosquitoes and rain were special agents of this nefarious force, determined to make me miserable and mock my efforts. The environment grinned at me, its biotic and abiotic components united in an invisible cabal that only I could detect. The first warning signs of this paranoia were anger, impatience, and curses directed at particular inanimate objects. This was a good indicator that it was time to camp, lay back, and tackle the work when fresh. Since this wasn't possible, I had to throw off the pack or canoe, take a drink of water, stroll around the woods, and begin seeing the country through which we were bulling our way.

But the immensity of the land and the exhilaration of working deeper into a trackless wilderness counteracted my tiredness. We climbed through an upsweep of rock and snow, with the Macmillan River far below and Mount Wilson drawing closer. The fish-hungry bald eagles perched in snags, and the whistled cries of lesser yellowlegs, scattered over lakeside marshes, caught the spirit of the land and soothed my fatigued body. In the late evenings came protracted sunsets that evolved through endless permutations of red, orange, and purple across the sky. To have seen so much, to have been drawn into a wonderful new world—already the adventure was fantastic. There were moments when the work seemed brutal, and I was discouraged by what lay ahead. Yet a view of my surroundings, or even a glance at the detail underfoot, would revive my spirits.

I recall one particular incident from the final portage to Peter Lake—a one-mile carry that took us through thick spruce and willow, in and out of a laddered creek, and over slippery boulders. It was at the end of a very long day. I was fatigued; the eighty-pound canoe threatened to topple me sideways onto the rocks; I cursed my tiredness. But when I was most exhausted and discouraged, and I desired nothing more than to abandon my burden, I noticed a tiny yellow buttercup and a sprig of heather with pink, bell-like blossoms. Somehow, that momentary flash of beauty invigorated me, and I wondered at how a seemingly insignificant sight could so profoundly penetrate a consciousness dulled by exertion.

We reached the Ross River on the evening of our fifth day out. This was the physical low point of the entire trip for me. I moved through chores in a catatonic stupor, trying to remember when I had last been so played out. After everything was done, I sat by the water, staring at my feet, preoccupied with a slow ritual, one performed in a silence broken only by monosyllabic grunts. Off with one boot. Place forearms on thighs. Stare at the ground for a few minutes. Off with the other boot. More ground gazing. Repeat the process, one foot at a time, until two pairs of wet socks are removed and replaced with dry footwear. From past experience I knew that this ceremony was reserved exclusively for moments of true exhaustion. I thought, "This is really getting to me. Thank God we're almost to the Nahanni. . . . Am I getting in shape or falling apart? Why so fast, why not ease back a little, maybe take a rest day? Well, there are schedules to adhere to, deadlines to make—we need to be in Simpson by July 8." So much for another day in what Gary termed the "Nahanni Death March."

It sounds rather masochistic—the bushes, muskeg, heavy loads, insects, and all. Was it really that bad? Did the others feel the same? Well, many variables are involved in remembrance and experience. Journals and memories tend to record only the most significant events; levels of conditioning and tolerance vary; perceptions change with attitude and pace. But everyone was fatigued by the constant exertion. Veterans of Boundary Waters and Quetico canoeing expeditions said that the individual portages were more difficult than any of the cross-country routes they had encountered. The Itsi-Ross carries totaled perhaps ten miles, and were consistently demanding; except for the lake paddling, there were no easy stretches between the Macmillan and the Moose Ponds. Gary seemed especially worn down—frustrated, negative, and at times cursing the whole undertaking. He feared that his back might go out on him and couldn't carry what he should have been able to manage. His lack of wilderness experience must have played a role in his frustration. He didn't have the skills that the rest of us had, or the reservoir of confidence born out of situations in which we had been soaked, bone-weary, scared, and yet had ultimately succeeded with the tasks that confronted us. The importance of such experience goes far beyond the acquisition of skills; it involves the development of an attitude that facilitates adaptation to demanding situations. This attitude may not manifest itself in stoical indifference; tolerance of discomfort is usually high, but I know many experienced wilderness travelers who may complain in miserable situations. I'm one of them at times—it helps relieve tension. But what develops is an acceptance of whatever may arise, a faith that conditions will get better—if not today, then tomorrow—and the confidence that you have the strength and the ability to follow through with the undertaking. There may be fear and anger, and the canoe may be thrown down in frustration, but you know how your mind and body react, that you will pick it up and trudge on. It's comforting to realize that you have the necessary reserves and patience, that you've been through it all before. Gary didn't have that knowledge, at least not initially, and it hampered him.

Yet this ability to deal with discomfort doesn't say much about questions of value. Why bother putting yourself in exhausting, uncomfortable situations? Answer: because it's all part of the experience, because of the sense of accomplishment that comes after completing a portage or difficult climb, or coming through a storm and into the following calm. Progress is easily measured, there is no wait for intangible rewards—they are there before you, in each foot of elevation gained, each mile traveled. It's partly a case of positive reinforcement, and the dividends of joy that come from a sweeping panorama after the last obstacle has been surmounted. And you can feel the muscles strengthen as civilization recedes; there's a sense of renewed vitality, a celebration of the physical being. Push the body; it will respond by moving toward strength and rhythm. In the Itsis, we were paid in something very precious—the view from the divide, progress traced on our maps, gathering strength and confidence. These rewards were not gained easily, but they did come.

All this is by way of denying that I attach any inherent virtue to suffering, like an austere Protestant. I have no love for pain, self-inflicted or otherwise. Expeditionary accounts are full of masochistic and heroic trials in intimidating environments. Perhaps these are necessary parts of adventure—the chance to measure yourself against adversity, to reach a rarely attained goal and celebrate your own abilities. Yet situations when the mind and body are pushed to the limit usually occupy only a small part of a trip or a lifetime in the wilderness. There are exceptions: those who always seek the most difficult way, or a trek through brutal terrain. The world needs its Reinhold Messners and Naomi Uemuras, its 5.13 climbs that force men and women to the limits of their skill and endurance, but there's more to it for me. The Itsi-Ross portages were demanding, stressful, and ultimately rewarding, yet they were only one part of the game.

As we worked through the portages, a closer group spirit began to evolve. This process had begun in the early planning stages, but our physical separation had slowed its development. Our camaraderie would always be tenuous, but its existence, however fragile, was due as much to the Itsi-Ross portages as to anything else we experienced. We fed off each other's energies, building a rhythm that carried us toward the Nahanni and the country beyond the Mackenzie Mountains. As the distance between us and the Macmillan increased, so did our cooperation and efficiency. We unconsciously adopted the best system for transporting loads, and there was little need for conversation. It was simply a matter of hoisting a pack or canoe (or helping someone else shoulder his load), carrying it to the drop point, and returning for another carry. A sense of purpose and shared experience pervaded our efforts and urged us on. I was encouraged by the strength and the humor of the others, buoyed up when my spirits were down. And at the end of a portage, there was not only a sense of individual accomplishment, but also of a successful group effort, a synergistic merging of desires. Ken Kesey puts it another way in in his description of loggers working together:

> The three men grew accustomed to one another's abilities and drawbacks. Few words were actually passed between them; they communicated with the unspoken language of labor towards a shared end, becoming more and more an efficient skilled team . . . becoming almost one man, one worker who knew his body and his skill and how to use them without waste or overlap.

Once to the Ross we tracked upriver for four miles, hauling the canoes along grassy cut banks and over gravel riffles, where the water sparkled in the sunlight. Tracking is the reverse of lining—moving upstream instead of down, the same playing in and out of the painters, maneuvering around snags, and maintaining an angle that allows the canoe to slide through the water with the least effort. Kurt and I worked our way along one bank until we encountered an obstruction, then hopped in the canoe and ferried across the river. We always sought the easiest path, and were constantly in and out of the water—trying to avoid outside curves and deep, fast currents that forced the canoe into the bank, searching for gravel bars and inside curves that meant shallow water and easy tracking.

Slosh, slosh, slosh—the tracking line taut over my shoulder, Mount Wilson prominent to the east. White-crowned sparrows sing from the forest margin as the sun drifts in and out of clouds and the afternoon cumuli build. We talk of women, of former lives. Kurt left a lover behind, back in Jackson; he wonders if she'll be waiting for him at the end of the trip, if a letter will be sitting in Fort Simpson. Did he do the right thing in taking off for the North? He dissects his feelings, searching for a realization and wishing for a more immediate way than letters to communicate. "Well, Kurt, that's fifteen months down the line; maybe you'll know then. Right now there's this canoe, these cold feet. . . ." We're alone, the others already around the next bend; it could be just the two of us on the river. There's a nice feeling as the conversation drifts along, silent stretches interspersed with musings and talk of the river. Up ahead, there's a sudden commotion: Mike and Robert are surprised by a cow moose and her calf—the moose swerve and ford the river, crashing through willows and disappearing into the forest. What was all that about? Soon the answer comes galumphing along: a cinnamon-colored grizzly, intent on the chase. Robert and Mike are about to retreat, but the bear stops twenty-five yards away, sniffs the air, and reverses course. Whew! Soon after, we break for lunch and build a fire to warm feet numbed by the icy waters.

In midafternoon we reached a spot where the gradient steepened and the river crashed through a boulder field; here we planned to strike out on a two-mile portage to the Moose Ponds, and here our first argument developed, over whether to portage or to camp. Although the day had been tiring, Kurt, Robert, Mike, and I voted for portaging. We were excited by the proximity of our goal and yearned to slip the canoes into the Nahanni and be done with the uphill slogging. John and Gary wanted to stay put; John was tired, and Gary was worried about his back, afraid to push it much further. In this situation, the majority gave way to the minority. A few angry, petulant words were exchanged—we were frustrated, psyched up for the final push, but with nowhere to go. I saw it as an arbitrary decision on John's part, influenced more by his own tiredness than overall group feelings. It bothered me, but I relented; there wasn't all that much reason to push on and it was better that Gary rest his back. Yet I suspected that an early halt meant the end of any hopes for climbing Mount Wilson. We were prodded by an unspoken need to cover miles, and this force of spirit had little tolerance for a stop at the Moose Ponds, unless we had been able to reach them that day.

Later on in the afternoon Kurt and I hiked up to the divide that separates the Ross and the South Nahanni rivers and the Yukon and the Northwest Territories. We found a well-worn game trail that passed through head-high stands of scrub birch and promised an easy carry. Although we would not take our gear across the divide until the morning, this moment marked my passage from watershed to watershed, and the attainment of our first goal. The pass itself was a broad, barely discernible swell; it was difficult to tell where one drainage ended and the other began. Yet there was a sense here of an absolute crossing, a passage into a new land. At our feet the waters parted, flowing west into the Yukon River and Bering Sea, east into the Mackenzie River. I stood among the birch, looking out over the land: Mount Wilson lay to the south, our route through the Itsi Range off to the southwest. To the west was the drainage of the Ross, bounded by rolling mountains, speckled with snow in a year of early melt. To the east was the Nahanni, an invisible stream flowing into an imagined land, its canyon dropping through parallel ridges that vanished in the hazy distance. A solitary bull moose browsed in a draw leading toward the Moose Ponds, hidden in a depression under Mount Wilson. What a land! An infinite expanse of mountains, endless fields of spruce and birch that stretched toward distant peaks and nameless valleys. I was swallowed by the vastness of the Selwyn Mountains, and I was supremely happy. The last week had been the most demanding, physical one in my life, at times a hated trial. Yet I had survived, and had done reasonably well. The group had coalesced; I felt close to Kurt and the others in spite of our recent disagreement. This was *our* adventure, and it was wonderful.

We broke camp early the next morning and crossed the divide under sun and scattered clouds. The frustration of the previous afternoon evaporated along the trail, and we reached the Moose Ponds by 10:30, less than six full days after leaving the Canol Road. We were happy with our progress and exhilarated by the sight of the Nahanni drainage, as it meant a downstream run for the next five hundred miles. We'd had a difficult time of it, but the crossing had been made.

At the outlet of the Moose Ponds we joined the young Nahanni as it meandered through marshy country, its willow-lined banks no more than fifteen feet apart. The marshes evoked a feeling of great productivity, of abundant life flowering in the first days of summer. Waterfowl dotted backwater channels, unidentified birds sang from thickets, and hidden noises announced the presence of unseen beasts: splash, splash, splosh as something approached the river. Splash, splosh, slosh: much closer! SPLASH, SPLASH! As Kurt stood up in the stern, a cow moose and a calf burst through the willows and came straight for the canoe. They spotted us, froze, and then turned away. The water swirled and eddied soundlessly as we drifted along and enjoyed the luxury of effortless movement—running with gravity, watching the miles go by without eighty pounds on our backs. As Mount Wilson receded into the distance, all of us were ebullient. The three canoes fell into a dance as they quietly passed one another and changed positions, and we began our Nahanni passage.

The next three days were devoted to whitewater: The river, brown and swollen with runoff, became a steep cataract that wound around sharp corners and crashed through field after field of boulders. The Nahanni was in flood, and its rapids were an almost continuous series of Class 2 to Class 4 drops known collectively as the Rock Gardens. Rapid followed rapid in what felt like an unremitting progression; the furious waters, constrained by the narrow banks of the young river, drove toward a more gentle gradient. We had little idea what lay ahead, except that it was bound to be more of the same; each turn seemed to reveal another rapid, often concealed by a curtain of heavy rain. I recall few details about this section of the river. It was impossible to relax, and I saw everything through a fog of water and adrenalin; the velocity of the current was so swift, and the demand for concentration so great, that I rarely had time to survey the surrounding landscape. The need to focus on the river, our small-scale maps, and the heavy clouds that obscured distant landmarks also made it difficult to determine our location. We were unable to evaluate our progress accurately, and I began to imagine that we were running down an endless, rain-soaked tunnel of whitewater. This was true wilderness, without the comfort of a guidebook or the security of a defined end, a wilderness that closed in upon our group and excluded everything beyond the river's banks. Many other parties had run the upper Nahanni, but that swollen torrent represented an unknown country to us.

It was dangerous enough work, and the consequences of a broached canoe or lost gear were so obviously serious that we ran conservatively—almost deviously. Two of the canoes no longer had spray skirts and swamped easily, so we ferried from side to side, sought out slow sections in the midst of fast water, and hung in close to the shore whenever possible. We stopped to reconnoiter the hardest stretches from the shore, but often darted from eddy to eddy, looking ahead from the canoe to judge the difficulty of the next section and the best route. And in the midst of that confusion of rock and water, Kurt and I were still learning. Our paddling was more proficient than on the Macmillan, but it remained erratic; fortunately, we were decent enough when we needed to be. We made the crucial moves, didn't flip, and only swamped once—feeling cold and disgusted afterward, as we braced to prevent the canoe from rolling. Our worst lapses came in the easier sections, when we were sometimes lulled into laziness. Mike and Robert were the best team; they executed well and tackled some difficult routes. In contrast, John and Gary had their troubles, and they spent a lot of time in the water. They ran in third position, and it was not unusual to paddle around a corner, pull into an eddy, and subsequently watch them float by, with foolish grins and here-we-go-again looks on their faces as they clung to the overturned canoe. Gary seemed mystified and intimidated by the whitewater, neither understanding the hydraulics nor paddling aggressively, although he grew more accustomed to it as the days passed. June 21 happened to be his thirtieth birthday, as well as the coldest, wettest, and most difficult day of the Nahanni run. He spent much of the day either in the water or sprawled on slippery rocks, and he remarked, only half facetiously, that it was one of his most unusual birthdays ever, and he hoped that he would survive until his thirty-first. But he and John managed, and they accepted our teasing with good humor. It wasn't long before they decided that there was something wrong with their canoe—Old Town had given them one that just wouldn't stay upright, and they christened it the "Dempster Dumpster," as its color matched the green of the famous trash receptacles.

We lined most rapids that appeared too dangerous to run; we portaged a few in an effort to stay dry. The lining was difficult, as the river was fast, the footing treacherous, and the shallow water choked with boulders. The rocks, covered with a slimy mixture of silt and algae, gave me the uneasy sensation that I was always verging on sprawling headfirst into the river. Kurt and I developed a lining system whereby one of us took the bow line and stuck close to shore, hopping from rock to precarious rock, ready to apply a belay on the canoe if needed. The other person attached himself to the stern, maneuvering it around the outermost obstructions and through narrow passages, easing it over rocks, and using it for flotation when the water became too deep for wading. While draped over the stern, I found that I was able to control the velocity of the canoe by dragging my feet over the bottom of the river and altering the surface area that I presented to the current. This method of lining was not aesthetically pleasing, but it was expedient.

The work was wet and cold; the waves that broke over the bow, the waist- and chest-deep wading, and the heavy intermittent rains contributed to a state of wretched soggification eased only by midday fires and the warmth of camp. My feet were particularly susceptible to the cold, and I often felt as though I were walking on my ankles. Much to our chagrin, water also worked its insidious way into our food through theoretically watertight canoe packs and three layers of plastic bags. Our losses weren't serious, but most of our pasta congealed into mucilaginous lumps of inedible starch. Some grains, freeze-dried vegetables, dried fruit, and desserts were also soaked and we had to spend the better part of one evening drying everything on a rack, checking plastic bags for leaks, and airing the packs. During this operation, the beach resembled a colorful open-air market, with piles of orange carrots and yellow corn contrasting with brown cake mixes and green peas.

All that frigid water! Sometimes I was possessed by visions of faraway desert warmth. Numb-footed, perhaps with a crotch full of cold water, or with rain pouring off my hat and down my back, I would reel off the objects of my desire, voice in cadence with paddlestrokes: "Death Valley! Grand Canyon! Organ Pipe! Canyonlands!" These fulminations had a beneficial effect on my spirits, for I saw the humor in our soggy existence, in what we had voluntarily subjected ourselves to: "Yes, sir, Norment, there must be a bit of the masochist in you; do you really like this stuff?"

As we worked our way downriver, I reflected on the qualities necessary to becoming a good boater. The repertoire of strokes required for canoeing is not extensive: the basic forward stroke, the J-stroke, the pry, the sweep, the draw, and the cross-draw, plus a strong brace to prevent undesired swims. With the possible exception of the J-stroke, there is nothing esoteric about any of these strokes, and it takes no great effort to master them. What takes practice and concentration is developing a sense of timing and value, a feeling for the proper moment and strength of execution. One must nurture an intuitive sense of how the canoe, water, and paddlers interact; understand the meaning of upwellings, eddies, holes, lines of foam, and subtle differences in current and surface texture; and learn which forces can be overpowered and which must be adapted to.

Perhaps the best river runners are Taoists at heart. Taoism considers a person wise if he accommodates himself to the rhythms of the universe. Likewise, a boater is wise if he accommodates himself to the river's flow: He must paddle with the water, not against it. Through practice and sensitivity come an intuitive understanding of the water's way. One important Taoist principle is *wu-wei*, which literally means "not doing." In practice, *wu-wei* means letting things be themselves and not forcing them. This does not imply nonaction; rather, there is an understanding of how to take the path of least resistance and apply one's strength correctly. This principle is embodied in the martial arts of judo and aikido. It is analogous to cutting up a chicken in the best way: Instead of using a dull knife and cutting through the bones, the wise butcher will use a finely honed blade and apply the needed force at the joints. The boater who understands water does not attempt to force his way through rapids, fighting the water and seeking to overcome it. Rather, he applies his strength at the proper moment and in the most efficient way. A light stroke, executed with finesse, will do more to control the craft than any amount of determined but insensitive flailing. The process is explained by Chuang-tzu, a fourth-century B.C. Taoist sage. He tells the story of an old man who fell into a terrible rapid and emerged safely downstream. When asked to explain his survival, the man replied,

> Plunging into the whirl, I come out with the swirl. I accommodate myself to the water, not the water to me. And so I am able to deal with it after this fashion. . . . I was born upon the land. . . . and accommodated myself to dry land. That was my original condition. Growing up with the water, I accommodated myself to the water.

I love the directness of river running. Few things are more satisfying than a good run—or more frustrating than a poor one. There is no one else to blame for your failure, there are no excuses to be made. You succeed or you don't. There is a basic commitment and acceptance of responsibility inherent in whitewater boating: Once you are in position and sliding down the tongue, the only way out is through the rapid. The adrenalin courses through your veins and there comes the exhilaration of being held by the power of the water, of executing a beautiful run. There is little opportunity for conscious thought, for dissecting your actions; there remains only the doing. When you push off into the river, nothing matters except the relationship among craft, flesh, and water.

Kurt and I sit in an eddy, looking downstream toward a rapid; the best route lies close to the opposite shore. We begin our ferry, keeping the bow pointed upstream at an angle of about thirty degrees to the current. We cross the river, paddling in a swift cadence and maintaining our position relative to the eddy we have just abandoned. Time to turn. I lean downstream, give a few quick drawstrokes while Kurt sweeps. A few adjustments and we are in position. We are committed, and there is little to do except wait. The rapid draws closer, and the roar of the whitewater builds. We can't see much of the river below the rapid except for "landmarks" that we must key on—the occasional dance of spray from a wave, or rocks at the head of the drop. Our velocity increases as we glide down the smooth tongue of water. It's an intense moment as we wait to be engulfed by the rapid: The quiet of the inverted **V**, and our inaction, contrast with the surrounding chaos of energy. Senses are heightened, time is suspended, muscles are tensed and ready. "Now!" A few quick strokes, and we swing around a rock and plunge through a series of waves. We take some water over the bow, skirt a hole by drawing strongly, and swing into a sheltering eddy—a counter-draw in the bow, being sure to lean with the opposing upstream flow, and we are safe for the moment. Only a few minutes have passed, but there is no sense of elapsed time. We bail out the water that we have taken in, survey the route ahead, discuss options, and move out into the main current once again.

On June 22 we passed a large stream entering from the north, its milky blue waters mingling with the brown Nahanni silt. The rapids were behind us and we would encounter no more whitewater until below Virginia Falls, some 150 miles downstream—and after ten days on the Itsi-Ross portages and the rapids of the upper Nahanni, we were ready for easier traveling. That evening, after the others were asleep and a light rain had begun to fall, I sat alone by the fire. A double rainbow arched across the Nahanni, shining against a backdrop of gray clouds; to the west the valley that we had descended was filled with a misty, golden haze. It was as though the land were offering a truce, an opportunity to dry off, relax, and devote our energies to something besides the immediacy of the river. I realized that I had been too long without a break, the last month having been devoted solely to getting from one place to another and completing necessary tasks. Now we were beyond the portages and rapids, and I no longer had to put all of my energy into movement and coping with the environment. I began to look around and wonder why we were moving so quickly. What was this urgency that propelled us? We had been pushing until we were too tired for exploration—almost every night had seen us set up camp, fix dinner, and stagger off to bed. Why? At first it had been a matter of ensuring that we would arrive in Fort Simpson by July 9, our scheduled rendezvous date with Bruce and Owen. An experienced party starting at the Moose Ponds and traveling to the Liard had taken four weeks to complete the trip; we had to finish the Itsi-Ross portages and canoe to Fort Simpson in less time. Since we had no idea what conditions would be like, we had needed to push hard during the initial stages of the Nahanni run. And there was also the urge to throw ourselves into movement after so many months of planning. But why now? Why continue at the same pace when it was obvious that we would reach Simpson long before scheduled, perhaps even before July 1?

The next morning, during a discussion about our pace and the need for rest, we decided to take a day off from the river if we could make Brintnell Creek, about seventy miles below our camp, in one paddle—a paddle that took us into another world, into a land that seemed less harsh and forbidding. The narrow, crashing stream gave way to a wider, gentler flow and the country opened up. Our views were no longer confined to the river margin as we paddled into a panorama of distant ranges and broad valleys. The river brushed massive walls of rock, where tongues of talus reached to the water's edge, then curved away through dense forest, into meanders and around islands, past oxbows and backwater channels. Spruce grew larger and poplars appeared—first in small clumps, then in large groves along the river, with new leaves, green as katydids, that caught the slanting light of evening.

Animals became more common; Bonaparte's gulls dove and fed in wheeling flocks; sandpipers flitted from rock to rock along the banks, their flight a stutter of blurred wingbeats. We discovered several sandpiper nests along the gravel shore, shallow cups lined with leaves and dried grass, the mothers fluttering off in broken-winged feints as we approached. Harlequin ducks, red-breasted mergansers, bank swallows, belted kingfishers, and mew gulls, oblivious to the rains, scattered as we paddled by. Moose made a renewed appearance; solitary bulls splashed through shallows, while cows and calves peered from thickets along the shore.

Our canoes came to resemble bits of debris as the river gathered its tributaries together, each swallowed in the growing volume. Creeks poured off mountain flanks, leapt over hundred-foot falls, and entered the river in a rush of foam tumbling over cobbled deltas. Larger streams joined more gently, their imbricated channels pouring meltwater into the Nahanni. Tiny headwater creeks poured into the Nahanni, the Nahanni into the Liard, the Liard into the Mackenzie, the Mackenzie into the Beaufort Sea: a gathering together of the waters. It was easy to follow the gravitational flow, and the miles slipped away.

We reached Brintnell Creek late in the evening, tired after a long, rainy day on the river. A few miles beyond our camp were the granite peaks of the Ragged Range, their spires and snow couloirs curving into the clouds. Massive, water-streaked buttresses rose six thousand feet above the Nahanni, above the tangled brush and charred skeletons of trees from some long-extinguished fire: a Patagonian scene, somber in the stormy light. I was drawn toward the mountains, and the next morning I started out with John and Kurt on a day hike to Glacier Lake, which lay six miles westward, below the highest peaks of the range. But I soon realized that my heart wasn't in the trip. I yearned for the chance to be still, to examine my surroundings in detail, and soon abandoned the pretense of accompanying them. It was time for some aimless wandering, and I spent hours poking around and photographing in the woods.

The forests along the Nahanni were impressive—trackless, impenetrable, dark and dank after weeks of rain. I stooped to gather a handful of litter from the forest floor. I let the needles, moldy alder leaves, and damp humus run through my fingers, and tried to appreciate what the rich, fecund odor of rotting vegetation represented. Plants remove nitrogen-containing compounds from the soil, incorporate them into protein, and part with some of the nitrogen as their leaves fall. Bacteria and fungi, their metabolic fires stoked by carbon compounds in the leaf litter, decompose the protein and return the nitrogen to the soil, where it can be assimilated by other plants. This was a portion of just one cycle among a network of complex, interwoven pathways—the large-scale carbon, nitrogen, oxygen, and water cycles contrasting with the intricate flow of required trace elements such as copper, iron, and cobalt. I imagined the millions of microorganisms in my handful of debris, and the endless cycles of growth and decay founded upon lives that I could not see—lives that, when multiplied an infinite number of times, supported the entire surrounding ecosystem.

I dropped the litter and continued through the forest, compiling a list of inhabitants and events. Towering above me were white spruce, the most important conifer across much of the boreal forest, seventy-five or one hundred feet tall, and occupying the better-drained soils. On wetter sites the white spruce gave way to black spruce, a smaller, more scraggly species. Black spruce is the characteristic tree of muskeg—that swampy bog that covers poorly drained areas of the northern forest region, and is the home of the mosquito and the miserable portage. Along the creek were thickets of mountain alder. Alders are important components of northern forest ecosystems because they often are early colonizers of disturbed sites; their roots contain nodules of nitrogen-fixing bacteria that stimulate the growth of spruce or hemlock, species destined to replace the alder as forest succession proceeds. Above the alder were balsam poplars, their silver-green, deltoid leaves restless in the wind, the female trees shedding silky clouds of feathered seeds. On through the woods I went, stomping noisily through the understory and wondering if there were any grizzlies nearby. Rain began to fall, and shrubby species shed water on my soaking pants as I worked my way along: Labrador tea, highbush cranberry, and wild rose. As the name implies, a brew can be made by boiling the leaves of Labrador tea—but it is a bitter concoction, worse than the rancid tea served in the assembly-line restaurants on the Interstate. Highbush cranberry and the pink-flowered rose were both common, but the most obvious feature of the understory was the sea of horsetails that spread over the forest floor—each stem one or two feet high, with radiating whorls of feathered branches forming a delicate woven carpet of green that softened the woods.

Lower down, among the moss and rotten logs full of fungal mycelia, were flowers whose leaves collected tiny beads of rain: bunchberry, a member of the dogwood family, with clusters of tiny white flowers surrounded by petallike bracts; twinflower; wild onion; and orchids. The latter—lady's slipper, bog-orchid, and ladies' tresses—were inhabitants of dark, wet places and lived off dead and rotting matter, as well as filtered sunlight.

The details of the forest had remained concealed by motion until I took the time to stop and look. It's the same with any form of transportation—car, canoe, or even your own two feet. Unless you are willing to stop and investigate, get down on your hands and knees and crawl around in the muck and dirty your clothes, you won't see much of anything. And the farther away you get from walking, the more your perception comes to resemble that of television. By the time you hop into a car or onto an airplane, you've arrived at a place where everything is experienced through a wall of plastic or glass that separates you from the environment. It's easy to slide into a padded seat, sit back, and let it all happen. The walls may not be as obvious if the glass is removed, but the more subtle partitions may remain. Movement is only part of the game; it can be pleasurable and satisfying in its own right, but it doesn't necessarily lead toward understanding. Other qualities are needed—concern, curiosity, perhaps even love.

Our rest day was a welcome break for most of us, yet it had unexpected consequences that were completely out of proportion to their seeming importance and dogged us for the rest of the journey. The first intimation of a problem surfaced the following morning, when Robert arose to make breakfast at four, two hours earlier than usual. While cooking, he rolled several empty fuel drums around camp, banged pots and pans, and made enough noise to make sleep impossible. Kurt was angry that he had been awakened early and accused Robert of insensitivity. Robert replied, "Yesterday was a rest day. You should have plenty of energy." Not a very tactful response, after John and Kurt had returned at 10:00 P.M. from their all-day bushwhack up Brintnell Creek, but he was burning to get going again after twenty-four hours of rest that he neither wanted nor accepted. What was going on?

Within any expedition, motivations and capabilities vary. Our group was no exception, as our Seattle discussions and performance on the Nahanni had indicated. We had different skill levels and ideas about the nature of the trip and our relation to the land, and these differences were manifested in Robert's frustration. From the beginning, he had more energy, strength, and intensity than anyone else. He carried the heaviest loads, was always willing to press on, and was the first one ready every morning. Robert hoped to complete the Nahanni as quickly as possible and push on to the Barrens. His vision looked east, to the Thelon River; its focus lay at Hornby Point and the huddled ruins of Hornby's cabin. He seemed to regard the Nahanni as a somewhat inconsequential stage in a more important quest. Before we stopped at Brintnell Creek, Robert said, "A rest day is one that could be spent building a cabin." He was committed to the idea of a memorial cabin to Hornby, Christian, and Adlard, and he saw a day off as a threat to his desire for an early arrival on the Thelon. The Mackenzie River, Great Slave Lake, and the Barrens—all were subject to storms that could slow travel, and Robert worried that we would not have sufficient time to prepare for the winter in the manner he envisioned. Robert felt that, through our stop at Brintnell Creek, we had lost our momentum and that the expedition had been jeopardized by what he called our "relaxed pace," and he became bitter, uncommunicative, and restless as we paddled toward the Liard.

While Robert believed that our pace was too slow, Kurt and I believed that we were traveling too quickly—participants in what Kurt termed "the Great Canoe Race Across the Northwest Territories," speeding on so that we could get to Simpson a week early and wait for Bruce and Owen. So what if there was a chance that we would be able to leave Simpson a week earlier than expected? Great Slave Lake and the Barrens would come in due time; we didn't want to chafe over future problems. Despite our rest day, we were making excellent progress. I didn't want the trip to become a headlong rush toward the Thelon, and in the process ignore everything along the way. One thing at a time! Over the next few weeks we battled out the issue—sometimes arguing, more frequently resorting to quiet gestures of defiance. Eventually, we effected a compromise: We paddled less than Robert felt was necessary, and more than Kurt and I felt was reasonable. And, as is true of many compromises, no one was completely satisfied.

Several hours after leaving Brintnell Creek, we entered Nahanni National Park, and more and more terrain features began acquiring names on our maps. Names are symbols of man's presence; they contribute to patterns of association that lend an area a particular feeling and maintain legends. Nahanni names, some behind us, some indications of what was to come: Sombre Mountain, Sunblood Range, Funeral Range, Headless Range, and Twisted Mountain. Broken Skull River, Hell Roaring Creek, Rabbitkettle River, Hole-in-the-Wall Lake, Hell's Gate (a rapid), Cache Rapids. The Splits. Deadmen Valley. Many of these sounded ominous and hinted of dark legends, of corpses and disappearing trappers, of an alien, hostile environment. And what does "Nahanni" mean? R.M. Patterson, in *Dangerous River*, an account of several years spent in the Nahanni country during the 1920s, gives three translations from the original Athapaskan. Two were from early twentieth-century books: "the People of the West"; and "the People over There Far Away." But the one that I preferred came from a resident of the upper Liard: "the People who Speak like Ducks." Somehow it seemed better to be canoeing "the River of the People who Speak like Ducks" than "the River of the People of the West."

About forty miles below Brintnell Creek we encountered the Sunblood Range, which runs parallel to the Nahanni as far as Sunblood Mountain, opposite Virginia Falls. We followed the escarpment for thirty miles, paddling beneath two-thousand-foot cliffs of striated, folded limestone and shale—450-million-year-old orange, pink, and gray sediments stretching down the river. In the late afternoon the current slackened, as though the water were resting and gathering itself for a tremendous leap into space. From downstream came a muted bass rumble—not loud, but with an aura of enveloping power. We had arrived at Virginia Falls, some two hundred miles below the Moose Ponds and three hundred miles above Fort Simpson. Below lay the lower Nahanni, visited more often than the upper stretches and frequented by an occasional jetboat, as there are no serious obstacles to up-stream travel until the 294-foot drop. Now would come the Flat River; First, Second, and Third canyons; and The Splits: familiar names gleaned from books, Albert Faille's country.

Faille may well be more closely associated with the Nahanni country than any other person. A Minnesotan of Swiss descent, he first came to the area in 1927, and he plied the waters of the South Nahanni well into his seventies. He spent more than forty-five years among the mountains and rivers, many of them alone. At first he overwintered on the Nahanni or one of its tributaries, going out to Fort Simpson only for supplies. Later on, he spent summers in the mountains and returned to Simpson in the fall, before freeze-up. He was a prospector and trapper, always looking for the elusive gold that formed the substance of many Nahanni legends. Each year he disappeared into the wilderness, working some new area, searching. Even as a stoop-shouldered old man, he managed to drive a scow up the Nahanni to Virginia Falls, dismantle it, and pack the pieces up a portage trail. At the top he reassembled the boat, threw his outfit aboard, and set off for a summer's prospecting. He never found gold, but he kept returning, as if he were engaged in a private pilgrimage. I can imagine his saying to some skeptic, "Hell, one more year and I'll give it up." Several years would pass and there he'd be, heading up the Liard toward Nahanni Butte on another spring day, and saying to himself, "Now I know where to look—this will be the year I'll find the lode!" Faille, you tenacious old fart, why did you keep on coming back? What motivated you? A prospector's dream? A love of the country and a simple way of life? An inability to cope with society? There had to be some strong force working inside him, pushing him up the river year after year, in a solitude that would destroy most people—forty-five years engaged in a quest few could understand. A few years after his last trip into the Nahanni country, he died in Fort Simpson.

In the natural world certain phenomena overwhelm the senses. Upon seeing one of these for the first time, or after a long absence, you are brought to a standstill by the sheer power of the spectacle, as though the mind cannot process the magnitude of the sensory input—it's so far removed from the normal range and scale of human experience that you have difficulty understanding your perceptions. The Grand Canyon is such a wonder; Virginia Falls is another. I got my first view of the falls in the morning, as we portaged down a well-graded, switchbacking trail with wooden walkways spanning boggy sections. After the Itsi-Ross portages, the trail seemed out of place, and a far cry from Patterson's and Faille's time. As I sauntered down the trail with my first load, I ran headlong into the view, and stopped; the Nahanni spilled over a drop of three hundred feet, a cascading explosion of noise flowing around a buttress of dark gray limestone—forty thousand cubic feet per second of water dividing into two great streams and tumbling into the huge pool below. There was a sense of absolute power about the falls. Here was the perfect illustration of potential versus kinetic energy: the pool of water above, silent, waiting. Then the acceleration through the preliminary cascades; the gathering momentum; the crashing roar as it fell, smashed into rock, leapt into space, and slammed into the pool below.

I imagined the ultimate whitewater run, an immersion in something more than water, in pure energy. There would be the quiet, drifting approach, the fear gathering as the void drew nearer. The canoe would flip as soon as it entered the first waves; then would come a gasping swim through a series of holes and over ledges, followed by complete disorientation as the body was flung about and the senses were overwhelmed by the sound and power of the water. Soon it would be difficult, impossible to breathe. No matter, as air would be inconsequential in that last fall through space and noise and foam—a final arc into oblivion, into a white merging with the water as body and mind were torn asunder. . . .

After depositing my load on a driftwood-covered beach bathed in mist from the falls, I climbed back up the trail and worked my way along the canyon rim until I stood directly above the falls, several hundred feet below. My camera was useless; how could I capture the feeling of the falling water? Too much of it was caught up in the touch of mist upon the skin, in the space below my feet, in the rumbling power of the water. When there is nothing subtle about a natural phenomenon, when it defies the separation into distinct visual units that is an inherent part of the photographic process, the camera cannot bridge the gap between art and experience. There's simply too much difference between what the mind's eye records and what emerges on the emulsion sheet. Virginia Falls did not lend itself to photographic interpretation; one might get a postcard-type photograph, a superficially pleasing image, but it would fail to portray adequately the majesty of the Nahanni.

So I ignored my camera and let my mind wander over the river—but after less than two hours at the falls, John was urging us on. I imagined Robert waiting impatiently below, chafing to continue the paddling. This was the height of my frustration—only two hours at one of the most spectacular places in North America, one that demanded days. We were becoming "Cadillac tourists," like those lost souls who rush from national park to national park in an effort to "do" as many as possible in one vacation, pausing only long enough for a few snapshots: "Let's see, Martha. We've already done Bryce, Cedar Breaks, and Zion today. Maybe we can make the North Rim of the Grand Canyon early tomorrow and the South Rim in the afternoon." Not exactly a fair comparison, as the Cadillac types don't have fifteen hundred miles of paddling and a Barren Grounds winter ahead of them. Still, I wondered what the country meant to the others. Was the Nahanni no more than a highway, and just something to be "done"? Kurt and I were bitter, convinced that the country was slipping away from us—an irretrievable loss. The preceding day we had wanted to scramble up into the Sunblood Range and look out into the vastness of the Mackenzie Mountains. But we had to click off those miles; there was too much momentum, and Robert's seething will, opposing our approach to the river, and we didn't bother to mention our wish.

Mingled with my disappointment about the pace was a disagreement with the way John was handling his position as leader. I felt that he was giving in to Robert's desire to push on and making too many arbitrary decisions regarding such mundane things as campsites and lunch stops. These executive decisions weren't necessary; the group was capable of deciding 99 percent of the issues that arose during a day. We were not clients on a guided trip. We were a group of six individualists, accustomed to being leaders and instructors, not followers.

Yet my resentment was partly a foolish expression of ego. I had definite expectations about the expedition and sometimes became frustrated if events did not go my way. John was in a difficult position. On the one hand, he had Robert, urging a faster pace and angry that he had assented to a rest day. On the other hand, Kurt and I were vocal about slowing down. John was also exploring his role. He had put so much time into the expedition that, to some extent, he had come to see it as "his," rather than "our" trip, and he needed to determine his relationship to the rest of the group. A problem of the ego then, for all of us—to know when to accept authority graciously and when to object, when to surrender to the collective will and when to resist. All of us were "right," given our different goals and expectations, but it was imperative that we all learn to subordinate our own desires to the goal of the expedition—to reach Chesterfield Inlet in the summer of 1978.

As we left Virginia Falls, group cohesiveness was very low. How odd. During the difficult days on the Itsi-Ross portages and the upper Nahanni, we had seemed united in purpose and spirit. Now, with easier traveling, that unity was gone. Why? Most expedition accounts tell of conflicts arising when conditions are most difficult and tensions highest. Perhaps at the outset we hadn't possessed sufficient surplus energy for argument. Perhaps our pace had seemed reasonable to everyone. Only when the blinders of constant movement were removed and we began to ease back did significant differences surface. Then again, on the first portages we were new to each other, still in the initial period of good grace that characterizes human relationships. Whatever the reason, our strained interactions were not encouraging so early in the journey.

On beyond Direction Mountain, Hell's Gate Rapid, and the Flat River, Albert Faille's home for many years. We camped a mile above the mouth of the Mary River; beyond its junction with the Nahanni stood the Funeral Range and the entrance to Third Canyon, one of three on the lower Nahanni. It was a beautiful evening, clearing after several hours of rain. The river flowed gently by our camp, muttering in its bed, an occasional gurgle of upwelling water breaking the stillness. Billowing cumulus stood over the high peaks, shining in the slanting light. I wandered through the forest, just looking, letting the day's anger and resentment dissipate. Virginia Falls began to recede into the distant past, as though part of a previous trip. I ended up sitting on the riverbank, tossing pebbles into the water. Plop! "Shouldn't let this bother you. Accept it; there's no other way. You're fortunate enough—how many have the chance to visit country like this?" Plop! "Yeah, but it's such a waste. To hell with Simpson! I didn't come up here to see the towns. Let me enjoy my anger." Plop! "Forget it! Don't play the martyr! There will be other trips, other times. You're only one of six; who's right? You must get along with the others for fourteen months." Plop! "Don't start this now—look at the river, the clouds, feel the rocks underneath you. Relax, relax." I had to abandon my anger if I were to enjoy the trip, the land, and my companions. It wasn't easy to give up my self-righteous indignation, but it was necessary. There would be recurring bouts of frustration and anger now and again, but they never approached the intensity of those on the Nahanni. The rhythm of the trip and the North itself acted to diminish bitterness and coax me out of myself.

The following day was one of continual rain, another in a long, soggy series; it had rained almost every day since we started the trip. On most days the rain lasted only a few hours, but it seemed that clouds were our constant companion. We decided that this weather pattern was part of the Nahanni's famous "seventeen-day clearing trend." The cycle was simple: rain for sixteen days, followed by one day of partly cloudy skies, then more rain. Each temporary break ("sucker hole") in the clouds convinced us that better weather was on the way, but we were constantly disappointed. Somewhere along the line—I believe it was the day we left Brintnell Creek—it had not rained. We were obviously in the middle of another clearing trend. . . .

On the day we passed through Third and Second canyons, a good upstream breeze drove heavy rain into our faces. Great fun—sitting on the canoe seat in a shallow pool of icy water, feeling the moisture gradually soaking through "waterproof" raingear and working its inexorable way toward arms, legs, and crotch, and driving warmth before it. Eventually it became a matter of endurance—cold-footed, hunkered over our paddles, and resigned to the soaking. Oh, well, there was really little to complain about; our raingear kept out some of the moisture (but don't ever believe those ads) and in the evenings there was always a warm fire, a dry sleeping bag, and a waterproof tent.

And there were many compensations. The massive walls of Third Canyon rose three thousand feet above the river in a series of gigantic steps broken by talus-filled gullies. We passed beneath craggy gray limestone and dolomite strata of Ordovician and Devonian seas, 450 to 400 million years old. Midway through the canyon was The Gate; here the river constricted, pouring through a sheer defile perhaps two hundred feet wide and a thousand feet high. On the left side of the river rose Pulpit Rock, a cylindrical monolith joined to the main wall by a narrow ridge. The Gate was spectacular, and I felt swallowed by the layers of rock that towered above. Second Canyon offered more of the same scenery: rock walls reaching thousands of feet into the air, their tops obscured by drifting sheets of rain. Waterfalls leapt off every cliff, each intermittent watercourse a torrent springing to life in the rain. Along the base of the cliffs were delicate salt seeps, where white encrustations and black water streaks trailed into the river. Light green lichens on gray rock, yellow and green moss beneath tiny stands of spruce and alder: Oriental scenes, a thousand macro-bonsai. The great and the small stood side by side, with the overwhelming void of Second Canyon's chasm, and the mass of its walls, alongside details of form. We passed six Dall sheep standing white and motionless, gazing down on us through the rain; hundreds of cliff swallows flew amid the canoes, just grazing the surface of the water as they fed. It was a world of gray craggy walls sheathed in mist, like a T'ang dynasty painting, or the far-off hills of Szechwan.

Below Second Canyon the country opened up into Deadmen Valley. After running through a series of gravel bars and channels, we camped in a grove on the delta of Prairie Creek. The still-simmering conflict over pacing resulted in the decision to take a rest day; in the morning Kurt and I walked up the alluvial fan of the creek to where it emerged from the limestone cliffs. It was a pleasant day devoted to walking, photography, and investigating flowers and fossils. In spite of its name, Deadmen Valley didn't feel very ominous; it was almost amusing to recall that until the publication of Patterson's *Dangerous River* in 1954, the Nahanni country was reputed to be particularly hazardous and mysterious. There were rumors of prospectors murdered for their gold, a hostile Indian tribe, and men who had vanished, swallowed by the land. Deadmen Valley had been at the center of the rumors; it received its foreboding label after the decomposed, headless bodies of the McLeod brothers were found (depending on the source) tied to a tree, shot in their sleeping bags, or shot while reaching for their rifles. But when the Royal Canadian Mounted Police investigated, they decided there was no evidence of murder and that the men had died of starvation. And there was another story of a man named Jorgenson, found dead near his burned-out cabin above the mouth of the Flat River, either with or without his head, or shot in the back. Patterson also mentions six others who vanished or were found dead in the Nahanni country in the 1920s through 1940s. What to make of all these suspicious deaths? Patterson believed that the muddled stories about the McLeods and Jorgenson prevented any positive explanations of their deaths; there were no witnesses, and the effects of weather and animals could have made any investigation difficult even within a year of the deaths. For the rest, several died of starvation, and it is easy to imagine a single man meeting with an accident on a trap line, or running into an angry grizzly. The Mackenzie Mountains are rugged; when they were even more isolated, many mistakes could have proved fatal for a person traveling alone. We encountered a more forgiving country, vastly different from how it was in Patterson's time. The days of the headless McLeods were long gone—jetboats, a national park, and six bozos in red, yellow, and green canoes had come to a once-empty land.

Early one morning by Prairie Creek: Smoke curled from the fire as we prepared breakfast and readied canoe packs for loading. I wandered off into the bushes to search out an odd sound—like the bleating of a lamb, but higher pitched. I pushed through some alders and slid down a steep bank onto a gravel beach. There, among the tangled plants, was the source of the mysterious noise—a young snowshoe hare, dark brown and plump, on its side and kicking feebly, grasped at the neck by a least weasel. The weasel was about six inches long, with another inch or so of tail; the hare appeared to outweigh it by a ratio of at least twenty to one. In spite of its weight advantage, the hare had almost ceased struggling. The weasel was dragging it, with much effort, toward a hole in the bank. I was surprised—

least weasels are the smallest member of the order Carnivora, and I would have expected the tiny predator to stick to smaller prey; the hare seemed a monumental undertaking. Tenacious little devil. However, my appearance distracted the weasel: It abandoned the hare, retreated to a hole, ventured out and ran between my legs, grabbed the hare again, released its grasp once more, and finally reentered the hole. There were no marks on the hare's body, but it lay still, as though further resistance were futile—the perfectly passive prey. Finally it rose and hopped away in a lackadaisical manner—hop a few feet, stop, feed, hop a few more feet, stop and feed. Eventually it made a casual escape. By blundering along, I deprived the weasel of a meal. I had not meant to do that.

Immediately after stumbling upon the scene, I felt an instinctive compassion for the hare, and I had to stop myself from breaking up the struggle. But as I watched, my sympathies swung over to the weasel. Why? I admired the weasel for its valiant attempt to subdue a much larger animal, for its sleek and voracious efficiency. Besides, there undoubtedly were many more hares than weasels in the area. Let the weasel have the young animal; for every one eaten, there were two or three littermates waiting to take its place. Why interfere with the "natural order"? The hare has always been the prey of the weasel, wolf, and lynx—why attempt to change the situation for a single moment? What right did I, a visitor to the Nahanni, have to deprive the weasel of its hard-earned meal?

Later, I related the incident in a letter to a friend. She replied that she thought I was correct in wishing not to interfere, but that an equally good case could be made for interference. Was not compassion part of my nature, and was I not part of the "natural order" of which I had spoken? Who's to say that good intentions leading to "interference" are wrong? The weasel may have needed the hare to survive, but then the hare needed to survive, too. She wrote that my description of the incident revealed two things: first, that I felt alien, in that I believed I had no right to interfere because I was not part of the natural order; second, that I infused the order with all of my impressions and in so labeling and classifying it in my experience, interfered in a most basic sense. Should I not accept the fact that I was a part of the order, that I had as much right to make an impact as anyone or anything else?

It's all a matter of values, and thus difficult to argue the point either way. Sure, compassion is part of my nature and I am part of the "natural order." But my bond to the hare and the weasel was tentative, born not out of necessity, but only out of an accidental presence. In contrast, the weasel and the hare were united by an intimate bond—one of the predator and prey, the life that is given so that another might live. Let them be, let my interference be confined to bumbling analysis.

Why dwell on one disrupted death? Was it that important? Not as a single event, but perhaps as a symbol. The environmental ethic teaches that we are a part of the natural order, the ecosystem of the planet. For many Americans this is accepted dogma, although most might not understand the true implications of the concept, or translate their vague beliefs into coherent action. Yet to ignore this relationship is to ignore the last thirty years of intensive research detailing the complexity of ecosystem structure and function—and to invite further oil crises, extinctions, Love Canal toxic dumps, and Ethiopian famines. And so a weasel and a hare in Deadmen Valley may not be very important (unless you are one of the actors), but our relation to the earth and its inhabitants is. Error invites tragedy, and right action involves the small as well as the great. Should we not strive to reduce our unnecessary impact, accept as much of the natural order as possible, and approach things with as much sympathy and understanding as we can muster?

Soon after breaking camp and leaving Deadmen Valley, we came to Cache Rapids, at the entrance to First Canyon. Here the Nahanni divided around a large island—to the left was a shallow passage, to the right the main channel. The rapid was easy to run—gentle riffles at the head, with some large, avoidable standing waves at the downstream end of the island. However, Mike and Robert decided to paddle out into the midst of the heavy waves. From shore, their canoe appeared dwarfed by the powerful hydraulics—easily the most spectacular bit of river running on the trip. Several irregular waves broke upon them in quick succession, and in spite of their attempted brace, over they went, through the waves and into the tailrace below. "Lunched" by the river! By the time they maneuvered the canoe into shore, they were a half mile downstream and had completed the longest swim of the Nahanni run. John and Gary were slightly jealous, although they continued to hold the record for the most swims and accumulated mileage. Not caring to dwell upon their achievement, Mike and Robert quickly emptied the water from their canoe, wrung out their clothes, and set off in fast pursuit of a lost paddle and bodily warmth. The rest of us followed more slowly, glad to be warm and dry.

First Canyon was even more spectacular than Second or Third Canyon, although my impressions may have been affected by that rarity of rarities, a clear day. There were no upstream winds, no rains, just pleasant paddling. Above us were huge solution caves—great indentations in the rock caused by the dissolution of limestone by carbonic acid in percolating groundwater. Bands of light and dark rock alternated, and the sun cast beautiful patterns on the curving walls. Kurt and I climbed up a steep scree slope to watch John and Gary drift by, nearly lost in the canyon's immensity. This, then, was the canyon that I had seen in that long-ago photograph, and had dreamed of running as I sat in a Las Vegas library some nine months before. . . .

We found Mike and Robert at Kraus Hot Springs, twenty miles below Deadmen Valley, with their canoe packs emptied and the contents spread out to dry. Evidently, our waterproofing system still wasn't completely successful. Since it was early in the day, we reorganized our food and equipment, then set off to explore the area. Gus and Mary Kraus had lived intermittently at the hot springs for many years, and had only departed in 1971, just before Nahanni National Park was established. Their cabin was rotting away at the base, and several Slavey Indians had been hired to dismantle the structure and cut the logs into firewood. Soon the only evidence of the Krauses' prolonged residence would be the exotic garden parsnips, which had turned the riverside clearing into a field of golden-yellow blossoms.

Kraus Hot Springs was a beautiful place, different from anything I had seen on the Nahanni. A trail led from camp through a tangle of bushes and into a meadow dotted with poplars. The area was a riot of green, the lush growth encouraged by the warm waters. A number of plant species reach their northern distributional limits here, relics of a warmer climate able to survive because of the favorable microclimate around the thermal area. Wild raspberry and currant bushes grew everywhere. Grass, a rarity on the Nahanni, was waist-deep in the sunlit glade. The streams emptying the hot springs were lined with richly colored muds infused with streaks of dark green algae and white salts, their mineral waters blue as robin eggs: a blending of blue and green hues like an impressionist painting. Yellow warblers, bright little beads of color, flitted in and out of the foliage. Dappled light, an interplay of sun and shadow: The forest and meadow lay bathed in soft colors.

After wandering through the meadows, we found a four-foot-deep turquoise pool. We had been anticipating the opportunity to bathe and regain some of the warmth lost during the "seventeen-day clearing trend," and the water, in spite of its sulfurous odor, looked inviting. Kurt, John, Mike, and I quickly stripped and plunged into the water, pursued by hordes of excited mosquitoes. Much to our disgust, the "hot" springs were only tepid, and the muck on the bottom of the pool whirled into suspension. Gone was the limpid pool and with it the prospect of a refreshing bath. Plop! A big gob of mud hit me in the back of the head. I reached down, grabbed a handful of goo, turned and fired it at the nearest body, innocent or not. Direct hit, midchest! Someone else received a handful of slime on the side of the head, and the battle was on, a laughing free-for-all in which alliances were made and broken, and nefarious treachery was commonplace. Within a few minutes everyone was covered with muck, so we declared a truce and smeared ourselves with layers of the stuff, disguising ourselves as legendary Nahanni Mudmen and foiling the mosquitoes. A single photograph of these savages survives. In it, they are wearing nothing more than mud and algae, gesturing angrily and threatening the photographer with handfuls of muck. So much for the hot springs. I ended up retreating to the river to wash, but the combination of alkaline water and slime proved resistant to cold water, and my final state of cleanliness was vastly inferior to what existed before my "bath." I hoped there would be showers in Fort Simpson.

Below Kraus Hot Springs, the Nahanni flowed into The Splits, a network of imbricated channels. Here the river meandered across a wide floodplain, with wide chutes and shallow snyes (channels) branching from the main current—a maze of waterways separated by gravel islands and great piles of driftwood. Sweepers—trees that had fallen into the water but were still attached to the shore—were common wherever the river cut strongly into a steep bank.

In the early afternoon, Nahanni Butte came into view, its rock cap marking the junction of the Nahanni and Liard rivers. Approaching the junction, we heard a generator in the distance and an Indian passed us, headed upriver in a scow. We had emerged from the Mackenzie Mountains; the vertical scarp of the fault-block Nahanni Range ran north from the Liard, while the great, gentle syncline containing Great Slave Lake and the Mackenzie River lay to the east. From here it was 110 miles and two days of paddling to Fort Simpson.

The Liard was not impressive—sluggish, with a thick brown current that swallowed the green Nahanni waters. After registering at park headquarters, we hunted for a decent campsite. Nothing looked attractive; we finally settled for a grassy meadow near an old cabin, reached by slogging through thick mud and climbing a steep bank. It was soon obvious that we had chosen to camp in Mosquito Heaven. They were thick and hungry, the first really bad case that we had encountered. After erecting the tents, everyone retreated to shelter except John and me, who were on cooking duty. Not to be intimidated by the bloodthirsty bastards, we decided to carry through on a promised sour-cream enchilada dinner. So we applied liberal amounts of government-issue insect repellent (75 percent active ingredients and able to dissolve many plastics) and went to work. As I rolled out and fried the tortillas, I noticed that the mosquitoes attacked each warm tortilla as it came out of the pan. Heh, heh: I quickly returned each cooked tortilla to the pan, thus frying my tormentors. This had no appreciable effect upon their population, but the revenge was satisfying.

Our first day on the Liard was gray and rainy, with an upstream breeze and a sluggish current that made the going slow. The Nahanni Range shrank into the distance and the country took on an almost monotonous regularity as it became part of a great plain of forest and muskeg that spread toward the edge of the sky. In the great sweep of the northern forest, the song of the land changes little. We traveled fifty miles in a long day, past the mouth of the Blackstone River, and camped on a miraculously mosquito-free island in midriver. After dinner, I went down to the river and rested against a canoe. The sky was still overcast; the colors of the river and forest had a dull, muted quality. But off to the west, toward the Mackenzie Mountains, lay a horizontal band of orange and red clouds. A flock of common goldeneyes wheeled overhead and settled into an eddy with a whistle of wings. It was the second of July, and we were twenty days out from the Canol Road. I had adjusted to the rhythm of the river; already it was strange to consider confronting civilization. In Simpson there would be mail, fresh food, and showers, but only the mail seemed important.

The river had begun to feel like my home, and as its current bore us along, the days merged into a stream of water, rock, and sky. Stay out long enough and the behaviors and thought patterns that you adopt in society change; there's no longer much desire to return to what's been left behind, and an acceptance of the wilderness and your presence in it grows. The "comforts" of civilization no longer seem very important, while the bouts of cold, insects, and rain become more tolerable. As your hands become calloused after days of paddling, your spirit becomes inured to difficulties that once were depressing and uncomfortable. There's little anticipation of the future or reminiscence about the past—only the present flowing on, day after day. A subtle attitude adjustment occurs, an evolution toward a more harmonious way of approaching the land and experience. Heightened sensory awareness is part of the process, but emotional, intellectual, and spiritual changes occur, too. Hard to describe, this transformation; it's not something that is done consciously or is forced upon the mind and body.

Over the previous three weeks our lives had become ritualized. Every day we performed the same chores, made the same automatic preparations for morning departure and evening camp. To increase efficiency, and to be sure that we all knew what was expected of us, the group was divided into teams of two, each assigned to one of three jobs: cooking, erecting and disassembling the tents, and gathering firewood and cleaning dishes. Teams exchanged tasks every third day, and at the end of two cycles, partners were switched so that the same people did not always work together. We were usually up by six. While the cooks prepared a breakfast of cereal (rolled oats, bulgur wheat, rolled rye, or granola), biscuits, and hot tea or chocolate, the others gathered personal gear, took down the tents, and changed into river-running clothes. About two hours generally elapsed between groggy risings and beginning the day's paddle. In the evenings, smoke curled from the fire and a hot brew was on the way by the time the tents were up, firewood collected, packs emptied, and the canoes moved to a safe spot for the night.

Before dinner we always joined in a circle of hands around the fire, a ritual meant to remind us that we could not operate alone. Often this small, quiet act calmed much of the frustration that had accumulated during the day and renewed my sense of commitment to the group. The dinners that followed were mostly one-pot affairs with a grain, noodle, or legume base; sometimes a dessert or cornbread was added as a treat. After dinner, bread for the next day was baked in an aluminum dutch oven and a more-than-ample lunch packed—bread; one pound per day each of nuts, raisins, dried fruit, and cheese; one-and-one-half cups of chocolate chips; peanut butter; honey; and fruit-drink mix. After chores came the limited time for photography, walks, journals, fishing, or relaxing by the fire. We often seemed more efficient in the evening. Perhaps it was the lure of hot food, dry clothes, and a chance to get off our butts and do something besides paddle.

All of the ritual, all of the gradual attitude changes meant something important. The trip had become an entity, a living thing composed of our movement, the flowing water, the daily tasks of living, our evolving relationships, and the North itself. Within the space of three weeks, these diverse elements had coalesced into a whole, each part influencing the others, building and merging like the voices of a choir. We had gone beyond ourselves, and the trip had gone beyond its separate components. It had become more than a "Traverse of the Northwest," more than a route on a map, a collection of supplies, and six men. There was a wholeness about it, one that would last for the rest of the trip. This wholeness had been, and would continue to be, threatened both by internal and external forces; it would evolve as we confronted new experiences and environments, but it would endure.

In the morning the current began to gather velocity as we approached Beaver Dam Rapids, a long stretch of large waves easily bypassed by a slot close to the right shore. The afternoon slipped away in the long curves and straightaways below the rapids, and cabins became more prevalent. As we swung around a last corner, we saw the white ferry that served the road to town. It churned across the Liard, its foghorn reverberating in the evening air, and we could see passengers and cars: so much for the wilderness and the first leg of our paddle. We were twenty-one days and more than five hundred miles out from the Canol Road, yet we were still in the infancy of our journey.

CHAPTER THREE
Interlude: Fort Simpson

Fort Simpson was our principal port of call on the Mackenzie River,
though it is of far less importance now than some years ago when it was the
chief post and headquarters of the Hudson Bay Co. for the Mackenzie River
district. There is a general air of listlessness, decay, and departed greatness
about the place.

—George Douglas, *Lands Forlorn*

OUR STAY IN FORT SIMPSON was a five-day hiatus, enforced mainly by logistical
concerns. We needed to rendezvous with Bruce Jamieson and Owen Williams,
resupply, and exchange our three smaller canoes for the single North canoe that
had been shipped to Simpson earlier. We had decided to use the larger canoe for
several reasons. Bruce and Owen were joining us for the section to Reliance, and
we figured that eight paddlers in a single canoe would make the 210-mile ascent of
the Mackenzie River easier and that the larger craft would perform better on the
rough waters of Great Slave Lake. We also wanted to experience something of what
the voyageurs had while paddling their twenty-five-foot freight canoes along northern fur-trade routes in the 1700s and 1800s. However, this created the problem of
transferring the smaller canoes to Reliance. Fortunately, Bruce and Owen arrived
earlier than expected, after successfully renegotiating the Canol and Alaska high-
ways and transferring our winter supplies to the barge company in Hay River for
the July 11 shipment across Great Slave Lake. This meant that the three canoes

45

could also be shipped on the barge, which was making the only trip of the summer to the eastern end of the lake, so Owen and Kurt headed back to Hay River in the *Yukon Rose*. Meanwhile, the rest of us waited.

Time in Simpson passed slowly, as though we had been absorbed by the lethargic, end-of-the-road spirit of the place. After we had read mail, taken showers, washed clothes, and readied supplies for the next stage of the trip, there was not much to do, so we wandered the streets and talked to residents. The atmosphere of Simpson was distressing; in spite of many friendly people, the town seemed desolate, as though on the verge of abandonment. One day, just before leaving Simpson, I ended up in Fat Daddy's Drive-In ("Best place in town to eat," said a local with a distended beer belly), munching on a burger and trying to make sense out of what I had seen during my wanderings. I was just back from a shower at the Koe-Go-Cho Friendship Center, the dormitory that housed Indian students from the bush during the school year. I was clean, restless, and ready to be gone from the oppressiveness of Simpson—the town smothered me like muggy heat. In the dormitory lounge I had found myself reading David Hume's *Treatise of Human Nature* (how did it ever end up there?) and listening to Fleetwood Mac on a battered record player. Contrasts: 1700s solipsism mixed with Stevie Nick's 1970s pop melodies, the spirit of a dog-day town clashing with the beautiful, empty land beyond its boundaries.

As George Douglas observed, Fort Simpson was once an important settlement. Founded in 1804, the town previously had served as the center of commerce for much of the Mackenzie River Valley, but its significance had faded. The dusty streets, old frame houses with broken windows, rusted-out cars, and garbage-strewn fields emitted an aura of decay—a frontier town on the way downhill, swept aside by economics and broken pipeline dreams. The ramshackle movie house was advertising *I Eat Your Skin, I Drink Your Blood*, and even the Hudson's Bay Company (or, simply, "The Bay") seemed to have deteriorated. Instead of counters jammed with the snowshoes, traps, woolen blankets, barrels of flour, boxes of nails, ammunition, and cast-iron frying pans needed for life in the bush, there were shelves filled with stuffed animals, wind-up toys from Taiwan, plastic dishes, greeting cards, and trashy paperback novels. What had happened?

Much of the decline can be traced to the decreasing importance of the fur trade, but there were more recent causes. In 1977 the Mackenzie Valley Pipeline, designed to bring natural gas from the Mackenzie River delta south through the Simpson area, was a fading possibility. It would have meant jobs and growth in a town with high unemployment, but the Berger Commission, a one-man federal advisory board comprised of Justice Thomas Berger of the Supreme Court of British Columbia, had just published a report calling for a ten-year moratorium on construction. Berger had held hearings concerning the pipeline in settlements throughout the Northwest Territories. Testimony was mixed, with many natives opposing the pipeline and most resident whites favoring it. Those opposed feared accelerated disruption of native life, and argued that the fate of the pipeline could not be decided until aboriginal land claims—a maze of conflicting arguments and demands—had been settled. Proponents argued that the energy would be needed to meet future needs, and that the Northwest Territories would reap significant economic benefits. Meanwhile, the temporary spurt of economic activity generated by the initial evaluatory phase had evaporated, and Fort Simpson's population fell by several hundred in a year. The only industries left besides subsistence-level trapping and seasonal transportation along the Mackenzie River were government and tourism; there were many agencies in the town (the Royal Canadian Mounted Police [RCMP], Postal Service, Northwest Territories Fish and Wildlife Service, Department of Transportation, Department of Indian and Northern Affairs), and a few southerners passed through during the brief summer.

Mixed in with my thoughts about the economy were recollections of people we met in Simpson. I remembered three Indian children who visited us in the campground outside of town—a boy and his two younger sisters, aged ten and twelve. They were polite, well behaved, and insatiably curious: "What's this?" "Where are you from?" "What's this?" "Can we have some more flapjacks?" Their parents were trappers in the bush during the winter, and their world was limited: one trip to Edmonton, a few to the territorial capital of Yellowknife. Later the parents came by to collect their kids—quiet and reserved, they sat at our table for a while, smoking and saying little, as though embarrassed. I wondered about their lives—whether the dynamics of Fort Simpson had affected them, whether they were happy, or whether they ever thought much about it. Later we heard that their boy had been arrested on a public drunkenness charge, and that the parents drank heavily and had shot at their neighbors after one spree.

Our first night in the campground, a group of six from the area held a party in an adjoining campsite, barbecuing meat and drinking wine. Robert introduced himself, talked for a while, and invited them to join us. Eventually they wandered over: John, an itinerant Dutchman working in a local sawmill; Joe, an Indian from Fort Franklin; and Alice, Louise, Elsie, and Elizabeth, Slavey women from Simpson and Wrigley, a village farther down the Mackenzie. It was interesting to talk with them, although there was a melancholy atmosphere about the gathering. The women were laughing but drunk, their bitterness only partially concealed beneath cheerful exteriors. The conversation began lightly, but turned serious: tales of Alice's thirty-five-year-old husband being treated for epilepsy in an Edmonton hospital, drinking while under medication and then dying, leaving behind his anguished wife and two little girls.

In the meantime, Louise was giggling and leaning all over me, asking if I'd "like to go for a little walk."

"I think I love you," she whispered, tottering on the edge of her seat.

"No, I'm not a good person to fall in love with; I'll be gone in two days."

"Well, I could love you for two days."

No, thanks, not my style, Indian woman or white woman. But there was a certain guilt in my response—as though our innocent, impromptu gathering and my conversation with Louise had somehow contributed to the whole white/Indian conflict, as though it were one more negative interaction upon which to build anger and mistrust. It wasn't the same as with a white woman on the make—not quite. Weren't her drunkenness, her loneliness, and her boredom responses to a particular widespread set of social conditions? And there was so much sadness; it flowed out of Louise and her friends like blood from a severed vein. Now the "party" was getting uncomfortable; the forces that had thrown us together, and our interactions, hinted at more than a chance meeting and people just having a good time. Finally, the six decided to leave; Louise asked me to come along, but I declined. Gary and John did go, though, feeling that the evening would not have been complete without seeing where everyone lived.

The following day, John related their experiences: a rundown house, Elizabeth throwing up in the bathroom, Louise transferring her affections to John, John backpedaling, more drinking, and the bastard Dutchman slurring out obscenities. Alice was morose and bemoaned her dead husband, while Joe was on the make for her and frustrated by her erratic fluctuations in mood and intentions. A desolate scene, and in the midst of it, out wandered Alice's two little girls, sleepy and wondering what the noise was all about.

In our mail had been a note for Robert from people named Nora Thorsen and Earl Dean, who invited us over to their house in Fort Simpson. Since none of us knew them, this came as a surprise. When we asked a Fish and Wildlife officer about them, we got raised eyebrows and a noncommittal response; it turned out they were an unmarried couple with a young child living in the "Indian section" of town. Not a conventional, white Simpson family—Nora had feminist posters on the walls, Earl talked of reading Marx (he had left a copy of *Das Kapital* under a rock on a Barren Grounds portage), and their little girl played with Indian kids.

Earl was from Hay River. A lean, soft-spoken man, he fought fires for the Forestry Department during the summer, did some prospecting, and ran a trap line in the winter. Or he tried to, as his trapping permit was in danger of being revoked. Permits were a delicate political issue, caught up in the problem of land claims. Who owns the land, or at least has the right to administer it? If the Fish and Wildlife Service has complete jurisdiction over the trapping permits, wouldn't that be a tacit admission that whites own the land? So let the local hunters' and trappers' associations decide who should get a trapping license, and perhaps the bush will become the exclusive realm of the Indians. There are not many white trappers left in the Northwest Territories (about 0.5 percent of all trappers), and those with whom we talked claimed that the hunters' and trappers' associations made it difficult for them to retain their permits. Reverse racism? Earl was one of those having difficulty maintaining his privilege, although he and Nora talked of "graduating to the bush" on a permanent basis. But there was a fantasylike quality to their conversation, as if they knew that their dream would not materialize: "If I got into trapping, purchased a good snowmobile, put five thousand dollars into supplies, I would probably make ten to fifteen thousand dollars a year. But I'd exhaust the land and have to move on in a few years. . . ."

Yet there were people making it in the bush around Simpson. Gus Kraus was up at Little Doctor Lake, a wedge of water splitting the Nahanni Range northwest of town. He had moved there with his wife and son after leaving Kraus Hot Springs. Earl also mentioned a fellow at another lake—lonely, he brought in a wife from the States after they connected through the personals section in *Mother Earth News*. They corresponded and then agreed to marry without having met: The story goes that when they met for the first time, she offered him some homemade cookies. He tried a few, liked them, and replied, "A woman who makes cookies like this will make a good wife." A vegetarian, she brought eight hundred pounds of grains and legumes with her. But the North is a land of meat, and when she ran out of grains, she turned carnivorous. She came north in the early 1970s, and Earl said they were still together in 1977.

The dominant sense of Simpson was one of economic dislocation and a stratified society: whites, métis (people of mixed ancestry, mostly Indian and French), and Indian ("The Dene Nation," or "The People"), all on different levels. Separate living areas, separate graveyards: Even the place where the dead are housed tells a lot about a community. In the smaller northern settlements that we visited, the cemeteries were either segregated (as Simpson's seemed to be) or contained very few graves of whites. Segregated graveyards occurred where the most active missionaries were Oblate Fathers. In these areas the Indians became nominal Roman Catholics, while the white traders and administrators were predominately Anglican or Presbyterian. As Justice Berger points out, the general lack of white graves is an illustration of different attitudes about the North: For the Indians, it has been, and is, a homeland. For many whites, it has been a frontier, a place in which to work and explore but not to settle and die: Up until the mid 1970s, only four whites were buried in the eighty-five-year-old graveyard at Fort Resolution. To some extent, this pattern is changing; more whites are moving north permanently, but historical patterns are still the source of present-day attitudes.

The pervasive sadness of the town was mirrored by the Indians gathered in front of the liquor store, the dilapidated buildings, the young men in their Cat hats, loitering and listening to the Rolling Stones in a town that had recently seen seventy juvenile court cases in a week. The Dene Nation was caught between two value systems, not knowing which way to turn—only that they must move. Ah, but where? Back to the bush, back to the traditional life? How easy is it to choose the harsh winters, the relative absence of material comfort, when the bush is no longer a necessity? And how do you educate your children—do you send them off to boarding school for nine months each year, to be taught by whites, however well meaning? Do you keep them in the bush, where they never learn to read and write properly and their later options are reduced? And suppose everyone did opt for the bush; could the land support them all? Do you choose to insert yourself into the wage economy even though your cultural heritage has no tradition of the eight-to-five-day, fifty-weeks-a-year routine? But you are without marketable skills in an area that produces little in terms of goods and services: "Everything flows into Simpson, nothing flows out," said one resident. It is a country where most youths are at best only marginally employed—so do you move south, away from your home, your relatives, your people?

This is limbo: Either path leads the wrong way. One possible refuge is to forget; stories and statistics tell a common tale of alcohol-induced misery and abuse. The Berger Report gives the average annual consumption of absolute alcohol in the Northwest Territories as 3.4 gallons per person, one gallon more than Canada's national average. Of course, the problem is not confined to the native Indians and Inuit. Some whites also drink too much and too often—but their drinking is generally not as obvious, and more frequently is confined to socially acceptable situations. Whatever the racial distribution of alcohol abuse, the problem reached such a magnitude in some villages—Rae-Edzo, Snowdrift, Fort Good Hope, and others—that the residents voted in "dry" ordinances. The social disruptions caused by alcohol make it all the more curious that liquor sales are a government-owned monopoly. Should the Northwest Territories make a profit from the misery of its people?

None of this is by way of supporting the stereotypes—the lazy, drunken Indian, or the racially intolerant white, out to make a fast buck in the North at the expense of the natives. We met good people everywhere, as well as some very unhappy ones. And I don't want to be one more transient southerner who visits the North for a month or a year, analyzes its problems, and then dispenses judgments and advice. Social problems rarely resolve themselves into either/or situations; there are few easily identifiable scapegoats or villains. All I can say is that there was anguish and division in Fort Simpson, that the town suffered from a general malaise of the soul. Individuals transcended this, but the community as a whole was absorbed by the greater flow of circumstance and history. But perhaps the situation wasn't much worse than anywhere else: Where don't alcohol abuse and social antagonisms exist? Maybe the emptiness and purity of the land magnified the human misery and made it seem worse than it really was because it contrasted so vividly with the beauty of our Nahanni run.

CHAPTER FOUR
The Mackenzie River and Great Slave Lake

Well, the wind is dropping a bit—I must push on. If ever I should experience a truly fair wind for any length of my travels I believe I would perish from surprise.

—P.G. Downes, *Journal of Travels North from Ille-à-la Crosse in 1938*

W E LEFT SIMPSON ON July 9, happy to abandon the town and our lassitude. Earl Dean and his daughter came down to the water to see us off—eight bodies and all of our gear stuffed into a twenty-five-foot green fiberglass canoe christened *Denise*. We made eighteen miles that first day on the Mackenzie, as we paddled head-on into a stiff current. It was hard and steady work all the way to camp above Green Island, and the struggle against the river was an intimation of what was to come. It is 210 miles from Fort Simpson to the head of the Mackenzie at Great Slave Lake, and it took us nine days to cover the distance, an average of twenty-three miles per day.

Soon after leaving Simpson, we began ascending the Head-of-the-Line, a sixty-mile section of fast water with currents ranging from two to seven miles per hour. (The name comes from the days when scows, canoes, and flat-bottomed York boats were rowed, poled, and paddled up the Mackenzie; fast water meant that the craft had to be towed from shore with lines secured to the bow and stern.) The paddling was a bit easier above Head-of-the-Line, where the current was generally slower, and the river pooled into the long slack-water sections of Mills and Beaver lakes. Once beyond these, we entered Great Slave Lake via a channel south of Big Island.

In spite of its name, we were able to paddle the entire length of the Head-of-the-Line; our only "shore work" on the Mackenzie came farther upstream, when we encountered the ten-miles-per-hour current of the Providence rapids. Paddling was possible on the fast sections only when we avoided the main current, by sticking close to shore, and took advantage of the upstream flow of favorable eddies. The work was like interval track workouts with alternating sprints and jogs. We rode each eddy to its upstream end (easy paddling), where we met a tongue of fast water flowing down from the eddy above. A burst of energy followed: Our paddles dug deep into the water in a quick cadence, and with straining backs, flushed faces, and labored breathing, we forced the canoe upstream against the current. Often the canoe's progress, measured against landmarks on the bank, was almost imperceptible, as though we were barely holding our own against the water. There was little talk during these efforts. I often wondered if my arms would hold out, if the others were working as hard as I was. But we always gained on the water; finally the current eased and we punched through into the next eddy. Our cadence then slowed, breathing was easier, and a rush of words poured out as we gathered our strength for the next push. It seemed like an endless progression: searching for the shallow water and eddies, fighting the fast stretches, taking all day to go twenty-five miles after having covered fifty or sixty a day on the lower Nahanni and the Liard. Each evening brought fatigue—not the bone-weary exhaustion of the Itsi-Ross portages, but a low-level, general tiredness that comes after long hours of steady work. On several days we went from six in the morning to midnight, and I was thankful for the perpetual light of the northern summer. A diurnal creature, my energy was sustained and renewed by the sun—as long as there was light, I could keep moving.

Denise had nice lines, but she was sluggish and unresponsive in comparison to our Old Town canoes. "She look like a Cadillac, but she drive like the *Yukon Rose*," said Kurt. In a small canoe, the stern person generally uses a J-stroke to hold a straight course. The name is derived from its pattern: a backward pull parallel to the side of the canoe, followed by a rotation of the wrist and a short, outward sweep of the blade. After some practice, it's easy to execute, although the final outward sweep doesn't offer much of a mechanical advantage for your arms, and you have to use relatively weak muscles to force the stern into position. Consequently, the J-stroke was useless when maneuvering *Denise*. We all took turns in the stern and found that the outward sweep couldn't persuade her bulk to swing into line. So we turned to the pry, drawstroke, and ruddering for control, all of which were less desirable than the J-stroke because they slowed the canoe.

A more satisfying discovery was that we could sail *Denise* in favorable winds.

We rigged a crude sail from two ten-foot spruce poles and a twelve-foot military surplus parachute. The poles were about eight feet aft of the bow and splayed out in a wide V; their position was maintained by a person who sat between them. The parachute was strung between the poles; tension was maintained on the sail by means of ropes attached to the poles and held in place by two people sitting in front of the sternman. It was enjoyable, and at times adventurous, and effortless progress for everyone except the sternman, who had to work very hard to keep the canoe running in a straight line. How nice to let the wind move us along and watch the miles drift by as *Denise* surfed on following waves: ah, movement. With our makeshift sail a white billow in the wind and our craft jammed with baggage and passengers, we were like a dhow rocking upstream on the Nile. The sailing grew exciting when the winds increased or suddenly shifted to port or starboard. We couldn't adjust the sail, and *Denise* wasn't beamy enough to withstand much side-to-side rocking. One day, when we were running through some large swells and an occasional squall, a sudden gust snapped a mast and the canoe listed sharply, spurring a frantic scramble to haul in the sail and steady *Denise*. Midriver was not a good place for a swim, and we quickly became more conservative in our sailing.

We were happy in the winds, but they were sporadic, so we paddled most of the time. Mills Lake, with about thirty miles of flat water and no perceptible current, was a welcome respite from the upstream pull, but Beaver Lake, which could have given us more of the same, was a long struggle against strong headwinds. It was only 210 miles from Simpson to Great Slave Lake, but another 1,050 miles from the lake to the Arctic Ocean. I thought of the time before steam and diesel engines made the ascent of the Mackenzie an easy affair, when it was an important commercial route and Head-of-the-Line earned its name. Alexander Mackenzie, who explored the length of the river from Great Slave Lake to the delta, took thirty-three days to ascend the river in July and August of 1789. His men towed the boats much of the way and sailed and paddled when they could—"hard and fatiguing duty," according to Mackenzie. Then why not use a motor, as some folks asked when we told them of our plans? Because the physical labor of hauling ourselves upriver generated a gut-level appreciation for history, for the sweat and tired muscles of men long dead. We were separated from Mackenzie's voyageurs by time and vastly different lives, but we were able to share the past with them, however briefly, and this sharing made the tired muscles worthwhile.

The Mackenzie passed through heavily forested country with little relief. During the first few days out of Simpson, the low purple outline of the Horn Plateau gave us occasional hints of distant mountains to the north, but our world was most often confined to the river: steep rocky banks, a line of spruce, and the sky, sometimes filled with thunderheads flung toward the horizon. Farther upstream, on Mills Lake, the view opened up: The expanse of the sky spread and we paddled toward heat waves that rose dancing from the water. There were days when rain buffeted the canoe, but we never suffered from the cold of the Nahanni's "seventeen-day clearing trend." And when the sun did shine, it felt like the land was caught in the height of summer. Then we lived in a world of blue and green light, and the colors of the water, sky, and forest filled our days.

It was summer, and the air and river waters were rich with birds. Bald eagles rose to flight from the tops of spruce, sometimes harried by angry terns. Sandpipers scattered along the shore and female ducks led convoys of young through streamside reeds. Rocky islets, covered with the nests of arctic terns, were common. If we approached too closely, the adults rose upward in an erratic flight of beating wings and raucous cries and circled overhead as their ungainly chicks huddled against camouflaging stones or scattered in a waddle of downy feathers.

Of course, good conditions for breeding birds meant good conditions for insects. Although we weren't bothered by many mosquitoes, we did encounter another species of Our Winged Animal Pals—a large and plentiful horsefly, slightly smaller than a hummingbird. These bloodthirsty devils, known as "klegs" or "bulldogs," inflicted painful bites when negligence gave them the opportunity. They were slow and easily killed, but many a warm, sleepy paddler's reverie was disrupted by a victorious kleg as it bit into unprotected flesh. Ugly and vicious, the only redeeming quality possessed by the species was its size. Mosquitoes are so tiny that a squashed handful provides the victim with little satisfaction to counteract his misery, but a trophy-sized kleg can bring pride and the thrill of revenge. Although the forehand slam was the most popular method for dispatching klegs, we discovered an alternative, more aesthetically pleasing technique. This involved capturing the offending pest with a sweep of the open hand, grasping it between the thumb and index finger, and then removing its head with a flick of the opposite forefinger. The only more satisfying type of kleg annihilation was watching a dragonfly capture one of the buggers.

In spite of summer's flush, the Mackenzie seemed impersonal. The river was too large for intimacy; it had the soul of an immense, brooding giant, silent and rather unexcited about life. The sheer volume of its waters was impressive, but its strength was too modest. The days were difficult to distinguish from one another because the country touching the river was so uniform; the skies varied more than the land and water. Only in the evening, when the slanting light set shadows and accentuated subtle terrain differences—when warm colors shone on spruce, water, and beige river sediments—could I feel close to the river that brushed our camps and fought our progress.

There was a different rhythm to our group on the Mackenzie. We were more tightly knit, as though exchanging three canoes for one had forced us to put aside our antagonisms. No longer were we separated by fifty feet or more of water, a distance that isolated us and provided time to brood over our worries. Robert was more voluble, less visibly concerned with the Thelon and the cabin issue; and there was less discussion about our pace. We were a single unit, paddling side by side for ten or more hours a day as we pushed *Denise* upriver. We sang songs; played word games, trivia games, and Minute Mysteries; and laughed at Robert's renditions of "The Goon Show." And it was nice to have Bruce and Owen along. Bruce was short and balding, with a curly red beard. A sometime Outward Bound instructor and computer programmer, he brought unassuming habits, a rumpled baseball cap, and a sardonic wit to the group. Owen, tall and gangly, was a part-time logger and student. Nicknamed "Cowboy," he was full of humor and the butt of many jokes, but he displayed remarkable self-confidence for a nineteen-year-old. Bruce and Owen had lived outside of our Nahanni conflicts and brought none of those frustrations with them. When they stepped into the canoe, the diversity of our group expanded immensely, and their cheerful presence relieved some of the pressure that had built among the rest of us.

Our divisions were buried or reduced not only by our physical proximity in the North canoe and the presence of Bruce and Owen, but also by the stage of our journey. We found ourselves in a part of the North conducive to long days of steady work. Great Slave Lake was another goal to be reached. We all wanted to be done with fighting the upstream current, and the repetitious landscape did not invite dallying, so there was little conflict over "faster" and "slower." It also seemed that the leadership issue had resolved itself. The night before entering Simpson, we had talked about our reactions to John's style of leadership; as a result, John had become more a group facilitator and representative than a dispenser of arbitrary decisions. Although at some point in the trip most of us disagreed with the way John handled his role, this was not so much a reflection upon his abilities as the result of the clash of our various egos and goals. In the end he did a good job, and I think that he was better suited for the position than anyone else in the group. John was a caring, competent man, and, most important, was reasonably humble and patient. He was willing to listen to suggestions, to examine himself critically, and to change when necessary. And he learned, both by example and experience.

The Mackenzie River and much of Great Slave Lake can hardly be classified as wilderness, and we were rarely out of contact with humanity for long. The Mackenzie is a major transportation artery during the summer, and huge barges, pulled by tugs, plowed by almost daily, their navigation aided by buoys, beacons, and massive aluminum tripods with reflectors and fluorescent orange markers. About 160 miles above Simpson, a ferry bridges the river with traffic bound for Yellowknife, and we slept one night with the sound of diesel engines and foghorns in our ears. Downstream canoeists, bound for Inuvik, were common, as were motorized launches that ran past us with a wave of hands and nod of heads from their passengers. Dotting the riverbanks were hunting and fishing camps, each little more than a lean-to, firepit, and platform cache. The camps were often strewn with litter—everything from old suitcases and ragged clothes to rusted-out refrigerators.

Seismic lines cleared by survey crews cut huge swaths through the forests in their determined march toward new sources of hydrocarbons, and abandoned cabins lay tucked in overgrown clearings—disintegrating log jumbles surrounded by thickets of wild rose, where the voices of former inhabitants seemed to whisper from the ruins.

The settlements along the Mackenzie were more pleasant than Simpson was. Fort Providence was a clean little town of six hundred, dominated by a white clapboard church and with little of the lassitude that pervaded Simpson. When we visited, people were fishing, gathering supplies, and bustling about on the dock. But our most enjoyable stop was in Jean Marie River, a Slavey Indian village with a population of sixty about fifty miles above the mouth of the Liard River. It seemed healthier than Simpson in body and spirit, a settlement that suggested some of the reasons for Simpson's problems.

We arrived in the late morning of a sunny day and were greeted by a bevy of curious Indian children. They showed us a baby duck they had found, and sat with us while we had lunch, asking questions as we ate. Later they followed us through the village, pointing out homes and telling of their families. What we saw was a cluster of neat log homes scattered through a field of mowed grass. The largest building in the village was the schoolhouse, a multiroomed affair for grades one through eight, with a Canadian flag flapping overhead. There was no garbage; there were no loitering youths, no outward signs of sickness. It seemed a peaceful northern village dozing in the warmth of a summer's day.

We talked for a long while with Sophia, the wife of the village schoolteacher. She had lived in Jean Marie River with her son and husband for four years, helping the village women develop their crafts business. The women produced beautiful leather goods—tanned moose hide decorated with intricate designs of dyed moosehair tufts and porcupine quills—that had been exhibited in museums throughout the country. Demand was such that a decorated leather jacket sold for anywhere from four hundred to six hundred dollars. She explained that the success of the craft work had given the village a sense of pride, helped some residents to get off welfare, and served as a good example for other villages seeking to break out of a morass of social ills. Here was a source of income and sense of purpose, dependent neither on the government nor on an eight-to-five routine. There was an atmosphere of community present in Jean Marie River, one that had not existed in Simpson. Partly it was a result of the village's small size and its less transient population, but the crafts program must have contributed to the cohesiveness.

Yet some of the same problems that affected Simpson—idleness, alcohol abuse, and family violence—were also present, although on a much-reduced scale, and the village was confronting the issue of an all-weather road. When we visited, Jean Marie River was accessible only by floatplane, boat, and a winter snow road, separated from the all-weather road to Simpson by seventeen miles of muskeg. To the villagers the road would grant access to the outside and cheaper prices. Louis Norwegian, a seventy-year-old carpenter and boatbuilder, complained that the government kept promising a road but never followed through. Road or no road? Many people in Simpson felt that the town's troubles multiplied when the road to the outside was completed in 1970, and Sophia was afraid that Jean Marie River could experience the same social disruption. Yet how often do people choose the path leading away from "progress"? How often do they decide to do what's best in their long-term interests? And how can anyone ask them to settle for less comfort and material wealth, particularly when those who do the asking lead middle- and upper-class lives?

Near the head of the Mackenzie we encountered rough, stormy weather. On July 16 we moved thirty miles up Beaver Lake, fighting a tedious headwind through hours of waves and soaking spray. The following day we began crossing the South Channel opposite Big Island, but we were windbound after covering only five miles. We completed the crossing on the eighteenth, but winds forced us to halt just short of Point Desmarais, at the western edge of Great Slave Lake. We had completed our ascent of the Mackenzie and were happy with our progress, but it appeared that the lake might not give us much easier traveling. At three in the afternoon, the winds calmed, and we set off along the southern shore of the fifth-largest lake in North America. For two hundred miles our route would be exposed to the prevailing northerly winds and the waves they generated, rolling unimpeded across the huge expanse of water that fills the western end of the lake. After passing Fort Resolution and the Slave River, we hoped to find more protected paddling among the islands lining Hornby Channel and beneath the north shore of McLeod Bay, which we would follow to Reliance.

The paddling was pleasant in the aftermath of the storm. Each of us was quiet, absorbed in his own thoughts. Rich light broke through the scattered clouds and *Denise* ran through the rhythmic swells and into the gathering peace. I drifted along, lulled by the gentle rocking of the canoe, humming songs in time with the waves. But all of this contentment disappeared at Point Roche, during Episode Two in the series *Bozos in the North*: "The Bozos Go Swimming."

The Bozos went swimming because they tried to skirt Point Roche too close to shore. It happened quickly—a wave hit *Denise* broadside, partly filling her with water. Kurt, in the stern, turned her to face the next series of waves, but it was too late. The canoe was wallowing in the water and couldn't rise over the incoming breakers; they smashed over the bow, knocking John backward into Owen's lap and swamping us. *Denise* floundered, then rolled over, a miniature *Titanic* scattering people, canoe packs, paddles, foam pads, and miscellaneous gear over the water. The entire sequence could not have taken more than two minutes; my emotions quickly progressed from contentment to disbelief ("Hey, this can't happen to us!") to concern ("We have to keep the canoe afloat!") to bemused resignation ("Nice evening for a swim, eh?"). Since we were only about a hundred yards from shore, it seemed that we wouldn't have much trouble collecting ourselves, the canoe, and equipment on dry land. We quickly donned life jackets, began working the canoe toward shore, and swam off in pursuit of floating gear. Only Bruce seemed a bit worried, and no wonder—he didn't have a life jacket. Hmm. Somehow, we had forgotten to get life jackets for Bruce and Owen before leaving Seattle. We had purchased an extra one in Fort Simpson, but Robert had said he would use the wet suit he'd brought along; it would provide plenty of buoyancy in case of a dump. But in the confusion of the dump, Bruce was left without a life jacket. As he swam toward shore, trying to carry a sleeping pad and some extra clothes, he encountered Gary. Since Gary was wearing a life jacket, Bruce (in his muddled state of mind) assumed that Gary "was the floating quartermaster" and asked him for one of the extra life jackets he had to be carrying. Actually, Gary had only the one he was wearing, but he wasn't sure if Bruce could swim well, so he valiantly surrendered his. Later, Bruce was a bit embarrassed by the incident: "My problem was not the lack of a life jacket or swimming ability; it was the lack of clear thinking." So we used it as an occasion to poke fun. "Women and children and Bruce first!" became the rallying cry for the Bozos as they paddled toward Reliance.

Even though we were close to shore and the waves washed us toward land, it took thirty minutes to get everyone out of the water. After the swamping, I grabbed a loose canoe pack and paddle and began heading to shore, but the going was very slow. The canoe pack was awkward to tow, my rain pants kept falling down around my ankles, and what began as a cheerful swim became a frustrating, chilling struggle. With my teeth chattering uncontrollably, I finally crawled ashore after a rocky, bruising landing. We were all on the verge of hypothermia as we gathered loose gear, dragged *Denise* onto the beach, and built a roaring fire. But soon a hot brew was on the way, clothes were hung to dry on an improvised tripod, and we were joking about the experience. Yet the incident's implications were very clear: *Denise* couldn't take big waves, and a swamping far from shore would be fatal. None of us would last long in the cold water, and the chances of being discovered by a passing boat were nonexistent.

We were in and out of Hay River in a day, pausing only long enough to take care of some logistical problems (just where was the peanut butter promised by Canada Starch Company?) and sell the *Yukon Rose*, recouping our investment in the process. Then it was eastward along the south shore, covering twenty-five miles in an afternoon of easy paddling. The next day we got in only eight miles before the winds and waves forced us ashore just east of Sulfur Point. We spent the next day and a half there, waiting out the wind and seeking to live up to our expedition's motto: "When all else fails, eat." We were able to leave on the twenty-third, breaking camp at 5:30 A.M. in the excitement over good paddling conditions. About twenty-five miles later, we were halted once again. It was frustrating, staccato progress, with no smooth flow. The swamping had left us doubting *Denise*'s seaworthiness, and even moderate winds blowing across the lake kicked up waves large enough to make travel foolish. There was no alternative but to accept the wind patterns patiently and travel whenever possible. So we waited—plenty of time to read, listen to the cries of gulls and terns as they flocked over the choppy surf, and explore the surrounding forest.

The eight A.M.-to-evening routine that had worked so well on the Nahanni and Mackenzie rivers was unsuited to the Great Slave Lake winds, and we had to do much of our paddling in the early morning hours. So we were up at three A.M. on July 24 and made Fort Resolution easily, paddling into its tiny harbor on a quiet Sunday morning. The Hudson's Bay Company had established a trading post at Fort Resolution in 1821, and it had once been an important settlement for northern commerce, but the sleepy town had no aura of past (or present) greatness about it. Its former importance was a result of geography and the fur trade: All water traffic headed into the Northwest Territories passed along a route that led from Fort Chipewyan on Lake Athabasca down the Slave River to Great Slave Lake and Resolution. From there, routes diverged—east to Fort Reliance and the Barren Grounds, west to the Mackenzie River, Fort Simpson, and Great Bear Lake. Many travelers had passed through the Resolution area—Mackenzie in 1789, John Franklin in 1820, George Back in 1833, Warburton Pike in 1890, Ernest Thompson Seton in 1907, and the Hornby party in 1926. For the later parties, Resolution had been an important resupply point—or at least a welcome haven providing a warm meal and new company—but for us it was just a brief stopover in another end-of-the-road village. We wandered the deserted streets, past the Catholic church, a garish purple-fronted store, and a cemetery of graves decorated with faded plastic flowers. As usual, the church was the most interesting building, clean, with intricate designs carved in the wooden pews and the fourteen richly detailed stations of the cross described in French. I imagined the years of masses, the long lines of Chipewyans taking communion and kneeling to an imported God, and the battle for souls waged by the Anglican and Catholic missionaries. The initial forces of exploration and settlement in the Northwest Territories were generated by religion and two rival trading empires, the Hudson's Bay Company and the Northwest Company. The two firms had merged in 1821, and now The Bay seemed like nothing more than a glorified northern supermarket, its romantic frontier spirit vanished in a cloud of prepackaged food and plastic gadgets. But religion had endured, at least superficially. The church retained its style; the days of dogsledding missionaries were recent memory, and dark-robed French and Belgian Oblate Fathers still said mass in tiny villages. Business, driven by the profit motive, changes to meet the demands of the present, and its allegiance to past tradition is ephemeral. Religion, for better or worse, endures, its values (particularly Catholic ones) locked in a vault of faith. This is no judgment of the relative merits of the two institutions, or their roles in the North, but for a sense of history, look to the Church rather than The Bay.

The church was only a small part of the town, though, and the past was just a faint murmur. Fort Resolution slumbered, but it was another end-of-the-road settlement drowsing into disintegration. Once again, alcohol was a culprit. The wife of an RCMP officer said that the town was a trouble spot, and that another officer was being brought in to help deal with the disturbances: four police in a town of five hundred, like a smaller version of Simpson.

Beyond Resolution lay the uplands of the Canadian Shield, well-drained country bearing the scars of the continental ice sheets that retreated less than twelve thousand years ago. The transition was sudden from low, poorly drained muskeg and thick forest to uplifted rock and a thinner cover of birch and spruce. The first hint of change came at Stony Island, a small dot of land less than a day's paddle east of Resolution. The mainland was much as it had been for the previous four hundred miles, but the island was different: an artist's palate of orange, black, gray, green, and yellow crustose lichens on brownish-pink diabase, and an open forest with an underlying carpet of moss and grayish-green reindeer lichen. Scattered pockets of crowberry and blueberry grew among the rocks, their fruits ripening in the short burst of July's warmth. Shortly after leaving Stony Island, we moved into the shield country for good: so much for the flatlands and their unchanging vistas of water and boreal forest.

Our route took us up Hornby Channel, so named by government surveyor Guy Blanchet after John Hornby pointed out the route to him in 1922. We paddled through a maze of islands, underneath cliffs hundreds of feet high: south of Preble and Keith islands to Pekanatui Point, across five miles of open water to Etthen Island, then up Hearne Channel, through Taltheilie Narrows, and into McLeod Bay. Because of the capricious winds, we often broke camp in near darkness and followed the gathering light into day. On these mornings, breakfast was a rushed, silent meal, consumed as we climbed slowly out of sleep. After we ate, the canoe packs were closed and *Denise* was dragged down to the water and loaded, each of us a hunched shadow moving through the routines of preparation. A creak of fiberglass and wood would follow as we wordlessly clambered aboard and settled into our seats, with the smell of cool morning air in our noses and Venus bright in the sky. The preparation was like a morning prayer, a ritual of quiet awakening and departure that no one wished to disturb:

> *I wake to sleep, and take my waking slow*
> *I learn by going where I have to go.*

When we were settled, the bowman pushed us off from shore. After a few strokes of backpaddling cleared us from the shallows, *Denise* was turned to face our destination and the day's work began beneath a faint shimmer of northern lights, with the three-quarter moon sinking huge and orange into a silhouette of spruce. In the early hours we paddled quietly but forcefully, compelled by the desire to keep warm; at these times we carried our world with us, its perimeter limited by our silent work and the vague light. Later, the eastern sky broke into fire and islands rose out of the half-light, gradually assuming shape and texture. The gathering day breathed life into intricate reflections as our wake trailed down long passages of stone, past pockets of green-leaved and white-trunked birch and dark rock splotched with orange lichens.

We generated several more installments of the series *The Bozos in the North* as we followed Hornby Channel toward McLeod Bay. Episode Three, "The Bozos Start a Fire," began when Kurt awoke at midnight and groggily asked, "Is someone cooking breakfast?" A quick glance out the tent door ascertained that no one was, but that flames were leaping high into the darkness. What followed was pure Keystone Cops, the first naked fire-fighting crew in the Northwest Territories stumbling out of the tents, shouting, stubbing toes, and stepping on wild rose bushes in the mad scramble to douse the conflagration. In the aftermath, we stood around in the thick smoke, panting and picking thorns out of our feet, and wondering what had happened. The Bozos had built their cooking fire on rock, but a tiny ribbon of tinder led from the firepit to thick duff nearby; when smoldering embers ignited the tinder, up went the duff.

Episode Four, "The Bozos Go Canoeing," happened later the same morning. We were up at 3:45, ate a quick breakfast, broke camp, and paddled from a sheltering bay out into the lake. Stroke, stroke, stroke—the hearty explorers paddled off into the morning. Unfortunately, they were met by wind-driven waves when they emerged from the lee of the shore. So they immediately reversed course, regained the shore, set up the tents, and went back to sleep. Maybe they would try again later.

Gary provided several more episodes in his efforts to retain dry feet. Throughout each day, he used various acrobatic techniques to enter and leave the canoe, contorting his body into postures that resembled esoteric yoga positions. Time and again he went to great length to avoid damp pinkies, once even allowing Robert to give him a piggyback ride to shore. But in camp he developed a magnetic attraction for the lake, and fell in several times: slowly working down a slanting rock to the shore, he would gingerly stoop to wash out a dish or get water. Suddenly there would be a curse, followed by a splash, and we would all break into laughter, for we knew that Gary would reappear, soaked to the waist and with a disgusted look on his face.

Our *Bozos in the North* episodes exposed us for the Batesian mimics that we really were. The classic textbook example of this phenomenon involves the viceroy and monarch butterflies. Predators have learned to avoid the toxic monarch, and in doing so they also ignore the viceroy, which has a similar coloration but is harmless. We were like the viceroys, then: We resembled competent outdoorsmen but were really mimics. Our dirty clothes, bearded and tanned faces, fancy equipment, and stories were all part of an elaborate disguise. In reality we were the stars of *The Bozos in the North,* running through a Jekyll-and-Hyde routine of competence and incompetence, yet always managing to get by.

During our Bozo period we also discovered canoe lag, a malady brought on by unpredictable winds and the necessity of traveling whenever it was calm, with or without sleep. The symptoms of canoe lag were similar to those of jet lag: exhaustion, and the inability of a confused body to adjust to sudden changes in its accustomed schedule. A brief description of our activity pattern between July 26 and July 30 will serve to illustrate the causes of canoe lag:

> *July 26.* Up at 3:45 A.M., out on the lake by 5:30. Strong winds prevented paddling, and we returned to camp (see *The Bozos in the North* number three). Slept until noon. Winds decreased and we began paddling at three P.M. Traveled until ten P.M., when we were windbound. Wait a minute, I thought that the winds decreased in the evening. . . .
>
> *July 27.* Windbound near the northern end of Preble Island.
>
> *July 28.* Up at midnight, off at 1:30 A.M. Paddled until early afternoon, when windbound again at Pekanatui Point. Waited to cross the five miles of open water between Keith Island and Etthen Island. Up at eleven P.M. after three hours of sleep, out of camp shortly after midnight.
>
> *July 29.* Paddled until midmorning; covered about twenty-five miles before being windbound. Camped on the north side of Hearne Channel and slept until late afternoon.
>
> *July 30.* Up early again, out of camp by four A.M. Got past Taltheilie Narrows before becoming windbound in midmorning.

The situation should be clear. Just how many midnight bowls of oatmeal and three-hour snatches of sleep can a body withstand before it becomes temporarily disarticulated and wildly out of synch with the mind? "I'm sorry, but we don't serve breakfast after eleven." Morning or evening? Descend far enough into the depths of tiredness, get five hours of sleep during the last forty-eight, and everything becomes slightly surreal. I remember the eleven P.M. wake-up on the twenty-eighth— silently scowling, frustrated with everything, my mouth tasting like stale socks. I think it was the only time on the entire trip that I was angry at everyone for no rational reason. I let the anger build inside and comforted myself with an imagined martyr's role.

Weary butt, bleary mind as we headed toward Etthen Island. No longer was the North canoe a craft that brought us closer together. Now it was a vessel of tyranny, and my companions pressed in on me mercilessly. I longed for isolation, for the red Old Town canoe and the chance to set my own pace, to reject the pressure for all the crazy motion. But I wasn't being rational—I knew that. We had to travel; the winds wouldn't wait for a leisurely awakening, and neither would the winter. Perhaps I needed my silent anger, perhaps it was a way of coping with a recalcitrant will. But after the miles were done, the tents erected, and a blessed, rejuvenating sleep finished, it was all worth it. We had made a safe crossing to Hearne Channel and I felt the exuberance that comes after recovering from exhaustion. The tiredness was just a memory, and a surge of energy pulsed through me. The world looked new and wonderful, tea tasted rich and strong, and I took great pleasure in the evening light as it shone upon the lake—a rebirth of the sensual, a tiny spring after a winter of depletion.

On our way through Taltheilie Narrows, the strait separating the ninety-five-mile-long McLeod Bay from the rest of Great Slave Lake, we saw an unexpected dock on the north shore. Curious, we stopped to investigate and found ourselves at Great Slave Lake Lodge ("Home of the Trophy Trout"), a destination resort catering to wealthy Americans and Canadians. Once a week a Boeing 737 flew in from Winnipeg and disgorged a load of eager anglers. We happened to pass by on the day that a new group arrived, and it was odd to see a large jet circle over the lake and land on a dirt airstrip 110 miles from the nearest road. Intrigued by the plush resort, we wandered onto the grounds, like rubes just in from the woods and seeing the bright city lights for the first time—which I suppose we were. It was soon evident that the owner of the "Home of the Trophy Trout" did not appreciate our presence, for shortly after our arrival he came by and told us to "get away from the windows and make yourselves scarce." Was he afraid that we would panhandle? Or that we would disturb his customers as they ate breakfast, like street urchins outside an Asian cafe? We may have looked and smelled a bit seedy, but we were in fact quite harmless, and reasonably polite. I guess we didn't look like subarctic explorers; perhaps he saw through our disguise, or perhaps he just wasn't interested. In any event, we left, puzzled by our reception. Later, a resident of Reliance mentioned that the owner of the lodge "could be difficult to get along with." We agreed, as we had been hospitably received everywhere we had gone in the North. Some northerners were suspicious of our motives, or didn't feel that we were experienced enough to succeed with our plans, but even they were willing to talk and listen. One of the most obvious traits of northerners—particularly those with experience in the bush—was hospitality. We always had invitations for tea, a meal, showers, or simply talk, and the generosity of others is one of the memories of the trip that I treasure most. The incident at Taltheilie Narrows stood out as an aberration, but it did make us more appreciative of future acts of kindness.

Shortly after skulking away from the lodge, we were windbound again—a perfect cap to a discouraging day. The next morning we began the long run along the north shore of McLeod Bay. Mercifully, the winds abated and we were able to cover eighty miles in two days of easy traveling. The weather was warm, the views expansive: scattered cumulus, a sweep of blue water, and the dark cliffs of Pethei and Kahochella peninsulas to the south, part of an escarpment associated with the massive MacDonald Fault.

We passed several waterfalls spilling directly into the lake from the north, the ends of rivers flowing out of the Barren Grounds. Treeline, that meandering border between boreal forest and arctic tundra, was less than twenty-five miles away. For the moment we were running parallel to it, but soon we would meet it. The Barrens were close at hand, the spruce and birch much shorter than they had been at Resolution, and the first dim stars of the season already hinted of autumn. It was odd: the warm days, the dry, almost xeric uplands wilting beneath the August sun, the smell of a forest sunk deep in summer, the cries of yearling gulls—within a week we would be beyond all of it.

On August 1 we camped within sight of Fairchild Point, which meant that we were almost finished with Great Slave Lake. Reliance, at the tip of the point, was where we hoped to find our three canoes and winter supplies, dropped by the barge from Hay River. It was exciting to think of waiting mail and the end to our herky-jerky progression across the lake. We had done well in spite of the winds—six hundred miles in twenty-four days, with many enforced time-outs called by the Great Umpire in the Sky. All that was left was a fifteen-mile crossing of the bay that separated us from Reliance—an easy shot if the winds were calm—or a slightly longer paddle along the margin of the lake if the winds were up. Yes, all that was left was another episode of *The Bozos in the North*, only this time it wasn't funny and no one laughed—at least until it was over and we could give thanks for being alive.

We were up at 12:30 A.M. and out of camp by two, hoping to reach Reliance before the winds rose. We were faced with an immediate decision—along the shore or across the bay? There was a gentle, innocuous wind blowing out of the northeast, but it was early enough in the morning that we had little fear of its rising. It had been unpredictable during the preceding weeks, but the mornings almost always had been still. The anticipation of finishing Great Slave Lake urged us to take the more direct route, and off we went. There was little discussion regarding the merits of this decision; most of us simply assented by virtue of our silence. There were a few questions, but no one forced the group to consider the alternative. It was as if we were drawn into our decision by a collective will to reach Reliance as soon as possible, and *Denise* was pulled out into the lake by our desire.

For the first hour things went well, although I felt a little vulnerable as the shore receded and we paddled through the dim light. Across the bay, perhaps ten miles, we could see a flashing red beacon marking the tip of Fairchild Point. This seemed easy enough.

And then gradually, what had been a light breeze became a moderate breeze, and the moderate breeze turned into a strong offshore wind blowing across our bow. The surface of the lake was no longer still; first we had light chop, then rough waves. We paddled harder, beginning to wish for the opposite shore and hoping that the wind and waves would calm. But they didn't; soon *Denise* was rocking in an uncomfortable, side-to-side motion and water was washing against the gunwales. The only alternative was to turn *Denise* into the wind—harder paddling, but to run with the wind would have launched us into the middle of the bay. Still the wind increased in velocity; waves began breaking over the bow—not much water, but enough to reinforce our sense of vulnerability. We paddled faster, harder. There were no halfhearted strokes; no one talked, and all of our energy was marshaled for the line that led into the lee of Fairchild Point. Under duress we had become a machine striving toward the limit of its efficiency and endurance. Our thoughts reflected back to Point Roche, of how a half hour in the water had left us on the verge of hypothermia. And here, in the eastern part of the lake, the water was much colder—the lake was deeper, the winter's ice more recently melted. There was no way we would survive a swamping; we were too far from shore, and no one would pass our way. Our hasty decision loomed very large, and I imagined the headlines: Eight Canoeists Perish in Great Slave Lake. Not a good way for the Bozos to end their trip, sinking slowly into hypothermia and a chilled sleep seven miles from shore.

The strain of muscles, the sweep of paddle blades as they dug for maximum effect: Fairchild Point seemed to hang in the faint light, as far away as it had ever been. Waves broke over the bow, and the winds held steady. We worked as hard as we could, and willed our way to safety. "Not like this, not in such a stupid way. . . ." And then, as if to calm us and take our minds off the cursed wind, Robert began telling the story of *The Count of Monte Cristo*. His poet's voice drew us into the tale, away from the waves and worry; it washed over us, and our minds wandered to a France of the early 1800s. We paddled on as Robert wove his tale—through the treachery that led to the count's ten-year imprisonment in the Château d'If, through his escape and subsequent revenge. The waves were still there, but they were less menacing; the uneasy minutes gave way to an hour, and our strained work brought *Denise* into the shelter of land. We were safe, and our pace slowed. We were tired but euphoric, riding the aftershock of adrenalin and the exhilaration of having survived. Reliance was less than a mile away, yet Robert was not done with the count, and we stopped the canoe, unwilling to let our arrival disrupt his telling of the story.

A close call. Or was it? Probably—and in looking back over the trip, it seems like the only time that our lives were obviously threatened. There may have been others, of course—thin ice underfoot, an aggressive sow grizzly with two cubs just around the corner—but I was not aware of them. If the wind had grown a little stronger we might have swamped, and that would have been it. I was worried at the time, but the incident seemed more dangerous in retrospect. Sometimes the worst fear comes after a close call, after the adrenalin has vanished and the imagination begins to roll. It can happen in the mountains: a head-sized rock comes hurtling down a gully, misses you by two feet, and explodes in a shatter of fragments hundreds of feet below. A slope that you crossed only a few minutes before avalanches, sending tons of snow roaring into the valley below. Your foot slips while traversing easy ground, and you almost tumble over a fifty-foot cliff. If you had been two feet to the left . . . if you had strapped on the skis a few minutes later . . . if you hadn't grabbed that handhold . . . if the waves had built. . . . You were very close to the boundary between life and death, but you were too busy reacting to realize it. Yet after the incident has passed there is a sudden rush of memory, and you shudder. It's here that you confront your own mortality, glance over that fragile cornice separating you from oblivion. These are experiences few welcome in advance, but most embrace in retrospect: You've seen the Beast, and you've survived.

Still, it's foolish to place yourself in overtly dangerous situations—unless you are overly fond of adrenalin or can't wait to use that burial plan you've been paying premiums on for the last ten years. Why did we choose the route we did? Why did we paddle out into the gentle breeze after our experience at Point Roche and constant exposure to the capricious winds of Great Slave Lake? Haste perhaps, or maybe overconfidence. Yet in rehashing the incident, it turned out that some of us had felt that we were making the wrong decision—but no one spoke up loudly enough to alter our course. We were sucked in by a collective desire; we acquiesced, and in doing so, assented. And acquiescence is worse than a conscious decision. Even if a decision gets you in trouble, it's a positive action—you've made a choice. Acquiescence is passive; you become a victim rather than an individual with free will. Better to die because of a stupid choice than because you were dragged unwillingly, but without protest, into a rotten situation.

We paddled into Reliance at five in the morning, just as the sun broke over the hills. There wasn't much to the place—a few cabins, a small fishing lodge, a weather station, and an abandoned RCMP post. Of course, there were also the requisite fifty-five gallon fuel drums ("arctic poppies") scattered about, a large radio tower, and a generator chugging away in the background. Across the way we could see our three canoes and an immense mound of boxes covered with plastic; our winter supplies had arrived and we were set for the Barrens. As *Denise* covered her last few hundred yards on Great Slave Lake, I imagined the scene as recorded in the style of an early nineteenth-century British officer:

> At five o'clock in the morning of August 2, in the Year of our Lord nineteen hundred and seventy-seven, we hove to in sight of Fort Reliance. Here terminated our voyage up the Mackenzie River and across the length of Great Slave Lake. After twenty-four days of the most fatiguing and arduous exertions, we were at once relieved by the assurance that our trials, if only briefly, were at an end. In honor of the occasion, we fired off a round and I ordered a ration of spirits for the men, who were thus heartened.

We remained in Reliance until August 5, resupplying for the three-week journey into the Thelon, re-sorting and packing food and equipment for the winter, receiving instructions on how to use the meteorological equipment supplied by the Atmospheric Environment Service, and making arrangements for meeting the air charter that would fly in winter supplies. By this time the resupply procedure was familiar. Kurt, "the Food Czar," directed the operation. First, consolidate any leftover food. Refill peanut butter, margarine, and honey containers, and restock the spice kit. Make sure that we have enough flour, breakfasts, lunches, and dinners to see us through to the next resupply, and that everything is waterproofed. Spread it all out on the ground, and wonder where it is all going to go. Fill the four food packs—one each for breakfast, lunch, and dinner, and one for condiments (flour, drink mixes, spices, and extra food). Test the packs, lifting each a few inches off the ground. Curse violently. Heft one onto your shoulders with someone's help, and struggle to get your arms through the straps. Curse and groan loudly. Stagger around for a few steps, moaning as the margarine container jabs you in the kidneys. Commiserate with the poor sucker burdened down with the condiments pack. Groan a bit more. Set the pack down. Laugh, shake your head and say, "They're not too bad this time."

We had hoped to meet Ron and Roger Catling, but they were off at Roger's camp in the Barrens. Ron had offered to make sure that our air charters came off as planned, and to pay the companies from our Yellowknife bank account, while Roger was renting us his dog team for the winter. Ron and Roger would prove to be very dependable and honest in their dealings with us, but we felt just the slightest bit uneasy about paddling off toward the Thelon and leaving our fate and money to people known to us only through letters and phone calls. We wouldn't be forgotten, would we?

Arranging for the charter meant that we needed to make a decision about our overwintering location. There were two obvious choices: Hornby Point, where Hornby and his companions perished, and "Warden's Grove," a small stand of spruce about thirty miles upstream from Hornby Point. There was a cabin there, built in the early 1960s. According to Ernie Kuyt, a Canadian Wildlife Service biologist who had done extensive research in the Thelon area, the structure was still in good condition. Robert argued for Hornby Point, saying that the spirit of the journey demanded that we winter there and build a memorial cabin to the three victims of the winter of 1926–27. The rest of us felt that Warden's Grove would probably make a better choice: A sound cabin was already there, making winter preparations easier and less rushed. As it was, there would be a great deal to do before the snow flew without adding the labor of constructing a complete cabin in six weeks. There was also the feeling that the Thelon did not need another cabin along its banks; the slow-growing forests near the northern tree limit would bear the scars of our cutting and building for a long time to come.

Both arguments were valid, but the group voted to go with Warden's Grove, unless it proved to be unsuitable for our needs. John, Mike, Gary, Kurt, and I felt the pull of the Hornby tragedy much less than did Robert. For me, the story, as told through Edgar Christian's diary, was an important aspect of the trip. But there were many other considerations, including environmental impact, the seemingly overwhelming list of projects that needed to be accomplished before winter set in, and our unfamiliarity with the Barren Grounds. Except for Robert, we all thought conservatively in this instance, and we opted for the cabin.

Robert acquiesced without arguing, but our decision hurt. He had been rebuffed when we decided to take a rest day at Brintnell Creek, and he told me later that our choice of Warden's Grove further separated him from the rest of the party. For Robert, the nature of the journey had been unalterably changed, but we did not realize the depth of his disappointment until we were well into the winter and the consequences of his disillusionment manifested themselves.

The staff at the weather station—three technicians and a cook—did their best to make us feel at home, inviting us in for meals, showers, and music. The music was a treat, especially after seven weeks around four other singing-impaired males, Robert being the only member of our crew with a voice suitable for public recital. Jim, the cook, went out of his way to be hospitable; we gorged ourselves on steak, fresh salad, ice cream, and cherry pie. Two gallons of ice cream and four cherry pies at one sitting wasn't a bad tally: Here was a genuine "Fat Daddy's," and we all looked like loyal customers, staggering off to our tents with bloated bellies and beards full of crumbs.

In spite of the hospitality and the satisfaction of having paddled eleven hundred miles from the Macmillan, the Reliance resupply was a melancholy time for me. I slipped in and out of a mild depression, and my confidence ebbed. Why? Part of it was the sudden transition from movement to sluggish, sporadic activity. We had paddled hard in traversing McLeod Bay, and there had been the exciting, draining finale. Somehow, it was difficult to move from that to pottering around with food and thinking about friends and family. I missed them and felt the great distance that separated us. The comfortable, warm relationships mocked my commitment to the coming winter of isolation, as did the pleasant meals, warm showers, and the attractive young woman who was on the staff at the weather station. Did I really want to do it? Wasn't I being a little foolish? Yes to the first question, no to the second, but I ached just the same. Fourteen months is a long time to be with the same small group of people, and to be away from those to whom you are closest. So I read and reread letters, and imagined the daily routines of the writers' lives. I yearned for the diversity and love of their companionship, while knowing all along that the feelings of loss would pass as soon as we were on the trail again.

CHAPTER FIVE
Into the Barren Grounds

The northern barrens have a beauty of their own. There is something in
the boundlessness of the rolling plains that is even more humbling than
mountains, and the monotony disappears completely on close inspection. The
strange light and cloud effects are constantly changing. Everywhere there are
lakes; to the natives who know the Athabaska and Slave Rivers so much
crystal clear water is in itself a constant cause for praise.
— C.H.D. Clarke, *A Biological Investigation of the Thelon Game Sanctuary*

ANYONE FACING A JOURNEY into the unknown—which is what adventures are
all about—must have a moment of doubt somewhere along the way. There must
be a crisis of confidence, when the spirit balks and the heart yearns for the familiar.
My worries peaked on the morning of August 5, 1977, as we prepared to leave
Reliance and travel north and east, toward the Barrens and the Thelon River. The
weather fit my mood: overcast, dark, and threatening rain. We had already said
good-bye to Bruce and Owen, and the weather-station crew had come down to the
dock to see us off. As we settled into our canoes, the emotional impact of the situation finally hit full force. I had always accepted my commitment on an intellectual
level—the trip would last fourteen months; the winter would be harsh, with temperatures down to minus 50°; we would be living three hundred miles from the
nearest settlement. Yet rational perception often lacks the impact of an emotional
realization. Previously, I had been preoccupied with the immediate demands of the
journey—the need to push toward the Moose Ponds, endure the winds of Great

Slave Lake, and reach the Simpson and Reliance resupply points. I always had known that we had twenty-two hundred miles and fourteen months ahead of us, yet I was usually too caught up in day-to-day concerns of life on the trail to focus on the Barrens and the coming winter. But as we traveled across Great Slave Lake, as the trees grew smaller and we approached Reliance, the feeling had grown: You will be casting off into the unknown, into isolation. You will leave behind all human faces except those of your five companions, and encounter a winter such as you have never known.

Thus, the enormity of the task hit. What some would do easily, with confidence, was intimidating to me. For a moment I was demoralized. The weather station looked inviting, and I envied Bruce and Owen their easy departures—they weren't committed, and they could fly out to Yellowknife without a second thought. But I was locked into the journey; there was no way to avoid the Barrens and the long winter. And then it was time to go: We pushed off from the dock, gave a last wave to the people ashore, and headed around Fairchild Point and into rough chop. Here again were the demands of movement, and a need to fight the winds and waves across the last six miles of Great Slave Lake to the foot of Pike's Portage, our route into the Barrens. Perhaps the waves were a blessing, for the energy I put into paddling cleansed my mind and brought relief from the doubt that had plagued me earlier in the morning. The day became much like most others on the trip, filled with paddling and portages. It was just another stage in the journey: from Reliance to the Thelon River, three hundred miles and twenty-five days to Warden's Grove and our winter resupply flight, which was scheduled for August 29.

Pike's Portage is actually a twenty-five-mile-long series of lakes and carries giving access to the southern end of Artillery Lake, and it was still used by the handful of trappers operating out of Reliance in the 1970s. Named for Warburton Pike, the first white to describe the route in detail, it had been a traditional access route for Chipewyan Indians traveling into the Barrens to hunt and trap long before Pike descended it in 1890. The first portage climbed to Harry Lake through the hills that rim the eastern end of Great Slave Lake. We swung easily into the rhythm of the work; although the carry was the hardest of Pike's Portage—three and a half miles long, with an elevation gain of six hundred feet—and our first portage since the Nahanni, it took us only three hours to reach Harry Lake. Since we each had to pack two loads up the trail, we averaged better than three miles per hour while ferrying loads. The long days of paddling had kept us fit, although the work was easier than during the Itsi-Ross portages. There was good trail much of the way, little brush or soggy ground, and we rose steadily through an open forest of birch and spruce, with nice views westward toward Great Slave Lake. Along the trail we passed sections lined with rows of horizontal poles, relics of what must have been a backbreaking effort to haul a large boat up the portage.

We crossed Harry Lake, French Lake, and most of Acres Lake, with short carries between each, and made camp on a lichen-covered point bounded on one side by a narrow arc of gravel. On the beach were two sets of bear tracks (a sow and a cub?) and on the hills was the rich light of a day turned from cloud to sun. These were good signs. I was happy to be on the move again. We had done well with the carries, and a day that had begun with doubt was ending with confidence and satisfaction.

Into the Barrens. We finished Pike's Portage the next day, making six carries and crossing Kipling, Burr, and Toura lakes. Between the foot of Pike's Portage and Burr Lake the trees thinned out, growing only in sheltered locations, and the land became more tundra than forest. Paper birch, a common boreal species, gradually disappeared as we moved toward Artillery Lake. As the birch vanished and the forest thinned, we started seeing Barren Ground caribou—*Rangifer tarandus groenlandicus*, the deer of the North (*tuktu* to the Eskimos, or Inuit, as the aboriginal peoples of the eastern Canadian Arctic prefer to be called). A beast of legends, tales of great herds moving inexorably across the tundra, thousands of milling animals driven by instinct and memory, swarming over the face of the North:

> . . . the land across the river as far as the eye could see was full of caribou.
> . . . The deer were storming up from the river at the foot of Hanbury Lake. The foot of Hanbury Lake was a moving mass, and there was herd after herd along the shore of the lake and the left bank of the river as far up as Lac du Bois. Caribou were streaming over the distant hills, to the limits of vision. The whole land, on the north side of the river, was full of caribou in large and small herds, some milling, some grazing peacefully, and some running in files. (C.H.D. Clarke, *A Biological Investigation of the Thelon Game Sanctuary*, 1940)

But these stories were of the giant post-calving aggregations of midsummer, when bulls, cows, and newborn calves come together into herds numbering upwards of 100,000 animals. What we saw were small bands of ten to twenty caribou, plus some lone individuals—male, female, and a few young—drifting south toward the forest, stopping occasionally to feed. When one sensed us, it raised its white tail flag vertically, tilted its muzzle into the air, jumped forward, and pranced along with a stiff-legged gait. After moving a short distance, it might stop and stare intently at the intruders. Caribou are such an integral part of the northern landscape, and so important to the people who live there, that the animals made me feel as though Pike's Portage had carried us into a new land, and we had entered the Barrens at last.

Spread out a map of North America and draw a diagonal line from the mouth of the Mackenzie River to Churchill, Manitoba, near the southern end of Hudson Bay. The line comes close to tracing the northern limit of the boreal forest; the 500,000 square miles of mainland Canada to the north and east are part of the Barren Grounds. In all this expanse there is only one interior settlement—Baker

Lake, with a population of about a thousand. The only other human inhabitants are a few technicians at two weather stations and a handful of trappers who winter at isolated camps. The scale and emptiness of the Barrens can be overwhelming; so much uninhabited space, so little to comfort and protect a traveler. Scan the horizon: hill after hill of frost-shattered rock; an undulating sweep of tussocked sedge; a maze of huge, naked lakes and tiny ponds. It is a land that has been stripped bare by glaciers, a land that is superficially monotonous, where "Barrens" seems an appropriate name. Travel a hundred miles, maybe even three hundred, and there might be little change in the texture of the earth. You'll encounter nothing to break the endless repetition of rock, tundra, and water. It just goes on and on, open to the bitter cold and fierce winds of winter, to the frigid air ripping down from the North. Spring is intense but fleeting, summer a brief intrusion that lasts two months and brings with it hordes of biting and sucking flies. Yet the tundra may also metamorphose into fields of flowers; the air may fill with flocks of geese; and wolves, grizzly bear, caribou, and musk-oxen may roam the land. It was once a familiar home for the Inland or Caribou Inuit, and for the Chipewyan Indians who traveled north to hunt caribou. And from the day that we crossed a final ridge and looked down upon Artillery Lake, it would be our home, too.

It took us two and one-half days to paddle the fifty-mile length of Artillery Lake. We traveled along its western shore, through a series of squalls, and fought winds much of the way. The showers approached in waves, hanging gray sheets of rain moving across the hills and onto the lake, enveloping the canoes in sudden torrents. The boundary between comfort and misery was as distinct as the advancing lines of the disturbances—from warm and dry to wet and cold in a few seconds, with my ineffectual raingear breaking the wind, but doing little to block the water.

Midway up the lake we passed the "Approximate Limit of Trees" as marked on our maps. Firewood became scarce, and we began carrying bundles of it in the canoes. There were still occasional pockets of spruce, but they were mostly tiny clumps of krummholz. Krummholz means "crooked wood" in German, and the name is descriptive: branches and needles beaten by the wind and cold, twisted into deformed shapes; trees stunted by the short, cool growing season. In more protected areas the spruce were wind-flagged—erect trunks, with branches on the leeward side only, rising six to ten feet above a thick mat of prostrate branches. Farther out on the tundra, the spruce were reduced to cushions, their contorted stems unable to grow above the protective level of the winter snowpack. The trees hung tenaciously to life, incapable of producing viable young from seeds. At the limits of spruce growth, seedlings cannot survive the harsh winters, and reproduction occurs by vegetative means: Prostrate branches spread across the ground, produce adventitious roots, and eventually separate from the parent plant. The vulnerable seedling stage in the life cycle is avoided, and the daughter plant is then capable of surviving on its own.

After two days of wind, rain, and fitful movement came a morning of absolute calm as we crossed the northern end of the lake and headed toward the Lockhart River, which drains Ptarmigan, Clinton-Colden, and Aylmer lakes. Gray-bottomed puffy clouds hung low in the sky, reflected in the mirrored surface of the lake. Our world was compressed toward two dimensions, the vertical lost in converging planes of cloud and water. The canoes and their inverted reflections ran toward the narrowing horizon; it was impossible to judge distances, as there were no reference points, no prominent landmarks to impart a sense of scale. What appeared to be five minutes away was actually fifteen minutes away, and sometimes what looked to be two hours distant was only one hour away. It was difficult to tell how large our world was, yet there was an intimation of limitless expanse, of earth and sky going on forever.

How to describe the space of the Barren Grounds, whether one is stuck in two dimensions or released into three? I find myself using words such as *expanse, vastness, sweep, panorama, limitless,* and *infinite*. All are appropriate, yet all fail to impart a true sense of the land. The best that I can do is to say that the Barrens was a vacuum that pulled my spirit into its great void. This may sound intimidating, but it wasn't. My body was swallowed by the arc of sky and earth, but my heart rushed into the emptiness, into a land that smelled of freedom. Perhaps this doesn't come any closer to conveying what I felt. Maybe one has to live it—somewhere out on the endless wash of Atlantic waves, a thousand miles from shore, among the moonlit sandstone towers of Monument Valley, or in the arid sweep of the western Great Plains, waves of wind over fields of wheat. . . .

We camped a few miles up the Lockhart, near where the river broke through the east-west march of an esker. Leveelike strands of sand and gravel fifty or one hundred feet high, eskers were formed from alluvial material deposited by streams running under continental ice sheets. Eskers are a dominant landform on the Barren Grounds; some trace the paths of Pleistocene rivers for seventy-five miles or more. Scraggly spruce sprout from eskers far beyond the forest limit, as they provide well-drained and sheltered growing sites. The conditions that favor spruce also attract animals, and eskers are popular denning sites for wolves, grizzlies, and arctic foxes. They are also useful for winter travel, as they may be the only reliable navigational landmarks in an otherwise-featureless terrain, and they often harbor the only accessible firewood for many miles.

The Lockhart esker was John Hornby's home during the winter of 1924–25. With J.C. Critchell-Bullock, Hornby spent seven months living in a cave excavated in the side of the esker. Their home was tiny, filthy, and smoky, and its ceiling constantly rained dirt. The cave meant a squalid, miserable existence for Bullock, yet Hornby seemed impervious to the conditions. Hornby was restless, constantly roaming the tundra and traveling the shores of Artillery Lake; hunting, gathering wood, and visiting other trappers overwintering under less trying conditions.

Bullock was often left to fend for himself and struggle with loneliness and despair. On Christmas Eve, Bullock wrote:

> Alone in this awful shack of continual discomfort with its subsiding walls and crazy roof likely at any moment to fall and entomb me in a living grave. Alone with sufficient wood to make only one more fire. Alone with a dying dog whose foot is stinking with the decay consequent on frost bite. Alone with but the howl of the blizzard outside to cheer me and the thoughts of peace and happiness and the faces of loved ones coming to mind only to remind me more and more of my deep loneliness.

The two men could have passed a much easier winter had they chosen to build a cabin thirty miles to the south, within the spruce, but according to George Whalley, Hornby's biographer, they wanted to experience the full force of the Barrens winter. During the following summer they traveled east to Baker Lake via the Hanbury and Thelon rivers, but not before becoming lost and spending two weeks wandering over the rotten spring ice that covered the headwaters of the Hanbury. It was on this trip that Hornby first saw the double bend on the Thelon where he would build his cabin and die less than two years later.

The esker had a sense of history about it, and Robert roamed its banks, searching for signs of Hornby's residence. Since leaving Great Slave Lake, and in spite of our decision about the wintering site, Robert seemed more relaxed and cheerful than at any time since early on the Nahanni—loose, full of quick humor, energy, and talk. He was nearing his goal, and every contact with Hornby's path brought out stories, speculations, and searches for evidence of the past. As Robert wandered, I poked about in the white and black spruce growing in the sandy soil, looking for cones (lots were present) and seedlings (almost none) and wondering about the sort of men who willingly chose to winter on the esker. Bullock was fresh from England; he had the ambition to test himself by wintering on the Barrens, and little idea of what he was getting into, but Hornby had been wandering around the North since 1908. He knew. Hornby must have been a man of great endurance, high tolerance of physical discomfort, and little common sense. What did Hornby want out of that esker? He must have longed for an arduous existence, and the brutal purity of the Barrens in winter. Looking down the esker, I imagined the winds, the struggle to find food and wood, and the cave falling in around its occupants. Ugh. A person could get cold just thinking about it. Later I found a passage from Whalley's *The Legend of John Hornby*, copied into my journal the previous April, when the trip was still a dream:

> From the time of his return to Dease Bay [on Great Bear Lake] in 1917 his life became more and more arduous, and deliberately so it seems, in the manner of an accident-prone neurotic: not that he went to more inaccessible places, but that he took no pains to avoid discomfort and disaster. Hardship and starvation seemed to take on a positive value for him, as though they were the only sub-

stantial values left, as though an ascetic and masochistic spirit were driving him to some impossible consummation with the country he loved.

I looked north into what the Chipewyans call *dechinule*, a word denoting an absence of trees. This was Hornby's country, a world of suffering and starvation, but much of that had been self-induced. Others had adapted more successfully, and I could almost believe that the land was benign—or at least capable of supporting a reasonably comfortable existence. The tundra was rich, berry-ripe, and just beginning to turn toward autumn. Tiny blueberry bushes hung heavy with fruit that we sprinkled on cereal and cakes. Cloudberries covered the tops of sedge tussocks, their rich, salmon-colored fruits borne on tendrils that crept through the thick turf. Caribou wandered past camp, and a pure-white wolf trotted across the Barrens, following the trail of its grazing prey. The air abounded with birds: rough-legged hawks, long-tailed jaegers, water pipits, and Lapland longspurs. But life's abundance was illusory. In four weeks the berries would be gone; within six weeks most of the birds would desert the tundra and caribou would be scarce. And a bad storm could hit at any time. Whatever peace the land possessed was tenuous; I enjoyed the precious moments of tranquility, while anticipating the sudden violence.

We ascended the Lockhart the next morning, portaged around several rapids, and reached Ptarmigan Lake before noon. The winds were still, but to the north a huge wave of black clouds roiled up, like an approaching wall of airborne soil in a Dust Bowl photograph. After a hurried lunch, we began paddling up Ptarmigan Lake in a strange and uneasy calm, just before we were hit by terrific gusts of wind and horizontal rain. Suddenly large waves were racing across the lake, and we were hard pressed to reach the nearest shore, a tiny island no more than fifty yards across. It was August 10, and we remained windbound until the thirteenth, held fast by an unrelenting storm.

Our temporary home was a rocky, convex bit of land, open to the weather. It was a poor place to wait out a protracted storm, and we hoped to move to a more protected site if conditions moderated. So we slung a tarp over a large boulder, secured it to rocks and a canoe, and huddled in its skimpy shelter as the winds increased. They ripped out of the north, a continuous, howling blast that tore into the island and beat against our refuge. Soon it was impossible to erect our tents, let alone escape from the island. So we spent the night under the madly flapping tarp, the six of us crowded together and draped over sedge hummocks. In the morning, conditions were much the same, although we managed to erect a tent during a slight lull and Gary, Mike, and I crawled inside. At first the tent was a welcome haven, but the winds continued to build and the incessant flapping of the fly became a jaw-clenching irritant. Whap whap whap WHAP WHAP. . . . There were peaks in the wind's velocity, but no gentle troughs; rain spattered against the nylon, the poles rattled, and with each gust the same thought came: "Will it stay up?"

Whap whap WHAP whap WHAP: Water leaked through the seams and our sleeping bags grew damper and damper. We huddled on foam pads, trying to stay dry and discussing how long the wind would last. Three days? Five days? A week? Whap WHAP WHAP Whapawhapa. . . . Robert had said, "The first two weeks of August are the best time to travel on the Barrens." This was some kind of "best time." I thought of Yvon Chouinard on Cerro Fitzroy in Patagonia—he had spent two weeks in a snow cave waiting out a storm. This was nothing. Yet it is one thing to read of fourteen days in a huddled refuge, another to live day after uncertain day of it, with no end in sight.

We talked and ate sparingly, as if the storm had pushed us into ourselves. How to fight off the boredom and weariness that accompanied the cramped inactivity, the roaring winds, and that goddamned flapping tent fly? Read? There was only one book, a history that I had already finished. Write letters? It was difficult to concentrate with the winds and the waves breaking around us, and concern for the tent's stability constantly intruded on my thoughts. There was no place to walk, even if it had been calmer, and I was consumed by lethargy.

Never had I felt so exposed and vulnerable. There was no place to hide, no escape from the wind; it tore into my soul. In the wilderness of the lower forty-eight states, one is never far from roads, shelter, and security. Often there is an easy out: A day (at most two or three) will bring you to a road and civilization. In the Sierra, Rockies, or Cascades, a storm may hit or a companion may be injured, but you can seek refuge and help in the lowlands. Not so on the Barrens. There is no shelter and help may be three weeks away. Down south, the occasional winter storm may trap the more adventurous wilderness travelers, but even then there's the comforting thought that a road is close by and a rescue team probably can get you out of a jam. Just wait it out and you'll be fine. On Ptarmigan Lake we had a different attitude. There was no shelter or retreat, there were no rescuers. We had to rely on ourselves, and wait patiently. We were truly "out in the elements," blown by the winds toward an understanding of that phrase.

One dictionary gives three definitions of the word *element*. The first, and most used today, is "a fundamental substance present in the natural world." The second definition is "an environment natural to or preferred by an individual." (Was I in my element on Ptarmigan Lake?) The third definition was most appropriate to our situation on the island: "The forces that collectively constitute the weather."

It is interesting to note that the Latin root of element, *elementum*, means "rudiment" or "first principle." *Elementum* equals first principle, which equals weather—and there we were! The weather was certainly the first principle for us, the difference between comfort and misery, between moving and not moving. At one time it had been the first principle for everyone: Without the right combination of warmth and moisture, crops didn't grow, livestock died, and wild game disappeared. The weather controlled humanity's happiness and destiny; no wonder ritual, prayer, and ceremony were invoked to influence its course.

But in the modern, developed world we have removed ourselves from the immediate effects of the weather through our all-electric homes, domed stadiums, indoor pools, supermarkets, huge grain reserves, all-weather roads, irrigation, warehouses, snowplows, air conditioners, central heating, and a thousand other conveniences and "necessities." Bad weather has been reduced to a mere inconvenience, and we are piqued when it doesn't cooperate:

"Oh, I won't be able to get to the market!"

"But I'll be late for work!"

"Our picnic!"

"We're paying too much for this beef!"

"I wish this damned fly would stop flapping. . . ."

But every once in a while, we are reminded: Weather is still the first cause. El Niño arrives, and with it a series of severe climatic changes. Australia suffers its worst drought on record while the western coast of the Americas is devastated by heavy rains. The upwelling of nutrient-rich water ceases and Peru's sardine fishery vanishes. On land, agriculture is disrupted by either too much or not enough water. A heat wave, with terrible humidity, settles across the Midwest and the South, and people die. Or a blizzard rocks the eastern United States and more people die, in rooms without heat or in stalled vehicles. The Missouri River overflows its banks in a year of heavy rains, causing billions of dollars of property and crop damage. Drought creeps down from the Sahara and engulfs the Sahel, cattle die, and famine ravages the land.

We are not removed from the first cause; the separation is only an illusion. Sooner or later the weather comes back to us, and when we are reminded of our vulnerability, we protest.

I feel sorry for the victims of climatic instability. Yet I am glad that droughts and floods occur (it's easy to be glad when you're not affected), for they are a strong antidote to hubris. We aren't ascendant over the earth—it only appears that way. A few degrees of global cooling and we're into another Ice Age and our ability to feed ourselves will decrease drastically. A few degrees of global warming, a slight decrease in the rainfall in critical areas, and our agricultural productivity will also suffer severely—enough to make the famines in Africa seem like small change. I'm not against comfort; I don't want anyone to die from cold or drought. Yet we must be reminded of our vulnerability. Complacency can lead to real disaster.

Out on the Barrens, we had to accept the weather as the first cause. Human arrogance was impossible. The winds beat us into compliance. Later, the cold would demand our allegiance. Only an idiot would inflate his chest and say, "I conquered the Barrens." You can only adapt to the land; if you are skilled and it is willing, you will survive. You come to realize that the margin of comfort and safety is only partly dependent on your abilities; it is also a matter of what the Barrens offers up in the way of wind, rain, snow, and cold. It wasn't easy for me to make the necessary attitude adjustment; I had been too long in the shelter of technology, was too accustomed to comfort. I was dragged into accommodation—grumbling, frustrated, often irritated by forced inactivity, and furious with uncooperative winds and drenching squalls. None of these emotions did anything to change the weather; I had to learn patience, and to gather the necessary skills and attitudes. It was a slow process, but as the trip lengthened into months, I began to understand more about acceptance, and life on the Barrens became easier.

We were able to leave the island on August 13, excited to be released from our island and hoping that the paddle up Ptarmigan Lake would be easy. Unfortunately, the wind was still kicking up and we encountered a strong downstream current flowing out of Clinton-Colden Lake—both of which meant more hard work. By the time we swung off a northeast bearing and headed southeast down a short arm of the lake toward the Hanbury Portage, I was in a thoroughly rotten mood. Once again it was a matter of desire, the wish for easy traveling on a day when the Barrens was not cooperating. Would I ever take the lesson of Ptarmigan Lake to heart, and learn to accept the weather?

My disposition wasn't helped by the long interval between meals; we had left camp at seven, and it was past one before we reached the foot of the Hanbury Portage and ate lunch. Analyzing my mood and its causes, I developed Norment's First Law of Wilderness Grumpiness: $G=(T^2)(B)$, where G=the magnitude of one's grumpiness, T=the time since the last meal, and B=bad weather. In other words, the magnitude of grumpiness is equal to the square of the time since the last meal multiplied by the severity of the weather. Note that as T approaches O, inclement weather will have a negligible effect on one's mood. It was like this on Clinton-Colden Lake: grumpiness, lunch, and then happiness. The day wasn't so bad, and I could cheerfully face the Hanbury Portage.

The portage was named for David Hanbury, one of the English gentleman-adventurers who roamed northern Canada in the late 1800s and early 1900s. Hanbury was an energetic traveler who spent the better part of four years exploring the boreal forest and Barren Grounds. In 1899 he sledded north from Churchill to Chesterfield Inlet, then turned west and ascended the Thelon—and what would later be named the Hanbury River—before crossing to Great Slave Lake via the portage that we were about to begin. In the spring of 1901, he left Edmonton, Alberta, and traveled down the Athabasca and Slave rivers to Resolution. From there he worked his way eastward to Baker Lake, where he wintered with an Inuit band. The following spring he began a sled trip that took him north from Beverly Lake to the arctic coast, which he followed westward to the Coppermine River. He ascended the Coppermine for seventy miles before crossing over into the Great Bear Lake drainage and making his way to Fort Norman on the Mackenzie River, thus completing a remarkable journey of more than three thousand miles.

The Hanbury Portage was a series of three easy carries across a divide that was low in relief but of great significance. For the first time since leaving the Ross River, we were out of the Mackenzie drainage. We would have no more upstream travel, and from here on, the waters would lead us toward Hudson Bay. By the time we finished the portage and threw our canoes into Deville Lake, the sun had broken through the clouds, and I felt that we were almost home, for it was downstream all the way to the Thelon and our winter camp.

In the middle of the portage, Kurt and I took a different route from the rest of the group. For an hour the others were out of sight—a strange feeling after the time together in *Denise* and our recent imprisonment on the little island in Ptarmigan Lake. There had been scant opportunity for solitude for many weeks, and the contrast between six people and two was striking. Kurt and I discussed what it would be like to do a long trip in the Barrens with a single companion—the greater isolation, the commitment to each other, and the importance of friendship in such a situation. It was an exciting prospect—to enter the wilderness and go farther out on a limb, to place yourself in a position where interdependence would be essential. With six, there was a greater margin of safety. In case of severe accident, there were plenty of bodies to go for help and stay behind to care for the injured. If a canoe were lost, we could still continue with three in each boat. And there were more personalities to dilute conflict and provide varied friendships. Six was a good number for our trip, but the level of commitment inherent in a two-person venture was attractive. Perhaps it was partly a function of our friendship; Kurt and I had regained the closeness of our college days. We approached the land in similar ways, and generally had similar reactions to other members of the party. We had our differences of course—Kurt was more emotionally volatile, whereas I tended to let things slide or bottle up my anger, but the long hours of paddling had given us ample opportunity to share our hopes, frustrations, and excitements, and to learn enough about each other to communicate nonverbally. More and more, we simply knew what the other was thinking about—the rapid up ahead, the actions of our companions, the overall quality of a day. I'm sure that John and Gary developed a similar closeness; although they seemed less alike than Kurt and I, their friendship went way back and they paddled for hours locked in private conversation.

I wasn't so sure about Mike and Robert. They talked, but there were moments when Robert seemed frustrated with Mike—as we all were at times. Mike was strong, apparently thoughtful, and a good canoeist, but his personality grated. In group meetings he often played the psychologist, analyzed everyone's feelings, and requested votes on inconsequential matters. He tended to speak in a convoluted manner, and sprinkled phrases such as "esoteric badness" and "you don't have a handle on the universe" throughout his speech. Even his passion for garlic, and his tendency to chew on his toothbrush for long periods of time—a classic petty complaint—had become important in our little world, and they could trigger a clenched jaw and muttered complaint if someone was tired or grumpy. These reactions were silly, yet they grew out of the peculiar chemistry of our interactions with Mike. Why do some people get along well, while others conflict? It's not just a matter of similar personalities and interests; these help, but friendships do exist between people who have little in common. There is an indefinable quality within each of us that makes friendship with a particular individual possible; when the right people meet, they mesh in a way that adds another dimension to what normally would be mere acquaintance. Kinship, maybe even love, develops; quirky traits and behaviors are accepted, even though they may not be tolerated in someone else. Whatever the cause, I didn't find it easy to get along with Mike, and I felt that it was better that his job commitment would take him south in a few weeks when we were resupplied. It wasn't his fault; not really. A random chain of events had gathered six people into an imperfect but necessary group. For me, Mike was a comrade but not a friend; we were united by common experience, but we shared little else.

From Deville Lake the Hanbury carried us eastward for the final 220 miles to Warden's Grove. Along its upper reaches, the river wandered through the treeless, granitic uplands of the Canadian Shield, and a maze of rocky islands and peninsulas. Often it was difficult to tell where the correct channel lay, or where one lake ended and another began; sometimes there was only the slightest hint of a current to point us in the right direction. Our first night in the Hanbury drainage was spent at Smart Lake, where Hornby and Bullock were lost for thirteen days during their frustrating search for the Hanbury River in June 1925. The next day, August 14, we paddled the length of Smart and Sifton lakes, through country that Gary said looked like "I-80 as it crosses western Nebraska." In a way, it did: wide-open views and rolling terrain, but there were eskers, and an even greater sense of space. And when we stopped to look around, we found pockets of lush vegetation that belied the label "Barren Grounds," and surprising variation in the form and texture of the tundra.

From a distance, much of the Barrens appears to be covered with an unchanging mat of vegetation and rock. Yet differences in soil and exposure combine to create an intricate mosaic of plant communities. On the well-drilled summits and upper slopes of hills is the rockfield community, a sparse collection of lichens, grasses, and woody subshrubs growing among exposed rocks. The low moisture, high winds, and lack of protective snow cover in these sites limit plant growth both vertically and horizontally. Many of the more common species have tiny, thickened leaves and matlike or cushion growth forms, adaptions that help them conserve moisture, trap nourishing organic debris, and resist the extremities of wind and solar radiation in exposed sites. Grading into the rockfield community from below is the tussock muskeg community, which occurs on moist sites without permanent standing water. Undulating soil hummocks, matted with sedges and thrown upward by frost action, can make walking tedious and awkward. Either you are up and down in a herky-jerky motion, like a person with one leg much shorter than the other, or you are tottering from hummock to hummock, ankles threatening collapse as the tussocks roll under your weight. The ground is covered with a carpet of thick moss, out of which grow dwarf shrubs and clumps of sedge and cottongrass. In late summer, favorable patches of tundra are covered with the fluffy white tufts of cottongrass seed heads, all aligned with the prevailing winds, like tiny white flags above a rich green sea. Alpine blueberries are common among the tussocks, and one finds purple-stained piles of grizzly dung during the early fall. The low sedge community occurs in flat areas where water accumulates. Sedges, low willows, and dwarf birch are common in these areas, which spring meltwater can convert to sloppy, foot-soaking bogs. These communities are easily recognized, yet they occur along a continuum of soil moisture and grade freely into one another; given the proper microhabitat, they may also occur as tiny islands in a more extensive community. The varying topography of the Barrens and environmental tolerances of tundra plants create rich species mixtures in many areas, but it's necessary to look closely to sort out the detail.

I remember one windbound afternoon on Artillery Lake; after a filling lunch and short walk, I dozed off in a soft, protected pocket of dry tundra, with my body wedged comfortably between tussocks. The sun was deliciously warm, the moss and lichen provided a good bed, and I felt both relaxed and sensuous. Rich, organic odors rose from the tundra—the acidic smell of fermenting vegetation being cycled back into the soil. Through half-closed eyes I surveyed the tangled detail of sedge, crowberry, alpine bearberry, and a score of other species: a tapestry of red, brown, and green woven into infinite permutations of form and texture. I was embraced by the tussocks, warm and secure in my refuge. As I drowsed away the afternoon, sunk in sleepy communion with my patch of tundra, I recalled a friend's description of a similar incident in the Canyonlands of Utah. Stretched over a piece of warm desert sandstone, he had felt a semierotic contact between his flesh and the rock. He was, at times, an admitted "lithosexual," one who took sensual delight in the earth. It was like that for me, and the experience gave me a perspective on the Barrens that I would hold onto throughout the trip. There would often be the harshness, the superficial monotony and bitter winds, but there would also be the gentle, erotic warmth of the tundra, the memory of a tiny hollow near the shore of Artillery Lake.

So maybe the upper Hanbury was like "I-80 as it crosses western Nebraska." But then, I like western Nebraska and its wide-open prairie sky. And if you are out in the Barren Grounds, paddling some godforsaken river that seems little more than a repetition of similar images, then get out of your canoe, lie down among the sedge tussocks (if the insects don't eat you alive), take a deep breath, and smell the living soil.

From Sifton Lake we continued eastward: thirty miles to Lac du Bois (But where were the trees?) on the fifteenth, twenty miles to an esker below Hanbury Lake on the sixteenth, across Hoare Lake to a camp below the Hanbury's junction with the Darrell River on the seventeenth. We passed the first spruce since the Lockhart River esker midway between Sifton Lake and Lac du Bois, a tiny clump of krummholz about four feet high and occupied by several tree sparrows—birds that follow the spruce to its northern limits. Once beyond Lac du Bois, spruce became more common, although we found few well-developed stands until we were within ten miles of the Thelon. The river also changed, gaining volume and losing some of its meandering nature; there were fewer lakes and more rapids. Most of the rapids dropped through boulder fields and narrow canyons, or cascaded over short granite ledges. On a sunny southern day we might have risked running similar rapids, but this was a world in which a dunking could have meant lost gear, hypothermia, and hunger. So we ran the easier ones and carried loads where we otherwise might have paddled—slow but relatively easy work that took us through tundra showing the first sign of autumn colors, with bundles of wood balanced atop our canoe packs.

Besides Hanbury, who was generously commemorated by a portage, river, and lake, the maps showed the names of many Barren Ground figures: the Darrell River, named for Hubert Darrell, an Englishman who accompanied Hanbury on his 1901–02 journey; Hoare Lake, named for W.H.B. ("Billy") Hoare, who wintered with A.J. Knox at Warden's Grove in 1928–29; the Clarke River, which flows into the Thelon just south of its junction with the Hanbury, named for the biologist C.H.D. Clarke, who undertook the first scientific investigation of the Thelon River area in 1936 and 1937; and Tyrrell Lake, twenty-five miles south of the Hanbury River, commemorating Joseph and James Tyrrell, Canadian brothers who explored much of the interior Barrens. Together or alone, the Tyrrells commanded small parties that surveyed three of the great Barren Ground river systems: the Dubawnt in 1893, the Kazan in 1894, and the Thelon in 1900. A short distance above the Hanbury-Thelon junction was the Radford River, which drains Radford and Street lakes; on the shore of Hanbury Lake was a wooden post bearing the carved inscription, "Lake Hanbury   Named Aug. 13, 1911   H.V. Radford T.G. Street." Radford and Street had passed down the Hanbury on their way to the Thelon and a winter camp at Schultz Lake with the Caribou Inuit; a year later, they were killed by Inuit in the Bathurst Inlet area. Radford was reported to have had a violent temper, and his whipping of an Inuit man evidently had precipitated the attack.

Because Radford supposedly had provoked his own murder, no attempt was ever made by the Royal Canadian Mountain Police to prosecute the killers.

As we paddled eastward, we passed many animals headed west along the Hanbury, or south toward the trees. Small bands of caribou moved along ridges overlooking the river, their antlers silhouetted against the sky. But there was evidence of much larger herds, of a season when the Barrens was covered with deer. Below Hoare Lake the riverbanks were lined with a foot-wide band of caribou hair—miles of it left by shedding animals as the great post-calving aggregation forded the Hanbury. How many animals would it have required to leave so much hair? I imagined their passage, the big bulls and cows with their tiny calves, fording in a press of struggling bodies, antlers and white tails held high out of the water. Each herd has traditional crossing sites, often where the land funnels the caribou to a narrowing of a lake or river. Although caribou are the most proficient swimmers of all deer, and can reach speeds of up to seven miles per hour if harassed, many perish at river crossings, and herds often appear reluctant to ford large streams. The Hanbury River, with its falls and cataracts, has claimed large numbers of caribou. In 1929, the RCMP patrol investigating the disappearance of the Hornby party counted more than 525 drowned animals in one five-mile section. Swimming caribou are also very vulnerable to human predation. The Inuit and Indians used to hunt them at water crossings, and sometimes killed many more than they needed:

> There is no idea of sparing life, no matter what the age or sex of the victim may be: the lake is red with blood and covered with sometimes several hundred carcasses, of which half are thrown away as not fat enough to be eaten by men who may be starving in a month. (Warburton Pike, *The Barren Ground of North Canada*)

Once, howls from a nearby hill alerted us to a pair of pure-white wolves moving in the same direction as the caribou. We beached the canoes, sprinted up a ridge, and watched the two lope out of sight. The wolves glanced back at us, then trotted a few yards, then glanced back again, as if waiting for the crack of a rifle. It was comforting to know that wolves were surviving on the Barrens. Between 1952 and 1960 a government-sponsored trapping program used strychnine baits to "remove" more than five thousand wolves from the southern Keewatin and northern Manitoba in an effort to protect declining caribou herds. But the costly program had little effect on wolf populations, and it was abandoned in 1970.

Flocks of Canada and white-fronted geese fed along the sedge-covered river banks; at our approach, they rose in choruses of goose voices and joined the thin upriver stream of arctic terns, yellow-billed loons, and pintails. There weren't many birds moving yet, but those we saw appeared to be flying purposefully, the heralds of greater migrations only a few weeks away. Other birds weren't migrating yet, and would remain on the Barrens until late September: herring gulls, rough-legged hawks, Lapland longspurs, red-breasted mergansers, peregrine falcons, robins, and white-crowned sparrows. The mergansers were molting, unable to fly, and paranoid about suspicious-looking canoeists; they paddled away from us in a mad, ungainly flutter of wings—WHACK-WHACK-WHACK across the water—or dove frantically to escape. One evening we camped near a peregrine falcon aerie. It was empty, but two adults and a fledged juvenile were nearby, circling and stooping in graceful dives, like archetypal predators. Fierce little falcons were still being raised to hunt over the tundra, but Canadian Wildlife Service biologists have documented a drastic decrease in peregrine breeding success along the Hanbury and Thelon rivers, with the percentage of known occupied nest sites dropping from 71 percent to 8 percent between 1964 and 1974.

On their northern breeding grounds, the birds are safe from organochlorine pesticides, but in the winter they migrate south to Central and South America, where there are few restrictions on the use of these chemicals. Then it becomes a familiar story. Prey species ingest the pesticides, and the peregrines concentrate the harmful residues when they consume the prey. These residues in turn lead to egg-shell thinning and increased embryo and nestling mortality; a decrease in the falcon population follows. It is not clear whether pesticides are the primary cause of the decline in peregrine populations along the Thelon, but it is interesting to note that their cousin, the gyrfalcon, continues to thrive in the area. Gyrfalcons generally move no farther south than the Canadian plains during the winter, and often remain in the arctic all year, far from the sources of most pesticides.

In addition to the many species of birds, we also encountered another of our Winged Animal Pals—the blackfly. The blackfly, a tiny biting insect half the size of the average mosquito, more than compensates for the size deficit with three times the cussedness of the most aggressive skeeter. The vicious beasts rose in clouds around us during calm weather, getting tangled in beards, stuck in eyes, and lost in ear canals. Their bite is more painful than a mosquito's, and it often left behind an angry red welt and a trickle of blood. Their tenacious pursuit of human flesh drove us all into headnets for the first time, and while carrying a canoe across a portage, I learned why caribou are said to be driven to a frenzy by blackflies. The canoe formed a sheltered haven for the bastards, and they somehow managed to work their way under the edge of my headnet: bite, chomp, munch, bite. I tried to balance the canoe with one hand and swat flies with the other, but it was an ineffectual defense. Eventually the canoe required both hands, and I was left open to their attack. Ah, for the bliss of hungry mosquitoes or klegs! And to complete my misery, the blackflies are so tiny that killing them gave me little satisfaction.

The blackflies were tolerable while we canoed, since they couldn't maintain our river speed, but they pressed home their attack on land. On windless evenings we ate dinner in the midst of blackfly swarms—and as they feasted, too. The only relief lay inside the tents, but a leisurely entrance brought in too many uninvited guests. So we developed the following tactic: (1) the person wishing to enter a tent alerted his tentmate, who was already inside; (2) the entrant took his position twenty-five yards from the tent; (3) he gave several feints and began sprinting toward the entrance; (4) the tentmate judged the approaching runner's velocity and zipped open the door just before he arrived (poor timing here would have meant disaster); (5) the runner dove in; and (6) the door was zipped shut as quickly as possible. Any blackflies successfully resisting the ploy were quickly dispatched, and the harried canoeists could relax as the frustrated flies outside beat their bodies against the protective nylon.

Below the Darrell River, the Hanbury cut more deeply into the granitic uplands, tumbling toward the Thelon through a series of falls and canyons filled with homogenizing, canoe-eating rapids. The rapids meant more portages, but they also meant fresh fish—huge lake trout and northern pike, taken easily with spinners. Never had we seen fish like these! We weren't out for sport, just animal protein, after weeks of vegetarian fare. Rice and lentils were fine (and a complete protein), but trout fillets dipped in cornmeal batter and fried in butter were a welcome change. On August 18 we were so pleased with our catch that we stopped early to feast on the results. It was midafternoon, we had just carried around Macdonald Falls, and the fish were more attractive than starting the Dickson Canyon portage. We tottered off to bed with bloated bellies, hoping that any grizzlies in the area weren't as enamored of fresh fish as we were.

Our final day on the Hanbury was one of long carries—two and a half miles around Dickson Canyon, one mile past Ford Falls, and one mile around Helen Falls. These were typical Barren Grounds portages—trailless routes over stony ground and through occasional bogs, with little impeding brush. We swung through the carries quickly and efficiently: From drop point to drop point, each of us hustled back for another load, offering a few words of encouragement along the way and otherwise staying silent in the rhythm of the task. Fifteen hundred miles of paddling and portaging had given us a matter-of-fact attitude about the work. Canoe packs, day packs, paddles, and canoes, their bottoms gouged by rocks and falls from weary shoulders, came across the carries—equipment whose summer's work was almost completed. We sensed the end of the season's travel, and Warden's Grove drew us toward the Thelon. One carry, then another; some hard work and rough ground; some pockets of bad flies, but soon we were into the last portage of the summer.

As if to welcome us to the Thelon, we came across our first musk-ox—a big bull feeding on bankside willows just above Helen Falls. He appeared unconcerned with our presence and allowed John and Gary to approach to within ten yards before wandering up the bank and across the tundra in a leisurely stroll. He seemed an anachronism, a shaggy Pleistocene refugee wonderfully adapted to the Arctic, with a thick coat of long outer guard hairs and dense, silk inner hair, called *qiviut* by the Inuit. The only bare skin is a small patch on the nose, and the insulating quality of the coat enables musk-oxen to stand immobile during long and furious storms. According to the ethologist David Gray, the phlegmatic nature of musk-oxen behavior may also be an adaptation to the cold, a way of sparing needless movement and conserving energy for use in staying warm. A massive boss of horn protects the skulls of males and females, then narrows and curves down and out in an intimidating arc. A lone bull musk-ox is a formidable opponent for a wolf pack; a herd gathered into a defensive circle—with the adults to the outside and yearlings and calves to the inside—is almost invulnerable if it holds its ground and doesn't stampede. Musk-oxen survived the repeated onslaughts of Pleistocene glaciations and wolves, but the very behavior that protected them from predators made them an easy target for humans. As long as the hunters were few and used spears and arrows, the musk-oxen survived. But with the advent of rifles, the procedure changed: Let loose the dogs, who chase the wooly beasts and cause them to circle, approach at your leisure, and slaughter the entire herd. Take the meat you need, as well as the skins, in great demand as carriage robes at the time:

> . . . there is a satisfaction in overcoming the obstacles which must be encountered before the musk-oxen are reached, but at the end, when you are within rifle shot of the long-sought game, you find after all that it is a cruel butchery; you do not feel the triumphant exhilaration which results from successfully pursuing the noble moose or elk. In fact, you can duplicate the sensation felt on such an occasion, at far less expense and hardship, by hiring a pack of hungry curs for an afternoon, and turning them into your neighbor's sheep pasture. When they have rounded up the flock, you can take your stand at a safe distance and shoot down the sheep. (Frank Russell, *Explorations in the Far North*)

Hunting pressure on musk-oxen increased to the point where their populations declined, particularly on the Canadian and American mainland. Musk-oxen were exterminated from northern Alaska by the mid-1800s, and alarming decreases in Canadian populations were noted by the 1890s. The species received complete Canadian protection in 1917, but there was doubt as to whether any mainland populations were healthy enough to survive. After Hornby and Bullock returned with news of large numbers of musk-oxen along the Thelon, the government established the 15,000-square-mile Thelon Game Sanctuary in 1927, with boundaries extending from Beverly Lake south and west to Artillery Lake. Since the area was almost unknown, Billy Hoare and A.J. Knox were dispatched to investigate; they spent the summers of 1928 and 1929 along the Thelon, and built a cabin for overwintering in the southwestern corner of the sanctuary, at a place later named Warden's Grove. The biologist C.H.D. Clarke followed during the summers of 1936 and 1937; he completed the first accurate faunal inventory of the area, paying particular attention to the status of musk-oxen and Barren Ground caribou. The boundaries of the sanctuary were "adjusted" in 1956, when the area between Artillery Lake and the headwaters of the Hanbury River were deleted because of the suspected presence of economically significant ore bodies. Still, the sanctuary protected a vast area, bounded on the north by the Back River, on the west by the Baillie River, on the south by a line running from the Hanbury River to Dubawnt Lake, and on the east by the Dubawnt River. Today it is the only fully protected area within the Barren Grounds, and home to one of the largest remaining mainland musk-oxen populations.

Our last portage took us around Helen Falls, a thirty-foot cataract tumbling over a beige sandstone ledge. Kurt and I carried on the left side of the river, past a cairn registering the passage of previous river parties: Eric Morse, author of *Fur Trade Routes of Canada*; Tom Price, former warden of Eskdale Outward Bound School in Great Britain; Alex Hall, who runs guided trips down the Hanbury and Thelon rivers; Earl Dean, our friend from Simpson; Richard Black, a solo kayaker out to "probe the silent places," who later returned to trap on the Barrens; and a French-English pair who had capsized their canoe just above the falls. They had managed to reach shore, but their canoe and gear had gone over the brink; fortunately, they were able to recover their equipment. And there were the ghosts of those who had traveled past Helen Falls before there was a register: Hanbury, Radford and Street, Bullock, Hornby, Adlard, Christian, and Clark. I felt an affinity for these men; they had seen the same country, felt the winds and isolation, been tormented by blackflies, and carried loads around Dickson Canyon. But ours was a more secure adventure, with the benefits of affluence and technology: unbreakable ABS canoes instead of canvas ones; warm Dacron sleeping bags instead of wool blankets; lightweight nylon tents instead of bulky canvas affairs; and the promise of a radio and resupply flights before the winter months. We considered ourselves out on a limb, but the old-timers would have marveled at our luxury. The ascetic Hornby felt that travel on the Barrens had become ridiculously easy, even by the 1920s:

> The days of hardship and exploration in the Arctic Regions are now a thing of the past. One can realize with what difficulties and hardships travellers used to be beset. Now the routes are mapped, transportation is easy and instead of months it is only a matter of days. Previously it was the Explorer, now it will be tourists who traverse these regions.

Perhaps it was a lot easier; perhaps we *were* tourists. I felt a great humility in the face of the accomplishments of those who had come before. (And what about those who were first—the Caribou Inuit and Chipewyans?) Yet we can only live within the framework of our own perspectives. We had leapt from civilization into the Barrens, and were sufficiently awed by what lay before us. Perhaps Hornby was jaded, and had exaggerated the ease of Barren Grounds travel: a little more than two years after he wrote the above passage, he starved to death forty miles below Helen Falls.

We reached the Thelon in the evening, and camped on a sandbar below the Hanbury-Thelon junction, only six miles shy of Warden's Grove. We could have covered the remaining distance easily, but it seemed better to save it for the morning. It had been a tiring day, filled with long portages and blackflies. We wanted to confront our likely winter home when fresh.

The view from camp wasn't much—just the low river, winding past exposed rocks and gravel bars, and a patchwork of scraggly spruce and boggy meadows, with a lone, barren hill off to the northwest. It was an overcast afternoon, the wind was up, and autumn stirred: the leaves of dwarf birch dusted with gold, the last of summer's flowers gone, and sparrows gathered into twittering flocks. It was time to stop moving. We had traveled fifteen hundred miles—from the waters that flowed into the Bering Sea to the waters that flowed into Hudson Bay, from the first flush of summer to its last days. I slept fitfully that night, half-dreaming of Warden's Grove and how the winter would go—and of the isolation that washed over me, the great circle of emptiness that spread over the tundra and merged with the horizon in all directions.

Next morning: down a gentle stretch of river and through a short maze of islands, the nervous anticipation growing with each mile. What would it be like, this place where we might live? How big was Warden's Grove? Would a floatplane be able to land on the Thelon? Would the cabin be in good repair? Past a long ridge of drifted sand on the right bank, covered with pockets of trees. We looked down a mile-long straightaway and scanned the western shore, where the cabin was supposed to be. No building. Kurt and I stopped paddling, and I drew out my binoculars to search for some sign of former habitation. Still no cabin. We drifted along, looking, wondering. And then I spotted it—a gray structure at the southeastern edge of a spruce stand shaped like an inverted **V**, with the leading point of trees aimed toward the summit of a rocky hill five hundred feet above the river. Surrounding the grove was a great sea of tundra; it broke against the island of wood and dwarfed the cabin. So this was it. We had arrived, and there would be little traveling for many months. The canoe ground into the sand below the cabin and I hopped ashore, filled with the happiness of the miles that we had traveled, and all the mysteries of the coming winter.

In the beginning were the waters. They stretched away from the Macmillan River, across the Mackenzie Mountains to Great Slave Lake, through the boreal forest and into the Barrens, toward Warden's Grove and the Thelon River. The rivers and lakes were our home: They bore us along, soaked and chilled us, gave us drink and food. And the waters told a story. They were the stuff of dreams—

endless waves that broke against our spirits and flowed north into an imagined land. But when the snows came, when the wind and ice spilled across the land, the waters would be stilled. So it was time to lay aside our paddles, time to embrace our solitude as the great winter's night came on.

CHAPTER SIX

Settling In

We have forgotten the use of axes and saws, forgotten the joy of doing
physical work. How few know the feel of an axe as it bites into a log, the solid
feel of it going into resin, the clean break of a chunk splitting in the cold.
How many know how to saw—that one must not ride the saw on its return,
only pull. These things have been forgotten, along with walking, paddling,
and carrying loads.

—Sigurd Olson, *Runes of the North*

WE HAD OUR FIRST EXCITED look at Warden's Grove after we climbed a steep
bank forty or fifty feet high, past a narrow band of spruce with an old platform
cache at one end. We found the main cabin on the far side of a soggy tussock
meadow, about one-quarter mile back from the river—a solid, fifteen-foot-square
building of weathered, grayish-blond spruce logs. The doorway was sealed by a
nailed board; we pried it loose, ducked under the low lintel, and entered. Inside,
the eight-foot peaked ceiling gave enough headroom to stand. The interior was
sparsely furnished—some battered pots and utensils, a small library of tattered
paperbacks, a table and several rickety chairs, and two crates of supplies left by
archaeologists who had spent the summers of 1970 and 1971 working in the area.
After poking around the cabin, we separated to investigate the derelict buildings
about thirty yards behind the main cabin and explore the spruce grove. As I wandered about Warden's Grove, the magnet that had drawn us east from the Yukon,
I tried to visualize what it would be like in the coming winter.

Settling In

Warden's Grove looked to be about ten acres, with a tangled understory of alder, willow, and dwarf birch beneath white and black spruce. The white spruce were up to sixty feet tall, with shorter, scraggly black spruce around the periphery; there was a good supply of standing deadwood; if we supplemented the supply from the surrounding groves there would be enough to keep our stoves roaring all winter. There were hare and ptarmigan in the woods, birds chattered among the trees, and piles of fresh bear sign indicated that grizzlies were frequent visitors. The cabin was at the southeastern edge of the trees, about two hundred feet in elevation above the Thelon, in a site that was well protected from the winds and would provide maximum winter sun. Twenty-five yards away was a spring that promised free-flowing water well into the fall. There were wonderful views eastward across the Barrens, toward distant sandhills lining the Clarke River. A glance at our map showed that Warden's Grove was surrounded by varied country that would provide an interesting focus for future explorations. Sandhills, scattered lakes, and well-developed spruce stands were all nearby. The Hanbury-Thelon junction was six miles south, the cliffs and cascades of Dickson Canyon less than a day's walk west. Only seven miles downriver was Grassy Island, a flat, willow-covered valley with excellent musk-oxen and waterfowl habitat. Knox and Hoare had chosen their wintering site well; Hoare later wrote that Knox "had been down the river for a distance of over ten miles and had not seen a more suitable place than the little stand of spruce in which we were then camping." Their two buildings were now fifty-year-old roofless shells, but they were still solid, and, once repaired, would provide plenty of storage space. Warden's Grove seemed ideal; its practicality and beauty reaffirmed the decision we'd made in Reliance about where to winter.

Yet there was a discordant note in our decision. We had turned our backs on Hornby Point; we had decided not to build a cabin, so we would be relying in part on the energies of others. I could not make contact with a sense of their onetime presence, even though the evidence from the buildings, the entries in the cabin's logbook, and the clutter of trash outside all pointed to Warden's Grove as a home or temporary refuge for a succession of visitors. The cabin seemed spiritless, as though its former occupants had left no lasting impression upon the dwelling.

That evening, I sat on the cabin steps and looked out across the meadow. A slight breeze touched the trees, and the sun cast long shadows over the tundra. I thought of our isolation—Roger Catling, our nearest neighbor, was 110 miles to the south; Reliance, the nearest settlement, was 180 air miles to the southwest; and the village of Baker Lake was 240 miles to the east. In all that space, there were no other people. . . . The river flowed on, past the curving spit of sand below the grove, north and east to Hudson Bay. It carried with it my thoughts of Hornby, the winter, and another home far to the south. Home—where one feels secure and comfortable, where there is an understanding born out of intimacy, where there is love. Warden's Grove wasn't our home yet, but time, energy, and emotion could

91

make it so. We had come to live among the silence and the wind, come to what Robert had said was "the place that we had chosen or that had been chosen for us." A peace and sense of place was here; it was our task to connect with it. And so we began to work.

Our inspection gave us a good idea of what needed to be done to prepare for winter: reroof one of the dilapidated cabins dating from 1928 to use as a cache; build an outhouse meeting the land-use permit specifications; and replace the plastic-and-sod roof of the main cabin. Rip out the cabin's interior, and add new furniture and shelving. Clear a platform for the twelve-foot-by-fourteen-foot canvas tent, which would serve as additional living quarters, and build furniture to go inside; build shelters for the six dogs soon to arrive by plane; cut some fifteen cords of wood for the winter. There was also a multitude of smaller tasks—set up the meteorological station, sew winter footwear and some clothing, reorganize the food and equipment for the next ten months, and start a botany project that would extend through our stay. All of these projects would have to be done with hand tools and a minimum of supplies.

The imposing list caused us to begin work with a rush, even though we lacked sufficient tools; most were in Reliance, still a week away from finding their way into the Thelon. Winter could come as early as mid-September; by then we needed to have the outhouse and cache serviceable, the arctic tent inhabitable, and a few cords of wood collected. Gary and Mike began cutting firewood, John and Kurt worked on remodeling the more solid of the two derelict cabins, and Robert and I started the outhouse. We chose a site in the lee of the cabin, protected from the worst of the winds, with good views upriver. There we built a tiny bombshelter stout enough to withstand the worst storms, a structure that John termed "a monument to our winter cooking." It was interesting to work alone with Robert—the first chance I'd had to do so since the trip began. As on the portages, his energy enveloped the project, and we dove into the work without much planning, making the necessary adjustments (there were many) as we went. Activity was bliss for Robert; it was almost as though he couldn't be bothered with the preliminaries—he lived for the doing, the swing of the axe, the pumping muscles, and the growing courses of logs. First came the four-foot-deep hole, excavated down to permafrost through layers of very stony ground. Then the search for proper logs, and the flying wood chips as the walls grew. (Gaps? Nothing that some moss chinking couldn't fix.) Finally a roof of wooden poles, a layer of plastic and sod, a seat of nothing more than two horizontal poles, and a door to block the winter winds—three days to complete a small but necessary task.

A week of work followed our arrival, most of it on bright days that began with crisp frost, rose to sunny warmth and blackfly torment, and then descended into slanting evening light: breakfast at seven, lunch at noon, dinner at 6:30, with the intervening hours devoted to axe and saw. Scant time for relaxation or exploration; we were as full of movement as we'd ever been on the Nahanni. Throughout that week I was filled with thoughts of snow and wind, plus the quietly insistent question—would the resupply plane find us, sunk so deep in the Barrens? But it came on schedule, a red-and-blue Twin Otter banking low over the cabin on the evening of August 27, after we had finished a long day of chopping and sawing. We were ecstatic to see it, but the thought of carrying loads up from the river to camp after twelve hours of work was not appealing. The plane made several passes over the river, buzzed the cabin again, then turned and disappeared to the west. Huh? It had to be our plane; the pilot had waved and dropped several boxes, none of which we were able to find. The only explanation could be that the wide, perfectly flat river was not suitable for a landing. If not the Thelon, then where? A frantic look at the maps and we were off and running toward two lakes more than a mile away, thinking, "How far are we going to have to carry all that crap?" Answer: Too far. Kurt found the Twin Otter at a lake two miles to the southwest; he crested a ridge just in time to see the plane taxi away from shore and lift off into the twilight. It had left behind a mountain of gear and it was bitterly evident that we would have to carry every blasted jar of peanut butter, every damned fifty-pound sack of dog food, every cursed tub of honey—all eight to nine thousand pounds of supplies—from what we soon christened "Cache Lake" to Warden's Grove.

Let's see: eighty-five hundred pounds at an average of eighty pounds per load works out to just about 105 carries, each a four-mile round trip. Figure four trips per day (that's sixteen miles of walking) per person, except for John (he sometimes did five) and Robert (he carried as many as eight in a single day). Total distance walked: 420 miles; total elapsed time to complete the megaportage and earn our Porter Merit Badges: four and a half days. Our routine varied little during the hauling. Robert rose at five, got a fire going, put water on to boil, and headed off for the lake. The rest of the group was out of camp shortly after a seven o'clock breakfast, following the line of cairns leading to Cache Lake. The next step was to fill a pack with as many boxes as possible, pick up a tub of honey (bad idea) or a lighter item, and trudge back to camp, as blackflies buzzed in your face and your feet were rubbed raw by hiking in footwear with inadequate support. Each round trip took about an hour and a half, although Robert (nicknamed the "Phantom 409") was likely to blow by while carrying thirty pounds more than anyone else and humming a cheerful tune—despite blistered feet that resembled the lava fields at Craters of the Moon National Monument. The work was utter drudgery, like a scratched recording of the Itsi-Ross portages: camp to lake, back to camp; click; camp to lake, back to camp; click. Kurt and I hung together, trying to talk our way through the tedium, but we were only marginally successful; a lobotomy would have been nice, or perhaps the Peruvian Indian's semicatatonic state, induced by munching coca leaves. At the end of the first day, our rush to get everything under shelter and out of the reach of marauding bears had reduced the pile significantly—but it blossomed past its original size with the arrival of a second planeload. This hardly seemed fair, what with the river so close to camp!

Yet soon there was more food and equipment in our camp than at the lake. We managed to manhandle almost everything—the bulky sacks of dog food, the massive canvas amoeba that would be transformed into a tent, the two barrel stoves, and the wooden Stevenson screen for protecting the thermometers. The only item that stumped us was the 450-pound barrel of kerosene. Even Robert wouldn't try that one, and we decided that it would be easier to fill smaller containers when we needed kerosene. One time, as I carried a load of cheese back to camp, I thought of the route that it had taken, of all the energy required to get it to Warden's Grove: by pickup truck from a cheese factory in Afton, Wyoming, to Idaho Falls, then on to Seattle via Garrett Freight Lines. From the Duffields' house to Hay River in the *Yukon Rose*, then across Great Slave Lake on a Northern Transportation Company barge. By La Ronge Twin Otter from Reliance to the Thelon, and finally the two-mile carry to camp on our none-too-willing backs—all in the name of "getting away from civilization."

We were waiting at Cache Lake on August 29 when the plane dropped out of a threatening sky to deliver its last load. It landed in a cloud of spray, taxied to shore, was secured, and disgorged our six sled dogs plus what looked like half the population of Reliance: folks from the weather station; Ted Butler, owner of a small fishing lodge; and Ron Catling, our unmet benefactor. The dogs looked a bit unnerved by the flight and the frenetic activity around the plane, but I was excited to see them in the brief interval before Robert hitched them to the sled and ran them to camp. I wanted to ask Ron about the team, but there wasn't much time to talk; the pilot was anxious to start back to Yellowknife as soon as the plane was unloaded. Our greetings and partings were simultaneous, but it was still reassuring to meet the fellow who would be our contact with the rest of the world during the winter. After final embraces and handshakes, our visitors clambered aboard, and then Mike joined them.

I wondered how he felt—headed south after almost three months in the North, and leaving us to the long, silent winter. There had been tension among the six of us, some of it directed at Mike. Perhaps he was ready to leave the stress behind, or perhaps he was reluctant to divorce himself from the group and from Warden's Grove.

The click of the plane door's latch signaled the moment of our withdrawal, the falling curtain that would shut us off from the Outside. For a moment I wanted to shout into the wash of the props, "Wait! Take me with you! I was just fooling!" But the plane taxied away from shore, accelerated down the lake, and was airborne into the angry clouds. We were left with the sound of water lapping against the shore and a discouraging mountain of supplies. As the Twin Otter rose and turned to the west, we smiled to each other, stooped to shoulder our packs, and walked into isolation.

We finished the carries two days later. After organizing the food, setting up the meteorological equipment, and erecting the arctic tent, which we planned to use as a temporary cache until the old cabin was finished, we returned to the business of preparing for the winter. In the aftermath of the resupply flights, the atmosphere changed at Warden's Grove. No longer were we waiting for anything; we were simply living, and working through the necessary tasks. As small bands of caribou wandered past the cabin and long vees of straggling geese passed overhead, Warden's Grove rang with the sounds of axe and saw as we transformed it from an impersonal point on a map into a home, a place in which we had heavily invested our energies and emotions.

There were other differences as well. The six dogs more than doubled the camp population. Chained to stakes set at the edge of the tundra, where there was more breeze to discourage flies, the dogs created a "northern" atmosphere. They would soon earn their food by hauling loads, but for the time being they functioned primarily as our BEW (Bear Early Warning) Line, and they filled the air with frenzied howls whenever wildlife appeared. The radio also made a difference. Although we used it only for relaying weather data, its twice-daily cracklings brought strange voices from the Outside into camp, and made Warden's Grove feel less isolated than a glance at a map might have suggested. The radio was rarely on, but the security that it provided drove a subtle wedge between us and the Barrens, and disturbed our developing sense of community. It was impossible to ignore the fact that we were connected to the Outside, and that in an emergency we could rely primarily on a machine instead of each other. Finally, Mike was gone. Even though he was a part of the group, the camp seemed an easier, far less crowded place after his departure. I felt that I should have missed his presence more than I did, but I gratefully welcomed the extra space and harmony.

We had a choice of two derelict structures to renovate for a cache. The one closest to the main cabin was roofless and, of the two, was in far worse shape. Thrown together hurriedly, it had large gaps showing between its unpeeled, rotten logs. Knox and Hoare had spent less than four weeks constructing it in the autumn of 1928, when their supplies were very low and they had to suspend building operations to hunt and return for food to a cache at Hanbury Lake. They finished the cabin on November 19 and left for Reliance three days later. In April 1929 the two men returned to Warden's Grove and built the second structure for use as a storehouse. This building was in far superior condition, so we decided to use that for our cache. Although it was also roofless, and had two rows of rotten logs at the tops of the walls, it was otherwise solid. There was evidence of good workmanship, especially considering the limited tools Knox and Hoare must have had with them. The logs were peeled, cleanly cut, and closely fitted. The entire structure had not a single nail: every log was secured by wooden dowels, and during the renovation we decided to maintain the integrity of the original construction. Kurt and John began the job by replacing the upper logs and adding a ridgepole and purlins to support the smaller poles that would form the main body of the roof. At first the work went slowly; we had to familiarize ourselves with the skills and tools used in cabin-building, and there were mistakes and false starts—improperly trimmed logs that left large gaps and wobbled after placement, inefficient use of manpower, and poor choices of building materials.

The most difficult task was shaping the cups at the ends of each log, where they fitted over the perpendicular course of logs below. All that was required was a simple, semicircular groove; the better the fit between overlapping ends, the tighter the entire structure, and the less chinking needed. But cutting these grooves proved a difficult skill to master. Their depth and arc had to be estimated by eye, then translated into wood chips with the axe, and both processes left plenty of room for error. Either we incorrectly gauged the dimensions of the groove, or the brain and muscles didn't do a proper job of translating the image into reality. With most logs, we went through a repetitious sequence: lifting them into place, testing them for fit, lowering them to the ground, trimming them, and refitting them.

Yet our skills improved, and soon we had a more efficient operation. Thin spruce poles were cut from a crowded clump of trees, delimbed, and hauled to the building site. After about twenty poles were collected, they were debarked and trimmed with drawknife and axe; at the same time, someone else was cutting dowels from discarded limbs. Each pole was then fitted on the roof, three holes were drilled with a brace and bit, and the dowels were pounded home with a hand sledge. After a good shake to see whether the pole was secure, we were on to the next one. The rows of roof poles grew slowly; after John cut his foot with an axe, I joined Kurt on the roof and had to relearn much of what John had already dis-covered. After the poles were set, a sleeve was added for a stovepipe and Robert chinked the logs with moss. Then came a layer of plastic, a thin layer of sand, and finally insulating blocks of sod. The roof was completed by September 11, and only a few details remained before the cache was ready—a small window fashioned by stretching two layers of plastic over a frame of scrap lumber, a door, a stone floor, and three gargoyles that Robert carved on the front purlins.

These projects were individual efforts through which we expressed a bit of ourselves. John sanded, planed, and cut for the better part of three days while building a solid, well-fitting door. I spent several days hauling rocks from the tundra and placing them in the dirt floor, digging out soil, and fitting them so that they wouldn't shift under my weight. It was good work—we didn't need a stone floor, and a less elaborate door would have done fine, but these tasks were the result of our respect for the cabin and those who had built it. It was wonderful to have the time to focus on a single project and work at getting it right. And finally there were the gargoyles, with their anguished and distorted features representing the enemies of Edgar Christian—despair, loneliness, and hunger. There was an obvious irony in these macabre carvings, which guarded the entrance to the storehouse that held our abundant winter rations.

As we worked on the cache, I tried to fit myself into the context of the lives of the past residents. The work that we had done since coming to Warden's Grove had helped to nourish a sense of connection that had been absent earlier. I envisioned Knox and Hoare picking the site for their headquarters camp, and then working on the two shelters. I also imagined the Hornby party rushing to complete their cabin in October 1926 as winter closed in upon them and they began running short of food. They had arrived in Reliance by June 23, but according to a message left in a cairn at Deville Lake, they did not reach the Hanbury River until August 5. In his note, Hornby wrote, "Owing to bad weather and laziness, travelling slowly." Since Christian's diary does not begin until October 14, it is unclear when they reached Hornby Point, but their slow pace must have allowed them little time to hunt caribou or prepare adequately for the winter after their arrival.

Curiously, I had more trouble picturing Fred Riddell, the government trapper who built our main cabin in the early 1960s. Perhaps the cabin was too new, and lacked the clear sense of history associated with the older structures at Warden's Grove, or with the events described in Christian's journal. Because the cabin dated from a time in my childhood that I remembered well, it was difficult to view it in an historical context; it was part of the present, rather than the past, even though I'd heard that the man who had built it was dead.

I also thought about the people who had lived in the Thelon River Valley long before the explorations and wanderings of nineteenth- and twentieth-century whites. Excavations conducted in 1970 and 1971 by the Upper Thelon River Archaeological Project suggest that the area around the Hanbury-Thelon junction was more or less continuously occupied for almost seven thousand years by aboriginal peoples dependent on caribou. The first groups apparently migrated into the region about 5000 B.C., following the retreat of the glaciers from the Barren Grounds and the hypothesized arrival of the first migratory caribou herds. About 1500 B.C., the climate cooled, these Indian groups retreated southward, and Inuit peoples of what archaeologists term the Arctic Small Tool Tradition moved south from the arctic coast. Evidence of their presence extends to 700 B.C., but it is not known whether they remained on the Barrens or overwintered in the boreal forest. The Inuit were followed by Indians, who returned to the southern Barren Grounds around 500 B.C., at almost the same time that the climate began to warm. Surface artifacts and burned pieces of spruce suggest that Indian groups did not abandon the Thelon area until approximately A.D. 1700, during the historic Chipewyan period, following decimation of their populations by smallpox epidemics and economic changes caused by the expanding fur trade.

In the more recent past, the Thelon was visited sporadically by natives. Indians living on Artillery Lake hunted as far east as the Hanbury-Thelon junction, and Inuit groups from the Back River, and Beverly, Aberdeen, and Schultz lake areas visited the upper Thelon River Valley to gather wood. These Inuit regularly cut timber in the vicinity of the Finnie River, about a hundred river miles northeast of Warden's Grove, and may have ranged southward past Hornby Point. However, establishment of the Thelon Game Sanctuary, and changing patterns of land use by the Inuit of the Baker Lake region after World War II, meant that the Warden's Grove area probably had not been visited by native hunting or wood-gathering parties for more than forty years.

After the cache was completed, we filled it with supplies and began furnishing the arctic tent and the interior of the main cabin. The tent was roomy, with double canvas walls for insulation and an asbestos-lined hole for a stovepipe. We planned to sleep three people in it, so we needed bunk beds, drying racks, and shelving. Kurt and I fashioned the bunks from spruce poles and scraps of lath. The pole framework was held together with a mortise-and-tenon joint, consisting of a rectangular peg (the tenon) fitted into a hole (the mortise) in a perpendicular piece and secured with a dowel driven into the peg—time-consuming work, particularly the chopping out of the mortise with a chisel and mallet. When the bunks and shelving were done, we added a desk, seating, and a barrel stove and moved into the comfortable, if somewhat dark, quarters with Robert. Meanwhile, Gary and John were adding shelving, a cook oven and second stove, a desk, bunks, and a kitchen work area to the main cabin. These projects maximized our storage and living space, but with no hardware stores in the neighborhood, many of them required some imaginative scrounging: A flattened piece of tin and a spike became a stove damper, while two small barrels nested together and fitted to the stovepipe served as an oven. After we replaced the sod and plastic on the roof and Robert built a covered entrance for shedding snowy clothes and storing equipment and wood, the cabin became our communal gathering-place and living quarters for two.

The tent could have become Kurt, Robert's, and my exclusive domain, and the cabin John and Gary's, but this seemed like a poor idea. The antagonisms of the Nahanni River had subsided, but we were aware that further tensions could develop if we allowed ourselves to form cliques—or simply from prolonged exposure to the same smells, snores, and idiosyncrasies. So we instituted a rotation scheme whereby one person from the cabin and one from the tent switched places every other week. This meant that no two people remained together for more than four weeks, and that no one would have to endure the respective drawbacks of either dwelling for months on end—the lack of privacy in the main cabin or the darkness and chilly mornings in the arctic tent.

By the end of September most of the construction was finished, and the major task remaining was wood cutting. Deadwood in Warden's Grove was felled with a crosscut saw, limbed, and bucked into sections light enough to haul to the log pile, where they were cut again and split. Wood in the outlying groves, the nearest of which was a mile downriver, was felled and carried to the edge of the stand, where it was stacked in tepees for later transport by the dogs. Woodcutting was demanding work. My back and arm muscles ached after long days of sawing and fighting a reluctant crosscut saw that seemed to seize up midway through every trunk. Heavy logs dug into my weary shoulders as we repeatedly hauled cut wood through thick willows, and my feet grew colder and colder as we worked on into October's snow. But the work was ultimately satisfying, made easier by gathering strength and small lessons. I felt the calluses growing on my chafed hands, and recalled how much sooner I used to tire. I learned that a well-sharpened saw sang its way through the wood and that the proper rhythm (Pull, don't push!) reduced fatigue and kept the blade running smoothly. To cut efficiently, a good partnership was essential—one in which each man knew his role and didn't interfere with the rhythm of sawing. Pulling a fraction of a second too early, or at an incorrect angle, could cause the saw to bind; at the end of a long day, such a mistake could lead to a heated exchange of words. It was the same with renovating the cache or building furniture for the arctic tent. I learned what I'd never known, or had forgotten: The most efficient and safest way to fell a tree; how to size up and trim a log so that it nested properly on a lower course of logs; how to use a drawknife without skinning my knuckles; how to sharpen an axe so that each swing would bite deeply into the wood; how to replace a broken axe handle. Slowly, awkward acts became easier, and muscles grew accustomed to new motions.

We fell into a pattern, absorbed in the immediacy of our tasks. We worked steadily, but except for hauling supplies from Cache Lake to Warden's Grove, we didn't hurry the process. Once it was evident that September would be a mild month, we knew that there would be enough time to complete what needed to be done without frantic activity. We also realized that rushing things meant redoing them, living with unnecessary mediocrity, or possible injury. Thus, each day fed into the following one, and the days of the week came to have no special meaning. Sunday, Monday, Tuesday were much the same, part of a steady stream of work flowing toward the winter.

The work was pleasing because it brought strength and skill but also because it was easy to see how our actions contributed to our comfort and survival. We were responsible for our own welfare; every axe cut, drilled hole, chinked log, and new shelf brought us closer to being prepared for the winter. The sweat and tired muscles were payments that contributed to later security; the dividends would come when a crackling fire and solid cabin sheltered us from a raging storm. We usually worked alone or in pairs, yet a cohesiveness emerged from the shared purpose that drove us to our tasks. We would make it work; we would make the woodpile grow, the cabin tight, the cache secure. The months of September and October were like a long, moderate portage: We worked toward a common goal, encouraged by each other's energies, living in and for the work rather than looking beyond it. And always in the back of my mind were images of Hoare and Knox building their cabin in the autumn of 1928, only two years after Hornby had paddled by on his way to his final winter. We had it easier, but the axes and drawknives hadn't changed; it was still a matter of cutting enough wood, chinking logs with moss, and waiting for the river to freeze. The sense of Warden's Grove's history grew in me, as though all that we were doing was part of a ceremony calling back the people and experiences of another time.

We came to feel more isolated and self-sufficient, but our isolation and in-dependence were in part illusory. The Twin Otter that had resupplied us was a reminder of this, as was the daily radio contact with Yellowknife. This sense was magnified by the events of a late-September day, when we were visited twice—first a mail drop by a plane chartered for water survey work along the Hanbury River, then by government officials. Both were surprising and disturbing; the first because it meant news from home, the second because it reminded us that we were very much subject to outside influences. The mail drew me away from Warden's Grove, into the very environments from which I had worked so hard to escape. We chatted happily about what was happening "out there"; the latest news from family, lovers, and friends; and memories and experiences thousands of miles from the Thelon. Only Robert seemed disinterested; he showed little excitement and retreated to the tent with his mail. Afterward, I felt happy, but also diminished, as though the mail was not part of our experience, and it had disrupted our lives.

Then came the second, more important, visit. In midafternoon the droning of another plane reached us, and we stepped out of the cabin to watch a bright yellow, single-engined Beaver circle the camp and set down on the river. Again it was John, Kurt, Gary, and I who responded, while Robert continued to cut wood. We trooped down to meet our visitors, officials from the Northwest Territories Wildlife Service, and the Land and Resources Office. We were in for an inspection of the camp facilities, which were fine—no problem with our privy, garbage dis-posal, or recent construction.

But it was another story with the Wildlife Service officer. We had two rifles instead of the one allowed by our land-use permit, and worse, one wasn't sealed. A sealed rifle cannot be fired without breaking the circle of string that runs through the breech and down the barrel. Since we were required to have our rifle inspected by a Fish and Wildlife officer at the end of the trip, the officer could determine whether the rifle had been illegally discharged in the sanctuary. The atmosphere immediately tensed as we struggled to explain our unsealed weapon. It had been with us since the Macmillan; Kurt had tried to get it sealed in Hay River, but the Wildlife officer there hadn't been able to find his seals and said that we could proceed with an unsealed weapon. The second rifle had appeared during the last resupply flight in August, a thoughtful and unsolicited (but sealed) loan from Ron Catling, who worried about our protection from bears. The officer didn't accept our explanations; he threatened us with the possibility of jail, slapped a makeshift seal on the offending rifle, and finished with an admonition: "The seals had better not be broken when you come out—the penalty is two to five! And I'd rather see you leave the sanctuary than shoot a bear!"

While Robert and Kurt were in the tent dealing with the angry officer, the rest of our group and visitors waited by the cabin. We had a curious conversation, made uncomfortable by the harshness of the one-sided confrontation in the tent, and a lack of communication between ourselves and our visitors. It was difficult to explain what earthly reasons, besides economics, could have motivated us to live at Warden's Grove. Our visitors felt that we had to be concealing some angle. Yet they were sympathetic to our plight—they didn't seem to care for the antagonistic Wildlife Service officer, either. One of the passengers, who had trapped on the Barrens in the 1930s, said, "I would have had the trees lined with caribou." He congratulated us on our ability to conceal evidence of our hunting—obviously, we couldn't pass a winter without meat, and we had done a good job of stashing it. Now wait just a minute! And the pilot said that he would refuse to take a confiscated rifle out of the sanctuary—"No man should have his weapon taken away from him."

What made me most uncomfortable was the conflict between my values on the Outside and those that I had unconsciously moved toward during the previous four months. As an unfamiliar observer safe and secure in the States, I would automatically have sided with the officer in his efforts to bring us into compliance with the law. The sanctuary was established for a purpose, and it is necessary to obey the letter and spirit of the regulations if the area is to be protected. An unsealed weapon could be used to poach game, and vigorous enforcement is needed to prevent abuse. But when this situation arose, I felt put upon by the authority I once would have applauded. We hadn't violated the spirit of the law, and were determined not to, yet an overbearing government representative had busted into camp and threatened to confiscate our protection. I found myself in sympathy with the hunters and trappers who had become antagonistic toward centralized authority after years of conflict over submitting to land-use and wildlife-conservation regulations. For me, the fundamental issue was not wildlife conservation, as important as that was; rather, it was a matter of freedom from restraint. The attraction of the bush is that the restrictions imposed by the impersonal demands of society are reduced, replaced by the demands of the land and one's companions. The physical separation from the sources of authority and the lack of day-to-day interference create a sense of independence. Yet the freedom to act as one pleases is only partial; it is impossible to be free from inflexible bureaucracies. There will always be the permits, the Wildlife Service officers, the bright yellow plane circling to land, uninvited, at one's doorstep. It is inevitable, and all for the best—left to themselves, many people would harm the land. Yet the intrusions still rankled. We just could not get away, at least not forever. Four months in the wilderness, freed from the obvious manifestations of authority, had changed some of my once-inflexible attitudes regarding conservation.

In political terms, I saw us as syndicalists—a group of individuals seeking to establish direct control over our lives, to the exclusion of the state. We had become like an independent union of workers, and the Outside represented authoritarian repression. Power to the people! Too many days with my focus directed toward the group, too many days of dealing with the elemental necessities of the Barrens, too many empty horizons had deflected me from the attitudes of a suburban conservationist and toward a variation of the frontier ethic. I desired freedom in a way that harked back to an older world and that would bring me closer to the earth. But the idealistic dreams of syndicalism were long dead, its last outpost destroyed in the bloody caldron of the Spanish Civil War; I supposed that my hopes were just as romantic, and as surely doomed, as were those of the Catalonian workers forty years before.

During September, before the search for wood took us downriver, our energies were focused on the cabin, cache, and tent, and most days saw us locked in work and rarely venturing beyond the spruce that marked the tundra's boundary. I'd be caught up in the work for days, only to realize suddenly that it was time to look beyond the head of my axe, and that I needed to be alone. So I would go out (feeling a bit guilty, perhaps, but going out all the same) into a land rushing into autumn. The first frosts had come weeks before, at the end of August. The first snow fell on September 13, deposited by a storm that passed into the mild, sunny days of an Indian summer. The colors of fall spread across the tundra—pockets of orange dwarf birch and yellow willow, swaths of brilliant red alpine bearberry, and patches of other tundra plants in endless permutations of brown. The fireweed sprouting in disturbed soil around the cabin died back, the last berries fermented and shriveled on leafless bushes, and we woke each morning to crisp frost. Fat arctic ground squirrels retreated into their hibernation burrows in early September. Most of the geese left at the same time, and the lonely cries of sandhill cranes grew fewer as October approached. Flocks of Harris' and white-crowned sparrows spread through the willows, then suddenly vanished. Willow ptarmigan molted from their dark brown summer plumage into winter's white; they gathered into huge flocks that exploded out of thickets and wheeled over the tundra. Although the days grew cooler, the weather held winter at arm's length as the autumn constellations rose farther into the night sky and the surviving blackflies delivered their last irritating bites before falling victim to the frosts.

It was a time of tentative intimacy, of precious moments snatched from work, and the first movement toward getting hold of the land in which we lived. But this attachment was one of emotion and knowledge; it could never be one of ownership. The sense of connection sprang from many sources. First there were the morning views as we stepped out of the cabin: the sun coming up over the edge of the world, its light gradually spreading across the empty land; the great silence that clothed the thousands of square miles of our isolation. To embrace the distance, to stride over the tundra and scan the horizon with binoculars, to live day after day beyond the sound of motors and the voices of others—we rejoiced in these things. The opportunity to be self-sufficient, to live on our own terms, to be responsible for our own lives: illusory or not, as diminished as it may have been by bureaucracy, the sense was strongest in the early mornings, during that first view with which we greeted each day.

Then there were the glimpses of wildlife, moments of bated breath and deliberate movement: a dark brown grizzly padding along a ridge, its muscles rippling beneath a supple coat; a bull moose crashing through some willows, staring at me for a second, then veering off into the tundra; the frenetic movement of a short-tailed weasel as it wound among the roots of an old spruce. We compiled a catalog of migrant birds, which grew fewer in species and number as the weeks rolled by, and counted the caribou as they trotted across the sandbar below camp. We searched for wolves and arctic hares, watched brown lemmings scurry along sedge runways, and wondered where the musk-oxen had gone.

Finally there were the intimate details of the tundra. One day I would shake off the fixation of work and wander out of Warden's Grove, only to stumble by some small, private place as if I couldn't see properly. Yet I might return the next day and strong patterns would leap out at me—bright sphagnum moss dotted with brown sprigs of crowberry and its black fruits, willow leaves floating in a small pool, stands of sedge suspended in fragile panes of ice. These patterns were made more vivid by a botanical research project that I began in September. Many plants growing in arctic and alpine environments, particularly grasses and sedges, pursue a growth strategy whereby green, partially expanded leaves are produced during one summer, mature the following summer, and die at its end. This strategy is an adaptation to the short, cold growing season because the plants are ready to begin photosynthesis as soon as snow melts in the spring; it had been found in plants growing in the Colorado alpine; wet meadows at Barrow, Alaska; and the polar desert of the High Arctic. I wanted to determine whether the same pattern held in the Low Arctic environment of the southern Barren Grounds. To do so, I had to mark plants in the fall, and return at monthly intervals to measure and note leaf conditions—work that required long bouts of poking through frozen tundra. The data gathering was sometimes cold and tedious—measure, scribble, measure, scribble for hour after hour—but I enjoyed the time spent investigating the minute details of the plants and following their lives into winter senescence. Once again I was looking for patterns and a sense of the tundra. This was a quantitative search, rather than an aesthetic one, yet there was a facility in both approaches, neither of which detracted from the other. Science and the process of reductionism (reducing a phenomenon to its smallest components) are often seen as inimical to "true" appreciation. But I've never understood the dichotomy. There can be beauty in data, which can add to a sense of place and process, just as emotion and harmony can positively affect the interpretation and understanding of myriad data.

And so the spectrum of understanding ran from tundra detail through wildlife to sweeping panoramas; all were part of the Barrens, and all were magical. Sometimes the magnificent scenes were easier to appreciate, yet the tiniest plants, the most insignificant events, were part of a pattern every bit as overwhelming. Narrow your field of view and magnify the image enough, and you find yourself traveling outward again, coming round to the infinity of space, as though you were falling into the tiniest crevices between bits of tundra soil and emerging on the other side, suddenly flying outward and looking toward the farthest eskers, and beyond. This process of coming to know was interrupted by work, by the need to get on with winter preparations, and by the occasional thoughts of people far from Warden's Grove. Yet it was the manifestation of a prayer: to let my surroundings become understood but not familiar, and always to see the purity and silence of the Barrens as something special. As with most prayers, there was a gap between the desire that spawned the hope, and the consistency of my actions and thoughts. Yet I unconsciously returned to the prayer so often that it came to provide a context for my stay on the Barrens.

As the pressures of work subsided, there were opportunities for exploratory trips to Grassy Island with Kurt in late September and down the Thelon with Robert in early October. Throughout our stay at Warden's Grove, the spirit of Hornby Point had tugged at us; I sensed it most in Robert, and we decided to do a trip before the river iced up. The thirty-five mile downriver journey required a moderate day: we left camp in midmorning and reached the Hornby cabin site at dusk. After having focused on Warden's Grove for seven weeks, it was both exciting and odd to drift by the willow-covered flats of Grassy Island and into the unknown, spruce-lined canyon that carried the Thelon north and east past Hornby Point. The afternoon sun cast long shadows and filled the canyon with soft, luminous light, while moose and white wolves moved along the banks, past indigo waters, through golden grass and leafless willows—the moose permanent residents, the wolves on their way south. By an evening fire, Robert and I talked of autumn stars, the spirits of the three dead men, and our isolation. The security of Warden's Grove seemed very distant from our little camp, and the emptiness of the land engulfed us. So many miles, such a deep silence—a silence that transcended the murmur of the Thelon and the crackling of the fire, a silence born out of the cold, out of the dying fall, out of three deaths.

In the morning we found the three graves huddled beneath a large white spruce and the tumbledown ruins of a cabin. All that remained were walls about three feet high and the rotten, collapsed roof beams; among the ruins lay a few scraps of metal and rubberized canvas and some caribou antlers. The cabin appeared to have been thrown up hurriedly. The logs were unpeeled and little attempt had been made to achieve a tight fit between them; bits of wood four to six inches in diameter had been used to cover the worst gaps. Three tiny windows about eight inches square were set in what remained of the north, south, and east walls. Banks of dirt were heaped against the west wall and parts of the north and south walls, apparently for added insulation.

I was glad we had decided not to live at Hornby Point. The trees were smaller, yet the site was surrounded by thick vegetation, near to the river, and afforded no views. The feeling of expansiveness characteristic of Warden's Grove was missing, replaced by a sense of confinement. And I couldn't ignore the three graves, the drifting memories of Adlard, Christian, and Hornby. I imagined their sufferings: Christian's devotion and loneliness, Adlard's moodiness and despair, Hornby's restlessness and fading will. It would have been a gloomy place to winter—and appropriately so.

I asked Robert what he thought of building a cabin at Hornby Point, now that he had seen the ruins and graves. He said he was relieved that we had chosen as we did—not because Warden's Grove was a more attractive location, but because another cabin would have dispelled some of Hornby Point's starkness and despair and given the place an attractiveness that it did not deserve.

I wandered out onto the Barrens west of the cabin, trying to rid myself of gloominess. Caribou paths crisscrossed the tundra, and back among the trees were recent sign of ptarmigan and moose: plenitude and famine, life and death. Coming out of the trees and away from the cabin was like finding myself in the lee of Fairchild Point: released from the spectre of death, no longer threatened by my own mortality or that of others. Out among the frozen tarns and rime-coated sedge, with the sun slanting over the endless hills and a raw wind coming up, I rejoiced in the day, in my life, in the land. It was difficult to believe that this place had once meant wastage and anguish, that Hornby probably had stood where I was and scanned the horizon in a futile search for caribou. Suddenly it was easy to smile, to look forward to the winter and the loneliness of our lives. But there would always be the image of those three graves, a flash of memory that would bring a little shiver.

The journey back to Warden's Grove was tedious, a day and a half of fighting a stiff southerly wind and paddling against the river. The canyon above Hornby Point wasn't too bad, as eddies gave us relief from the opposing current, but these disappeared below Grassy Island and we often found ourselves in shallow water, struggling to overcome frictional drag as the canoe grazed the sandy bottom. Indian summer had finally vanished, and there were pockets of ice in the river's shallows, and thick gray clouds building in the south. On the way downriver two days before, we had passed many different species of waterfowl—tundra swans, common loons, red-breasted mergansers, herring gulls, a lone mallard and a Canada goose. Now there were only the swans, and they rose and turned to the south as we struggled by. The sky was ominous, the air chilly, and, even when paddling, I wore all of my clothes to stay warm. We seemed to be racing the weather, fleeing from cold with the last of summer's birds. I was happy when we finally beached the canoe below Warden's Grove. As we came up the last slope, I smelled the woodsmoke and waved to Kurt and John, who were standing in front of the cabin. And as we set down the canoe on the wooden supports where it would rest for the next nine months, I felt the Barrens hover on the far edge of autumn, and then turn toward winter.

CHAPTER SEVEN
Winter

When God made time, He made lots of it.

— Gus D'Aoust, Barren Grounds trapper

Dawn was theirs,
And sunset, and the colors of the earth.

— Rupert Brooke, "The Dead"

I HAVE THREE STRONG memories of the rapid transition from a gentle autumn to a hard winter, the first as the Thelon began to freeze on October 12, 1977. Out for a walk by the dying river, red-faced and runny-nosed in a northeasterly wind, I watched ice floes up to seventy-five feet across swirl slowly past the bend below camp, collide with one another, and jam in the narrow channel below. The ice groaned as it buckled under the pressure of collecting floes pushing downstream, and water dammed by the ice spilled over the sand and froze in large sheets. It was a day of lead-gray skies, of snow flurries and scattered sunlight that broke through the scudding clouds and sent crystals of light dancing across open patches of dark water. Later, in the waning hours of the storm, as the wind tore over the tundra and the snow fell in horizontal clouds, I followed a female caribou and her calf as they slowly fed and moved southward with the storm. They worked the terraces above camp, selecting drift-free areas and keeping their distance from me, and soon vanished into the falling dark. Like us, they seemed at home on the Barrens, yet

107

at the same time, alone and lost in the blowing storm, far from their fellow creatures and swallowed by the land.

The second memory is from late October, after ten days of intermittent storms, when the river was solid enough for careful foot travel and the temperatures had fallen to 0°F—temperatures that brought icicles to my beard and a sharp, crisp sensation to my nostrils with every inhalation. Alone on a clear afternoon, I climbed through loose, shining powder snow to a ridge above camp. I could see the sweeping ocean of white all about me; the scattered, frozen lakes; and the small bands of dark green spruce tracing the lines of streams. The Thelon wound through the narrow canyon below camp, past Grassy Island and into Hornby's country, and the rolling hills faded into the horizon. The snow was alive with light as I traveled toward no particular destination, my snowshoe tracks tracing an aimless path.

The final memory is of long lines of caribou moving along the Thelon in the first days of November, headed south with a bitter wind at their backs. They traveled in single file, trudging slowly through the morning shadows—heads bent, hooves crunching in the crusted snow, the sun shining on their rich, brown coats. The herds were mixed—great bulls with magnificent antlers and long white manes below their swollen necks, drab females with much smaller antlers, and five-month-old calves—but all were moving with the same patient, plodding gait. They were the last of the stragglers working southward toward the taiga after the rut—an inertial mass following the memories of their youth and the ancestral past of a thousand earlier generations. And with the deer came the wolves, feeding well as they followed the herds toward Saskatchewan. In the evening we heard their howls, and in the morning we found the carcasses of those unlucky enough to be chosen.

Sitting in the tent by a kerosene lamp after everyone was asleep, I thought about the Barrens, the dying river, the great expanse of winter that had engulfed us, and the migrating caribou. The quiet was wonderful; after the constant chatter of voices, I appreciated the silence made richer by the occasional creaking of wood as John or Robert turned in his bunk, or the riflelike cracks of river ice as it settled into an uneasy bed. Rising quietly, unwilling to wake the sleepers and break the peace, I threw aside the canvas flap and stepped outside to look at the constellations: the course of the heavens, their slow spiral as Virgo and Bootes fell away and Orion and Taurus rose in the eastern sky. I'd never before followed the stars, and I felt their dance, just as I'd felt the migration of birds, the senescence of plants, the freezing of the river, and the fated movement of the deer. This was like Cold Mountain, the dwelling place of Han-shan, a Chinese hermit-poet of the seventh century:

> *Cold Mountain is a house*
> *Without beams or walls.*

Winter

The six doors left and right are open
The hall is blue sky. . . .

My home was at Cold Mountain from the start,
Rambling among the hills, far from trouble.

For Han-shan, Cold Mountain was both a place and a state of mind. The Barrens were becoming my Cold Mountain; I was being pulled into it by the silence, the physics of the stars, the groaning ice, and the passage of life as it fled south. Cold Mountain was in my heart, exploding into the dark and spilling over the snow with the cycles of the earth. Cold Mountain, with its bitter beauty, and an isolation lonelier than the female caribou and her calf, yet somehow consoling: Locked into Cold Mountain, dwelling on its slopes, I was ready for the long winter.

Barren Ground caribou occupy a range in Canada extending from the northern Yukon eastward to Baffin Island and the shores of Hudson Bay. Within this area are ten separate populations or herds, each of which consistently calves in a traditional distinct location. The thousands of caribou that passed by Warden's Grove in early November were among the last remnants of the Beverly Herd, which has an estimated population of 120,000 to 165,000 animals. One of the largest herds in Canada, it has a range extending over six hundred miles in a north-south direction from near Chantrey Inlet on the Arctic Ocean into northern Saskatchewan, and three hundred miles in an east-west direction from Dubawnt Lake to the eastern regions of Great Slave Lake.

The animals we saw were completing a migration cycle along traditional routes that some biologists and archaeologists hypothesize have remained unchanged since the retreat of the continental glaciers from the Barrens some eight thousand years ago. Although the exact timing and route of these movements vary from year to year, depending on weather and snow conditions, we could assume that "our" caribou began their cycle of movements last spring, when the pregnant females, accompanied by yearling calves, juvenile males, and barren females, started northward from the herd's wintering grounds in Saskatchewan and the southern Northwest Territories. Migrating caribou move steadily whenever conditions permit, but delays caused by bad weather can mean that pregnant cows must increase their rate of movement to twenty miles per day as they near their calving grounds, which, for the Beverly Herd, are located about two hundred miles northeast of Warden's Grove in the tundra between Beverly Lake and Garry Lake on the Back River.

Few yearlings travel as far as the calving grounds—they cannot maintain the pace of the pregnant cows and lag behind, or they drown while fording a river in the full flood of breakup, or they fall victim to the wolves that follow the herds northward until they reach their denning sites. Yet the movement of young caribou is important because they must learn to migrate. Somehow, caribou develop the ability to return to the same site year after year. How they navigate—whether by the stars, magnetic orientation, or topographical features—is not known, but the calves must travel through a full cycle of movement with the herd if the crucial learning process is to occur.

The calving period lasts about two weeks during the first half of June. Once calving is complete, the cows and their wobbly legged calves join with the non-reproductive stragglers and mature bulls—who leave their wintering grounds several weeks after the females—in one or more giant herds. These post-calving aggregations generally pass through the Warden's Grove area in late July, fording the Hanbury River near Dickson Canyon and leaving behind a band of white fur like the one that we had found in August. Following the breakup of the giant herds, the caribou scatter in smaller groups, some drifting southward toward the forest, others remaining on the tundra until the first snows. A more purposeful southward movement comes then, with the rut peaking in mid to late October.

As in the spring, wolves follow the autumn caribou. While wolves catch a wide variety of prey during the spring and summer, including rodents and small birds, many wolf populations are much more dependent upon caribou during the winter. Consequently, we saw or heard few wolves after the last of the caribou passed by Warden's Grove—none in December, and very few in January, February, and March. The wolves that followed the November herds must have fed well, for we found many caribou carcasses around camp. Most were only partially eaten, with the liver, heart, and tongue consumed first. Studies have shown that the eating habits of wolves are related to prey availability; in the winter, when conditions are most harsh, prey will be consumed completely. On the calving grounds, where hunting is easy and about 30 percent of the calves are killed by wolves, a third of these may go uneaten, perhaps even killed for practice or play. Yet what the wolves leave behind is quickly consumed by ravens, arctic foxes, and red foxes. The red foxes were permanent residents around Warden's Grove, but the ravens and arctic foxes came and went, peaks in their numbers coinciding with the passage of caribou. I followed the condition of one carcass that had been left half eaten; within two weeks there was little left, and by spring, the remains had been reduced to bone and scattered fur. When we discovered the carcass, a red fox and an arctic fox were haggling over the treasure, watched from a respectful distance by several ravens. The arctic fox, although tamer, was also more aggressive; it hissed and darted at the red fox, which ran off and left the victor to gnaw at the frozen meat. The fox tolerated our approach to within twenty feet—it glanced nervously in our direction, then stuck its blood-smudged muzzle back inside the rib cage. Another nervous glance was followed by hunched gnawing for scraps of meat that clung to the pelvis. If we moved suddenly, it darted from the carcass with a peculiar, bounding gait like that of the cartoon character Pepe la Pew, and then slowly edged back to resume feeding. Even the presence of strange creatures couldn't keep him from a bountiful meal.

But foxes and ravens weren't the only scavengers; we collected one of the better carcasses, carted it back to camp, and hung it to thaw in the cabin. It was not very pleasant to live for a day in close proximity to a mangled lump of meat, fur, and partially consumed viscera, as the contents of the digestive system slowly warmed and plopped into a pan, but the results were worth it—several meals of the meat upon which many northerners still depend.

So it's a hard life for the caribou. Intensive studies of the Kaminuriak Herd, which ranges to the east of the Beverly Herd, have shown that annual calf mortality may reach 80 percent—including 40 percent during the first winter. Wolves take about 40 percent of the calves and 5 percent of the adults, and others fall victim to humans, grizzlies, inclement weather, disease, swollen rivers, and malnutrition. Then there are the blackflies and mosquitoes, which torment and weaken them throughout the summer, driving the animals to move restlessly or stampede in efforts to escape persecution. But apparently they are most frightened by two other insects—the warble fly and the nose-bot. The warble fly is a parasite that lays its eggs on the fur of the caribou. After the larvae hatch, they tunnel to the back or rump of their unfortunate victim, chew a breathing hole through the skin, and continue their development. The nose-bot has a different strategy; it deposits larvae in the nostrils of caribou. These move to the throat, where the maturing larvae can form a grapefruit-sized mass that interferes with breathing.

Yet somehow, in spite of all this adversity, the caribou persist much as they must have for thousands of years, moving through an endless cycle of tundra and taiga, fed upon by wolves, grizzlies, parasites, arctic foxes, ravens, and humans. Although circumstantial evidence suggests that caribou populations have fluctuated drastically through time, only since the mid-twentieth century have some Barren Ground herds been threatened with extinction. Several factors appear to have negatively affected the caribou, including more efficient weapons and methods of travel, as well as the concentration of native peoples in permanent settlements. Studies conducted in the 1970s showed that the most heavily hunted herds were declining, while herds subject to low hunting pressure were increasing. At the same time, the management of caribou populations had become a sensitive political issue involving aboriginal hunting rights. The Beverly Herd appeared to be secure, but as I watched the caribou make their way past Warden's Grove, I wondered about their future. Would the herd continue to migrate, continue to feed the animals and people of the North? I believed that they would endure, but I could also imagine a desolate land without caribou, a land as perpetually bleak and empty as it was during Hornby's last winter.

And so we followed the last caribou into winter. October's cycle of storms alternating with mild weather ended with the passage of the deer; we began a period of 180 consecutive days without temperatures above freezing, as the snows deepened and the rivers and lakes froze solid. The thermometer dropped to minus 20°F and then minus 40°F, and we exchanged wool sweaters and windbreakers for heavy down parkas. Looking eastward past the sandhills along the Clarke River, we watched the sun's course as it rose a little farther to the south each day. In early November, the sun was above the horizon for seven hours, from nine until four, although there was enough light to add one and a half hours of working time to either side of the day. By the winter solstice, the sunlight had decreased to just over three hours per day. Since the sun rose only a few degrees above the horizon, it had little warming effect. Maximum temperatures were often only a few degrees higher than minimums, and for a month we lived in a world of perpetual twilight. Often the sun made the cold seem more intense, because the light didn't bring the expected warmth. I felt I could almost see the cold as it lay huddled on the land. Nonetheless, the psychological effect of the sun's appearance was wonderful; it was always heartening to welcome the morning light to our isolated, frigid world.

The major winter preparations were finished by late October, although we continued to cut wood until mid-November. Once this task was finished, we adopted a rhythm of daily life that we maintained until thaw. This pattern grew out of the requirements imposed by maintenance activities, the necessity of getting along with one another while living in cramped quarters, and the psychological and physiological changes accompanying the decreasing daylight and deepening cold. During the long summer days we rose early, traveled hard, and went to bed late, as though we were photosynthetic beings who ran on light energy. As the photoperiod shortened, we became more inclined to relax—as though our physiology was somehow influenced by the decreasing daylight. But we avoided sluggish bodies and spirits by filling our time with physical and mental activity.

Days in camp were structured around two meals, a late breakfast at ten and dinner at six. Lunch was discarded once woodcutting and intensive work on the cabin and cache were completed, in part to decrease our obsession with food. In spite of our diet—with its weekly cycle of grains, legumes, and pasta—we didn't crave fresh or exotic foods, but there was a tendency to maximize the rate and volume of intake. As had been true for George Douglas, who wintered on Great Bear Lake in 1911–12, "Eating was our chief amusement. The amount of food we could put away was perfectly amazing."

Meals varied in complexity, depending on the motivation of the current cook, who had a two-day duty shift beginning every tenth day. Sometimes dinner was a simple one-pot meal; at other times, four hours or more would be spent preparing more exotic dishes such as pizza, yeast breads, cinnamon rolls, and sourdough pancakes. John's baking oven was very useful, as the dietary emphasis was on carbohydrates—partly because we had lots of flour and partly because the cold imposed increased energy demands upon our systems.

In the Itsi Range on the fifth day of the trip. Looking west past Willow Lake from near the start of the portage to the Ross River.

Mike and Robert paddling in the Rock Gardens on the upper South Nahanni River.

Winter preparations at Warden's Grove—a new roof for the cache.

Resupply, late August. Unloading food and equipment
from the Twin Otter at Cache Lake.

John and Gary's canoe, dwarfed by the limestone walls of First Canyon.

Arctic fox feeding on the carcass of a wolf-killed caribou, November.

Caribou migrating past Warden's Cove, early November.

John discussing life on the trail with one of the dogs, March.

Warden's Grove, September. The main cabin is nearest the edge of the grove;
the cache and arctic tent are farther back in the trees.

Inukshuk above Aberdeen Lake, July 1978.

Female musk-ox "gland-rubbing," May.

Rainbow over the South Nahanni River
from our first camp below the Rock Gardens.

Journey's end, at Finger Point on Hudson Bay, August 1978.
Kneeling (left to right): Robert, Kurt, and John.
Standing (left to right): the author, Mike, and Gary.

The more complex meals required lots of fuel, and extended bouts of cooking often drove temperatures inside the cabin well past 80°F. It wasn't unusual for the noncooks, clad only in T-shirts and pants, to cluster as far from the stove as possible; or to see a sweaty, red-faced, and bare-chested cook, looking like a stoker in a coal-powered steamship, run out into minus 20°F weather to drain a pot of noodles. Thanksgiving dinner was our maximum effort, consisting of roast caribou (courtesy of the wolves), green-bean-and-almond casserole, brown rice, peach and honey bread, Boston cream pie, and apricot kuchen. Afterward, we were "bunked out"—reduced to a state in which only a horizontal position brought relief.

To escape from constant involvement with food, some of us fasted periodically. John was the most conscientious about it, fasting two to five days each month. (He once wrote in his journal: "Third day of fasting—periods of cleanliness and energy, alternated with times of spaciness, lethargy, and weakness. Quite difficult to concentrate.") I fasted one day each month, and I welcomed the break as an opportunity to regain my hunger and to be alone while the others ate their meals in the cabin. Sometimes I'd read Christian's diary and think of his winter:

> *May 5th.*   Today I resumed my digging and again had luck in finding more good food which had been discarded. 1 very fat wolverine Gut + Kidneys and heart and liver and 1 Fox gut. A quantity of meaty bones and enough fish for 1 meal. . . . I now have, Guts 1 day, heart and liver 1 day, meat scrapings 2 days and bone boils to go along with anything insufficiently greasy.

But we did not spend all of our winter preparing and eating food. A tremendous number of projects always were underway, and I don't ever recall being reduced to boredom by forced inactivity or the lack of distractions.

First there were the necessary chores—cooking, splitting wood for the three stoves, fetching water from the spring, sharpening tools, cleaning the cabin and tent, feeding the dogs, and a multitude of miscellaneous tasks. The wood had to be split into three sizes—thin slivers for kindling, slightly larger pieces for the cookstove, and eighth- or quarter-sections of logs for the barrel stoves. Our three water buckets had to be filled at regular intervals. We anticipated that the spring would freeze solid during the winter, and that we would have to melt snow for water, but it kept flowing, protected by a thick layer of snow; each morning someone had to chop a new hole in the ice.

One small but important task was cleaning the stovepipes. Because the spruce that we burned produced a lot of tar and soot, and the baking oven impeded smoke flow, deposits accumulated quickly in the pipes. This led to two problems: a smoky cabin and potential chimney fires. The first was just an irritant; the stove would begin to smoke without warning (usually during meal preparations), and after a few chokes and groans, the fire would be extinguished and the pipe removed for a good scraping. The second problem was serious, as it could have led to the destruction of the cabin. Only once did a roaring conflagration, fueled by an accumulation of volatile compounds, start in the pipes. Robert saved the day by grabbing a bucket of water, scrambling onto the roof, and pouring the bucket's contents down the flue, which sent a billowing cloud of smoke into the cabin.

There was a constant stream of clothes to sew, snowshoes to repair, and leather dog harnesses to mend. None of us had ever lived so long without the opportunity to replace broken or worn possessions, or used our belongings so intensively. Consequently, we soon ran short of repair materials, such as extra wool and nylon fabric, thread (nylon fishing line was an adequate substitute), sewing needles, and awl needles. Because two pairs of pants (one for the summer and one for the winter) had to last more than a year, patches eventually covered patches—first in the knees and seat, then in the thighs and cuffs. Gloves, mittens, and socks constantly needed darning; sparks burned holes in shirts, jackets, and pants; and buttons disappeared into the snow. By winter's end our clothing was shabbier than that of a freight-yard vagrant.

A major project for everyone was sewing mukluks, designed with an emphasis on warmth and lightness. The bottoms were made of moosehide, to which were sewn canvas uppers extending to the knee. A thin felt innersole and three layers of duffels, sewn from wool fabric of blanket thickness, provided insulation. To reduce weight, one set of duffels covered only the foot, another pair came to mid-calf, and the third extended to the top of the canvas uppers. The system was held in place by a toggle closure at the top and laces that ran from the foot up the calf. Although we all used the same basic pattern to sew our mukluks, design variations reflected the differences in our personalities. John began his mukluks in October and worked with extraordinary care and patience, using a traditional moccasin pattern that required more sewing, and tucking the leather in small, even gathers. Kurt and I used a simpler design for the foot section, attaching the canvas to a single, elliptical piece of leather, as if we were more interested in function than design. Gary sewed a well-crafted pair of mukluks, but he put off working on them until after Christmas and didn't finish the project until February—a pattern similar to his relaxed approach to most work.

One other job helped structure our lives—gathering daily weather data and relaying it to Yellowknife or Reliance at six A.M. and six P.M. Weather duty shifted every two weeks, with one of the cabin residents taking observations, which included maximum and minimum temperatures, barometric pressure, cloud cover and type, precipitation, wind speed, and visibility. On duty days, I awoke quietly and fumbled in the dark with my parka and boots. After dressing, I stepped out into the bitter air, glanced up at the sky, and moved to the Stevenson screen to read the thermometers. The only potentially unpleasant part was measuring the wind speed, which meant walking into the middle of the meadow and exposing myself to any gale-force winds that happened to be screaming out of the north. After the observations were complete, I then made the clipped radio transmission:

"Yellowknife, Yellowknife, this is Warden's Grove."

"This is Yellowknife; go ahead, Warden's Grove."

A string of numbers followed; after confirming that the message had been received, it was "Warden's Grove clear." After the data were transmitted, I'd usually start up the stove, put on water for a hot brew, light a kerosene lamp, and settle down for an hour of quiet. This was a pleasant aspect of weather duty, because it provided the best opportunity to be alone without stepping outside into an environment that made reading or writing impossible.

Initially, the radio was an unwelcome intrusion, but I soon adjusted to, and sometimes welcomed, the voices that floated into the cabin from hundreds of miles away. We often listened to other transmissions from outlying weather stations— Reliance, Coppermine, and Contwoyto Lake. More rarely, we switched to the Fish and Wildlife frequency and picked up Inuit conversations from Coral Harbour, Cambridge Bay, or Gjoa Haven, or raised Roger Catling at his camp on Double Barrel Lake. Listening to the voices made me feel like we were part of a scattered northern community, one whose members lived in isolation but still required the reassurance of human contact. I wondered about the owners of those voices; what were they like? And if they heard transmissions from Warden's Grove, did they wonder the same about us?

The daily tasks by which we structured our lives were in a sense liturgical: They were part of a pattern of worship that helped define our world and give sense to our stay on the Barrens. The scope of our existence extended far beyond cutting wood, filling water buckets, cooking, sewing, and recording weather data. Yet these were our elements of necessity, and central to the purpose of our stay at Warden's Grove: to accept responsibility for our own welfare, and to find a life whose rhythm fitted with the pulse of the land.

Unless we had cooking duty, chores occupied only a portion of most days and there was plenty of time for other activities. Cabin fever and crushing boredom are part of the myth of northern winters in the bush, but we never suffered from these afflictions. The preventive prescription was to spend a minimum of several hours outside every day, most frequently on exploratory trips, either by snowshoe, ski, dog team, or—as the winter progressed and the snows hardened under the force of the winds—on foot. We usually traveled alone or with one companion, sometimes wandering aimlessly, more often with a goal in mind—south to Helen Falls or the sandhills nearer to camp, east to the Clarke River, north to Grassy Island, west to Steel Lake, or just up to the summit behind camp. These trips, if human-powered, usually covered under ten miles, but the dog team more than doubled our cruising radius. Such excursions provided us with exercise and relief from our crowded camp, and they drew us into a more intimate association with the land, if not one another.

Winter became a familiar mixture of the great and the small—the brutal storms that swept out of the Arctic, bringing more wind than snow, wind that demanded a face mask to prevent a frozen cheek. The red sun rising through a translucent gray ice fog, spreading a diffuse orange glow through the air. Brilliantly clear days without a breath of wind, when the temperatures fell to minus 40°F and sun dogs (vertical arcs of light reflected off atmospheric ice) danced on either side of the sun. Sastrugi—wind-sculpted mounds of hardened snow. Aligned in rows, with their long axes parallel to the direction of the prevailing winds, sastrugi began as forms resembling frozen sand dunes, but often grew into two-foot-high pillars that made travel (particularly across their grain) a jarring affair. Hoarfrost crystals that blossomed on spruce branches during calm weather, giving backlit trees a halo and transforming small forest openings into miniature cathedrals of light. Tiny flowers of snow on dried, nodding sedge heads; last year's brown and curling willow leaves clinging to otherwise naked branches; contrasting circles of green and yellow lichen splashed across a snow-spattered rock wall; patches of krummholz bent to the screaming winds.

Familiar places began to acquire names associated with our experiences as they became part of our history: Beddingstraw Creek, where we gathered dried grass to line the dog shelters; Cache Lake, where our supplies were dropped in August; Eagle Cliffs, where we spotted several golden eagles; North Grove; Bonanza Grove, where we discovered an unexpected supply of firewood; Sled-Dump Riffle, an open section of water on the otherwise-frozen Thelon River near where we over-turned a dogsled; and Home Hill, the prominent landmark overlooking our camp. Gradually we came to know all of the corners of our world—the small grove of poplars that lined a pond at the base of the nearby sandhills, the only stand of deciduous trees for more than a hundred miles; the short cliffs above camp where the snowdrifts built into impressive waves; tiny forest openings where the trees towered and the Barrens seemed miles away; the small clump of spruce near Warden's Grove where we always surprised an arctic hare; the best place to find ptarmigan. . . .

Our wanderings gave us the opportunity to observe our fellow inhabitants of the Barrens. There weren't many; the last of the migrant birds—snow buntings—disappeared in late October, the caribou were gone, and the hibernators were underground. Arctic ground squirrels had vanished in early September, and we saw our last grizzly on November 3. We saw only seven species of birds and eight species of mammals during the winter, and some of those were only sporadic visitors. Yet time and patience granted us experiences that we otherwise would have missed: two jet-black wolves cresting a hill and staring intently at Robert and me before loping off; a red fox listening for the sounds of voles scurrying beneath the snow, then leaping upward and plunging through the crust to capture its prey; gray jays gliding silently from a tree where they had cached winter food; ptarmigan exploding out of the snow where they had huddled during the night. Like watching the caribou, following the pattern of the animals' lives gave further sense to the winter and the cycles of the land. Getting out told me that rock ptarmigan, which breed on exposed tundra, moved into willow stands, apparently replacing many of the willow ptarmigan that had migrated out of the area a month earlier. Yet many of the latter species remained, and I could count on finding them in the taller willows, while rock ptarmigan remained in the shorter stands away from the river. Patient stalking allowed me to approach to within ten feet of an arctic hare, which was nibbling away at the willow twigs and buds that form the bulk of its winter diet. What struck me most was their size; the largest of North American hares, they weigh up to twelve pounds and have massive hind feet, size 14EEE platforms that give them excellent "flotation" in the snow. I was surprised that they invariably were solitary around Warden's Grove, as the same species is sometimes seen in groups of up to fifty animals on Ellesmere Island and Greenland. Another difference between northern and southern populations is that animals from the North remain white throughout the year, while those from the South molt into grayish-brown summer pelage.

Developing a sense of how and where the animals lived, and appreciating the adaptations that allowed them to survive in a harsh and brutal environment, was another aspect of my growing intimacy with the Barrens. After a night out at minus 40°F or a day of sledding into a bitter wind, I wondered how the creatures found food, tolerated the cold, and avoided getting eaten. Of course, many didn't— a fox skull still wrapped in a grimace of hide and fur, the scattered ptarmigan feathers beneath a gyrfalcon aerie, the frozen carcass of a gray jay, the intersecting tracks of a weasel and lemming all told similar stories, but enough got by to perpetuate the species, in spite of all the elements on the Barrens that promised death.

The desire to explore distant parts of the Barrens also led to longer trips lasting anywhere from three to ten days. During the winter months we traveled, usually with the dogs, north to Hornby Point, far up the Clarke River toward Dubawnt Lake, to Dickson Canyon, south to Eyeberry Lake and the Radford River, and finally to Reliance. The journeys grew longer as we gained experience and the daylight lengthened beyond six hours, and they gave us relief from one another. Those who stayed behind felt that camp was an easier, far less crowded place; those out on the trail also felt a diminution of the pressures from living in crowded conditions. The trips were also a good opportunity to develop winter traveling skills. The cabin and arctic tent were insulators that provided an easy escape from harsh conditions; security grew out of the warmth, light, and food we knew waited only a few miles away. But it was different on the trail: no easy refuge, and life in an environment where you had to rely on your own abilities and those of your companion.

My first trip, in mid-November, was a humbling experience with Kurt that destroyed some of the self-confidence that I had built up since the first snows. My illusion of competence was destroyed, or at least severely mauled, by temperatures that dropped from the minus 10°F range I'd known during winter trips in the States to the previously unknown world of minus 40°F. We began our planned six-day outing thinking like ski tourers in Colorado, but we returned to Warden's Grove after only four days—severely chastened, with our adventurous tails tucked between our shivering legs, and realizing that the Bozos would have to learn a number of lessons before they could be comfortable on long winter journeys.

Lesson number one: A team of six dogs will have great trouble pulling a fully laden sled, plus a passenger, through powder snow, even with a fine runway of smooth ice six inches below the snow. It wasn't enough for the team's driver to trot beside the sled and help the dogs along by pushing it through drifts and up hills; the passenger had to abandon his easy seat atop the gear. Even if the dogs had been stronger, though, the cold would have forced the passenger out of the sled; a thick parka provided inadequate insulation for a resting person. On the first day, with the temperature at a mild minus 10°F, Kurt and I got about a mile out of camp before we realized that our Grapes of Wrath sled imitation wouldn't make it, and we would have to follow the sled on foot.

Lesson number two, of which there will be more later: Watch your dogs closely, and learn their quirks well in advance of long excursions. We discovered one dog's bad habit on the first day, when he (Pemmican) chewed through the leather traces connecting him to the next dog. We repaired the line with nylon webbing—only to have him do it seven more times during the remainder of the trip, despite frequent hints administered with a willow stick that such behavior was not acceptable. At minus 10°F, such mittenless work is frustrating and painful; at minus 40°F, it becomes almost impossible.

Lesson number three: At minus 30°F, blocks of cheese and loaves of bread cannot be cut into edible pieces. They assume the density and consistency of bricks and are equally nourishing; no longer food, they might be better used as building materials or anchors. Since we had planned lunches around these staples, the only solution available at the time was to build a fire and thaw out the surfaces of our bricks, which we then gnawed like hungry rodents. The fire was welcome anyway, since we became cold after standing around for just a few moments—which leads into the next lesson, a two-part one.

Lesson number four: To stay warm, don't sweat and don't wear rubberized, insulated boots. Not sweating meant reducing heavy and even moderate exercise to short periods; avoiding rubberized boots meant mukluks. Kurt had already made the switch, but I had procrastinated and thus suffered the consequences—thick liners that became progressively damper as moisture from my feet accumulated inside an impermeable barrier, and feet that tingled whenever I stopped moving. Rest stops came to resemble a performance by Freddy and the Dreamers, a sixties rock group, as I waved my arms and feet to keep warm blood flowing to the extremities.

Lesson number five: If at all possible, avoid making camp in the dark. Darkness meant that everything took twice as much time, on top of the prior doubled effort caused by the cold itself. Anything that required manual dexterity and, consequently, mittenless work, became a fumbling, frustrating epic—mitten liners off for thirty seconds, on for several minutes, then off again. Erecting the tent, getting the dogs squared away, and preparing dinner were major efforts, accomplished with much grousing, tripping, and foul humor. Our tasks were not made any easier by the fire that refused to flare into bright warmth, but instead filled the air with smoke that made us feel like a couple of semiasphyxiated Tibetans sitting around a choking blaze in a chimneyless house somewhere in the Himalayas.

Lesson number six: Make sure that the dogs are securely chained, so that you don't have to leave the warmth of your sleeping bag to retrieve an errant pooch. Getting up was no simple matter, as it involved reversing the standard process of wriggling into the three layers of our tight-fitting nylon cocoons: (1) remove parka and boots; (2) crawl into vapor-barrier liner of waterproof nylon; (3) slide into a down inner bag; (4) slide into a Dacron outer bag; (5) close up outer and inner bags (each of which rotated independently of the other and had to be positioned correctly for comfort); (6) wriggle hips and pound snow with fists to create a level sleeping surface, and position pillow; and (7) close up vapor-barrier liner. Whew! In line with this lesson, it was also important to refrain from that last cup of tea before bed, to prevent being awakened at two in the morning by an insistent bladder that would, on no account, wait until morning.

Lesson number seven didn't sink in until much later, at least not completely: Arctic explorers, at least real ones, should not have long beards, because facial hair acts as a focal point for the condensation and freezing of exhaled water vapor. The results of this process were an expanding glacier stretching from cheek to cheek and parallel rivulets of frozen snot below each nostril. While neither of these was particularly uncomfortable, and they did contribute to a certain romantic air (Amundsen and Stefansson surely looked the same), the accumulated ice was potentially dangerous, as it made warming one's face next to impossible. If I was sledding into a wind and felt the telltale numbing, or if my partner noticed a white spot on my cheek or nose, the only effective treatment was to turn my back to the wind, remove my mittens, and warm the affected part with a bare hand. A personal glacier, however aesthetic, made this impossible. In January I grew a nice set of frostbite blisters on my chin in such a situation and shaved the next day.

There were many other lessons, of course, some gained from that first trip with Kurt, others not learned until later. But the all-encompassing moral was that traveling at minus 30°F or colder was a much more serious proposition than I had imagined. It demanded skill, determination, and scrupulous attention to mundane details. In the extreme cold, seemingly easy tasks became extraordinarily difficult, frustration and anger thresholds decreased dramatically, and concentration became increasingly hard. The margin of safety was thus reduced considerably in an environment that left little room for error; it was difficult to make intelligent choices and anticipate potential problems, and it was even more difficult to relax and enjoy being outside—which was an important part of the trip.

Kurt: "It's six-thirty; do you want to get up?"

Me: "Another half an hour—it's still dark," as steam rose from the tiny opening of my sleeping bag.

Kurt: "Umph!"

Kurt: "It's eight-thirty!"

Me: "Oh, damn!"

So began the last morning on the trail, which was the nadir of the excursion; we had both slept restlessly and were ready to get up, yet we were also reluctant to face the cold that seemed to have deepened overnight. We struggled to escape from our sleeping bags and don clothing as our bulky jackets knocked frost off the tent and down our backs, and our frozen fingers struggled with boot and mukluk laces. The fire was anemic, breakfast took forever, and my feet felt like they were immersed in ice water. Every half hour or so, I'd explode out of camp, tear down to the river, and jog upstream for a hundred yards in a futile effort to generate warmth in my agonized toes. It was after ten when the sun made its reluctant appearance, rising slowly through a dull haze, with no warmth in its weak rays. Three hours after rising, we broke camp, intending to push on toward the Hanbury. But we abandoned our plans and decided to head for home after lunch. We were both miserable, the dogs were sluggish, our frustrations were building toward critical mass, and the trip had degenerated into nothing more than a survival course. It was a blow to our prides to admit defeat, or at least a partial drubbing, but we felt much better after having made the decision, and were further mollified when we heard that temperatures had fallen to minus 40°F on our morning of misery. We had learned a great deal about winter travel, and we expected that the next trip undoubtedly would be much easier.

We added to our collective knowledge by discussing experiences and impressions every time a party returned from a long trip, and testing refinements on shorter outings. The most important changes we made were to lighten the sled load as much as possible, and to wear mukluks instead of much heavier insulated boots. We then adopted a system of travel whereby partners alternately jogged and stood on the back of the sled, switching positions every hundred yards, and helping to push the sled through difficult terrain. This reduced stress on the dogs, kept us comfortably warm—even at minus 25°F, a windbreaker, wool sweater, and wool turtleneck were adequate protection on windless days—and increased travel speed. We also reduced the length of our lunch breaks to a few minutes. We filled a water bottle with hot tea before breaking camp, wrapped the bottle in a down parka, and buried it deep in a pack, so that we could have a hot drink at midday. Gone were bricks of cheese and loaves of bread, replaced by a mixture of chocolate chips, raisins, nuts, small bits of dried fruit, bread, and cheese. Ten minutes after halting, we could be rested, fed, and ready to move again. Even with less than six hours of light, we could cover thirty or forty miles per day—not impressive by Iditarod standards (dog racers would have laughed at us), but we were carrying relatively heavy loads and exploring the countryside as we traveled.

We became much more proficient at setting up camp. Fifteen minutes after deciding on a suitable grove of spruce—one with adequate deadwood and protection from the wind—we would have the dogs chained to trees (securely) and be unpacking gear. First the tent would go up. Then one of us would work on digging a firepit extending down to soil, with a diameter large enough to accommodate two people and supply sufficient oxygen for a smokeless fire. Since snow depths usually were less than three feet, this task wasn't too exhausting. Sleeping bags were then laid out and a hot brew started while more wood was gathered; within an hour and a half, the dogs were fed and we would be relaxing by the fire, cooking a one-pot meal that featured lots of margarine for added calories. The walls of the snow pit reflected much of the fire's warmth, and we were usually comfortable in sweaters or unzipped parkas. After dinner came a slow ritual of hot drinks (but not too many) and drying the clothes dampened by the day's exercise. Most important were mukluk liners, which were dried carefully layer by layer; then came mittens, hats, and socks, the latter replaced earlier by a dry pair.

Another aspect of our winter's education was learning how to read the land and determine where the best traveling conditions were. Deciding between two routes often required evaluating how subtle variations in terrain, coupled with prevailing wind patterns, affected snow deposition and texture. An incorrect choice sometimes led to a sweaty wallow through deep snow and a bogged-down sled—or it could have meant an infinitely worse dunking. We decided that the fastest traveling was generally along ridge tops and large drainages, although the latter meant increased danger of either plunging through the ice or getting soaked feet in overflow.

John and Kurt had a bad experience in late October, after striking out across a newly frozen lake. Two-thirds of the way across, they encountered wobbly, slushy ice; water gurgled to the surface with each step, and they had some long, anxious moments before reaching shore. But we didn't need such an experience to tell us that a soaking at minus 30°F could be a potentially lethal mistake. The worst scenario was losing the sled and the entire team through the ice; the best was a shivering race to build a fire and shed ice-encrusted clothing before the body sank into numbing sleep.

As the cold deepened and December passed into the New Year, the chances of breaking through the ice decreased, although there were occasional weak places that shifted under our weight or oozed water as we crossed over them. There were times when we were saved from wet feet only by a quick hop onto the sled as the dogs pulled it free from slush. But one danger remained prevalent—overflow, or water that had seeped up between cracks formed when water levels fell and large ice sheets collapsed under their own weight. Steam and sheets of bright blue water often made fresh overflow easy to spot, but older areas were covered by an insulating layer of snow. For the dogs, stumbling into hidden pools of water meant only a break to chew the ice from their paws, but for us the same error could have led to frostbite, so we were always alert for hidden water.

You make mistakes, you bumble through initial incompetence and move slowly toward an understanding of the land's character and an acknowledgment of your own limitations. Presently you begin to relax; you accept the cold and the wind, become more adept at remaining comfortable and confident under conditions that were once intimidating. There comes a time when the environment is no longer foreign, and you are no longer an alien—when you can exult in the harsh cold, in the three-quarter moon sinking into the hills, in your aloneness as the dogs carry you across the frozen earth. A jingle of harness bells and the crunch of crusted snow as the team crests a ridge and the Barrens lies before you, glowing with a soft, luminescent light as the sun climbs toward the horizon. There is the love of movement, the brittle beauty of the land, the still-fresh sense of adventure, and the chance to see what few have seen before. But beyond all else is that sense of belonging to a place, of coming to know it so well after those first fumbling encounters, of holding it in your heart and feeling that you are not a stranger and that the vertical shaft of sunlight arcing into the sky in advance of the coming day is somehow just for you.

Returning home from a long trip always meant the welcome sight of Warden's Grove as we climbed the riverbank from the Thelon or descended from Home Hill. The omnipresent wisp of smoke rising from the cabin's stovepipe meant a stream of associations: warmth and shelter, the daily flow of chores, the aroma of hot bread baking in the oven, idle conversation and philosophical discussions, reading, journal and letter writing, games, and a host of other activities with which we occupied ourselves during the winter. As we unhitched the dogs and carried gear inside, we anticipated hot cups of tea, stripping off layers of bulky clothes, and the warm, red flush as circulation returned to chilled skin. With feet propped up on a bench, we would relate the inevitable war stories and discuss minutiae that seem unimportant in retrospect. Out on the trail, I sometimes pictured the many permutations of the cabin scene: John working on a pair of snowshoes, Gary reading in his bunk, Kurt sewing canvas patches on his tattered pants, and Robert playing his pennywhistle, while the kerosene lamp glowed and a pot of tea simmered on the stove. There was a comfortable clutter everywhere—shelves crammed with blackened pots and the month's rations, boots tucked beneath benches, red or blue down parkas and wool shirts hung from every nail, rows of books above the compact orange radio, a rifle supported by two wooden pegs, binoculars easily available for scrutinizing any wild-life that might wander by. A smell of woodsmoke permeated everything—hair, clothes, sleeping bags—mixed with a faint odor of sweaty, most likely unwashed, bodies. There was always time to spend outside, but there were also long bouts indoors, often enforced by howling storms, when we withdrew into silence, when we laughed, and occasionally when we argued with bitterness and anger. But life inside added up to never being bored, and rarely restless.

Our library was a major source of entertainment. Some of it was inherited from previous visitors, but most of it was imported on the resupply flight. We had books of every description, from novels (*David Copperfield*, *Shogun*, *The Count of Monte Cristo*, *Lord of the Rings*) to philosophy (Russell's *A History of Western Philosophy*, the *Tao Te Ching*) to essays on the land (*A Sand County Almanac*, *Reflections from the North Country*, *Desert Solitaire*) and accounts of the North (George Back's journals, *The Legend of John Hornby*, *Dangerous River*, Pike's *The Barren Ground of Northern Canada*). There was time to read books slowly and in depth, time to tackle intimidating works such as Russell's philosophy and Thomas Pynchon's *Gravity's Rainbow*.

All of us kept extensive journals and wrote prodigious numbers of letters. Never before or since have I felt capable of the correspondence that I generated during that winter. At Christmas, the five of us sent out more than 250 letters, many five or ten pages long. I think that our letter writing was more than a way of passing time; it was a reaffirmation of our contacts with the Outside and a strategy for dealing with the isolation that forced us into constant contact with one another. Even if the letters were not sent for three or four months, they still allowed us to vent emotions and transcend the limitations of our social environment.

If we weren't in the mood for writing or reading, then there were always games: bridge; backgammon, played with a set of homemade spruce pieces; Scrabble, a gift from the Outside; euchre; cribbage; and poker. None of us normally were very interested in games, but we played frequently and set off on binges whenever a new game was suggested. After beating the new passion into the ground during marathon playing sessions, we moved on to the next one before returning to the former attraction weeks later.

Other indoor projects included crafts (the predictable whittling and not-so-predictable musk-ox-turd necklaces for the ladies back home), exercising and yoga—

pull-ups, push-ups, sit-ups, and intensive stretching to keep the food and inactivity from turning us into lumpy slugs—and washing, which occurred more and more infrequently as the winter progressed. I washed my face, armpits, and groin once a week, and my clothes and entire body once a month, and I wasn't the least enthusiastic bather. Our lackadaisical approach to washing was due to the combined effects of the long months of snow (and, consequently, little dirt), habituation to altered states of cleanliness, and the inconvenience of bathing in cramped quarters. A full wash meant heating enough water to turn the cabin into a steam bath, which usually irritated the other, clothed occupants. The end result was great, but the means of getting there seemed like too much bother to pursue frequently. A March journal entry describes the process:

> There's a good storm blowing, so it's a poor day to run the dogs, and I decide to take my monthly bath. I collect some kindling and a few small logs, start a crackling blaze, and cram every available pot onto the stove. After several trips to the water hole to fill all the buckets, I peel away the four layers of clothing that I wear continually: wool sweater, wool turtleneck, long underwear, and T-shirt. It's interesting how the frequency of my baths has decreased since our arrival at Warden's Grove. Initially, I vowed to wash once a week; then it was twice a month; now it's once a month. If I stayed in this neighborhood long enough, I might give it up entirely. Why the change? Well, it's colder and there's less dirt around than when we were working on the cabin and the cache. Second, who is there to wash for? Besides, I don't stink. The others do, though; I wish they would bathe more often. When one of them is nearby, I can smell spruce smoke, mingled with sweat, dirt, flatulence, dog, and a collection of other scents too subtle to identify, but I'm positive that I have remained odorless.
>
> As I strip, I confront a body almost twenty pounds heavier than when I lived and worked in the desert. I'd like to think that the majority of the weight gain represents added muscle, rather than fat, but I feel as though my body has compensated for the cold by adding extra bulk and insulation. Perhaps there's something to this: The lower the surface-to-volume ratio of an organism, the greater its ability to conserve heat. In our own species, inhabitants of desert regions—the Bedouins, Aborigines, and !Kung people of the Kalahari Desert—tend to be thin; those of mountainous or northern areas—the Lapps, Inuit, and Sherpas—are usually stockier.
>
> Anyway, I'm much heavier and whiter than I was before the trip. *Pale* isn't a strong enough word to describe my condition; except for my hands and face, I'm striving to attain the uniform color of pork lard. But the water's ready. I remove a pail from the stove, pour the steaming liquid into several large bowls, add cold water to each, and put more water on to heat. I dip my hands into the deliciously warm water and begin to wash my face: This does feel very good, and I decide that I'm not quite ready to abandon entirely the habits of my past.

Finally, there were the innumerable hours spent in conversation, on topics ranging from the business of living in the Barrens to esoteric philosophical matters.

But, like a Kansas wheat farmer or a Maine lobsterman, we were most often concerned with our immediate world—how the dogs were running, ways of staying comfortable in the cold, chores that needed doing, logistics, and above all else, the weather, present and future. How much longer would the storm last? When would the cold moderate? How were the winds, and were they shifting direction? Because the weather dominated our lives, we focused on its patterns and vagaries. Yet our talk could easily shift 180 degrees and wander into the aesthetics of photography, the nature of adventure, Anglo-French Canadian relations, the history of English royal families, Taoism, or conservation. We talked a lot about our past histories and present, suspended relationships—another way of reaffirming our connection with the Outside. Scattered throughout these conversations were the inevitable digressions on our womanless existence, a subject whose importance waxed and waned during the course of our journey.

Curiously, one of the most common reactions that I encountered from men before our trip was an incredulity that we would voluntarily choose to be away from females for so long: "Hey, it sounds great, but I couldn't stand to be away from women for fifteen months—I'd go nuts!" Some of this undoubtedly was male posturing, but there was an element of perceived deprivation—mostly sexual—in their statements. The concern seemed ridiculous, and none of us questioned our participation for such a reason. There may have been strong doubts about sacrificing or postponing particular relationships, but abandoning sexual contact was not a worry. And there were responses even more ridiculous than that: friends of John's parents worried that fifteen months without women would transform us into homosexuals. To me, these reactions pointed toward our society's overemphasis on the sexual; there were plenty of good reasons for not doing the trip, but a lack of sex wasn't one of them.

Read through expeditionary literature and there's rarely mention of sex, other than vague references to bawdy fantasies generated while stormbound in a tent, or abstract dissections of relationships left behind. Yet I know that the subject comes up frequently. Maybe it's a matter of the author's reluctance to discuss elements of private lives in front of an audience, or perhaps the issue wasn't judged important enough to the central story. Or it might be that the author was simply too tired to care about sex during the expedition. During our first summer's paddling, I was generally disinterested in sex or even in seeing women—my energies were poured into movement. With the arrival of winter, there were more opportunities to think about women, and a greater inclination to do so. Yet the subject rarely dominated my thoughts—partly because of other concerns, partly because of the isolation that enfolded me. I'd felt the separation from women much more strongly in cities, when surrounded in my loneliness by the apparent happiness of all those mated pairs.

Of course, there were moments of longing that came and went with no obvious pattern. I'd awaken remembering a dream, or suddenly find myself longing for someone I'd "left behind." (Maybe this was just playing up to the explorer's mystique.) The only predictable response came when we were temporarily exposed to civilization and brought into contact with women again. Yet the response, whenever it did arise, was curious—more of a longing for the feminine aspects of humanity than for the carnal. There were times when I was simply tired of the constant companionship of four or five sweating, farting, belching, hairy males. They were my friends and comrades, but there was just too much testosterone floating around all the time. It wasn't the foolishness of the *Cosmopolitan* image that I wanted; only a warmth and tenderness to counterpoint the culturally induced aspects of our masculinity. Although I imagine that we would have classified ourselves (in the language of today's popular psychology) as "sensitive males," there were barriers among us—barriers to any sort of physical tenderness or exposure of our hidden selves—that remained surprisingly resistant to time. Gary once remarked, "We have done an amazing job of maintaining a distance between us." The barriers were not complete, and friendships flourished under the influence of shared experience, yet we were reluctant to share much of ourselves. And so, I think I yearned more for overcoming some measure of this isolation through familiar acts of tenderness than for satisfying any tug of the gonads.

Thirty below on a windy December night, with the waxing moon high in the sky. I climb out of the spruce, away from Warden's Grove and the Thelon River. Hard snow crunches underfoot, and each inhaled breath is ragged in my nose. Overhead the aurora dances in ribbons of color—purple, yellow, and green curtains streaming through the sky. From the crest of the hill, the Barrens lies clothed in a liquid, silver light—a great, undulating sweep of land locked in the grip of winter. Below, the Thelon gleams gently, its frozen current shining in the brittle night. And everywhere is a silence so deep that it has become palpable; the wind is here, but as a part of the silence that streams out of the desolate land. It is as though I could reach out and hold the silence, cupping it, ever so gently, in my mittened hands. I recall the words of Meister Eckehart, a fourteenth-century German mystic: "There is nothing in creation so like God as stillness." His words hover in the quiet of the expectant night; I huddle in the lee of some stunted trees and drifted snow, desiring warmth yet unwilling to leave the ridge and hear myself move. No matter how many days and nights pass, no matter how many sunrises and sunsets greet me, no matter how many disappointments there are—moments when the fabric of the trip seems to be ripping apart under the strain of our disagreements, or outside forces—there will always be this view, and a sense of having come to an appointed place, drawn by whatever it is that marks the stillness and the course of my life. I tell myself to hold onto a quiet heart, and the empty land, for they offer the hope of grace at times when grace does not seem possible.

Winter

When I become conscious of my shivering, I begin the descent, walking back as quietly as possible, guided by the familiar landmarks and the soft lamplight from our cabin—a single beam that rushes out into the night, only to be swallowed by the Barrens, by the empty land that seems to go on forever, until it finally dissolves in the winds of space.

CHAPTER EIGHT
Of Dogs and Men

One's experience of dogs in civilization is quite inadequate to give any idea of how a dog's character may develop and how acute his intelligence may become under the stern conditions of life in the North. . . . Certainly I had never before seen dogs of such pronounced individualities as those we had now got together or who in their traits and behaviours so exactly resembled certain types of men.

—George Douglas, *Lands Forlorn*

THERE ARE MANY EXOTIC legends associated with the Arctic, but few are quite so ingrained in my imagination as those concerning sled dogs. Yukon King and Sergeant Preston on patrol; an Oblate Father struggling through a storm to reach his isolated mission; an Inuit crossing the sea ice with a load of walrus meat, his team strung out in a fan-shaped arc—these are images of my romantic North. It was difficult (and still is) to picture a northern winter without sled dogs, yet by the time of our trip, working teams had all but disappeared from the Northwest Territories, replaced by snowmobiles in villages and hunting camps from the Mackenzie River Valley to Baffin Island. For several reasons, the two-cycle engine had established primacy over working dogs: Travel is quicker, and there is also no need to feed a snowmobile when it's not working, or to worry about two of them getting into a fight over a female in heat. Instead, dogs had become the focus of an avocation, bred and trained for racing rather than hauling loads. In spite of this trend, we had the great fortune to run what must have been one of the few remaining working teams in the Northwest Territories. In the early planning stages of the expedition, we had not envisioned using dogs; they came to us unexpectedly, offered by Roger Catling, who was switching to snowmobiles for his trapping operation. So we had the pleasure of seeing the unexpected become an integral part of our lives at Warden's Grove.

The dogs gave us vastly increased mobility, the ability to haul heavy loads of wood to camp, plenty of entertainment, and companionship. The dynamic between man and dog was the source of many lessons, much amusement, and occasional frustration that deteriorated into fury. Without our six furry companions, life on the Barrens would have been far poorer, and the story of the winter remains as much theirs as it is ours.

When the team was delivered to us at the end of August, our total experience with sled dogs was nil. We were utter novices, our only guides the little that we had read, and a short letter from Roger urging us to "have patience" and giving the basic commands: "Okay!" (Go!); "Whoa!"; "Yee!" (Right!); and "Chaw!" (Left!). Armed with this vast reservoir of knowledge, we set out to "train" the team of three experienced adult males (Krackedy, Woofer, and Rusty) and three male pups completely new to the harness (Potash, Pemmican, and Dewey). This was like trying to drive a bulldozer without understanding the bewildering array of levers and pedals—lots of false starts, curses, and confusion before anything resembling motion occurred. There were many hard moments for both men and dogs; I am sure that they suffered from confusion as often as we did. And in their own frustrating way, the dogs did as much to teach their theoretical masters as the masters did for the dogs; there were other ways to instruct besides reliance on a whip, loud voice, and promise of food.

We began training the dogs as soon as all the food and equipment had been hauled to camp from Cache Lake. Robert volunteered to take charge of training and feeding the dogs, and building their shelters, but we all joined in the effort to prepare man and dog for winter. The objective of the training program was to get everyone into running condition; expose the puppies to life in the harness; convince Krackedy, the lead dog, to do the driver's bidding; and acquaint human and canine mind. Initial attempts at running the team convinced us that these few succinctly stated objectives concealed the promise of much hard work, and that the threat of anger-induced apoplexy. A September journal entry reveals something of the initial frustration:

> Ran the team today, over the muskeg, down onto the beach, and up through the muskeg again. A real workout, as I had to trot along with the sled on the sandy and uphill sections—not easy in a pair of heavy boots and after three months without running. The start was hilarious—Krackedy not wanting to go, testing us, looking cowed when the whip was brandished, but still not responding. The pups were either tangled up in the harness, or almost completely

out of the contraptions. The command was given—"Okay, come on!" The team began to move, one of the pups being immediately knocked down and dragged along the ground with no hope of recovery. Halted and untangled the mess while fighting off blackflies, Robert finally getting everyone organized. Only Rusty and Woofer seemed to know what was going on. Tried again—"Okay come on!" Again there was confusion and tangled dogs. We waded into the melee, straightened the team out, and tried a third time. Better—everyone was pulling hard and moving well; the sled careened along at a fast clip, pounding and bouncing through the tussocks. I was laughing at the newness and ridiculousness of it all—running a dog team without any snow on the ground.

Robert said that training the dogs "was like working with schoolboys." Someone else compared the experience to dealing with juvenile delinquents. The process was one in which man and dog came to a mutual understanding of one another's personalities and capabilities. Each dog was an individual; each responded differently to discipline, had different attitudes toward work, and belonged in a different position in the team. Likewise, each human approached the dogs differently; patience varied, as did the will to instill discipline and push the team toward its maximum performance. The dogs sensed this, and their response to one of us could not be used to predict their response to another driver; each of us was tested, some more severely than others. Gary's first attempt at a solo run with the dogs turned into a fiasco. He spent forty-five minutes traveling less than a hundred yards out from the shelters and finally retreated in the face of his own frustration and the dogs' intransigence—even though they were running well for the rest of us.

The dogs could be "cheeky bastards," as we often commented, and control necessitated the use of a loud, sharp voice, willow switch, open palm, and whip, in descending order of frequency. Yet the dogs didn't need to be brutalized; firmness, consistency in training, and affection brought increasingly good responses as the winter progressed, and we soon abandoned the whip entirely. I suppose that old northern hands would have been scandalized by the way that we treated the dogs. Early in their training, we even took individual dogs (mostly the pups) for walks in order to exercise them and work at basic obedience lessons. They were never completely working dogs, and became more like pets, talked to and petted frequently. Theirs was not the hard life described in many accounts of the North—dogs let loose on an island to fend for themselves in the summer, beaten severely for any transgression, and worked to their limits:

> The ordinary lot of dogs in the North, despite their great service, is not a pleasant or happy one. Their only caress is that of a club or the lash, their only reward as they grow old is abandonment and starvation or death at the jaws of their own kind when they become unable to defend themselves. Although in the winter when they are in constant use they are fed and bedded with something approaching care and certainty, in the summer they are not always treated with the same consideration. Some Indians go so far as to leave the dogs on

islands and allow the dogs to fend for themselves. Whether in summer or winter they are the complaining recipients of constant and countless beatings. (P.G. Downes, *Sleeping Island*)

Sled dogs also have a reputation for viciousness that we never saw; ours were almost always friendly, greeting us with a wag of the tail and an excited bark. Perhaps we would have gotten more out of the dogs if we had been firmer and less affectionate; perhaps the relative ease of our life allowed us the luxury of kindness. Yet we did work them, and we could have pushed them harder—but our inexperience allowed us to approach the dogs without preconceptions and the habits of prior generations. I sometimes wondered if the described treatment of sled dogs had something to do with the harshness of the North; perhaps it was a response to life in an unpredictable and overwhelming environment. It would be futile, and even dangerous, to express anger toward an environment that was completely beyond one's control; perhaps the dogs represented a convenient outlet for frustration and anger, much in the way that abusive parents may strike out at their children in the face of the despair generated by the larger world.

As our experience with the team grew, the personalities of each dog became more and more familiar. Krackedy—a Chipewyan name of unknown meaning—was the lead dog; his position was crucial, as it was his role to respond to the driver's commands and alter direction accordingly. He was a black-and-white mutt with floppy ears; an ancient, grizzled face; and a stout build that gave him the appearance of a four-legged sausage. But behind Krackedy's oafish exterior lurked the mind of an extremely willful and crafty manipulator that constantly tested his drivers. If Krackedy didn't want to go, it was very difficult to persuade him to change his mind. I recall one such instance in late October; we had made three trips to North Grove, bringing back four-hundred-pound loads of logs each time. Krackedy decided that he'd had enough; after the third load was dropped in front of the cabin, he headed for the shelters. I wanted to fetch one more load, and tried to turn the team to the left with repeated shouts of "Chaw!"—but no such luck. I halted the team (Krackedy didn't mind stopping; he would obey that command) and strode up to discipline the miscreant; he cowered and I gave him a light whack, to which he responded with howls of agony. These howls were the heartrending cries of a tortured dog, and would have alerted any A.S.P.C.A. member within ten miles. However, they were meaningless; he would also howl if I tried to hit him and missed, so he received no sympathy from me. I trod back to the sled and gave the command to go, and go to the left. Krackedy responded by heading uphill to the right for the second time. I halted the team, gave Krackedy a harder swat, and tried again. Same result, followed by another swat. This wasn't getting me anywhere except frustrated. I finally manhandled Krackedy into a position where he was facing in the general direction of my desired destination; this convinced him that he would have to work for another hour, and he took off for North Grove with ears back and tail held low. Little did he know that he had come close to winning the battle—but I knew that capitulation, as attractive as it seemed, would only have led to later problems.

Krackedy was basically a lazy dog that didn't care for hard work. His traces—the leather straps that connected him to the following dog—were usually slack, an indication that he wasn't pulling his fair share of the load. Yet he had the tiring job of breaking trail, and could not turn well if he was pulling hard; we forgave his lapses because his lazy intelligence meant that he was masterful at selecting the best routes. Krackedy seemed to have a sixth sense about finding the easiest and safest traveling; when faced with two choices, he invariably chose the path with the hardest, most wind-crusted snow. We usually let him have his way in these matters, because overriding his decision often meant exhausting wallows through soft snow—or, occasionally, ventures onto thin ice or areas with concealed overflow. Krackedy was also a master at following a previously traveled route over long distances, even if it was six days old and had been obliterated by wind and drifting snow. His skill was most evident when we were running toward home. Even if we were thirty miles out from Warden's Grove, he would unerringly go in the correct direction, and could travel for hours without needing a single directional command if he knew that the end of work lay ahead.

We usually ran another adult, Woofer, in the second position. Woofer was the antithesis of Krackedy in personality and appearance. He was thin, with long brownish fur; he rarely misbehaved; and he was always ready to run and haul loads. Woofer's trademark was a forward leap at the shout of "Okay, come on!" and this momentum always got the other dogs and the sled moving. His loyalty and passion for work made him the type of dog that would have died in harness if circumstances had called for such devotion. Woofer's lean build left him particularly susceptible to the cold; a night out on the trail at minus 40°F would leave him shivering and anxious to get moving again. Woofer was always eager for attention, and he loved to be petted and praised; his only aggravating traits—fawning behavior and a whining, yippy bark—grew out of his desire for human contact.

The third adult ran behind Woofer. Rusty was the sort of fellow that doesn't get noticed right away, and often is taken for granted. Small and homely, with bloodshot eyes, he was a consistent but undistinguished worker that seemed to possess few unique personality traits. But months of working with him revealed that he was a tough bugger with much more spark than was initially apparent. First, Rusty was the concertmaster that led the canine chorus in its response to animals and passing planes. The barking yip of a red fox or the howls of a wolf would always draw a reaction from him, and he seemed most intrigued by the animals that a chain or traces prevented him from reaching. There was also his aggravating habit of rolling and twisting in his traces whenever the team halted for a rest; Rusty was constantly having to be untangled and repositioned, and no amount of scolding could persuade him to act otherwise. He could also be a grouch; he resented discipline and was the only member of the team ever to snap or growl at us. A torn eyelid, ragged ears, and body scars showed that he was a scrapper unafraid of a fight; he was quick to take offense and turn on the other dogs. Yet he loved attention and a pat on the head after a good run. I often felt sorry for Rusty because he had such conflicting personality traits—a desire for affection, yet a demeanor that isolated him. Perhaps his behavior had been influenced by his puppyhood experiences; we heard that he had been mistreated by a fellow who had owned him before Roger.

Next in line were the two snow-white pups, Potash and Pemmican. They were nearly identical in build and facial features, and their personalities seemed interchangeable. One day, Potash would play the ne'er-do-well—disobeying commands, not paying attention, and standing up facing backward in his traces after a rest—while Pemmican was being a "good old boy" and pulling strongly. The next day, roles would be reversed and Pemmican would become Bozo For a Day. Pemmican did have one tendency that set him apart, though—the aforementioned habit of chewing on his traces. This was frustrating at any time, but particularly while out on the trail at thirty below. We tried dissuading him with hard swats and a concoction of cayenne pepper mixed with Vaseline that we smeared on the traces, but neither of these tactics fazed him. We finally replaced the leather in his traces with a section of dog chain; it didn't take him long to discover that frozen metal was not much fun to chew on.

The final team member was Dewey, a.k.a. Master Dewey or Dewey Decimal. Dewey was a handsome pup, with a thick black-and-white coat and stout build. He bore a strong resemblance to an Alaskan malamute, was larger than any of the adults, was strong, and could pull for long stretches without tiring. Because of his size, we placed Dewey last in line, in what is known as the wheel position: His strength was useful in helping to pull the sled into a new track after the team had turned to the right or left. Yet the decision to make Dewey the wheel dog was made only after lots of experimentation and with some hesitancy—for Dewey was very slow in being trained to the harness. His lessons were filled with tangled traces, stumbles, crashes, collisions with the sled, and being dragged sideways across muskeg or through snow. But we soon learned that disciplining Dewey did little to speed his education; it generally retarded the process because even a loud voice caused him to collapse into a cowering ball incapable of standing, let alone working. Dewey's extended apprenticeship was not a matter of low intelligence; although his size, happy-go-lucky attitude, and mental lapses made him seem a bit thick, I suspect that his disposition rendered him less suited to the task of pulling a sled than the other dogs. Dewey may have looked the part of a magnificent sled dog, but he was a family pet at heart, with the personality of a golden retriever.

In the best of all possible worlds, Dewey would have earned his keep not by hauling sleds, as physically suited to the task as he was; rather, he would have lived out his days playing with children and romping in a suburban neighborhood far to the south of the Thelon.

The combination of personalities (both human and canine) made each run with the dogs an interesting one—particularly during the fall, when control over the team was what we termed "approximate." Preparations for a run began with harnessing the dogs, placing them in the proper sequence, and attaching the string of six to the sled. The first step in the ritual was to remove the sled from the top of two fifty-gallon drums, where it spent all resting hours—a precaution against marauding red foxes that loved to chew on anything smelling even faintly of food or humanity. Even canvas and polypropylene rope, two major but seemingly inedible components of the sled, were not safe from their depredations.

The sled was very solid, with wide oak runners that formed the bottom of the baggage compartment and curved upward in the front much like a toboggan. Several vertical posts two feet high and a rope meshwork helped secure the white canvas sides; the back of the compartment was sealed off with plywood. The driver stood on the rear end of the runners, which formed a platform about eighteen inches long, and gripped the handles extending upward from the runners. A short two-by-four with a piece of caribou antler at one end served as a brake. This was attached to the sled with nylon webbing, and normally carried face-upward on the rear platform. The team could usually be halted by flipping the brake onto hard snow and standing directly over the antler.

After the sled was set on the snow, the harnesses were carried from the tent and placed next to the proper dog. This was usually the occasion for great excitement and a chorus of frenzied barking. Ears up, tails wagging, the dogs would dance at the ends of their chains in anticipation of the coming run—oh to be free of confinement and out on the Barrens! At least this was the case when a day trip was in the offing. If, in addition to day packs, we loaded the sled with sleeping bags, a tent, large packs, an axe, snow shovel, dog food, and all sorts of odds and ends, then the reaction was very subdued. The dogs knew that a long trip and hard work were in store, and they greeted the prospect with utter silence, ears back and chins resting between outstretched legs. The lack of enthusiasm was complete; each dog acquiesced to the harness only grudgingly, except Dewey—he usually rolled up into a ball and had to be dragged into position.

If the dogs cooperated, harnessing them was a simple matter. A padded yoke was pulled over the head, paws lifted through a chest strap, and a belly strap clipped into another strap that ran across the back. The harnessed dog was then placed in his proper position. We ran the team in single file, rather than in a fan radiating out from the front of the sled, as favored by the Inuit, so each dog was secured to those in front and back by parallel leather traces. The fan-shaped arrangement was unsuited to areas outside of the High Arctic; the dogs pulled less efficiently because they weren't running in a single direction, no single trail was broken through deep snow by preceding dogs, and the team could not maneuver in woods. The harnessed dogs were never left unsecured; we clipped a trace around a tree to prevent a premature, driverless start. Once the team was in place, we attached the wheel dog to the sled, released all restraints, and gave the command—"Okay, come on!"

The initial explosion was like the start of a horse race—the dogs tore out of Warden's Grove as though they sought to exhaust their store of pent-up energy in a fifteen-minute sprint. Unfortunately, the resemblance vanished as soon as Krackedy braked to urinate on one of his favorite bushes. Since the team was traveling downhill at the time, momentum carried the rest of the dogs past Krackedy and into an inevitable collision with one another, with the sled usually plowing into the wheel dog from behind. The ensuing Gordian knot of tangled traces and growling dogs could only be unraveled by unclipping each dog and reassembling the team—by which time Krackedy usually had circled back to visit another bush and caused further entanglement. When the mess was finally straightened out and the go-ahead command given, Woofer and Rusty often charged past a relaxed Krackedy—resulting in more confusion and a stream of invectives from the infuriated driver. Further swats and scoldings straightened out most of the team, at least temporarily, but caused Dewey to collapse into his characteristic mound of quivering fur; once he was propped up and encouraged, some progress might finally be made. I held up restraint toward the dogs as an ideal, but when I was surrounded by a seething, spaghettilike mass of dogs and traces for the third time in ten minutes, I wanted to kick and maim each uncooperative pooch—or perhaps to follow P.G. Downes's suggestion: "Some drivers, both white and Indian, in fits of exasperation with recalcitrant dogs, are wont to seize the animal and bite its ears, but this practice is not as common as the desire, for it is hard on the teeth."

No matter how hard I tried to convince Krackedy to behave otherwise, he would not abandon his ritual urination. Along with the other dogs, he needed to rid his system of misbehavior, but once the first quarter mile was dispensed with and his bladder was empty, Krackedy usually broke into a steady trot and the rest of the team fell in with his pace. If the weather was clear and calm, the sled light, and the traveling conditions good—either wind-hardened snow or a thin layer of snow over water ice—the dogs needed little discipline and pulled well. These were the moments that I loved the best—running with the team toward a blood-red sunset or a rising moon, my eyelashes and beard coated with rime, clouds of exhaled air rising into the frigid air, Krackedy's harness bells jingling in time with his gait, the dogs grabbing mouthfuls of snow on the run. I could feel myself moving in time with the dogs, and with the winter. It was more than simply enjoying running the team; the flow of movement given by the dogs became an indispensable part of the place, and our motion blended with the rhythm of the land. We would snake along a winding riverbed of ice, struggle up a steep hill, then careen down the other side—on the sled for a hundred yards, off for a hundred more to give the dogs a rest or help push up the hills, my breathing deep but not labored, the miles rolling away into the empty hills, all past canine transgressions forgiven or forgotten. . . .

After an hour or so of traveling, we would stop to rest the team. The dogs would lie down, eat more snow, roll onto their backs to cool off, and chew ice off their paws. Afterward, there would often be a few tangled traces, and one or two dogs to discipline and straighten out. Krackedy was usually a culprit, but we increased his willingness to cooperate by picking him up and giving him an airborne roll 360 degrees to the right or left to untangle his traces; the unfamiliar motion and subsequent landing made him reluctant to forget about his traces. During stops, we were careful not to leave the sled unattended, as a moment's lapse could have given the dogs enough time to escape. John almost had the team get away when they unexpectedly tore off in pursuit of a red fox; in spite of a fully loaded sled and an uphill path, they could accelerate quickly when sufficiently motivated. We had also heard about a trapper who had left his dogs unattended for a moment while he checked a nearby set; the dogs bolted toward camp, where there was a bitch in heat. He was left with a long walk home, and by the time he arrived, several of his dogs had been killed or severely injured in the melee over the female.

The dogs were less enthusiastic about running when the winds were hard out of the north and our course took us directly into the fiercest conditions. Then they were reluctant to move away from shelter (as we also were), and tended to veer off at an angle from the prevailing winds—yet they performed as bidden, with heads turned to one side to avert the worst gales. In these situations, and on the harshest nights, I marveled at their resistance to cold. At Warden's Grove they generally chose to sleep outside their shelters, even during storms, and nights on the trail found the dogs chained to trees and curled into compact balls with tails wrapped around noses to protect the only hairless skin on their bodies. On the coldest nights, when I had trouble staying warm in three layers of down and Dacron, I sometimes awoke and listened to the dogs as they shifted positions or barked at a passing fox. How exposed and lonely it seemed outside the tent. It was a wonder that a layer of fur, no matter how thick—plus a few cups of dog food and one-third pound of pork lard—could keep them warm and power them through the long days of hauling loads and longer, motionless nights of minus 40°F. The books I had read told me much about their hardiness, but experiencing the harshness of the winter made their resilience all the more impressive.

If a long day of work, bitter winds, or too many nights on the trail had sapped the dogs' energy and enthusiasm, two things invariably perked them up:

a homeward course or an animal coming into sight. No matter how far we were from Warden's Grove, the dogs always sensed the moment when we made the turn toward home. Their lethargic pace would quicken, ears and tails would climb higher into the air, and even bitter weather wouldn't deter them as they followed Krackedy's lead; like us, they must have been encouraged by thoughts of food, rest, and shelter:

January 22 [journal entry]:

Tendrils of snow snaking across the tundra as we moved past tiny groves of spruce and over rocky ridges, the sun shining occasionally through a veil of clouds. A gray, spindrift day, filled with thoughts of home place [Warden's Grove]. Fighting off the windchill blues—chin and cheeks very cold, constantly having to be warmed with mittenless hands—as we headed into a bitter storm. But the hands got cold quickly; back into overmitts they'd go until the dog harnesses needed rearranging or rime had to be cleared from my eyelashes. So wonderful to pop over Home Hill and see camp! The dogs knew that we were close long before Warden's Grove came into view; they were eager to be off whenever we stopped, and disobeyed "Whoa's!" as Krackedy unerringly followed the obliterated trail into the gale.

After the arrival in camp came the ritual of unhitching the dogs, chaining each by his shelter (pups between adults to prevent fighting), and feeding. The dogs always stared at the food with rapt attention and barked eagerly as we prepared their meal. The regular rations of a few handfuls of hard chow mixed with melted lard were gobbled almost instantly, with even less grace than we displayed at the table. The processed food seemed a poor substitute for caribou, but we couldn't hunt, and raw meat also meant worries about intestinal parasites, which had affected the adult dogs and kept them looking undernourished until we dewormed them at Christmas. Yet we did scavenge several wolf-killed caribou, and fed the carcasses to the dogs; they attacked the remains with unbridled enthusiasm, inhaling large chunks of meat within milliseconds and snarling at their neighbors. Afterward, the bones kept them occupied for long hours of contented crunching: Here was proper food, not some commercialized nonsense.

The second cure for canine drudgery was even more effective than a homeward run. Imagine the team struggling up a hill with a load of wood; they have already made three runs to North Grove and back, and appear played out. The driver feels sorry for the exhausted dogs; the poor fellows are having trouble keeping the sled moving through some deep drifts, even with assistance. Suddenly, a red fox trots into view; the dogs immediately burst into a flat-out run, straining at their harnesses to catch the fox. The driver screams, "Whoa!", is ignored, and plants the brake firmly. No response; the team keeps moving. So he dumps the sled onto its side and the load of logs spill out into the snow. This halts the team; they dance in the air and bark frantically at the fox, which pauses momentarily in its leisurely travels and calmly sits down to survey the chaos. The driver, meanwhile, is afraid to move away from the sled to retrieve the logs out of fear that he'll lose the team, and is wondering if he would rather strangle the disobedient dogs or the disdainful fox.

Although the dogs occasionally stumbled across caribou or arctic hares, red foxes were the most common and frustrating objects of their attention. The foxes seemed to know when the dogs were restrained, and how close they could approach and still remain safe. This knowledge instilled in them a casual, aloof manner that drove the dogs wild—whether the foxes were encountered on the trail or in camp. If fox and dog crossed paths on a run, it became a matter of controlling an immediately disobedient and frantic team; in camp it became a matter of dealing with the impotent, frenzied howls of chained dogs.

The foxes first became a camp problem in the fall, when food became scarce on the Barrens. Although they quickly scavenged any available carrion, and we sometimes saw them with the carcass of an unlucky ptarmigan, the foxes grew thinner, hungrier, and peskier as the cold deepened. Soon nothing was safe from their depredations; there was little logic to what they chose, as the edible and inedible were consumed with equal gusto: varnished leather on snowshoes, nylon rope on the dogsled, a pair of wind pants, candles, and even a package of dental floss. We soon learned to protect our equipment by keeping everything out of reach of their teeth, but the foxes combined their searches for nourishment with visits to the dogs, which created a more intractable problem. Trotting in from the Barrens, they stationed themselves ten feet from the chained dogs, which were instantaneously worked into a yelping frenzy by their inability to give chase. The din was unbearable inside the tent, so someone had to get up and chase off the fox—which insolently returned to his station as soon as the muttering human had reentered the tent.

This cycle of advance and retreat wasn't broken until we decided to let one of the dogs roam at night. Rusty was chosen for the job because he was the most insistent barker and we hoped that his freedom would bring silence. Our first experiment with this tactic was conducted during the day, when a fox was nosing around the cache. As usual, Rusty was creating a one-dog ruckus, and the fox was unconcerned. This was the fox's undoing, because Rusty took off in determined pursuit of his long-sought target as soon as he was released from his chain. Rusty was on top of the fox within a few seconds, and before we could separate them, he had severed the animal's spine with a bite to the midback. It was a sad affair, as there was no reason for the fox to die—we hadn't expected that Rusty would react so quickly, or that the fox would be so careless. Yet it was obvious that Rusty would be a good deterrent and that we wouldn't be bothered by nocturnal pandemonium again; our vulpine pests would learn to keep their distance, and we wouldn't release our watchdog until we were sure that there were no foxes in the area.

The foxes were fun to bark at and chase; caribou were also interesting, although very wary; but the most enjoyment came from musk-oxen. Now there was a quarry worthy of a dog's complete and enthusiastic attention! Since the Thelon Game Sanctuary had been established to protect a large musk-ox population, we had expected to find lots of them roaming the tundra near Warden's Grove. However, we saw only two solitary bulls and a little sign between our arrival and the end of January. Where had all the shaggy beasts gone? We found out later that during the winter the musk-oxen move far out onto the tundra—where winds reduce snow cover and make vegetation more accessible—and return to the lush stands of willow and sedge along the river once thaw arrives and the snows recede. So in early February, when Robert reported that he had seen a bull musk-ox near Cache Lake, I was excited. Circumstances prevented an immediate investigation, but Kurt and I harnessed the dogs and set off on a search two days later. We suspected that the bull had moved out of the area, so we were surprised to stumble across musk-ox tracks at the western end of Cache Lake. The tracks were partially filled with snow and looked several days old. We began following them, losing and relocating the trail several times. It looked like a long, fruitless search.

But when we popped over a small rise, our bull was feeding less than fifty yards ahead. "Whoa! Whoa!" The dogs stopped, but only grudgingly—with ears and tails up, and bodies tensed, they stared at the bull, which started and raised his head from the snow. He stood motionless, intent upon his sudden adversaries; the impasse persisted for a minute or so while Kurt and I decided what to do. Back off? It hardly seemed possible, as a sudden move would probably send the bull and dogs running. Move to a better position to photograph the musk-ox? Remain where we were and hope that the bull retreated? There were more "Whoa's" as the dogs whined and shifted their weight from foot to foot; they were ready to break.

Somewhat illogically, we decided that Kurt would circle around to the side of the musk-ox, in hopes that he could approach close enough to get a few good photographs. He quietly gathered the camera gear and moved off to the right—but as soon as Kurt stepped away from the sled, the bull wheeled and departed for the nearest horizon. The dogs broke at the same instant; I was caught off guard and had to lunge for the sled to avoid being left behind. The dogs were racing as fast as they could, and the sled accelerated as we rocketed down an icy hillside. In spite of my vehement shouts, commands were useless, as was the brake—it ineffectually bounced off the hard snow—and we rapidly closed on the fleeing beast. Things were moving very quickly. A vision flashed through my mind—of eight hundred pounds of bull musk-ox, plus six dogs, a sled, and me meeting in a colossal pileup. Since this was a very unattractive prospect, I dumped the sled on its side, hoping to halt the chase. The sled slowed, then hit a rock, and I was thrown off. For a moment I lay in the snow, wondering what had happened. But when I looked up from my prone position and saw the dogs and the driverless sled careening after the bull as he galumphed through deep snow in the bottom of a draw, my world darkened considerably. I imagined an eight-mile slog in pursuit of the vagabond team, pounded my fists in frustration, screamed insults and curses at the dogs, and swore terrible vengeance upon Krackedy when (or if) I caught up with him. This was the ultimate episode of *The Bozos in the North*, with me as the star of the show!

I interrupted my reverie by scrambling to my feet and starting to run. One hundred yards ahead were the dogs, and fifty yards beyond them was the bull—but the dogs were closing in on their quarry. I lost sight of the team as I descended into the draw and floundered through thigh-deep snow; Kurt, burdened with camera gear, was far behind. Soon I was gasping up the hill; I could hear frenzied yelps and barks as I followed Kurt's shouted directions toward the ridge crest. The dogs obviously had stopped, and my anger changed to concern when I realized that they had caught up with the musk-ox. Oh, shit! Picturing dead and maimed dogs being ground to a pulp beneath the musk-ox's hooves, I was frantic as I crested the rise and saw the chaos in front of me: a mass of dogs tangled in their traces, a snorting bull, and an overturned sled. The dogs were in a semicircle around the bull, barking wildly and leaping into the air—whether to nip at the bull or in an effort to get out of their harnesses and be free from his attacks, I couldn't tell. The musk-ox was doing his best to defend himself with short, furious charges and attempts to hook or butt the dogs with his horns. The dogs were in an extremely vulnerable position because the traces restricted their movements and they were literally underhoof. Only Potash was safe; he had managed to work free from his harness and was busy tormenting the bull from a respectable distance.

For a moment I stood motionless, mesmerized by the pandemonium and the apparent hopelessness of the situation—surely this was the end of our team. I had to make some effort to save the dogs, though, so I circled around to the side of the bull, darted to within about a yard of him, grabbed a harness, and began dragging the barking, hyperactive tangle of dogs out of the immediate vicinity of horns and hooves. As I struggled to get clear of the musk-ox, I flailed and kicked at the dogs and screamed at them to quiet down. Anyone that misbehaved was whacked or kicked with as much force as I could muster, and soon the team was under tentative control.

Once the dogs were out of immediate danger, I stopped and watched as Potash continued to hold the musk-ox at bay. The bull behaved much as I imagined he would have if faced by a pack of wolves. He had selected a high, relatively snow-free piece of ground for his defensive position; from there he made short, quick feints at Potash, then suddenly wheeled to charge the rest of the team. With each feint and subsequent charge, he butted the sled, knocking it farther down the hill and forcing the team and me farther away from his stance. Between charges, he snorted, blew clouds of steam into the afternoon air, and rubbed his preorbital gland with the inside of his foreleg—standard musk-ox aggressive behavior.

Wham! The sled rolled a few feet before stopping. This triggered barking and angry shouts from me to quiet the dogs. Gland-rubbing, then another attack—the bull charged Potash, then suddenly switched directions and bore down on the sled. Wham! Man and dogs scrambled to move farther out of range. The cycle of attack and retreat was finally broken after Kurt arrived, when the bull charged directly at Potash, who fled in terror. Potash was a dedicated barker, but when he saw the intimidating bulk of an angry musk-ox coming straight for him, his puppy bravado vanished. He retreated with his tail between his legs, ran down a steep slope as he glanced over his shoulder to see if the beast was still in pursuit, and plowed head-first into a snowbank. He quickly struggled free from the drift and slunk back to the sled with a spot of blood on one leg and a noticeable limp, looking utterly chastised by his loss of courage.

The bull appeared none the worse for his experience, and when last seen, was galloping off at full speed. We were left to survey the damage, which was less than we expected—a few broken traces, a badly beaten sled, and several limping dogs. The lack of serious injuries was surprising, and it meant we could return to camp with laughing tales of narrowly averted disaster instead of unhappy news about a death or serious injury. I supposed that the bull continued to beat his hasty retreat for some time, and that the experience left him feeling nervous for days afterward. For our part, Kurt and I felt fortunate to have come through almost unscathed, and resolved never again to go looking for musk-oxen in the company of dogs. Life hadn't been dull enough to require that kind of excitement.

The dogs were with us until late March, when Robert and Kurt ran them out to Reliance and returned them to Roger Catling—a 180-mile, six-day journey via Eyeberry, Tyrrell, and Artillery lakes. For the next few weeks, camp was a much quieter and lonelier place; their absence made us realize the extent to which Krackedy, Woofer, Rusty, Potash, Pemmican, and Dewey had become an integral part of our lives. They cost us a lot, at least in relation to our meager funds—a seven-hundred-fifty-dollar rental, an extra Twin Otter flight in August, perhaps fifteen hundred dollars for food and incidental expenses. But their worth to us could not be measured in dollars; how could a monetary value be placed on mobility, the joy of long sled trips across the Barrens, the loads of wood hauled, or simply learning how to work with and appreciate them? They were good dogs—gentle, usually strong workers; their mischievousness, and the frustrations that it engendered, were just part of the winter's experience. Even their peculiarities remained special—Krackedy's floppy ears, grannylike face, and subtle impertinence; Woofer's whining sycophancy; Rusty's incessant barking and scarred muzzle; Pemmican's mildly sleazy character; Potash's happy-go-lucky playfulness; and Dewey's docile, long-suffering tolerance of work.

They weren't quite pets, but I came to feel closer to them than to any other dogs that I have known. Why? Mostly it was a matter of what they gave us, and the shared experiences: gasping up steep hills, floundering through bottomless snow, heading into a stiff wind at minus 30°F, sleeping outside on a bitterly cold night; the joy of running out into the tundra after days of inactivity; the happiness of popping over Home Hill after days on the trail and seeing Warden's Grove far below. Surely there was some basic connection between canine and human emotions in these situations. Surely there was some primal, shared joy when the jingle of harness bells, the soft cadence of breathing, the rhythm of the pace, and the flow of the passing miles blended with the land, blended into a harmony of motion: Oh, for those times of perfect peace, when everything seemed to fit, when the Barrens seemed like the most beautiful place on earth.

CHAPTER NINE
Slouching Towards...

In this closed world, good manners were more crucial than true feelings.
—Peter Matthiessen, *At Play in the Fields of the Lord*

EXPEDITIONS ARE MICROCOSMS of a larger world, where a harsh environment and the forced intimacy of inescapable contact act as magnifying lenses that focus the light of human emotion on particular personalities and events. If a group of people are thrown together into a demanding situation for an extended period, it is almost inevitable that conflict—as well as bonding—will occur. The initial days of the expedition may be filled with goodwill, and the excitement of a fresh adventure may unite disparate personalities. It is easy to sail along, buoyed by a common goal and the wonder of launching into the unknown. Each individual wants to be accepted, and is unsure of his position relative to others. Energy levels are high, tolerance is easy to find, and one can hide behind a veneer of politeness. Sooner or later, though, cracks appear in the protective facade; there will be harsh words, less reluctant displays of anger, the clash of egos and desires. Under the pressure of physical exhaustion, and sometimes danger—and as familiarity encourages us to relax our defenses—we become more human. We may show our best, and sometimes we may reveal our worst. There may be moments of deep camaraderie and friendship, moments that spiritually unite people for the rest of their lives. But there may also be moments when the anger within each of us emerges, and threatens to rupture the interlocking web of relationships that holds the journey together.

There were times when the beauty of the land and the necessities of our lives brought us closer to one another. Those brutal portages between the Macmillan and Ross rivers, long hours of bucking wood with a crosscut, moonlit walks on the Barrens, straggling vees of geese slicing southward into winter, and snatches of intimate conversation were the basis for friendships that will last through decades of intermittent contact. And even if I were to meet one of the expedition members who did not become a friend, the bond of shared experience would still exist. There would be the memory of having come all that way together, and I would hope that we would have a basis for communication that people who did not make the journey could never fully understand.

However, we also had our moments of anguished and bitter disagreement; at one time or another, each of us failed the others, and ourselves. The dissension and anger that first surfaced on the Nahanni River receded when we left Fort Simpson; it lay mostly dormant as we crossed Great Slave Lake and moved into the Barrens. As we settled into life at Warden's Grove, there were occasional flashes of tension, but the five of us appeared to be developing a stronger community. We worked hard and well together, we had long discussions, and we were even quite silly now and again. Yet some of this amity was perhaps illusory, for as autumn gave way to winter, we were more often troubled by echoes of the Nahanni. This wasn't a result of the cold, darkness, and cramped quarters of winter; rather, it was the effect of decisions that we made, and the conflicts of our desires.

Yet it is very difficult to write about any of this. I do not want to violate the privacy of my companions, nor do I want to accuse anyone—beyond myself—of any particular failure. What passed between us occurred in the absence of expectations that any of it would ever become public; thus there is much that should remain private. There is no reason to become involved in the intimate dissections of some recent expedition accounts, where the lurid details of human conflict are laid bare. Such an appraisal would be unfair to my companions and would miss the point of the trip. Yet a comrades-in-arms approach isn't quite right, either, for there are lessons to be learned from our conflict. Because our reactions to later events were influenced by the dynamics of our relationships, and because our ultimate success meant transcending discord, it is important to examine what transpired between us. The task is to get it right, to do no one a disservice, and to be faithful to the spirit of our journey.

In the aftermath of failure, we often look back on our behavior and wonder: "Could I have done better?" So I pick through the journal pages, and memories of conversations and events, and piece together the sequence of thoughts and actions that led to our contention. It seems that we could have done a much better job of communicating, that we sometimes made wrong choices. Yet our mistakes were mostly understandable ones, and we rarely violated the spirit of our collective commitment to the journey, as general as it may have been rendered by individual desires and values.

But there is one decision that stands as an anomaly, and that most of us regretted after the fact—perhaps the only time during the expedition when we chose a course of action that clashed strongly with our collective morality. This was the decision to have a resupply flight at some point during the winter. There are other choices that I question in retrospect, while understanding that, at the time, they seemed correct; but this one went against the spirit of our venture. I know now that, in agreeing to, and even pushing for, the flight, I violated my own deeply held values. And I see much of the conflict that developed during the winter as attributable to the decision.

The remnants of our disagreements on the Nahanni undoubtedly contributed to the dissension that came during the winter—yet the flight acted as a catalyst, as though its reality brought the group to critical mass. This is often the way: A single action has consequences extending far beyond its apparent locus. In Graham Greene's *The Heart of the Matter*, a caring, deeply religious man makes one crucial error in judgment. He betrays his moral code, and in doing so, betrays his God— and the long chain of compromises that leads to his death follows. Our failures were less spectacular, but I wonder if the consequences weren't just as inevitable. Or so it seems in retrospect. The odd thing is that neither my journal, nor John's, mentions the initial discussion about a winter resupply flight, which occurred before we left Reliance in early August. I recall little of the conversation, except that I was in favor of a flight. I knew that the flight wasn't needed, that we had sufficient supplies to see us through to the following summer, and that it could not be justified— only rationalized by my own uncertainties about the winter. The knowledge of contact with the Outside, although contrary to the nature of our quest, was reassuring, as though it would moderate the anticipated rigors of isolation. I shouldn't have wanted the flight, but I did; my fears and the world that I had left behind were still tugging at me, and I went against what I knew was best. Even though I knew that my argument was unsound, I justified it on the grounds that we were already committed to the September resupply flights and the use of a radio to report weather data. A winter flight was an additional disruption, one that would break the continuity of our isolation. Yet the group opted for a flight; I don't recall if Robert was silent on the issue, but I am certain that he would have disapproved.

In early November we confronted the issue again; a flight was probably going to come, but what would it bring? We were worried about running low on several staples, particularly flour, and kerosene for the lanterns—in addition to the sewing supplies, material for mukluks, worm medicine and food for the dogs, paper, and miscellaneous other items. The concern about food was frustrating for Kurt, since he regarded it as a slight upon his planning, which had proven to be excellent. And he was right; we didn't need the extra food, and we finally canceled our order in early December. What seemed much more important was the opportunity to send and receive mail—even though we had settled into a life much happier and more comfortable than I had ever imagined, and the thought of a plane flight still made me uneasy.

Thus we laid the groundwork for the dilemma carried in a radio message relayed to us after our morning weather transmission on November 21: A flight would be coming some time in December, and Mike would be aboard. This was a complete surprise; we had understood that he planned to remain out until spring. We had to make an immediate decision: Should we accede to this change of plans, or ask Mike to stay out for another five months? On one hand, we had grown accustomed to a style of living designed for five people—with different members rotating into and out of the cabin at two-week intervals. A sixth person would disrupt this pattern and add measurably to our crowded conditions. In this way, we were a bit like stereotypical old-timers, wanting nothing to disturb the set pattern of our ritualized lives. We also wanted to preserve our cohesiveness. We had prepared for the winter together, and we were reluctant to disrupt the sense of shared purpose and belonging that had grown out of the months of sawing, chopping, sweating, and living with the Barrens. Thus, I don't believe that anyone would have been welcome at this time, but it was particularly difficult with Mike. We all had experienced trouble adjusting to his personality during the summer, and it wasn't easy to contemplate the increase in tension that might accompany his return to Warden's Grove.

Yet we also felt an obligation to Mike. He was part of our group; he had paddled fifteen hundred miles with us and had spent a week at Warden's Grove—he should have been able to rejoin us. He was obviously expecting to do so; something must have gone drastically wrong with his job in the States. If so, he probably wanted nothing more than to be back in the wilderness. And we had never asked him to stay out until spring, only expected that he would do so. We discussed our quandary for hours—let him come in, or ask him to stay out? In the end, we voted unanimously to ask him not to return in December; the magnitude of the disruption seemed too great, and we felt that some of the winter's special quality would disappear. So, after many false starts, we drafted a telegram for transmission from Yellowknife:

> Mike: Change of plans. Please come in on spring flight. Group needs space. Over-crowded. Under pressure. Deeply sorry at trouble this will cause you.

Looking forward to paddling with you in spring. Letter to follow. Affectionately,
T.N.T.

Having made the choice, we were relieved—and hoped that Mike would not
fight our decision. But on November 25, there was another message from Ron
Catling in Yellowknife: Mike wanted to know why we had made our decision, and
he asked us to reconsider. So we debated the issue again, discussing it long into the
evening; there were arguments back and forth, and solitary walks out into the
snow. After much agonizing, the majority of the group gradually swung over to the
position that Mike had the right to return to Warden's Grove. Eventually we called
Catling back with the message: "Our previous commitment to you, Mike, super-
sedes our present situation."

The decision was a very difficult one for me. My emotions pushed strongly
for rejecting Mike's request, as I valued the extra space and harmony that might
be lost if he returned. Yet my conscience argued for accepting him; he was part of
the expedition, and we had not made our expectations clear to him in September.
The selfish part of my being struggled against the decision, but eventually was
dragged into grudging acceptance by what seemed to be the correct choice. I imagined that life would be much more difficult than it had been, but resolved to do
my best to reach an accommodation with Mike.

Only Robert demurred from the decision to accept Mike's return, arguing that
"the milk of human kindness is being given in the wrong situation." He felt that
Mike had made his choice when he left in September, and that we should not back
down on our resolve. Robert's initial reaction to the reversal was anger; afterward,
he began his long physical and emotional withdrawal from the rest of the group.
This withdrawal, manifested by prolonged silence and solitary activity, was sporadic
and varied in intensity, but it still lasted for the remainder of the journey. I saw
it as an outgrowth of the differences that he perceived between his own values and
those of the rest of the group.

During the first five months of the expedition, several decisions had gone
against Robert. Our insistence on a rest day at Brintnell Creek, our choice of
Warden's Grove as a wintering site, and our decision to have a winter resupply
flight were all difficult for Robert to accept, as they violated the spirit of his journey,
which revolved around a commemoration of Hornby's death and Edgar Christian's
courage. His views on issues ranging from politics to religion and morality were also
different. He was a strong Christian, was adamantly opposed to premarital sex and
any experimentation with drugs (however moderate), disliked swearing and drinking, and had strong patriotic ideals. While none of us would have qualified for the
Marquis de Sade Memorial Award for Debauchery and Decadence, we all had
come of age in the late sixties and early seventies; to some extent, we had absorbed
the prevailing values of the times. Thus our attitudes and experiences tended to

clash with Robert's moral code. For him, our decision about Mike was the final demonstration that an ineluctable gulf separated him from the rest of the group; it was another matter of, as he termed it, "one against five." Robert felt isolated; we appeared to be on completely different wavelengths, and to approach the trip from entirely different perspectives. And once he was convinced of this, there was little that anyone could do or say to dissuade him from this view.

Perhaps Robert and the rest of our party could have understood each other better if the foundations of our moral codes had been less different. Robert was a true romantic, a man who believed in The Good and judged issues in terms of an absolute dichotomy between right and wrong; once he had made up his mind, no gray areas of doubt were acceptable. He clung passionately to his ideals, with a strength that paralleled his physical prowess; he refused to watch television or read newspapers because he did not want them to influence his vision negatively or modify his values in any way. Robert was a modern knight who took his quest and vision seriously, and he was intolerant of what he viewed as the moral lapses of others. The rest of us had ideals—ones that I would still defend as good, ones that we had pondered and modified through the years—but some of these conflicted with Robert's. And we accepted the value of situation ethics: Morality was not absolute; it was relative to the particulars of the situation. Whatever the weakness of a moral code based upon this belief, we all wanted to be reasonably good human beings, were committed to the trip, and saw the importance of doing it in a decent style. Yet these attitude differences made it difficult for Robert and the rest of the group to find a common ground. The very passion of Robert's beliefs, though decent and noble, created an intolerance that prevented him from understanding and accepting other viewpoints. I remember a conversation I had with Robert toward the end of the trip. I said that I was truly sorry that a division had come between us, and that his journey had been diminished by some of the decisions that the group had made; although I differed with him on many points, I could still accept the legitimacy of his beliefs. I asked him not to agree with me but at least to respect my convictions, and understand that I had struggled with the decisions that he had come to resent so vehemently. He remained silent, and I was left feeling that he could not respect me, or any other member of the group. We were on the far side of Robert's moral code, and he would not accept the idea that we operated with any of the same basic concerns for the necessity of right action.

Robert's isolation was compounded by his disappointment with John's leadership, which he saw as not measuring up to that displayed by Robert Falcon Scott or Kurt Hahn, the founder of Outward Bound. Whatever critical historians may now say about Scott's abilities to lead, Robert believed that he possessed the qualities that John lacked. John was prone to belching, made occasional childish jokes about farting, and did not stand up for Hornby and Farley Mowat in the face of our occasional skeptical comments. In the past he had taken drugs, which Robert felt was spiritually wrong and out of step with the philosophy of Outward Bound. And by not pushing the group harder on the Nahanni, John had prevented the expedition from reaching Hornby Point and building a cabin there. Finally, Robert saw John's ego as having caused him to be overly domineering much of the time. The criticisms may have had some merit from Robert's point of view, but the rest of us saw nothing wrong with any of these behaviors or attitudes except for the latter one, which became a much less significant issue after the Nahanni. I felt that John had grown into his role and dealt successfully with the problems that had arisen early in the journey. What Robert faced was the realization that leaders aren't perfect; some are better than others, but all are fallible human beings. Rather than accept this view, Robert lost faith in John's leadership. If he had retained his faith, perhaps John could have pulled Robert out of his isolation and into a more willing acceptance of decisions that ran counter to his wishes. For Robert's ideal was the necessity of complete obedience to the leader of an expedition—if the leader retained the moral right to lead. But, given the intensity of Robert's vision, I wonder whether anyone could have retained his allegiance during fourteen months of isolation.

Robert's response to what he saw as his spiritual isolation was to withdraw into a concurrent physical separation. After we had decided to readmit Mike, and as the resupply flight drew nearer, Robert became more and more morose and uncommunicative, and spent most of his time alone in the tent or occupied outside with solitary tasks. Gone was the jovial Robert, the one who sang, played the pennywhistle, imitated Peter Sellers, and discoursed on English literature and royal history. Instead, Robert appeared in the cabin only at meals, which he ate silently, with his head bowed. He spoke only when addressed directly, and his responses were usually limited to a few excruciatingly polite and quiet words—unless we mentioned anything having to do with Christianity, relations between French and Anglo Canadians, or Hornby, in which case he often misconstrued what had been said and responded aggressively. The effects of such behavior, when drawn out over many weeks, were oppressive. The atmosphere at meals became more and more tense, and Robert's sense of isolation, as expressed through his actions, became a self-fulfilling prophecy as his sadness and depression affected the rest of us. Attempts to breach the wall of his reserve were always deflected; he would not talk about what was bothering him, and we began to feel as though we could do nothing to drag him back into the community. In place of our companionship, Robert seemed to rely more and more upon his emotional connection to the Hornby party, spending long hours pouring over *The Legend of John Hornby* and *Unflinching*, and whatever conversations we did share revolved around the Hornby party.

Robert was disconsolate; his dreams of what the trip would be like—its style and purpose—were shattered. He evidently had lost something very dear to his heart, and the damage was irreparable. In a way, he was in mourning for the cabin at Hornby Point, and the ideals of leadership and companionship that had propelled him into the journey. The black mood with which Robert greeted the resupply flight and the New Year would eventually fade, and he would gradually regain some of his old cheerfulness and become a functioning member of the group, although the fragile nature of our relationship to him persisted. Not that he would ever have failed to see the trip through to Chesterfield Inlet—but it was likely that other incidents could bring renewed withdrawal, so our interactions with Robert became much more guarded from December onward.

The resupply flight was scheduled for the third week in December, but its presence was felt long before it touched down on the wind-packed snow of the Thelon. First there was Robert's reaction to the flight, and Mike's arrival; second, the disruption of our connection to the Barrens. For the first time since starting down the Macmillan River, we were concentrating on something besides the land and our place in it. The lure of communication with the Outside was strong; it was difficult not to think of the letters and packages that undoubtedly would arrive, and for many days prior to the scheduled flight, we mostly stayed indoors and spent long hours busily scribbling letter after letter. The last few days prior to its arrival on December 19 were particularly frustrating, as a bitter storm made flying impossible. Like a nagging injury, the thought of the plane constantly intruded upon my thoughts and interfered with any projects and excursions that I attempted. Curiously, I also felt that my previous desires were foolish—I easily could have gone four or five more months without mail. My life had become increasingly divorced from friends, family, and current events; what was going on Outside had little relevance to my winter.

But even as I thought about this, the La Ronge Twin Otter was flying northeastward from Reliance, past Artillery Lake and toward the Hanbury. The storm was still blowing, and the pilot had trouble keeping his bearings among the low clouds; he was just about to turn back when he spotted trees along the Hanbury drainage, and soon he was flying along the Thelon. The distinctive hum of the Twin Otter brought us out of the cabin in the afternoon dusk, and we watched the plane break through the clouds in a blaze of landing lights. It came in low over the tundra, circled camp once, then immediately set down on the rough landing strip that we had stamped out on the river and marked with spruce boughs. There was a roar and a cloud of snow as the engines reversed, and we set off to meet our visitors.

On board the plane were Mike, Ron Catling, a Wildlife officer, the pilot, and the copilot. Greetings were rushed as the crew hurried to unload cargo and secure the plane for the night, and we began hauling supplies to camp. Robert didn't stop to talk with anyone, and he appeared to be barely tolerating the situation. His sole response to Mike's "Hello, Robert!" was a chilly "Oh, you're here."

The plane brought a large quantity of supplies, including a fifty-gallon drum of kerosene, four mailbags, fresh vegetables, four hundred pounds of dog food, a barograph, miscellaneous equipment, and extra food for Mike, as his presence had not been foreseen when winter rations were planned. It took seven trips with the dogs to get everything up from the river, but the confusing jumble was finally temporarily cached and we all crowded into the warm and smoky cabin.

In spite of my ambivalent feelings about the charter, it was exciting to have guests at Warden's Grove. Curiously, we spent little time discussing politics, sports, or other aspects of life on the Outside. Instead, over dinner and innumerable cups of tea, the nine of us (minus Robert, who had retreated to the tent after fulfilling his cooking duties) talked of the North—of flying and the near-misses that our pilot had experienced, Reliance, hunting and trapping (wolf pelts were bringing three hundred fifty dollars, arctic fox about fifty dollars), northern characters, history, and our life by the Thelon. This phenomenon—the conversational emphasis on the North among veterans of the country, even those who had been long in isolation—had once puzzled me, but now I understood. We were becoming northerners, if only temporarily, and what was happening "down south" had lost some of its former significance.

Our visitors left after an unhurried and congenial breakfast. We said our good-byes in front of the cabin, as the pilot had risen in the early morning to warm the plane's engines and had taxied up to the meadow below Warden's Grove. The blue-and-red metal beast looked alien as it sat waiting on the tundra; it was strange to watch from our doorstep as it accelerated and bumped over the snow and rose into the clear, windy sky. The roar of the engines faded as the plane headed south toward Roger Catling's place on the upper Thelon, and we were left with the familiar silence of the Barrens.

We spent the rest of the day opening mail and sorting through the food and equipment that Mike had brought in. Robert did not participate in any of this. The volume of mail was overwhelming; in the huge mailbags were packages crammed with books and food, although they also contained everything from handkerchiefs and T-shirts to magazines, Christmas ornaments, and puzzles. The outpouring of love and good wishes was heartening, and I imagine that all of us were drawn away from Warden's Grove by thoughts of those who had remembered us. But there was a discordant note: Even though many of the gifts were thoughtful, others seemed unnecessary and out of place—copies of *Newsweek*, *People*, and *Playboy*; chewing gum, candy, and prepackaged junk food. These things were superfluous, but they did clarify what was truly important—notes of love and support, needles and thread, moosehide and wool duffel for mukluks, mantles for the lamps, writing paper, food and worm pills for the dogs, and a cloud atlas for predicting weather patterns. "Have you guys got your priorities straight?" whispered all the little doodads that I would gladly have done without.

The appearance of debris from the Outside further colored the plane's visit, and disheartened me. The great irony, though, was that the mailbag with most of the letters had been left behind in Yellowknife. I felt deflated—I was uncomfortable with my decision about the plane flight to begin with, and then frustrated because I didn't get what I most desired.

As we plowed through the mail, we quizzed Mike about his time in the States. He had returned to his job only to find that the program had changed direction during his four-month absence, and he had lost much of his responsibility. He fled after a single day, reeling under the severe blow—to have left the expedition, only to return to a world of which he was no longer an important part. He had nearly been excluded from both the expedition and his program; now he seemed happy to be back at Warden's Grove, and pleased with his role as Santa Claus. In addition to his rations, he'd brought fresh produce, equipment that had been promised to us before the trip, and news of contacts with friends, *National Geographic*, and sponsors. He had done a lot of work on behalf of the expedition, and we appreciated his efforts. On the personality side, he seemed more low-keyed than in August. He talked a lot, but he also listened and questioned, as if searching for his place in the scheme of our winter: We had firmly established ways of doing things and months of experiences that he had not shared. Would he be able to fit into our life? Some of the summer's tension was still present, and camp was a measurably more crowded place, but there was also an opportunity for improved relations between Mike and the rest of the group.

Over the next few weeks, as Mike settled into Warden's Grove and Robert's withdrawal deepened, I thought a lot about the resupply flight. I knew that we had diminished ourselves, that our winter had been tainted when we violated our goal to make do with what we had brought with us. We could have gotten by, but decided not to; as a consequence, we had disrupted our life at Warden's Grove, and our journey had lost some of its purity and innocence. I was angry with myself, in spite of attempts at rationalization. Yes, we had existed completely on resources from the Outside throughout the trip; the civilization from which we were seeking a temporary refuge had enabled us to be at Warden's Grove in the first place. The radio and fall resupply flights also tied us to the Outside; we had isolated ourselves to a degree much greater than most people ever experience, but we had still dragged the modern world along with us. And we had no economic ties to the land; we neither hunted nor trapped, and thus were not dependent upon it in a most basic sense. We were just on an extended vacation. . . . I ran all of this through my mind, but still came up feeling as though I'd erred. There was a qualitative difference between the radio and the autumn flights and what had happened in December; a vision had been violated, a vision of a winter's isolation.

I wondered how we could have done a better job of charting a course through the temptations and dissension that had become a part of the journey. Some if it undoubtedly was inevitable, but we could have avoided our worst mistakes. We had not been very good at discussing our expectations, and understanding other points of view. We were reluctant to reveal too much of ourselves; we acted out our frustrations, but usually did little to work through them on a day-to-day basis. So much of how we behaved had been aimed at avoiding confrontation and soothing over disagreements, but in not being more open, we reduced the chance for better understanding and more gracious compromise. We tended toward a crisis approach to problems—let them slide until there was an explosion or an unavoidable need for discussion or confrontation. This pattern extended all the way back to the pretrip planning stage. In Seattle, I had wondered whether our different motivations for doing the trip were important; did it matter why we were charging off into the North? Now I realized that these expectations were vital to understanding each other, and that the seeds of discord were there, hidden in our initial interactions and conversations about why we were part of the "Traverse of the Northwest." Robert's all-consuming focus on the Hornby tragedy, Mike's frustrating and convoluted language and tentative commitment to the trip, even Gary's sometimes relaxed approach to work—all were recorded as quotes and perceptions in journal pages written seven months earlier. Could we have saved ourselves from some conflict if we had recognized that competing desires would make it impossible for us to attain all of our individual expectations? Were we too willing to gloss over differences in attitude and style during the first, heady flush of excitement and goodwill? Perhaps we could have understood Robert better—and he could have accepted alternative points of view more easily—if we had listened more carefully to what everyone had said. This was not to ignore absolute differences in personalities and attitudes; there is no way to avoid the particular chemistry of interactions among individuals, yet more discussion might have eased our passage.

But we did endure. In spite of some rather bleak moments, particularly surrounding Robert's withdrawal and the eventual resurfacing of frustration with Mike, we came through more or less intact as a group. Sometimes we were driven mostly by individual worries, but our feelings and actions were moderated by our mutual commitment, and a basic concern about how our behavior affected others. While I am not happy with several decisions I made, or how I interacted with my companions, I am proud that we were able to transcend our differences. We put them aside often enough to keep functioning as a unit, to find moments of closeness, and to withstand an intrusion that would make the December flight seem like a minor irritant. We began the journey as a nascent group, lining our canoes down the rocky headwaters of the Macmillan, and we would end it together, paddling past the rocky headlands of the Canadian Shield and into Hudson Bay.

Winter solstice and Christmas came and went: We passed into January, a month of cold, wind, and subdued light. Less than one inch of snow fell during the month; the air was too cold to hold much moisture, and no fronts from the south displaced the mass of arctic air that settled over the tundra. Days of absolute calm were followed by periods when the wind dominated the land; it sculpted and packed exposed snow to the point where we could walk without snowshoes; it drove animals to shelter and made traveling a brutal affair. The most violent storms kept us indoors, unless we were on the trail and had no choice but to keep moving—and even then we sometimes had to wait out the worst conditions.

The winds soon obliterated the last traces of the Twin Otter's ski tracks, but the impact of the flight was with us for a month. Only after weeks of runs with the dogs, moonlit walks onto Home Hill, and absorption in the daily routine of our life did I feel as though I had regained my connection with the Barrens and our journey. Robert slowly began to emerge from his depression. He became more sociable and lingered in the cabin after meals, although he was much livelier when John was not around; his disappointment with John remained. Slowly the days began to take care of themselves once again; the winter deepened and the Outside began to fade away.

One January day Kurt and I walked over Home Hill to Cache Lake in a gusty wind that measured over forty-five miles per hour on our anemometer. We dressed as warmly as possible to face windchill temperatures of at least minus 100°F—wind suits, insulated overpants, down parkas, leather face masks, and thick overmitts— and set out into the storm. As soon as we left the shelter of the spruce, we were blasted by winds tearing out of the north. It wasn't snowing, but the winds seemed to have plucked away every loose particle of snow and sent it flying in long tendrils that snaked south across the river and out onto the Barrens. We trudged along, searching for the slight mounds of wind-packed snow firm enough to support our weight, leaning into the gale but suddenly stumbling forward whenever we broke through the crust or the winds momentarily abated. After a second of relative calm, the winds returned, gathering intensity as we lurched across the tundra like drunken men. The roar built in my ears; I had to shout to make myself heard to Kurt, only a few feet away. I felt completely isolated, beaten into a tiny, vulnerable sphere of huddled life by the great storm.

Now and then, a tiny cone or a curled willow leaf went skittering by, bound for Saskatchewan; perhaps I would be next, sent cartwheeling across the tundra by the wall of wind and snow. Body bent, parka hood drawn tight, I focused on the snow in front of me and struggled to shield my face and keep my footing. At my feet were areas where the winds had stripped away the snow, leaving behind a thin crust of rotten, granular ice. In many places the hoofprints and droppings of November's caribou were visible, along with tiny yellow mushrooms of ice—urine deposits left by some passing dog, fox, wolf, or man. (We had tramped around

Home Hill for many months, and had frequently marked our territory.) Occasionally I stopped to examine exposed tundra vegetation—bare umbels of a stunted species of Labrador tea; faded, brittle leaves of bearberry; brown branches and shriveled black berries of crowberry; crustose lichens that covered large blocks of rock.

Aeolian vectors, the ragged power of a storm more intense than anything I had ever known: The winds tore through cracks in my defensive insulation, cold struck at the corners of my eyes and through the ice that clogged my beard and nostrils. I felt my chin numbing, but could do nothing; I was unable to get at my skin through the ice, and in any case didn't want to risk exposing my hands. As the sun sank toward the horizon, trails of spindrift glowed copper and the slopes and flats to the south were clothed in a flowing, orange-red gauze of snow. Tiny patches of spruce shuddered erratically under the force of the wind; how could their exposed branches survive such an onslaught? How could the musk-oxen survive—long, shaggy coats and all—in the face of such power? Could I have lived for long, dressed even as I was, without shelter? I was battered and tossed upon waves of frozen water, a lonely being lost in the crushing cold of winter as I lurched homeward, seeking the warm security of the cabin and a refuge from the violence.

Ah, but after the great winds had vanished, the Barrens lay silent and utterly calm, illuminated by the quarter moon, the gentle light touching the groves of once-battered spruce and the curving river. Like the aftermath of a great battle, the peace was all the more intense because of the lingering memory of great violence; instead of discarded cartridge shells and twisted bodies, there were only fresh drifts of snow and a subtly altered landscape. I could step from the cabin clothed only in a thick wool sweater, with a cup of tea in hand, and look out over the Thelon and toward the Clarke River—I could imagine the storms to come, and the winds that could, by virtue of their power, cleanse us all of memories of conflict and failure.

Or I would awaken to empty my bladder long before dawn, step out into the minus 30°F air, and look up into the night sky. Above me were constellations that spoke of the flow of time and the slow passage of the winter: the Serpent, Libra, and Orion; Sirius, the Dog Star, shining on the horizon. And rarer and more precious was the shimmering miracle of the aurora, spreading curtains of light across the heavens. On some nights the displays were subdued—faintly shining bands of green light slowly flickering above the horizon. But on other nights the skies exploded in torrents of red, green, and yellow light; endless permutations of shape and color arced across the boundaries of the heavens. Ribbons of light danced above the horizon; balls of color leapt out of these banners in rapid succession and raced across the sweep of night, while showers of yellow light fell from the western sky, steady as a spring rain. It was as if a celestial sorcerer were waving an enchanted wand through space, its path trailing a tail of magical light.

During these displays I stood transfixed, listening for what I knew I could not hear—the hiss of charged particles as they slammed into the earth's magnetic field and danced their light-giving dance along invisible lines of force. My heart leapt with those particles; I felt joy in the beauty of their light and imagined the frustrations and disappointment of the past month rising toward them, into the cold eternity of the arctic night.

After New Year's we began making longer trips away from camp. John and Mike took six days to explore the area between Warden's Grove and Hornby Point in early January, traveling much of the way through deep snow, temperatures down to minus 44°F, and heavy winds. Unable to locate the ruins of the cabin, they were nonetheless encouraged by how they had handled the weather and the necessity of traveling in the dark. It was interesting how often we were drawn northward: John and Mike would set off for Hornby Point once again at the end of the month, and Robert and Kurt had made the trip in early December. They even saw white-winged crossbills chattering away in spruce near the ruins, almost fifty years to the day after Edgar Christian had spotted them:

> 4th December. I had intended to day to go out on barrens to look at traps but before going, to get in some wood. While packing a Log I slipped and the log hit me plumb in the middle of back laying me out for some time and keeping me indoors resting. The monotonous silence was broken during the day by a flock of little American white winged crossbills coming around.

On January 20, Kurt and I set off on a three-day trip to the southwest, traveling past Helen Falls, which was completely frozen, and up the Radford River. This was my first overnight trip since the end of November, and I was pleased by how much easier it was to deal with the cold. The weather wasn't much better—temperatures down to minus 32°F and heavy northerly winds on the return leg—but we felt more comfortable with life on the winter trail. Evidently, we had learned something from our previous experiences, and those of Robert, John, and Mike. Yet there were still several reminders of the need for caution: frost-nipped cheeks while heading into the wind, and two close calls with thin ice. The first, and most serious, happened just below Helen Falls, as we were crossing the Hanbury. Kurt was running the dogs when the ice beneath him shattered, exposing a two-foot drop into the river; he had to heave himself onto the sled, which had just slid onto a solid ice shelf, to avoid plunging into the water. We had run into an area of thin ice and open water, and had to reverse directions gingerly. The dogs were very aware of the danger; Rusty froze and had to be dragged along when we turned the sled around to backtrack. The memory of a sudden glance down into the dark waters, and confronting the consequences of a dunking or a lost team, was with us for the rest of the winter—a valuable reminder of our vulnerability.

We had gone on the trip in search of musk-oxen, but saw no trace of them; the Barrens were devoid of almost all animal life. We counted one raven, six rock ptarmigan, and one arctic fox during our wanderings across miles of windswept tundra and frozen lakes. The animals had migrated south, become inactive, or retreated into hibernation, and the plants were dormant—the willows leafless, the spruce senescent through the months of deepening cold. It was the zenith of the winter, yet we could still go out into the cold, and there was something exhilarating in this—to carry a small measure of life and warmth with us as we crossed what looked to be an abandoned, lifeless landscape, and to have accepted a harshness that I never could have imagined before coming to Warden's Grove.

On January 25, I went for a long walk up onto the ridge south of Eagle Cliffs, where there were good views in all directions—northeast down the Thelon toward Hornby Point, east beyond the Clarke River dunes, north into the uplands of the Hanbury drainage, south toward the headwaters of the Thelon and the forests of birch, spruce, and jackpine that stretched into Saskatchewan and Manitoba. It was a bitterly cold but beautifully clear day, and I took solace in the vast fields of winter. I felt peaceful, as though I had finally regained my equilibrium. The plane flight was five weeks behind us, and the bitterness generated by the event had dissipated. In the intervening days there had been skies that danced with rivers of light, storms that blew hard out of the north. The cold was as severe as it would ever be, yet the sun had already begun its long climb toward summer, and the days were noticeably longer and brighter. Robert was more cheerful than he had been at any time since we had decided to readmit Mike, and Mike was fitting in better than I had expected. The omens were good as I stood on that ridge and watched John and Mike begin a second sled journey to Hornby Point. Far below me were two small figures and a string of six dogs traveling downriver. I gave a shout and waved, but they were too far away, and didn't respond. Later I would look back on that moment and re-create the scene in my mind: men and dogs a long way off, running purposefully in the bright sunshine, as the faint jingle of harness bells drifted up from the river. They were running as if they hoped to cover the thirty-five miles to Hornby Point in a single afternoon, and beginning a journey that would take all of us farther than we could ever have imagined, far beyond the Thelon and deep into another country.

The Thelon River Blues

I've been to the tundra and the mountains too
I've been in Paris doing what the Frenchmen do
I've been in Boston where the buildings grow so tall
Everywhere you go the blues got the world by the balls.
 —Bruce Cockburn, "The Blues Got the World . . ."

January 25, 1978. John and Mike left Warden's grove this morning with the dogs and food for nine days, headed north along the Thelon to Hornby Point, then back upriver to Grassy Island, where they plan to cross over into the Hanbury drainage.

January 26. At 2:30 in the morning we are awakened by a large, four-engined plane passing low over the cabin; it appears to be flying in a grid pattern, as if it is conducting a search. A radio call to Yellowknife Aeradio confirms this—a C-130 Hercules transport is searching for the wreckage of Cosmos 954, a Russian nuclear satellite that crashed somewhere east of Yellowknife on the twenty-fourth.

 In the afternoon we receive an unexpected visit from a bright yellow Ptarmigan Airways Turbo Beaver carrying several Land Use officers out with the pretext of making another inspection of the premises—but they seem primarily interested in the goings-on relative to the mysterious Cosmos.

 During our evening weather broadcast, the A.E.S. [Atmospheric Environment Service] requests that we increase our reports to four per day in order to assist with search efforts being conducted east of Great Slave Lake. We are happy to comply, although we feel as though we are becoming involved with the affairs of the Outside once again.

January 27.   A quiet day at camp; we gather the additional weather data, but mostly go about our normal activities. I think about John and Mike, and wonder how things are down toward Hornby Point.

January 28.   Winter evenings are the time for fat masterpiece novels, and I am deeply involved in *War and Peace* when the unexpected jingle of harness bells breaks my concentration—John and Mike are back early from their journey, so I don a parka and step outside to help unhitch the dogs.

"Howdy! What are you doing back so early?" as I grab a dog, work the legs through the girth strap, and pull the collar over the head.

John says, "Well, we thought that we should come back because there were some weird things going on downstream."

"And here," as I chained the pooch by his shelter.

"On the first night out we were sitting around the fire when a huge plane flew right over us. It looked like it was conducting a search—and then this afternoon we found a strange object in the river ice just below Grassy Island, not more than a hundred yards from where we'd passed three days ago. There was this crater, six or seven feet across, where something hot had hit and melted into the ice, and several charred metal struts were visible."

Oh, no.

I quickly put two and two together, come up with five, and lapse into babbling excitement. I've reached a painfully obvious, yet ridiculous conclusion: "You guys have found a goddamned (etc., etc.) Russian satellite!"

John and Mike are skeptical, and rightfully so, but as I explain the events of the last few days, they're partially convinced that this isn't some April Fools story coming two months early. And so we scramble down to the cabin to inform the others, and the scene descends into the pandemonium that will mark the following days and weeks.

Mike puts in a call to Yellowknife via Reliance, as our signal isn't very strong. Reception is poor, but he still uses his typical, obtuse approach: "We found a particular object that may be of interest."

Big deal. The fellow in Reliance sounds confused: "Would you repeat that? You're garbled."

For some reason, Mike seems to be striving for a lack of clarity, and I figure that his next line will be, "I'll give you a hint. It's larger than a breadbox but smaller than the *Queen Mary*."

"Say it clearly! Tell him that you found the goddamned (etc., etc.) Russian satellite!" comes a chorus of voices.

And so the message goes out. We wonder if anyone will believe us; perhaps the report will be considered an irresponsible joke by the Bozos at Warden's Grove or Spruce Grove or whatever it's called. Eventually, contact is made with Yellowknife for further consultation. When told to stay a thousand feet away from the object, as it might be emitting harmful radiation, we inform them that two of us touched it. There is a second or two of silence, followed with, "Stand by."

Several hours later we receive the following message: "Your group is requested to come to Yellowknife January 29 for medical check for radiation exposure. Department of National Defence Twin Otter will depart YK 0730 MST and expect arrival 1100. No contact has been made with group people in the south."

I am incredulous. Yellowknife? All of us? But I hadn't been within five miles of the damned thing! I don't want to go! Suddenly we're all bouncing around like addled rodents with overactive thyroids. Robert and I shave, and we all change into relatively clean underwear: Goin' to the Big City, got to be inoffensive when the medical folks start poking around. . . . We scuttle around the cabin jabbering, packing, and trying to prepare for the unimaginable. The wheel is beginning to spin and there is this sense that some very odd happenings are coming our way. . . .

January 29.   The morning is spent in fidgety anticipation; the Twin Otter is late, and doesn't arrive until two P.M., coming in hard on the snow in front of our cabin. After a brief interval, two boffins in full protective regalia emerge with radiation detection devices and begin measuring contamination levels; the other passengers remain on board, awaiting word that it is safe to deplane. I can see faces peering out of the plane's windows, and I feel like an animal on display in a drive-through wildlife park. The scientists run their instruments over the dogs and sled, and take readings on John and Mike. One of Mike's mitts is found to be very faintly radioactive, and it's confiscated. There is a strange contrast between the older, primitive technology of dog team, sled, and harness, and the modern one of scintillation counter and Twin Otter. . . . The scientists announce that readings are zero everywhere, and that the other passengers are free to emerge. We are no longer considered unclean.

An hour later, a twin-engined Chinook helicopter comes whopping into camp with a Hercules flying support and making large circles overhead. The Chinook disgorges twenty people out of what looks to be its anus—scientists, military types, photographers. Everyone is outfitted in what will become familiar attire: white insulated boots, regulation green overpants and parkas, and white-and-tan mitts with synthetic fur backing. A big conference convenes while Lieutenant Colonel Davidson, the Man in Charge, gives directions; his compatriots stand around looking knowledgeable while Hasselblads and Nikons click away, motordrives whirring.

As Robert runs up to welcome Davidson to Warden's Grove, his two false teeth fly out of his mouth and land at the colonel's feet. Davidson does not appear to be impressed. Before we realize what is happening, the conference breaks up and John and Mike are spirited off in the Chinook to point out the satellite debris; we will not see them for a week.

After the helicopter departs, Kurt, Robert, Gary, and I await a decision as to whether or not we must go to Yellowknife. One of the pilots casually crumples a paper cup and tosses it onto the snow near the plane. I retrieve the trash and hand it back to him: "Excuse me, but did you drop something?" This is our home, not some Canadian Armed Forces garbage dump.

For a while, it appears as though we can remain—after all, we had not been exposed to anything more than the earth's own radiation; no RADs (radiation absorbed doses) for us. However, the order comes over the plane's radio: "Take all souls." Fine! Can we leave our material bodies behind? But it's off to Yellowknife and those big-city lights for the Bozos; we are given just ten minutes to prepare, as it is getting dark and the plane has to refuel in Reliance. We are admonished to take nothing except the clothes on our back, as all else might be confiscated if contaminated. For a moment I contemplate civil disobedience; perhaps we could chain ourselves to the bunks and begin chanting, "Hell, no, we won't go!" But everything happens too quickly; one minute we're thinking that we can stay, and the next we are being ushered on board the plane and leaving our faithful pooches behind. There's too much force pushing us out of our home, and resistance is impossible; this is obviously a Big Thing. Once the CAF assures us that the dogs will be cared for, we go like docile sheep being herded toward the corral. As Kurt and I trudge to the plane, we lock arms for a minute and laugh. We have these idiotic, disbelieving grins on our faces and there is nothing worth saying, no way to express what's happening.

The plane climbs above the river and Warden's Grove vanishes from sight. We head southwest, passing above the Hanbury River and last summer's canoe route. Below, the Barrens stretches on—a sea of rolling white hills and frozen lakes fading into the gloaming light. It is a horizontal, almost featureless, world; our cabin is a solitary speck lost in the vastness. Once beyond the Hanbury and its scattered spruce, there is little to remind me that there are living things below, coping with the winter as they always have. The Twin Otter is insulation, an aluminum and plastic tube shielding me from the land. The plane's window is my television screen and the tundra below is an inaccessible, flickering image. Soon thick forest appears, and I know we are approaching Great Slave Lake. We have covered the distance from the Thelon to Reliance in an hour and a half, instead of the sixteen days that we needed in August. The miles that earlier had been achieved with so much effort (How many paddlestrokes, how many pounds carried across the miles of portages?) have come so easily this time around. Has the mechanized ease of the flight negated all that we had achieved during the summer, and made our journey into a fools' quest? Not really; for I realize how much I saw and felt as we crossed the miles of tundra and water—so many experiences that otherwise would have been lost. And the flight gives me a perspective on our isolation—so fragile, yet so immense. At Warden's Grove our world extends to the edge of the horizon. We can increase its boundaries by scattered trips to Hornby Point or Dickson Canyon, but for the most part, the sand dunes on the Clarke River mark the edge of our lives. Yet as we fly westward, our isolation takes on a new aspect; in one brief interlude I can examine all that separates us from the Outside.

After refueling in Reliance, the Twin Otter is airborne again. Ahead lies Yellowknife, a splotch of light in the frigid night. How long has it been since electricity, cars, and running water? Not long enough. We are informed that the RCMP will escort us to the hospital and protect us from the media, who are down below, waiting. At the airport we are whisked off the plane and into a four-wheel-drive carryall amid the glare of portable floodlamps and the pop of flash units. Our destination is the Stanton Yellowknife Hospital, where we will be examined and housed for the night. Our RCMP escort drops us off in front of the hospital and we amble into the sterile receiving room in our mukluks, wool trousers, and down parkas, trailing a wake of pungent odors from seven months' worth of woodsmoke, sweat, and dirt.

The hospital staff is kind and interested. There are blood tests and physicals; the doctor who examines us doesn't appear the slightest bit worried about our condition—but neither are we. The medical check seems a mere formality, and I wonder why we are even in Yellowknife. A CAF officer informs us that John and Mike went on to Baker Lake and are now in Edmonton, and he requests that we not say anything to the press until ten o'clock tomorrow morning, when a statement will be released in Edmonton. Fine with me—I don't want to talk to them at all. The officer has no information on when we will be allowed to go home.

Then it is off to the surgery ward, where a room has been readied for us. Things are beginning to get very giddy, and I am descending into a dazed state of chronosynclastic infandibulation (to borrow a phrase from Kurt Vonnegut), and the atmosphere has a sense of temporal and spatial disarticulation. We are issued funny green pajamas and offered showers. ("Smells really good in here," comments a nurse.) My first shower since Reliance, and the hot water feels wonderful as it washes away the grime. Out on the Barrens I haven't felt at all dirty, even though sponge baths are isolated events. But in town, later, among people with different standards of cleanliness, I immediately began feeling like something the cat dragged in and forgot to bury.

Soon there is pizza and beer—our hospital hosts are very accommodating. Oh, boy, have to have some of that alcohol and pepperoni, celebrate my return to society with a secular communion. . . . We flirt, without serious intent, with the nurses who are attending to us, the first women we have seen since August. I receive a backrub that ends much too quickly; lots of tight muscles have accumulated during the canoeing, woodcutting, and portaging. The nurses remark that we are the healthiest patients they have ever had; I'm ready to bounce up and down on the beds and go sprinting down the corridors screaming at the top of my lungs, as there's a nervous intensity in me that refuses to dissipate. I can't concentrate on anything, feeling as though I'm suffering from sensory overload. Then it is time to call home; we've been asked to assure families that we are in the best of health, even if somewhat confused. It is strange to phone those with whom I didn't expect to speak until August 1978, and difficult to carry on a normal conversation after the events of the previous twenty-four hours:

"Hi! Guess who?"

"Oh, I'm fine—just got a little bored and decided to hit a movie in Yellowknife. No, but seriously folks, this Russian satellite crashed near Warden's Grove and we found it and we just got examined for radiation exposure and now we're dressed in green pajamas and eating pizza and gosh, I'm really not sure what this all means and how's life down south. . . ."

In the aftermath of the calls, showers, and food, we roam the halls in bathrobes—petty hoodlums in from the bush, unable to sleep and searching for mischief and diversion. While watching the late news, we hear the first garbled mention of Warden's Grove—there it is on a map, in bright capital letters. We have been discovered, at least for a day or two.

January 30.   In the morning we are served a bland hospital breakfast and told that we are free to go—but a news conference awaits. We're given the option of a clandestine escape but decide on an attempt to be done with the media once and for all; if not now, then we probably will be hounded incessantly. We are ushered into a room jammed with television cameras, microphones, and floodlamps: ABC, NBC, CBC, an all-news Canadian radio network, and a host of others. I feel like a fool, wandering into the midst of the expectant crowd in a grubby parka with an idiotic look on my face. What am I doing here? What is this all about? I don't even look like a subarctic explorer since I shaved off my beard. The predictable questions are asked about the discovery of the satellite, our companions in Edmonton, the expedition, the Barrens. Finally the session is over, the cameras are packed up, and the gaggle of media folks disappears, off for some other hot news item. Whew!

But wait a minute—that's not all. Those were the television people; the newspaper reporters missed the conference, as they had heard it was to be at ten A.M. instead of 9:30. Several reporters bicker with one another and cluck around the table like chickens, squabbling over us as though we are some special type of feed. "Why wasn't I notified," etc. etc. Grumble, mumble. . . .

"Don't worry, folks. We don't have anything else to do and we'll be glad to go through it again." And so out come the same questions, but this time in greater detail. The newspaper reporters are a different bunch than those from the television networks, who, for the most part, were just *there*. Some of these reporters are quite annoying—aggressive, obnoxious, and with a frustrating tendency to interpret our expedition in terms of "man against the wilderness" and all that nonsense. On the other hand, several reporters, especially those from local papers, appear sympathetic to our plight and interested in us as individuals rather than as inanimate bits of news, and I enjoy talking with them.

Eventually it is over and we are notified of our immediate fate—free room and board in the best hotel in Yellowknife, the Explorer (naturally), courtesy of the Department of National Defence (DND). The hotel turns out to be a huge plasticized edifice with windows that won't open and decor that might be found in a Holiday Inn in Kansas City—except that silent, stoical Indian women drift up and down the corridors changing linen and cleaning bathrooms. The scene is definitely odd after eight months in the wilderness; too many elevators and flush toilets, and I feel like a rube in town for his annual trip to the Big City.

Once in my room, I flop on a bed and try to make sense of what has happened to us. It is obvious that we are enmeshed in an important event, particularly John and Mike. A Russian satellite carrying a reactor containing some hundred pounds of highly enriched uranium 235 has crashed, perhaps scattering radioactive strontium, cesium, iodine, and plutonium over large parts of the Northwest Territories. No one seems to know how much radioactive material survived the satellite's re-entry, and how much risk there is to the public's health. The authorities are concerned with the possibility of large-scale radioactive contamination, the media thrilled with the prospects of a Big Story, the public worried by the lack of information on the fate of the satellite and general nuclear hysteria. John and Mike had had the misfortune to stumble across some of the first debris to be located, and here we are. (Later we will find out that airborne sensors had detected the first hit site north of Reliance on January 26, and three more in the same area on the morning of the twenty-eighth—but John and Mike had made the first ground contact with any of the debris.) We are temporary celebrities by virtue of the discovery; as Gary commented, we are easily "the most famous campers of 1978." However, we are also peripheral; our concerns are of minor importance to the agencies and personnel involved in the search and cleanup operations. We could easily be tossed aside and ignored, much as the media would soon abandon us. Nobody would purposefully interfere with our journey, but it would be very easy for the "Traverse of the Northwest" to be overwhelmed by forces released by the death of Cosmos 954.

February 2.   Our stay in Yellowknife has descended into tedium. Sleep is restless, and our meals are consumed with more than the usual haste. The days drag on and we wait for some word as to when—or even if—we will be allowed to return to Warden's Grove. Each morning we wander down to the Northern Regional Headquarters of the DND for a briefing by the current information officer—they are CAF Reserve, and come and go with amazing rapidity. We are told that four paratroopers have parachuted into Warden's Grove to "secure the airstrip"(!) and are feeding the dogs. Several additional pieces of the satellite have also been discovered near Reliance; a couple of them are quite radioactive, much more so than the debris John and Mike found, which gave off a mere fifteen roentgens per hour, or the equivalent of about two chest X rays. Lucky for them. Although the military is noncommittal, each passing day does bring a slightly greater conviction that we will be allowed to go home. The satellite's mystery is disappearing, and it seems more and more likely that its core disintegrated upon reentry.

We get to know some of the military people quite well; they are almost relieved to see us when they realize that we aren't reporters bent upon badgering them. They've been having a difficult time with the media, and I can sympathize. For several days after our arrival in Yellowknife, reporters followed us around like a flock of imprinted ducklings, and we had to close down our hotel-room phones to avoid early morning disturbances. During this pursuit, I developed a scenario to fit my mood:

The announcer steps to the stage. Applause. He looks like a cross between Walter Cronkite, Johnny Carson, and Ted Mack, and indeed, that's what this show is all about. The audience is composed of reporters with a few moms, relatives, and friends thrown in. "Ladies and gentlemen—let's hear it for the Satellite Heroes!"

In come our six boys, dressed in traditional subarctic explorer garb: mukluks with canvas uppers and moosehide soles, baggy wool trousers, woolen long johns, balaclavas, glacier goggles, and capes embroidered with a three-colored replica of Cosmos 954. They have put together some kind of vaudeville routine and a ragged and uncoordinated chorus line lurches across the stage, a poor attempt at a soft-shoe number: shuffle-stomp, shuffle-stomp, shuffle-stomp.

"Say something for the folks out there in media land, fellahs!"

The Satellite Heroes stumble to a halt and immediately break into a series of tired old jokes:

"Had to shoot my sled dog yesterday!"

"Why, was he mad?"

"Well, he wasn't too happy about it!"

Oh, ha.

This goes on for a while and falls entirely flat. At first there is embarrassed laughter from the audience, but soon only silence. The Satellite Heroes look confused and awkward. Finally the audience begins to drift away, having lost interest entirely; only moms and friends remain behind. The announcer is disgusted and walks offstage. These boys aren't any fun—back to the Barrens with them, and good riddance. . . .

Actually it's not like this, but we soon tire of the interviews and attention. Luckily, our value as media celebrities declines steadily, and after a few days we are left alone. (But some bitterness lingers: *People* didn't even bother calling.) However, John and Mike are still hot commodities in Edmonton; they spend much of their time hobnobbing with the powers-that-be in the CAF and the American N.E.S.T. (Nuclear Emergency Search Team) and Canadian N.A.S.T. (Nuclear Accident Search Team) groups. The recovery operations (dubbed "Operation Morning Light") are being directed from Edmonton, and this is where the action is. Our two compatriots could join us in Yellowknife, but it is better that they remain where they can look out for our interests, which consist of returning to the Barrens as soon as possible.

February 4.   We seem to be confined to limbo—an open-ended residency in Yellowknife. This is like being sentenced to an indefinite wait in the lobby of the Greyhound bus depot in downtown Chicago, but the inhabitants are much friendlier in the Northwest Territories. And in the background, the requisite musical accompaniment can be heard: bleak, atonal works performed by an orchestra of mud-filled tubas and violins strung with parachute cord. Blah, umpah, blah, umpah, blah. . . .

John and Mike are up from Edmonton for an overnight visit to brief us on recent developments; we've been in contact by phone, but it is good to see them again. John seems a bit uneasy with all of the publicity he has been receiving, and he is ready to get back to Warden's Grove, while Mike appears more comfortable with his sudden prominence as a media personality and the opportunity to rub elbows with the directors of the search operations. A few days ago, Mike's imagination was captured by the suggestions of two American public information officers attached to Operation Morning Light on "how to take advantage of your notoriety." Johnny Carson? Merv Griffin? Or how about contacting the Soviet embassy and trying to arrange a wilderness trip in the Soviet Union? Mike was excited about the prospects of such a venture, but when the idea is presented to the rest of us, there is no enthusiasm whatsoever. Russia? But what about the Barrens? We have a trip to finish; Robert sums up our feelings when he says, "Krackedy speaks Chipewyan, not Russian." And so the idea is permanently shelved.

I have come to know a bit about the town of our imprisonment—the curious mixture of ramshackle cabins and modern homes in Old Town, the high-rise government buildings downtown, the dull red sun rising through a sea of steam that drifts from a multitude of heating systems, the monolithic headframe of the Giant Mine. And everywhere are flocks of ravens playing on the wind and haggling over garbage—more ravens than I have ever seen in one place. We wander the streets, dodging cars, gazing into store windows at the clutter of goods that we had left behind. I feel alienated among the crowds; perspectives and environments seem so different, even in this frontier town on the edge of the wilderness. Midwinter in Yellowknife: forty below, cars have trouble starting, and the consumption of alcohol is very high.

The town is crawling with CAF personnel, the media, and a smattering of scientists, all connected with Cosmos 954. It is easy to spot the newspeople, as they usually are dressed in immaculate new parkas, overpants, and boots, either military issue or the après-ski variety, and they invariably have a few cameras handy for instantaneous use. Many of them are from the States and obviously not used to the cold; they carry looks of suffering wherever they go, and they seem out of place.

All of the hotels are booked full, taxis are in great demand, and while business isn't as good as it would be if the town were gearing up for the indefinitely postponed Mackenzie Valley pipeline, it isn't bad for early February. Local entrepreneurs quickly produce several items for the tourist trade, including a T-shirt showing a raven riding a Russian satellite and waving a YK beanie; underneath is the caption, "What, me worry?" However, the best curio to hit the shelves is a piece of caribou antler mounted on a plywood base. Glued to the antler is a small metal plaque of the type found on tacky trophies given out by local bowling leagues. On the plaque is inscribed, "Yellowknife. Satellite City. 1978." Oh, boy! Gotta get me half a dozen, send 'em home to folks and friends. The money thrown around by the visitors is amazing. Beyond the general high cost of living are extravagances such as a Lear jet supposedly chartered at eight thousand dollars per day to fly television footage to Edmonton, and taxis rented for an entire day to shuttle reporters here and there. I begin to appreciate the money and effort that go into assembling the news that is fed to the American public—those reporters and camera crews are serious about their current events!

In spite of the media's earnest pursuit of news, lots of misquotes and misinformation appear in regard to our participation in the affair. At various times we are billed as biologists employed by the Canadian government, meteorologists, scientists, environmentalists, or adventurers. We are obviously difficult to fit into a convenient category. Lots of incorrect statements are made about the Hornby party—that they perished in 1925, that they were attempting to canoe across Canada, that Hornby was an "explorer," that their wintering site was Warden's Grove.

The *Edmonton Journal* carries a quote by a CAF officer: "Those fellows have been out in the wilderness for four weeks and I understand that they are glad to be back in civilization again." You bet. A New York paper refers to the "dirt landing strip at Warden's Grove," and there are ticky-tacky errors in most every article. Perhaps the errors are due to the manner in which the DND is giving, or not giving, information to the press, but I suspect that the real reasons are related to journalistic sloppiness. Our problem is of little importance to the satellite incident as a whole—we are a peripheral curiosity—yet it still pains me, and I am led to wonder about the general accuracy of reporting. Question: If those incidents of which I have immediate knowledge are reported incorrectly, what assurances do I have that the news stories I come across in my normal life are any more factual? Answer: I have none, and acceptance of the "news" becomes more of an act of faith than anything else.

Yellowknife does have its saving graces. The people of the town are friendly, and they invite us into their homes for conversation, meals, and music. We get to know Ron Catling and his wife, Jean, much better and talk with Bill Carpenter, who is actively involved in a breeding program to save the Eskimo breed of dog, which is threatened with extinction by the transition to snowmobiles. We also meet Gus D'Aoust, a bent and crippled old man who, in the 1930s, trapped in the area Roger Catling now uses. He has many stories to tell—of getting lost and wandering foodless across the tundra for days, of dogs and Indians, of what it was like to live on the land during a time before radios and airplanes changed everything. There are opportunities to forget about satellites and expeditions, to let go of some frustration, to take the edge off my anxiety. It is especially soothing to lose myself in the music that I hear; it creates associations, and memories return—memories of friends from another life. I also take great pleasure in the company of people from outside our group—I feel a yearning for new faces, and a society other than the one composed of the same five grubby men. The months of constant contact, and the troubles with Robert and Mike, have taken their toll; I am still committed to the trip and my companions, while at the same time longing for more diversity in my personal life.

February 5. Morning brings a call from a CAF captain: "If you can get out to the airport immediately, there is room for one of you on a Chinook going out to the hit site."

We have wanted to secure a seat on a helicopter for several days, mainly to pick up some needed equipment and check on the dogs; what we originally anticipated would be a two- or three-day stay has turned into a much longer exile, with no end in sight. I volunteer; an hour later I am airborne, heading eastward over Great Slave Lake. The helicopter is crammed full of outhouses, food, snowmobiles, and other winter equipment, as a tent city is going in adjacent to the hit site, only ten miles from Warden's Grove. It is to be a base for further search and recovery operations, and it's obvious that things around Warden's Grove won't be as we remembered them for some time.

Below are Taltheilie Narrows, McLeod Bay, Artillery Lake, and the Barrens, plus an occasional herd of caribou—the country and animals of last summer. I am painfully aware of the contrast between different modes of travel—the quiet canoe and the deafening helicopter. I'm sitting in an intricate machine, a product of twentieth-century technology so loud that headphones must be worn at all times. There are fuel systems, hydraulic systems, fire-control systems, electrical systems, and the connections for weapons systems. In the rear, two five-hundred-gallon rubber fuel bladders jiggle and bounce, making me uneasy with thoughts of a sudden seam failure. In the cockpit are instrument panels with more than fifty different gauges and innumerable dials, knobs, switches, and buttons; flip a switch and the entire panels glows a soft, eerie red. I have made a quantum leap, from a simple way of traveling and living to an infinitely complex one. The months of isolation seem part of another lifetime as we clatter and whirl toward our spruce oasis along the Thelon River.

At the hit site, several tents guard the debris and a Chinook is immobilized by the cold. After our cargo is delivered, big tubes are run from kerosene heaters to the engines of the crippled chopper, in the hope that the heat will allow the mechanics to get it airborne. I remember something that Lieutenant Colonel Davidson told reporters: "The big problem is operating in cold weather. The machines don't function and the cold weather gets at instruments pretty badly." Well shucks, Colonel. No problems with our dogs in the cold—they work quite well at minus forty. No trouble starting them as long as they're fed well and treated kindly, and not in the vicinity of a female in heat—and we've never had to hook them up to kerosene heaters.

Eventually the Chinook carrying me heads for Warden's Grove, and I have ten minutes to gather everything together once we're on the ground. As soon as I enter the cabin, I realize that the paratroopers have occupied our dwelling. We had been told that they were living in their own tents, and for a moment I'm taken aback. I suppose that it's only sensible, but it is still disconcerting to have strangers living in our home and burning our wood, while their submachine guns hang on the wall and most of our equipment lies piled on a bunk. They mention that they had tried running the dogs, but hadn't had any luck because they couldn't figure out which one was the leader. (Actually, it's the feeble-looking one that resembles a black-and-white mole with absurdly long legs.) I don't like this—no one asked if they could stay in the cabin or use the team—but I'm not in any position to argue, and the cabin technically is public property. It's obvious that the paratroopers are tired of their accommodations and would rather be in Edmonton. Fine—I would rather be back at Warden's Grove. But there is no time for discussion as I frantically gather cameras, boots, pants, and day packs and scramble back into the Chinook.

Then it's back to the hit site and another four hours spent in refueling before we head off toward Yellowknife. I arrive at the airport twelve hours after leaving the hotel—a day of weary sitting in exchange for ten minutes at Warden's Grove, but at least everything is okay and the dogs are still alive.

February 6.   Early this morning there is another call from the CAF—this time with the unexpected message that today one of us can return to Warden's Grove for good. Fantastic! Robert is the one chosen, and in a few minutes he is off for the airport and home—one down and five to go. The three of us still in Yellowknife will probably be able to return tomorrow, so we spend the rest of the day running errands and preparing for departure. In the evening we invite three of our new-found friends over to the Explorer for a final dinner in the hotel's fancy dining room and run up a one-hundred-five-dollar tab. Luckily it's on the expense account, and we will have skipped town before the damage is reported. I feel a bit guilty, but I rationalize it by recounting all of the military personnel whom we have seen eating there in the past week.

February 7.   Off to the Barrens on another noisy Chinook. It is a blustery day and streamers of snow flow across the tundra in a two-dimensional dance. The clatter of the rotors makes conversation impossible, so we just gaze at the drifting snow. It's wonderful to be heading home, to have left the enforced confinement behind. There were brief moments of despair in Yellowknife, when I toyed with the idea of abandoning the journey, but I knew that would never work: There would have been no proper end, just a gradual trailing off into negation. My heart told me there must be a positive way to finish this; otherwise, it would simply be one more unsatisfying case of *coitus interruptus*.

At Warden's Grove we find the paratroopers gone and Robert out running the dogs. The pilots are so eager to be off that we are barely able to get our gear unloaded before the Chinook is airborne. Unfortunately, a box of papers is left beside the helicopter; as it rises, the blast of air from the blades sends a twenty-foot-high wall of paper marching across the meadow. We frantically pursue the debris and manage to recover the most important items, but some are gone for good, scattered on the wind.

An inventory of camp reveals one machine-gunned ptarmigan (had to keep their sights adjusted), lots of wood burned, our last bottle of whiskey consumed, and some missing items: a pair of sunglasses, several face masks, and some lens filters. Oh, well, this is probably inevitable with uninvited houseguests. Luckily, there were no clean towels or silverware lying around. Wonder what those sub-machine guns were for? Certainly not to protect the dogs. To guard our "airstrip," that hummocky track marked by two eight-hundred-foot-long parallel lines of spruce boughs? Okay, but from whom? Marauding foxes and wolves? Maybe the dead ptarmigan was caught sneaking onto the runway while engaged in a little nefarious avian subterfuge. Hell, half of the Barrens is an airstrip in the winter, as almost every frozen lake and large river can accept a Twin Otter on skis.

February 8.   Ah, but it is grand to be back; my heart leaps as we run the dogs over wind-blown snow, the jingle of harness bells dancing in the air. Before my first run with the team I'm like a little kid, bubbling with enthusiasm and eager to be off. Kurt and I take the team up past the Hanbury-Thelon junction, into an area of pinkish-beige sandstone cliffs and aquamarine water ice, where daggered icicles hang from sedimentary rock. We are stopped by a band of steaming overflow that spans the river and decide to return via the sand dunes on the south side of the Thelon. A beautiful day—calm, bright sun, only about minus 10°F. The sun's inclination is noticeably higher than in early January, and I seem to feel more incident radiation in its rays. The dogs are lazy after their nine-day vacation, but we are still able to cover twenty miles in less than five hours on the trail. The trip infuses me with energy, and all the inertia of Yellowknife is stripped away as we run on, into the frozen space.

In the evening I step out of the stuffy cabin to clear my head. A faint curtain of northern lights shimmers off to the east and the winter constellations hang bright and glowing overhead. It is deathly still; the peace of the land washes over me, and I mumble a quiet thanks for my escape from Yellowknife, for being able to continue the journey. Yet there's an irritating disturbance, for I know that a group of strangers have settled in for a two-month stay not ten miles from where I stand.

February 15. John and Mike are finally back from Edmonton, their Chinook almost landing on top of the cabin in the evening's half light. They've been hired as "consultants" to Operation Morning Light, but seem to have little idea of their duties. Evidently, the authorities prefer to have them on the payroll as a means of keeping track of our group while the recovery operations proceed. It is a good feeling to be reunited again, to have the six of us together in our home, and we sit around talking about the last few weeks until late in the night.

February 28. Operation Morning Light has produced the anticipated disruptions in our lives—Hercules transports rumbling over the cabin on their daily runs to "Cosmos Lake"; the reverberating whack-whack-whack of helicopters as they prowl the Barrens in search of satellite debris; trips with the dog team to Camp Garland (as the neighboring village is called); visitors, invited or otherwise, to Warden's Grove; and occasional radio contact with the folks downriver. Our contact with the Outside has also brought us the first illness of the trip; about a week ago, John, Kurt, Gary, and I started passing around a bug that blossoms into a runny nose, sore throat, and fever. It is particularly vexing because it forces John and me to postpone twice a long sledding trip up the Thelon. Operation Morning Light has also intruded in other ways: the six of us have numerous protracted conversations about our relationship to the cleanup—to what degree should we strive to maintain our isolation? A certain amount of contact is inevitable; it would be impossible to

171

ignore completely what is going on at Grassy Island, what with C-130 transports rattling the walls, John's and Mike's status as Operation Morning Light employees (although they haven't had any business yet), and our inability to discourage visitors without seeming unduly rude. Yet we still have choices to make, particularly in regard to the frequency of our trips to Camp Garland, and inviting guests to Warden's Grove.

Beyond the physical manifestations of our disrupted winter, which are irritating but tolerable, there looms a nagging sense that something has gone very wrong, that a great misfortune has befallen us. Cover up a festering wound and it's still there, slowly poisoning your body; get through a day without an overflight or contact with Camp Garland, and there is still the knowledge of its existence, and the memories of the last fractured month. And our involvement with Operation Morning Light has been the catalyst for renewed conflict among us; John, Kurt, Gary, and I are getting along well, yet we are back at our wrangling, with Robert drawing into silence and Mike's relationship to the group threatened by his attitude toward the Thelon River's version of Disneyland. The once-restored stability of January has vanished, emotional debris scattered along the "footprint" of Cosmos 954.

From the start, Mike has been the most interested—*fascinated* might be a better word—in the recovery operations. I don't know much about what transpired in Edmonton, but the film clips I've seen portray two different reactions—John subdued, Mike enjoying the limelight. And Mike was the one who showed up in Yellowknife excited by the prospects of a trip to the Soviet Union. Since his return to Warden's Grove, he's traveled to Camp Garland more frequently than anyone else, refers to his "dear friends" among the CAF and scientists, is the only one to carry a dulcimeter (a radiation detection device) while traveling, and seems to have a sense that he and John are somehow important to Operation Morning Light. He has also pushed to have visitors from Camp Garland, and he issued an invitation several days ago without consulting the rest of the group. I don't blame him for his interest, as it is exciting stuff—an international incident, the sophisticated technology necessary to search for radioactive debris, the attention of the media—and under other circumstances, I imagine that I would be just as excited. Or, as I remind myself, perhaps the whole affair would have grabbed me just as much if I had been the one to stumble across those metal struts. But Mike's interest has exacerbated the split that developed last summer. I see his willingness to involve himself with Operation Morning Light as an outgrowth of his absence during the fall—he put less energy into preparing Warden's Grove for the winter, experienced less of its solitude, and thus is less inclined to protect it. It is easy to question his commitment to the journey, much as I did when he left in September. Perhaps this is grossly unfair—he has argued all along against such an interpretation—but whatever his ultimate loyalties, his involvement is perceived negatively, and he is aware of this. He seems defensive, insecure, and at times depressed by our coolness toward what's going on at Grassy Island. He's had several drawn-out talks with John, in which he has accused John of misrepresenting him, and of not leading the group properly. Today he also had a run-in with Robert—ostensibly about whether or not to feed scraps to the dogs, but most likely brought on by his ill-considered dinner invitation, which he didn't discuss with us.

Then there is Robert; Kurt and I returned from a four-day trip up the Clarke River on February 24, only to find him obviously depressed again. The behavior that manifested itself during December is back; long hours alone in the tent, a despondent demeanor, silent meals with his gaze focused on the table, and measured politeness. In the midst of conversations that degenerate into hysterical laughter, he hardly cracks a smile. The cause apparently is the spectre of visitors at Warden's Grove—another decision that has gone against him, although I am with him on this one—and Mike's relationship to Operation Morning Light. Robert's outward expression of anger toward Mike was very unusual; it is about the only uncontrolled outburst I've seen on the trip, and it shows how bitter he is as more of his expectations evaporate. I feel that Robert is in part responding to a situation beyond our control, as we cannot seal ourselves off from what's going on ten miles downstream, yet we still suffer the consequences of his unhappiness and can do nothing to penetrate the shell of his sorrow.

March 2.   The aggravating intrusion of overflights continues—110 decibels blasting the cabin as a Hercules roars by a few hundred feet off the deck, or as a chopper skims the Thelon. In the afternoon, one too many flights trespasses into "our" airspace, and Kurt bursts out of the cabin and brandishes a rifle (sealed, of course) at a passing helicopter. Poor manners, perhaps, but an understandable expression of feeling. The most nettlesome thing is that we can have no influence on the situation; it's very difficult not to feel like a passive victim.

March 5.   We had a visitor yesterday—Dr. "Beanie" Cavendar, a soft-spoken man in his sixties, and a friend of John's and Mike's. A specialist in nuclear medicine, he is one of the two men who first examined Warden's Grove for radiation contamination on the day that we were "evacuated." He later spent a lot of time with John and Mike while they were in Edmonton, and he showed a great deal of concern for their welfare. His friendship with them obviously means a lot to him; he came all the way from Las Vegas, on the pretext of Operation Morning Light business, to spend the night here. It was hard to maintain much opposition to visitors in the face of such sentiment, but Robert remained quiet and withdrawn and retreated to the tent for most of the day.

Beanie left for Cosmos Lake earlier this morning aboard a Kiowa helicopter, which had landed in the front meadow. John, Kurt, Mike, Gary, and I walked him out to the waiting chopper, while Robert remained by the woodpile, separate, staring. Looking at this image—the helicopter; the five of us in a group; Robert alone—I felt as though the division in our group suddenly was drawn into perspective. There was Robert, aloof with his vision, watching as his dreams were about to rise and vanish in the clear Barrens air, while the rest of us were down below, fraternizing with the enemy.

March 6.   Camp Garland shows no signs of disappearing, and my curiosity finally draws me to the site. It is an absurdly impressive operation, complete with almost every modern convenience that a C-130 can transport. By the middle of February, the CAF had bulldozed a five-thousand-foot runway on the ice of Cosmos Lake and begun bringing in up to three flights every day to supply the military and scientific population, which fluctuates but remains above eighty. There are snowmobiles, four-wheel-drive pickups, portable bathrooms and hot showers, electric lights, disposable dishes, an inflatable hangar for the helicopters, radio beacons, a two-and-a-half-ton cook truck connected to the mess tent, movies (tonight it's *Butch Cassidy and the Sundance Kid*), a satellite telecommunications system, a burning garbage dump, and enough beer and whiskey to keep the entire occupation force drunk for a fortnight. And just to remind everyone that Camp Garland is an outpost of civilization in the wilderness, there is even an outbreak of the crabs. (Fortunately confined to the bathroom facilities, we're told.)

The dogs are a big hit with the troops and the scientists. The cooks give them huge chunks of ham and cheese ("Hey, what about us?" I want to shout) and everyone has to pet them after being assured that they will not attempt to remove unfamiliar hands. Some of the boys even go for rides in the sled: "Getcher free dog-team trips right here, folks! Step right up and don't be shy! Don't miss this once-in-a-lifetime chance to travel with gen-u-ine Northwest Territories Sled Dogs!"

Kurt loads two scientists into the sled and the dogs haul them down the smooth, black ice of the runway to a waiting C-130. The dogs aren't fazed by the noise of the idling engines and lie quietly in the snow a hundred feet from the behemoth. The plane begins its takeoff just as we reach the end of the runway on our return trip; once again, the dogs don't react as the Hercules climbs into the air directly overhead with an ear-numbing roar. We cringe and grit our teeth, but they act as though nothing is different.

The scientists are employees of the Atomic Energy Board of Canada, the Department of Energy, the Environmental Protection Agency, and private engineering firms. Many of the Americans, especially those from the nuclear test site near Las Vegas, are intimidated by the cold; it is a dramatic transition from a warm desert spring to a frigid Barrens winter, and they are feeling it. One fellow even talks of getting back to his lawn, which desperately needs mowing.

There is a great deal of dead weight around Camp Garland. Many of the scientists appear bored, as they have had little success locating more debris; several pieces were found on Douglas Lake, about a hundred miles to the southwest, but that's about it. Apparently, John and Mike stumbled across the only large piece to make it to the Thelon River. Many of the enlisted men wander around with little to do; others sit in the mess tent drinking coffee, smoking, reading copies of *Penthouse* and the *Edmonton Journal*, and discussing the previous night's alcohol consumption. The conversations often drift toward "nymphomaniacs driving beer trucks" and the like—good, clean fun for the boys on the front. Most of those with whom we talk are counting the days until they can go home, and so am I.

We urge several fellows to walk out into the Barrens for a little while, to get away from the noise, crowds, and distractions and perhaps catch a hint of what this country is all about, but there is no interest. A CAF photographer in the operations tent says, "Shit, no, I know all about snow. Spent ten years in it. I live on Vancouver Island and there's snow up on the mountains—that's where I'd like it to stay. I've had enough!" The vehemence in his voice discourages a response. It's a case of different ways of perceiving land; most of the military men and scientists seem like outsiders who have come here to live in opposition to the Barrens instead of with it. There is no sense of belonging; no one is here by choice. There is no love for the land, and that is evident in actions and attitudes. I recall lines by Tu Fu, a T'ang dynasty poet watching a brilliant moon rise above a country overrun with war:

> . . . *The moonlight*
> *Means nothing to the soldiers*
> *Camped in the western deserts.*

March 12.   Warden's Grove remains a tourist attraction, but we can't feel too proud—after all, it's the only one within two hundred miles. Every few days a helicopter drops by for a visit, disgorging a few well-intentioned military types. Most head straight for the dog shelters; the six of us are a sidelight, and our pooches receive most of the attention. We answer the same questions a dozen times and come to expect unannounced visitors. It is impossible to avoid frequent reminders that we aren't isolated. Hercules transports still ply the air and Kiowa helicopters zoom up and down the river, like flies in search of carrion. It would take more effort than seems reasonable to avoid contact, as the Thelon River Valley is a jumble of activity and we are at the center of it. Besides, most everyone is friendly and courteous; we are always treated well during visits to Camp Garland and have received lots of exotic edibles—boxes of pork chops and cutlets, a cut of beef, cans of peas and corn, even a dozen loaves of white balloon bread. The officers are solicitous and willing to look out for our interests as much as they can. Efforts have been made to replace the gear that disappeared during our absence, a few pieces of military clothing have been donated to replace our worn garments, and the CAF is transporting our mail. Our contacts with Camp Garland, and the resultant surplus of goods, have made my concerns about the winter resupply flight seem ludicrous—but I still remember the context of our debate and the spirit of the fall. Another reality existed then. . . .

March 13.   Robert left on the eleventh on a solo trip to explore the area north of Grassy Island and west of the Thelon, where he suspects that the Hornby party made a last, desperate search for game exactly fifty-one years earlier:

> *March 13.*   Seeing how conditions were in Morning it was obviously foolish to carry on. All feeling tired from want of sleep and little grub, heavy packs and soft snow. After a breakfast of hide we started to make tracks for the River. Travelling very bad making packs feel heavier. Took turns at beating trail and struck river at 2 p.m. about 8 miles from Camp. Here we spelled and had a cup of tea and frazzled hide with a little bit of sugar.

Robert's departure fit his recent mood. On the morning he left, he presented John with a map showing his route. Without further explanation, other than "I'm going out for a walk for a few days," he departed; we figured out his probable intent from our knowledge of the Hornby party's activities and Robert's obsession with the story. What was surprising was the report later that day from the commander at Camp Garland, who popped in for another in the series of unannounced visits—he told us Robert had stopped by to post a letter and had stayed to eat lunch. We were amazed that he had made the visit at all, considering his aversion to Camp Garland, and that he hadn't volunteered to carry anyone else's mail.

A further surprise was in store for us when Robert returned earlier today as a passenger in a Kiowa helicopter. On the way home, he stopped by Camp Garland again, was offered a ride, and accepted. Apparently Robert was quite talkative until he returned to Warden's Grove, when he lapsed into silence and vanished into the tent. The camp commander, an observant major back for his second visit, commented on Robert's sudden change in demeanor and his failure to post any of the group's mail. In an indirect way, he was seeking some understanding of Robert's behavior and the status of the group. So are we.

March 17.   John and I are out on our long-postponed trip; I'm sitting on a gentle hill overlooking the southern end of Eyeberry Lake, some sixty miles from Warden's Grove. The moon rises high into the evening sky, translucent behind thin altostratus clouds. Our dogs, tied to spindly spruce and tamarack, are restless as they finish their evening meal; there are wolves in the area, close by and howling their haunting, eerie song. There are few trees here, only isolated clumps in the shelter of hummocks and ridges. The white expanse of winter reaches out across the imbricated river delta, the ice and willows spread toward a distant esker and the hazy line of red and purple marking the setting sun.

Today was a long haul; we got lost in the confusing maze of islands near the outlet of the lake, and later, under a flat gray sky, had trouble telling if we were traveling on the lake or on land. The absence of landmarks to orient by, the treeless country that we traversed, and the miles of steady running on a southward course have caused Camp Garland to recede into the murky past. A sense of isolation washes over me, as in pre-satellite days. This journey offers a new perspective, an opportunity to remove myself from the immediacy of Herculeses and Chinooks and recall that there is much more to the Barrens than what exists at Cosmos Lake. It feels wonderful to be on our own, away from the security of the cabin, swallowed up by the land.

It is difficult to imagine what Hornby, Christian, and Adlard must have gone through during their despairing winter and spring of 1927. At this time fifty-one years ago, they had just returned from their unsuccessful upriver venture, struggling with snow, cold, and hunger in the vicinity of Grassy Island:

> *March 15th.*   Starting about 12 noon with sleigh we found travelling very bad indeed. All feeling as weak and feeble as anything and Intensely cold. Pulling hard for a long time in soft snow certainly showed we had the stuffing knocked out by this but we have to get back home as making open Camp tonight means too much work and we would all be in the next day. At about 8 p.m. we had to dump the food and pack on with bare necessities. On way home Jack fell and must have hurt himself badly. On arrival I could hardly do a thing.

Now Camp Garland is there and what the three suffered is obscured by the noise of helicopters, the smoke of burning garbage, and the haze of change. What was once an empty sea of leafless, snow-covered willows holding no promise of game is now a modern community, complete with the comforts of home. My, how far we have come. Yet being out on the trail makes remembering and imagining a little easier; there is a bit more understanding now that the occupation forces are far away and the wilderness is before me.

March 23.   In the afternoon a chopper circles Warden's Grove and settles down in front of the cabin. We emerge just in time to see an enlisted man hop out and set four boxes on the snow. Without acknowledging our presence, he clambers back aboard and the helicopter immediately lifts off and heads toward Camp Garland. Upon inspection, we find that the boxes contain 24 frozen pies—twelve apple and twelve blueberry. No ice cream, though. Damn.

April 4.   The planes have stopped flying. Camp Garland is gone and the silence returns. More than two months have passed since our evacuation and I have grown accustomed to the sounds of aircraft, unexpected visits, and the perpetual annoyance of a tent city ten miles downstream. My concept of the Barrens has undergone a metamorphosis, evolving from one of peace and solitude to one of noise and disturbance. But now there is only the wind, the chatter of white-winged crossbills in the grove, and the occasional howl of a wolf. We are alone, and finally it is possible to examine the contrast between Camp Garland's presence and absence, to understand the nature of an inevitable abomination.

Is there any significance to our discovery of Cosmos 954 and its subsequent effects upon our journey? Perhaps it was simply a quirky coincidence—the satellite just happened to find a final resting place on the Thelon river, we just happened to spend the winter of 1977–78 at Warden's Grove, and John and Mike just happened to stumble across debris that the C-130s had failed to locate. It is difficult to comprehend the odds working against such an intersection of trajectories, human and mechanical—there were so many tenuous paths that had to be followed toward the eventual conclusion. Yes, perhaps it was simply an isolated incident, and one single event, no matter how astounding, can never prove an hypothesis. And it will never happen again. Yet this doesn't seem quite right, for there are intimations that the satellite's impact extends far beyond the hit site and the mauling of our dreams. Maybe Cosmos 954 was a courier; it fell tumbling out of the sky, died in a fiery stream of radiation and glowing metal, and left its message strewn across the Northwest Territories: Things will never the be same. The relationship of the individual to wilderness, and to society and its technology, has changed. This change has been a long time coming, but there's no mistaking that its day has arrived. It is finally impossible to seek refuge from the clatter of machines, the incessant demands and restrictions of society for any length of time.

Once the Thelon River area was part of a great *de facto* wilderness, protected not so much by legislated boundaries or administrative regulations as by the extremes of the environment, the sheer expanse of the land, and the perception that the tundra contained little of economic value besides fur. Prevailing social attitudes placed little importance upon conservation, but human impact was concentrated in small pockets or made insignificant by the immensity and power of the land. Without governmental protection, musk-oxen thrived along the Thelon River into the 1920s, after they had been extirpated in many other parts of the North, because the area was made inaccessible by the surrounding sea of tundra and taiga. The tide of exploitation had not yet spread west from the coast of Hudson Bay or north and east from inland waterways, but the establishment of the Thelon Game Sanctuary in 1927 recognized an inevitable change: *the people will come.*

Now, a metamorphosis has occurred and isolation is measured in days and weeks instead of months and years. Prior to the 1930s, relatively slow and inefficient methods of travel ensured that only determined effort would grant access to the region, and that widespread exploitation of resources, other than fur-bearing mammals, would not occur. Today the tundra is only a few hours away if the necessary funds are available. It is difficult to emphasize how very different life on the land must have been before air transportation became commonplace. Certainly the Hornby tragedy could not have occurred in today's world of mining exploration flights and Land Use inspections. Much of the land remains pristine, but its isolation is conditional; a plane equipped with floats or skis can always pick out a landing spot on water or snow, and discarded aviation fuel drums litter the shores of many lakes and rivers.

The ease of access creates a different perspective than what must have existed earlier. There is little need for commitment and for long approaches by paddle and portage, and one cannot always expect to be alone on the land. For instance, parties canoeing the Hanbury-Thelon river system no longer have to deal with a windswept traverse of Great Slave Lake from Resolution, and the twenty-five miles of Pike's Portage. Most groups now fly directly to the head of the Hanbury River—presto-chango, instant Barrens. And, it must be admitted, the airplane made possible our winter at Warden's Grove, as we could not have transported all of our supplies from Reliance to the Thelon via canoes. Thus, the advent of the airplane presaged a radical change in the quality of the wilderness, and the more recent arrival of Cosmos 954 seems like a logical extension—while at the same time representing a quantum leap, one that somehow changes everything.

I am alternately grieved and amused by what has befallen us; there is sadness, yet I have to laugh at the absurdity of it all, like some bizarre plot twist in a Vonnegut novel. But one emotion that has not been easy to generate is anger. I suppose this is because it is difficult to trace lines of responsibility and there is no focus for my frustrations. Perhaps the Russians are responsible for the Cosmos 954 situation, since they launched the damned thing, but it easily could have been an American satellite. Or perhaps I can blame the scientists and technicians, whoever they are. But it's not this simple, for the designers and builders of satellites are following the wishes of our political, business, and military leaders—and, ultimately, the majority of society.

So what I come to is the realization that what we have here is another action directly attributable to Them. By "Them" I am referring to the folks who have brought us Glen Canyon Dam, the Santa Barbara oil spills, the flammable Cuyahoga River, toxic waste dumps, and a thousand other insanities. They have been around for some time—thousands of years, really—mucking up the earth through Their various misdeeds. Sometimes the guilty party is easy to spot, but other times the culprits are too amorphous, and the lines of responsibility seem to lead everywhere. This is the case with Cosmos: obviously the work of Them, but I'm not at all clear who They are. Hmm. There appears to be a bit of paranoia present, but after the satellite I find myself more than willing to cast a cautious glance over my shoulder. When is paranoia no longer paranoia? When They really *are* following you. In *Gravity's Rainbow*, Thomas Pynchon writes of the V-2 rockets that fell on London and the rocket cartel that launched them: Royal Dutch Shell, I.G. Farben, the military, politicians, and a host of other individuals, companies, and agencies—

not all of them German. Maybe there is something similar here, intentional or otherwise—a satellite cartel. And we are to be assured that They, or It, know what is going on at all times and in all situations. "Heh, heh. Don't be alarmed, folks; nothing at all to be worried about. Plutonium 239 only has a half-life of 23,640 years, and nothing like this could conceivably happen again. Honest."

Yes, but there is a discordant note somewhere. It's not just the Russians' problem; things are starting to get a bit out of control and the satellite is one more creation of a society that has chosen a certain way of relating to its tools and environment. The direction is obvious, and Cosmos 954 tells me that no wilderness is truly inviolate. Unless there are some radical attitude changes, They will destroy whatever wilderness is left by whatever means are available, be it the smog that creeps up the valleys of the Sierra foothills, the acid rain that falls on New England's forests, the antiquated remnants of the 1872 Mining Act, or—as inconceivable as it might seem—a satellite. Wilderness has always been prey to economic considerations and now They have the means at hand to do a proper job of destruction. And perhaps the system has accumulated enough inertia to resist any change in motion, no matter what the wishes of the majority are. No, I can't believe that the task is impossible, and I will not allow myself this pessimism—yet the dilemma remains. Wilderness-protection laws in and of themselves will not accomplish the goal; rather, it is a matter of changing the way in which we relate to the land, to our needs, to our luxuries, and to a finite resource base.

I'm not a reactionary, arguing against satellites and all they stand for; I actually like the things, at least when they stay in orbit. As Robert Pirsig writes, there is nothing inherently wrong with technology—be it nuclear fission, snowmobiles, beer cans, or satellites. What dehumanizes and injures people and desecrates the earth is our relationship to these things, the manner in which we approach, or fail to approach, our tools and their products.

April 20.   As the Barrens begins to turn toward spring, the immediate memories of satellites and helicopters have begun to fade, and I am confident that much of my disappointment and frustration will be swept away by the tide of returning life and warmth. And friends who have written assure me that the Barrens will remain the Barrens, long after the Canadian Armed Forces, the mining exploration companies, and the six of us have disappeared from the scene. Yet I know that my outlook will always be different, that Cosmos 954 and Camp Garland have wrought changes within me, changes in the way that I view my relationship to wilderness and to society. I have crossed an absolute watershed and I sense that it will be impossible for me to regain my innocence, no matter how strong my desire.

CHAPTER ELEVEN
Spring

"This is my favorite place in the whole world," Doc says quietly. "I don't
think I have to tell you what that means. . . . Once the land touches you, the
wind never blows so cold again. You feel for the land like it was your child."
—W.P. Kinsella, *Shoeless Joe*

I AWOKE IN THE EARLY morning to the sound of rain and lay in my sleeping bag,
listening to the voice of spring as it fell upon the Barrens. Soon a breeze began to
build, a warm chinook blowing from the south, pushing the white edge of winter
before it. I felt the winds sweeping over the prairies and the lakes of Saskatchewan
and Manitoba, through the boreal forest, and out onto the tundra—winds that
spoke of melt and flight and southern dreams. And I listened for the muted breath
of the senescent soil as it stirred from sleep, and as the warm, wind-tossed rain
began to coax life out of the frozen land. Long before I arose, and much longer
before the Thelon ice went out and the first birds settled upon their nests, I imagined great skeins of honking geese, a flowing river, and a flush of green spreading
across the Barrens. It was April 29. Exactly six months had passed since temperatures were last above freezing, and when I stepped from the tent and out into a
morning of scudding clouds, I felt as though I had been released from winter and
caught up in a wondrous song of life and light.

How little time was needed to change the face of the tundra, and how few additional degrees of warmth! Within twelve hours, dark swaths of vegetation and rock had spread across south- and east-facing slopes, mounds of snow resting on the purlins of the cache had shrunk, and the meadow in front of the cabin was dotted with the brown noses of sedge tussocks. Water dripped everywhere—off rocks, trees, and cabin eaves. The bow of the red canoe poked free from a retreating snowbank and a fly buzzed along a windowsill. How wonderful to climb Home Hill and feel earth underfoot, to look out upon patches of snow-free ground and see spring clouds, fluffy with vertical development, clouds that held rain and not snow. Yes, and how wonderful to smell the tundra again, six months after its odors had been locked up by the cold—fertile scents brought suddenly to life; the smells of a drowsy, wind-blown afternoon by Artillery Lake. . . . And that evening, Robert walked into the cabin, grinning, and asked us to step outside. Across the river were our long-awaited musk-oxen—a herd of seventy spread along the crest of a hill three miles to the northeast. We watched through binoculars as the shaggy beasts fed in snow-free areas and then, as a herd, settled down to rest and ruminate—the final heralds of spring on that April day. Excitement kept us up late into the night, and I finally went to bed feeling that the long bout of winter had been worth it—if for no other reason than to taste the joy of life's reaffirmation as it returned to the North.

April had been a month of impatient anticipation of thaw. Robert and Kurt flew back from Reliance on April 15, hitching a ride with a Land Use officer on a round of camp inspections, after finishing their sled trip and returning the dogs to Roger Catling. Although they reported that conditions at Reliance had moderated considerably, temperatures still dropped below zero every night at Warden's Grove, and almost continuous winds blew from the north; average wind velocity was greater in April than in any other month during our stay. Although we spent many hours attempting to perfect our crash-and-burn ski techniques on a sheltered slope near the edge of Warden's Grove, and still got out on long walks, there was a touch of aimlessness in our activity. We were awaiting spring, whose appearance was promised by scattered bits of evidence: daylight that lingered until past ten P.M., increasing numbers of ravens, and protected pockets where solar radiation collected and melted back the snow.

Spring, when it did arrive, was fitful and tentative. After the first glorious week of warmth came a week of storms with bitter winds, temperatures down to minus 8°F, and four inches of snow. The tundra froze solid and the migrating birds disappeared; I felt that suddenly we had been returned to late October. Conditions moderated around the middle of the month, but then another blustery storm followed, and so on. One of the worst storms hit on June 16, after three days of delightful weather; in a few hours, temperatures plummeted from the seventies to the twenties, blue skies turned to snow and freezing rain, and the winds built to a howling frenzy, bending the tops of spruce thirty degrees out of vertical. On Home Hill the winds knocked John and Mike to their knees and supported their weight when they leaned into the gale. The velocity of the gusts can only be guessed at, since the needle on our anemometer was "pegged" at the instrument's upper limit of seventy miles per hour. Small streams froze solid, and ice and snow coated the tundra; momentary breaks in the clouds revealed huge whitecaps beating upstream through the Thelon's grim waters. It was a world of inhospitable violence—intimidating to humans, fatal to some animals. After the chaotic storm had spent itself, I found dead horned larks, Lapland longspurs, and gray-cheeked thrushes among the tussocks—like drowned shipwreck victims tossed upon the shore. Those that I examined had empty stomachs; they had not been able to feed and keep warm during the storm, and probably had succumbed to hypothermia.

The storm may have been extreme by southerly standards, but not by those of the Barrens; in 1970, biologists studying the Kaminuriak Herd of caribou had their camp flattened by June winds in excess of a hundred miles per hour. Toward the end of every spell of good weather, as the barograph plummeted and the high cirrus built, I imagined cyclonic waves of arctic air forcing back the spring. I longed to hold onto melt, to the species of birds that arrived with each sunny day, and to the renewed growth of sedge, so I mourned each advancing front. I didn't expect a balmy, gentle spring, but conditions seemed harsher than reasonable; average temperatures at Warden's Grove were only 25°F during May. Afterward, I read that temperatures at Barren Grounds weather stations were as much as seven degrees below average during May and June, and that the spring breakup was two weeks later than normal.

Yet warmth prevailed; each succeeding storm spoke less of winter, and every break in the weather was milder and more hopeful. Each day of melt saw soft, muted browns, tans, reds, and yellows spread across the breadth of our horizon. These were autumn's colors, but now they held the promise of growth instead of senescence. Everywhere I walked were patterns—orange and tan sprigs of moss contrasting with dark brown leaves of cloudberry and dwarf Labrador tea; a latticework of ice overlying a background of black mud; a green mat of alpine azalea intersected by weathered gray spruce twigs. And everywhere was the long-forgotten sound of running water—rills and rivulets of meltwater that collected in pools among the tussocks, tumbled down steeply cut banks, and flowed onto the Thelon's ice. And on those days when the sun beat down on my back, before the first mosquitoes appeared, there was always too much to do. Sleep came to matter less and less; I was driven to wander among the sedge and rock and touch as much as I could of spring's rebirth.

As the snows retreated into the shadow of north-facing slopes, buried tales appeared. Signs of caribou littered the Barrens, left by migrating herds and victims of the cold and wolves: droppings, matted hair, the mandible of a month-old calf, skulls of bulls with massive "double-shovel" antlers, scapulas, and femurs. A carcass that fed foxes and ravens in November had been reduced to a chain of vertebrae, skull, and tufts of hair; every scrap of food left by the wolves had been consumed. There was also evidence of our winter—carbon deposits from the stovepipe, dog turds, mounds of wood chips, and scraps of garbage. The debris combined with the gooey mud clogging the path from the cabin to the tent to create an aura of squalor about Warden's Grove. A similar situation must prevail in hunting camps throughout the North during melt, particularly if the rotting remains of caribou, fox, wolverine, and muskrat are added to the slop.

By mid-May, the flowering heads of cottongrass were beginning to appear in favorable spots, borne on stalks several inches high, with minute yellow stamens—the first flowers of spring. Cottongrass was one of the species that I had followed through the winter during my botanical research; along with other sedges and some grasses, it had maintained a core of tiny green leaves surrounded and protected by withered leaves from the previous summer. Now these wintergreen species, as they are termed by botanists, were able to take advantage of May's sporadic sun, and were well on their way to producing pollen and setting seed. Species that didn't pursue this strategy were many weeks behind in their development.

Crowberry and alpine bearberry, procumbent, matted species, flowered on south-facing slopes in mid-June, before they had developed leaves. This is another adaptation to the short growing season; some perennials rely on stored nutrients for the energy needed to flower and set seed, rather than waiting for the growth of the season's new leaves in order to begin photosynthesizing. This hastens the production and germination of viable seed, and increases the chances that seedlings will accumulate sufficient reserves to survive the winter. But the unusually cold spring delayed plant growth, and the Barrens did not take on a lush green hue until the end of June. By then alders, dwarf birch, and willow had catkins and new leaves, and the purple blossoms of bog laurel and lingonberry, whites of cloudberry and avens, and yellows of cinquefoil brightened favored pockets of tundra.

Melting snow, wildflowers, warmer days—all were welcome signs of spring, but none were quite so precious as the animals that returned from the South or rose from their long sleep. One by one the migrants and hibernators appeared, pulled north or pushed out of their dens by interactions between endogenous rhythms and environmental cues. The long winter, with its dark cold and absolute stillness, fell away into the past as the tide of life spread across the tundra, ebbing and flowing with the weather. Each good day seemed to bring at least one new species of bird to Warden's Grove, while inclement weather meant a hiatus during which all movement stopped. Sometimes I ventured out into the storms—fighting the wind, sleet, and snow—looking for the new arrivals. But except for a few sparrows pecking at grain we had scattered in front of the cabin, the Barrens seemed as deserted as in midwinter. Yet the end of each storm always brought a stronger chorus, as if the survivors were raising their voices in defiance of the winds.

Once again I confronted the contrasts of the Barrens: the storm and its aftermath, blackfly hordes and their sudden disappearance after September's frosts, fierce cold and sudden warmth, solstice darkness and the gathering light, the absence of life and its miraculous return. The abruptness of these transitions made their impact all the more intense; one day the skies and spruce were empty, on the next they were filled with flocks of geese and sparrows. Thousands of caribou passed by a point in one day, but then they were gone, leaving only stragglers behind. Winter brought the deep silence when no waters ran, no winds ransacked the spruce, and no living thing sounded—yet this quiet was broken by fierce winds roaring down from the Arctic, and then by the gathered song of spring.

As late April's weather gradually warmed, wolves began appearing at their traditional denning areas in the Thelon River Valley, where their pups would be born in May. We saw several distinctive individuals repeatedly, and there were probably several active dens in the area; the loose, well-drained soil of nearby eskers and the sand deposits downstream from the Hanbury-Thelon junction would have made excellent sites for the network of tunnels that make up most dens. The three-month period between the arrival in May of tundra-breeding wolves at their denning sites and August, when the cubs are able to travel with the adults, is the one time in the life cycle of most tundra wolves when they do not remain within the area of caribou distribution. This is advantageous to the caribou, as it reduces the number of predators on the calving ground—although nonbreeding wolves still kill substantial numbers of calves in the weeks following the major birth pulse. Recovery of ear-tagged wolves and observation of traveling animals suggest that tundra wolves track the migrating caribou south toward the tree line in the autumn, and return to their denning sites the following spring, before the caribou move north again. The restricted movements of breeding wolves means that they cannot rely entirely on caribou, their staple food during much of the year. Wolf scats collected by biologist Ernie Kuyt show that caribou still comprise almost 50 percent of summer wolf diets, but that a wide variety of other prey is eaten, including musk-oxen, arctic ground squirrels and hares, lemmings, ptarmigan, and other birds. Why don't the majority of wolves den farther north, nearer to the calving grounds? Apparently, the rocky uplands that cover much of the calving grounds in northern Canada provide few suitable denning sites. Also, the two- to three-week calving period would not be long enough to support many breeding wolves. Since few other major prey species inhabit the calving grounds in high densities, and female caribou and their young drift out of the area soon after birth, more northerly denning areas might offer little nourishment for the pups at a crucial time in their lives.

Local grizzlies were out of hibernation by May 11, although Kurt and Robert reported that trappers had seen bear tracks near Aylmer Lake in early April. The bears that we saw assiduously avoided contact with us; the scent—or what must have been a blurry view—of a human (bears have very poor vision) always sent them galloping off in the opposite direction. One morning I followed a set of bear tracks, with hind-paw prints more than twelve inches long, to within forty yards of the cabin; here they stopped, changed direction, and veered off through the spruce. The reluctance of bears to investigate our camp reassured me and calmed my bear paranoia, which had been nourished by tales of Yellowstone and Glacier parks. Although the possibility of an encounter with Griz always added a bit of excitement to my walks, I felt reasonably secure venturing out with nothing more than a Swiss army knife for protection.

The first caribou appeared on May 12—a herd of twenty-eight moving slowly northward, picking their way around snowbanks and stopping to feed in the amber light of evening. These were the first caribou that we had seen since early November, although John and I had found sign from a small herd near Eyeberry Lake in March. Their six-month absence made the Thelon seem like a poor place to overwinter if, like the Hornby party, one missed the fall migration and was forced to rely on stragglers for food. No further caribou were seen until early June, when occasional groups of yearlings, cows, and immature males passed by camp. The cows were probably nonbreeding stragglers far to the south of the calving grounds; we heard later that the main body of pregnant cows in the Beverly Herd had passed to the east of the Thelon on their way north in May. In November the caribou had rich, tawny coats, but in June their beige coats looked pale and scraggly as they drifted across the umber tundra and descended to the river, where they collected in milling bunches before plunging into the water and crossing in single file.

Arctic ground squirrels emerged from their dens by May 14, after eight months of hibernation. They are reported to be out and about during the latter part of April across much of the Arctic, but as was true for most plants and animals, the late spring appeared to have delayed their cycle. The ground squirrels were frantic in their pursuit of food after their long winter fast, but they were also quick to scurry to shelter if disturbed. They are a primary prey species for many predators; grizzlies excavate huge quantities of earth in search of ground squirrels, and they are common food for wolves when caribou are scarce. If we approached foraging squirrels, they chattered nervously—hence their Inuit name, "siksik"—but careful stalking allowed an advance to within twenty feet. Any further movement sent the siksiks scrambling for shelter, but they reemerged, often with great hesitation, after reassuring themselves that they were not about to become someone's meal.

The first migrant birds to arrive were snow buntings on May 1. Flocks of a hundred or more of these small, black-and-white passerines were common during the first half of the month, when they stopped to feed before proceeding to their breeding grounds on the northern Barren Grounds and Canadian Arctic islands.

The weather had undoubtedly delayed them, as buntings are the first migrant birds to appear in the High Arctic, and are often seen at the edge of the tundra before mid-April. Other species followed in rapid succession: rough-legged hawks on the third, herring gulls and northern shrikes on the sixth, sandhill cranes on the seventh, and Canada geese and a lone robin on the thirteenth, after a week of rotten weather. Willow ptarmigan, although permanent residents in the Thelon River Valley, also began showing signs of spring as they molted from winter's pure white plumage to the brown and white of summer. Their mottled pattern blended well with the equally variegated tundra, and we later found that the females used their protective coloration to great advantage during incubation, when they remained invisible unless a close approach caused them to explode off their eggs. Yet male ptarmigan abandoned any advantage conferred by their coloration when they courted prospective mates. During fits of hormonal ecstasy, they flew to the cabin roof, radio antenna pole, or nearby spruce and delivered grating, rattlelike calls. Males further announced their intentions by displaying against competing suitors while a female crouched nearby. The combatants would rush toward one another with raised tails, drooping wings, and distended red eye wattles, and during these moments of careless passion, we could have approached within easy clubbing distance. The males seemed like the ultimate buffoons—a ridiculous call blended with a lack of concern for their own welfare—and I wondered about the selective advantage of such behavior.

Four species of arctic-breeding geese visited the area in May, although none apparently bred nearby: the Canada goose, snow goose, Ross's goose, and white-fronted goose. Of these, the Canada goose was the earliest arrival, and the most common until the end of the month. While some of the birds probably were members of a smaller race on their way to breeding grounds in the Low arctic, most appeared to be larger nonreproductives from populations nesting in the northern United States and southern Canada. Banding recoveries suggest that these individuals undergo a molt migration that carries them north to the Thelon River, where they replace their plumage while foraging on summer's lush vegetation.

Snow geese, or "waveys," appeared on the eighteenth; their numbers peaked on the thirtieth, when Kurt and I counted two thousand in a single flock gathered around a tundra pond. Although the species has both white- and blue-plumaged color phases, we saw only a handful of the darker birds. If the Canada goose has the most stirring call among North American geese, then the white phase of the snow goose possesses the most beautiful plumage—pure white except for black wingtips. On clear days, flocks of snow geese formed brilliant white vectors against the blue sky as the birds flew north toward their breeding grounds. In Canada, snow geese breed mainly in discrete colonies of up to four hundred thousand birds scattered across the Barrens, along the coast of Hudson Bay, and in the High Arctic islands. Many of the birds probably were heading toward the High Arctic, while smaller numbers may have bred in colonies around Baker Lake; in July we encountered adult snow geese and goslings once we passed beyond the limit of trees and entered the series of big lakes leading toward Chesterfield Inlet.

Of all the birds that we saw, the Canada goose came closest to capturing the feeling of the tundra spring. We raised our eyes toward great vees that filled the air, then turned to watch as the flocks set their wings to glide over the still-frozen Thelon and land on the banks to feed. On the ground, the geese were alternately raucous and quiet, and they stared intently at observers before edging hesitantly across the ice and rising into flight. Once airborne, the "guh-luke! guh-luke!" of their great chorus spilled over the Barrens, carrying with it a message of life's great renewal. There was an indefinable quality in the music of Canada geese that set it apart from the calls of other species of tundra waterfowl; it touched a part of my heart that remained aloof from the higher-pitched "wah wah wah" of the white-fronted goose, or the muffled whistle of the snow goose. There was a celebration in the call, a shout: "Here is spring, and here is life!"

Once, as I crouched quietly to photograph a ground squirrel, I glanced up and saw a flock of Canada geese circling to land nearby. I pressed myself closer to the tundra and lay motionless. The birds continued their downward spiral, gliding directly toward me. As they went into a last-second stall before settling on top of me, there was a rush of wind through their wings, and what I took to be the sound of goose breaths. I looked up and saw the fine, reticulated pattern of their breast feathers, and the silhouette of outstretched wings. The geese were suddenly about me, and for an instant I was part of the flock. And then I flinched. Suddenly I was no longer a simple lump of tundra; I was Danger. The geese were startled, rose above me with panicked cries, and were gone. I lay there, my heart pounding; if I had been a wolf, or even a hungrier, slightly more patient human, I easily could have grabbed one of the great birds. But why did I flinch? Perhaps it was the surprise of their unexpected descent, or an unconscious response to the approaching collision—after all, who wants to be a landing pad for a startled goose? But, more important, I wondered if they had crossed an interspecific boundary and had gotten closer than wild animals should ever be to a human—and I had recoiled from such intimacy. Human and goose should maintain a physical separation; without this distance, the idea of wildness vanishes. I wanted to understand more about the lives of the geese, but I had no desire to eliminate the caution and sense of "otherness" that made them rise fearfully into the air when they become aware of me. I was glad the geese were afraid, and separate. There was no sense of alienation in my reaction; on the contrary, the fleeting contact had nurtured a strong sense of connection in me. But if the view of a least weasel struggling with a snowshoe hare, or the rush of goose wings over my face were commonnplace events, if wild animals had no fear of humanity, then some of the magic of the Barrens, and its creatures, would have vanished. Thus I treasured the momentary breaks in the boundary between human animal and wild animal because they were so rare. If the symbolic, ideal Eden embraces a less adversarial relationship with the rest of life, one in which humanity is more inclined to moderate its impact and work toward protecting the other ten (or is it thirty?) million species on this planet, fine. But if the ideal envisions a world where wild animals have lost their ferocity and fear—no thanks. The seventeenth-century vision of a peaceable kingdom where predator and prey live on friendly terms with each other, and with man, may seem ridiculously romantic and unnatural to our modern sensibilities. But don't our parks, however necessary, encourage a similar vision? For how much wonder is there in panhandling deer, garbage-eating bears, or rotund squirrels begging for sugar-coated peanuts from the hands of Yellowstone tourists?

One of the glories of life at Warden's Grove was the opportunity to go out as often as I wished, to revisit the same sites again and again, and pursue whatever projects interested me. So I returned repeatedly to what we called "Musk-ox Hill," the rounded summit where Robert had noticed musk-oxen on the first day of thaw. Kurt and I were off to investigate the musk-oxen herd on the morning following Robert's sighting, and although we approached from upwind (good Bozo wildlife observation technique), the beasts did not seem overly concerned by our presence. By keeping low and halting whenever they raised their heads to stare at the intruders, and not proceeding until they resumed feeding, we were able to approach to within seventy-five yards of the herd. From our vantage point we counted sixty-six animals, including adult bulls and cows, subadults, yearlings, and three calves. The adults looked magnificent. They had not yet begun to shed their underhair, a process that the biologist John Tener describes as giving them a "weird and moth-eaten appearance." Their long coats streamed in the wind, and their massive, light-colored horns and tawny saddle hair gleamed against the background of dark brown and tundra, and the somber, overcast sky.

The herd was almost synchronized in its movements: The animals fed as a unit, then followed the lead of several instigators, which lay down to rest and ruminate. Although most of the musk-oxen were preoccupied with feeding, the tiny calves nuzzled for milk at their mothers' abdomens, while a few bulls jousted with one another and gently butted heads before breaking off their engagements and resuming feeding. Although mating season generally does not commence until August, the first stirrings of musk-ox passion were already evident in the tentative butting contests and the sniffs that several bulls directed toward the genitals of a few cows.

On May 6, John, Kurt, and I again headed off toward Musk-ox Hill, as we had spotted a small herd through binoculars. Near the top we found three adult musk-oxen. As we approached, a big bull and one female ambled off leisurely, as if indifferent to our advance; the remaining cow retreated to the highest nearby ground, where she assumed a defensive position facing us. I was surprised that she had separated from the others; lone bull musk-oxen are common, but solitary cows are rarely seen in the wild. We took a few photographs and edged closer to the cow; she responded by bending her head and rubbing her preorbital gland against the inside of her foreleg. When we were ten yards away, she made a short feint in our direction, then retreated to her stance and resumed her gland-rubbing. All of this was standard musk-ox aggressive behavior, with which I had become all too familiar during February's Great Musk-ox Chase—but there was a strange listlessness about her actions. Her attention wasn't focused on us; she seemed preoccupied, as though her heart were not in defense and its prescribed patterns of behavior. So we abandoned Musk-ox Hill, in hopes that she would rejoin her companions, and I puzzled over what was bothering her as we began the three-mile hike to camp.

Thoughts of the solitary cow brought John and me back to Musk-ox Hill four days later. We didn't expect to find her again, but she was still in the same exposed spot, despite a fierce storm that had settled over the Barrens. Her condition had deteriorated noticeably. She was very lethargic, made no attempt to defend herself, and lay with her back to us as long as we remained twenty yards away. If we edged closer, she simply retreated an equal distance; there was no defensive stance, gland-rubbing, or charge. Her movements were awkward and weary; she moved her hindquarters with difficulty, and walked with an arthritic, stiff-legged gait. Blood and fecal material were matted in the hair around her vulva, and she left a spot of blood in the snow each time she struggled to her feet. We watched for three hours as she slowly fed and rested near the summit, the three of us battered by the gusting winds and below-zero temperatures—conditions almost as harsh as during a full winter storm. I wanted to stay with her, but the cold was agonizing; my heavy parka and insulated boots were ineffectual against the onslaught of the weather, so we had to retreat from the hill. Conditions were somewhat better below the summit, and the walk to camp warmed me up, but all the way home, as I trudged through the frozen tussocks, I thought of the cow, sick and alone amid the snow flurries and bitter winds.

Although the storm continued through the night, I was drawn back to the hill the next morning, both from curiosity (Just what was wrong with the cow?) and the desire to keep her company. This notion was foolish; how could my presence do anything but compound her fear? There was no rational answer to my question, but it was far too lonely up there, far too desolate a place for sickness. So Kurt and I went out into the storm, and found her still alive, lying with her hind legs folded forward, and her forelegs bent backward under her body. As we walked toward her, she raised her muzzle and sniffed the air, but she made no attempt to rise and face her potential assailants. Not wanting to disturb her any more than we already had, we backed off, sat down with our backs to the wind, and waited. For what? I had no idea, but I realized that I was as close to a dying creature as I'd ever been, that my thoughts and emotions had become linked to the cow and her ordeal. And so we sat on the frozen tundra, with the frigid winds tearing at our parkas. Each gust rocked our huddled bodies and sent tendrils of ice crystals streaming past us and out across the Barrens. I imagined the storm building as it roared out of the North—waves of wind sweeping down from the High Arctic islands, across the sea ice of the Queen Maud Gulf, over the thousands of square miles of frozen tundra, now suspended between winter and spring. Torn shreds of cloud fled through a sky streaked with glimpses of blue as the weather broke against us, as we watched, and waited.

The cow moved very little during our two-hour vigil. She grabbed several mouthfuls of snow and vegetation and attempted to rise once, struggling onto her hind legs before collapsing again. Afterward, she extended her forelegs and placed her chin on the ground, as though utterly, infinitely weary. Too exhausted to turn her body, she lay facing into the wind, with her flanks coated with rime and her muzzle encrusted with snow. She was wonderfully adapted to life in the Arctic; her insulating coat of long outer guard hairs and silky inner hair enabled her to remain immobile during long, furious storms; yet now the protection only prolonged her agony, allowing her to lie motionless for hour after hour without sinking into the relief of a numbing sleep. The gusts rippled through her beautiful coat, and she closed her eyes as a slow, shuddering contraction spread from her shoulders along her flanks. Another contraction followed fifteen minutes later, and I wondered if the clotted blood, stiff-legged gait, and contractions were evidence of a complicated pregnancy.

So it was to be a slow, lingering death on that hill—six or seven days to die as she awaited a final contraction and wave of pain, or confronted a marauding pack of wolves. I stared at the musk-ox across the evolutionary gulf that separated us, the tens of millions of years that had passed since the lineages leading toward modern primates and ungulates diverged. Just how wide was that gulf? Could I, in any way, bridge it? As I watched the dying cow, I tried to focus on her eyes: Were pain and fear present in them, or just the mirrored reflection of my own humanity? I refused to believe that she was not experiencing some sensation akin to what we encounter on our own deathbeds; there had to be some primordial sense of passing, some stark emptiness that all living things confront at the end of their days. I couldn't comprehend what form this might take in a mollusk, an insect, or even a reptile—the phylogenetic distance that separated me from them was too great— but the dying musk-ox was much closer to home. In our chests beat almost identical mammalian hearts; in our brains were similar neurons, and many of the same neurotransmitters. There must have been a commonality connecting us, a thread of existence that linked our very different lives. There was a harsh irony in this feeling, for the musk-ox's imminent death reminded me of my own mortality, and linked me to her in a way that would have been impossible if she had been healthy. If this feeling was anthropomorphic, so be it. I simply could not accept the idea that some mortal terror and uncomprehending agony was not concealed beneath her placid exterior. It wasn't entirely a matter of screaming neurons, genes, and programmed behavior; somewhere within her slow bovine brain must have been a fear and loneliness far beyond what ethologists are able to describe and catalog. Scientists may capture some of the essence of being, but there's much that will remain inviolate, forever removed from the domain of empirical knowledge.

These thoughts tumbled through my mind as I cowered from the assault of the wind. I felt completely ineffectual, consumed by an impotent compassion. In my most imaginative moments, I pictured myself as a veterinarian, able to reposition the hypothetical calf—or, failing this, that I could have comforted the dying cow, provided relief from her pain and some reassurance that she was not alone. But surely a closer approach would have brought only more terror, and a futile effort to rise to her feet, for I was not kin. I could not communicate, I could not bridge the gap that separated us. Frustrated, on the verge of tears as the wind and ice beat against me, I thought: This is death, very direct and no longer expressed in the language of biology, the phrases to which my university training has exposed me. This was not only a statistic from a life-expectancy table, an event predicted from adult morality rates. Equations and data are necessary for understanding and conserving musk-oxen, but alone they are insufficient; they may summarize or predict, but they do not adequately describe the spirit behind the events that make up the lives and deaths of animals. The dying cow forced me beyond numbers, beyond the bleached, weathered caribou bones scattered across the tundra, the tufts of ptarmigan feathers strewn beneath a gyrfalcon's perch. Her sufferings bore little resemblance to the glossy photographs of a wildlife calendar, or even the celluloid deaths recorded in a thousand nature films. Instead, her agony was related to the entrails streaming from a zebra as it is disemboweled by a pack of African hyenas. It was closer to the patient, careful consumption of a caterpillar's organs by the parasitizing larvae of a braconid wasp, or the surplus killing of caribou calves by wolves on the calving grounds—at rates of up to one calf per minute—with the carcasses often uneaten and left to carrion feeders.

We want to love nature, but it's difficult to embrace the death and agony—particularly when most of us expend considerable energy avoiding these things in our own lives. But perhaps I didn't have to do this; maybe it was just a matter of understanding that a search for meaning would bring no answers, only another look at the deaths themselves. Edward Abbey quotes Baudelaire as saying, "There is no beauty in nature." Once I was baffled by this statement—wasn't nature full of glory and wonder? Now I understood what the poet meant; at least the dying cow had given me this. The natural world is neither "good" nor "bad," "beautiful" nor "ugly"; it simply exists, dispassionate and disinterested, beyond the realm of human thought. Yet out of necessity, we infuse it with our values and perceptions, which are crucial for establishing relationships with the land and its inhabitants.

In turn, these relationships can cause us to see either a dollar sign or a national park, the sublime or the tedious, strychnine-baited carcasses or free-ranging predators. Even though we are a part of the natural order of things, our intellect has also given us the ability to live, at least partially, outside of it. This is both a blessing and a curse, for depending upon one's point of view, it is the source of either intimacy or isolation.

But what was I to offer the musk-ox in her helpless pain? Perhaps nothing more than a prayer, and a willingness to carry some small measure of her agony in my heart, as partial compensation for all the times that such pain had happened before against the backdrop of an indifferent arctic world. My mother once related a story about finding a scrawny and bedraggled kitten when my sister and I were young. In spite of our best attempts at nursing it back to health, the kitten soon died—but my younger sister said, "I'm glad that we had it for a little while. At least it had someone to cry for it when it died." Was I fooling myself to think that it was better that Kurt and I were there, sharing something of her death? No, for perhaps this was where my humanity—the very qualities that may be a source of alienation from the natural world—offered up the chance for a momentary sacrament of passage. Perhaps this was all that I could hope for, and it was enough. Perhaps, like Buddhist prayer flags fluttering in the wind and sending out messages of hope and praise, our sorrow and compassion somehow touched the world of pain and death enveloping the musk-ox.

Kurt and I finally were driven off the hill by the cold; we left depressed, and I brooded over the dying cow for the rest of the day. Why was it taking her so long to die? Why hadn't the wolves found her, and ended the agony? The natural world may indeed be neutral, and exist beyond "good" and "bad," but the dying cow had entered our hearts and we felt her pain. The next morning we decided to return to Musk-ox Hill, armed with a rifle and enough bullets to end her ordeal. The rifle was still sealed; we understood that we were risking a fine, or worse, if we shot her and did not have a good explanation for how the rifle had lost its seal. How could a wildlife officer, especially one like the fellow who had visited our camp in the fall, understand what had transpired up on the hill, and why it was necessary for us to contemplate violating the letter of the law?

It was another storm-wracked day; I felt weighted down by a burden of cold and death and didn't speak to Kurt while we crossed the tundra. As we climbed the slopes of Musk-ox Hill, I encountered the spirit of a place that had been consecrated by the solitary yet momentous event that was occurring there—the pain and dying had bestowed an atmosphere of sanctity on the summit.

There was no need for the rifle. The cow was dead, lying in the same position in which we had left her, although somehow she had managed to rise and drag herself twenty feet to her final resting place. Her chin lay on the ground between her extended forelegs, and her rump was coated with snow and clotted blood. For a minute I stood at a distance and gazed at her corpse. I walked up to her, took off a mitten and felt the solid boss of her horns, then ran my hands through her thick fur, letting my fingers rest in the soft, luxurious underhair. She was a beautiful animal, well nourished and powerful; she was not yet stiff, and there was little about her that suggested death, except for the lidded eyes and motionless form. Perhaps we should have let her be, but the wolves would have found her eventually, and my biological training spurred me to find out why she died. So out came the knives. It was terribly cold, and our hands froze as we worked, but we slit open her abdomen from the sternum to the public bone. As we cut through the layers of skin and muscle, I felt as though I were conducting an autopsy on a friend—guilty for violating the privacy of her death, and for substituting a clinical approach for one of simple mourning. Yet I worked quickly, and with determination; I had to know. Inside the ruined uterus was what we expected to find: a fully developed female calf jammed in the birth canal, with its hindquarters forced against the pelvis and the hind legs bent at the hips and thrust forward. The tiny creature was still warm, her hooves soft, eyes closed, teeth unworn. Behind a veil of burst placental membranes, she looked to be perfectly formed—but there would be no emergence into a world of light and snow and wind. It was the end for both of them, nine months after conception and seven days after the cow had come to her final hill.

Later we watched from a distance as wolves and ravens fed on the cow and calf—four faraway, gray wraiths and six black, dancing birds haggling over their treasure, ensuring that the deaths were not wasted. When I returned to the hill for a last visit, the storm was breaking up and the air was warmer than it had been in more than a week. And near the summit was another herd of musk-oxen—five mature cows, several yearlings, and three tiny calves. All that remained of the dead musk-oxen were scattered bones, picked clean, and balls of soft fur tangled in the low tundra plants. As I stooped to feel a tuft of hair, I said a prayer for those that died, and for those that still lived: for the calves that roamed those slopes, the calves that would survive the wolves and cold and go on to become yearlings and then adults. They would help carry the genes of a Pleistocene beast forward, toward the next century, perhaps into another Ice Age. . . . The pain and death seemed farther away; I felt cleansed, and much better. I shouldered my pack and started down the hill, almost running across the terraces and rock ledges and wanting to shout: thanks be for the end of the storm, for the calves that still lived, for the geese whose cries were gathering into a song, for the wolves that consumed the dead. Thanks be for this day, for this joyous spring, and for my place in it.

Near the end of May, Kurt and I left for a trip to the Hanbury River. Our first day's hike took us to Ford Falls, a mile below the bottom of Dickson Canyon. The walking was easy except in areas with rotten, bottomless snow, where we found ourselves postholing through thigh-deep slush. This was particularly frustrating because the crust was often hard enough to support my weight for a split second before collapsing—up, pause, DOWN, up, pause, DOWN—a bit like having one leg a foot shorter than the other. As we strode across dry uplands and wallowed through drifts, I mused about the previous two weeks and about how, once again, our behavior appeared to be at least partially explainable by the weather.

After the cow's death, snow flurries, blustery winds, and below-freezing temperatures alternated with short windows of warmth. The cycle of storm and sun fit the group's mood—like the weather, our relationships were in flux. The long winter and months of close contact had decreased our tolerance for confined living and inactivity. As with the returning birds, a migratory urge seized us: We were ready to roam the countryside, to seek solitude and movement as antidotes for restless tension. Consequently, Robert, Mike, and John each made solo trips lasting a week or more during May. I felt little need for this kind of isolation, but did take several trips with Kurt, and I spent many hours off by myself, botanizing, working on a bird census project, and observing wildlife. The need for distance also led us to spread out around camp. Robert established quarters under a tarp in back of the dog shelters; John moved into Hoare's and Knox's old residence, a ramshackle ruin that he christened "The Hovel"; and Kurt sought refuge in the half-empty cache, where he placed a desk and a small stove.

Yet our increased physical separation did not mean that we had withdrawn into private worlds. Instead, the distance was necessary for examining our various concerns—the cycles of the land; the impending return to lives on the Outside; the deaths of Hornby, Adlard, and Christian. We were a contemplative bunch, and we sought solitude, but we were also more jovial and congenial than at any time since autumn. Robert's cycle of moods gradually worked into an outwardly cheerful state, with a return to animated conversations over dinner, laughter, puns, and recollections of *The Count of Monte Cristo*. Mike's mannerisms, the cause of some frustration during the winter, seemed less irritating, and such statements as, "You guys are as metaphorical as dirt!" no longer elicited a slight shake of the head, but instead struck me as amusing. When Mike erred in preparing a meal—as we all did now and then—and served up a dinner of undercooked rice and a canned cake with a ghastly, whiskey-flavored icing, there was good-natured ribbing instead of frustration.

Mike: "I beg your indulgence, but this isn't going to be one of the best dinners served at Warden's Grove."

Gary: "As long as it's not one of the worst."

Silence, as we sampled the fare.

Gary: "Is this rice, or did you boil some popcorn?"

Me, pulling out a box of tapioca: "Dessert, anyone?"

Only Kurt did not appear to brighten with the improving weather. As we wandered toward the Hanbury, I recalled his flashes of anger during the previous few months—sudden outbursts over someone banging a skillet with a spoon, how a fire was laid, an uncooperative branch, or a broken axe handle. The magnitude of his responses seemed disproportionate to the irritants. Why? Part of it seemed to be rooted in Kurt's personality, which was usually good-natured but given to occasional bouts of moodiness. But Kurt also appeared to be more concerned, in a quiet way, with the return to the Outside than were the other expedition members. He had received disappointing news about the "woman left behind" during the winter, after months spent questioning his commitment to the relationship. He also worried about what he would do professionally when the trip was over: Would he go back to carpentry or Outward Bound or strike out in a new direction? Perhaps the Outside was tugging at him; he had lived with his concerns for months, and had become frustrated by being unable to address them while he was thousands of miles and three months or more away from any resolution. But what good was any of this? What good was the anger? Wasn't it enough to be where we were, rambling among the eskers and lakes, far from trouble? Didn't the anger interfere with appreciating the land and our relationships with one another? Had anyone's anger during the trip produced positive results? I thought not. And hadn't those occasional outbursts directed at me created subtle barriers in our friendship, one built from memories that would always remain? Perhaps—but maybe I was too easily intimidated by displays of temper, too quick to seek refuge in the natural world when things among us turned at all sour, or when the Outside intervened. Why did it have to be like this? The ideal of the smoothly functioning group, united in purpose and spirit, had dissolved long ago, replaced by a reality composed of six disparate, imperfect men trying to live with each other and with the land. We were searching for a vision as pure as the cries of geese drifting over the Barrens, yet more often than not coming up short. So much for perfection—but Kurt was still my good friend, and we were still hiking together in a wild land. . . .

Later in the day, we found John camped near Ford Falls; he was happy to see us after six days of solitude, and we agreed to spend part of the following day exploring Dickson Canyon together. The morning found us crossing some very dubious river ice—through slush up to our boot tops, over large cracks and uplifts that had appeared during the night. It was like being caught by darkness in the wrong section of town: I was uneasy, and paranoid about a seemingly hostile environment. We crossed the ice as quickly as possible, hoping that we would be able to find a better crossing place on the way back to camp, and not have to retrace our tracks.

During our walk we found the first evidence of spring breeding activity—gyrfalcon and rough-legged hawk nests with eggs, and a pair of ravens tending three downy nestlings. The gawky young were about seven days old. Since ravens have an incubation period of about twenty days, egg-laying must have been completed around May 1, at the very beginning of thaw. Ravens are often the first bird to nest in the Canadian Arctic, and although eggs have been found in early April in northern Greenland, I was still impressed that the female had brooded her eggs during some very harsh weather. The south-facing location of the nest had probably helped, since it would have received maximum insolation and protection from the northerly winds.

In the evening the three of us sat around a fire and talked of spring, John's solo trip, and recent events. It had been a very good day—the river crossing, with its lingering aftertaste of excitement; the active nests; and a walk Kurt and I had taken after dinner, when we climbed to a series of small lakes in a basin west of the Hanbury. There we had found a resident pair of peregrine falcons, circling above us and filling the air with sharp cries. It was a mild and lovely time. To the east was Home Hill and a vast panorama of barren summits spread below gray clouds that dropped curtains of rain among random windows of blue. The land was clean, washed in the rains of spring; there was a freshness about it, a sense of falcon eggs and the year's first flowering. I was transfixed by a burst of happiness—to have been in that spot, cast adrift in a sea of solitude, blessed by the songs of birds and life's ascendance. Afterward came a pleasant feeling of tiredness, the comforting warmth of a fire on a still, cool evening. Small flocks of snow geese and tundra swans passed overhead, their white bodies sparkling in the soft light. I felt close to those two men, thankful for the chance to share that place and time with them; the musings on anger that had occupied me the day before were suddenly alien, as if I had forgotten the language of doubt.

The following day we worked our way down from Ford Falls to a camp by Helen Falls, investigating ice-free potholes for ducks: We'd seen pintails on May 26. We had also found the first shorebirds of spring—semipalmated plovers and least sandpipers—foraging on snow-free sandbars along the Hanbury. The migration of both species conforms to a common pattern among Arctic-breeding shorebirds, many of which winter from the southern United States south into tropical South America. Adults arriving on their breeding grounds in late May spend two months or less before heading southward by early August, after the great peak of insect abundance has passed. Although the long-distance migration of these two small species—neither of which is over eight inches long—is impressive, it is not quite as remarkable as the movements of two other species that arrived at Warden's Grove in early June—lesser golden plovers and arctic terns. The golden plover winters on the Argentine pampas, after making a continuous flight of two thousand miles from southeastern Canada to South America, while arctic terns may fly more than eleven thousand miles, across the Atlantic Ocean and along the west coasts of Europe and Africa, to their winter range, which extends south to the Antarctic Circle. This tremendous peregrination means at least twenty-two thousand miles of flying each year; as I contemplated a lunch stop after five miles of wobbling through the tussocks, I decided that the little devils made our canoe trip all the less impressive: "Two thousand miles—why you've just started! Only twenty thousand more to go!"

Next day's walk back to Warden's Grove was filled with music rising from flocks of snow and white-fronted geese feeding in meadows adjacent to the Thelon. For some reason I was played out, as though my body were running at seventeen and a half rpm. I felt as though my pack were filled with eighty pounds of sand, and my veins clogged with sludge. Yet when we popped over Home Hill, my spirits were revived by the sight before us—a great lead of open water on the Thelon. A small channel curved past the sweep of sand east of camp and broadened into a wide expanse below. Chunks of ice drifted slowly downstream, jamming into a creaking mass opposite Beddingstraw Creek. After almost eight months, the river was edging toward breakup, opening to welcome the returning waterfowl that suddenly graced its waters: oldsquaws, yellow-billed loon, scaups, and red-breasted mergansers.

Once again the river was set to become the focus of our world. We would follow its waters into June, into a month of leisured preparations for a July departure, long rambles across the Barrens, and many hours of bird censusing—and a month in which we noted the passing of Edgar Christian and the anniversary of our departure from the headwaters of the Macmillan. But what comes back most clearly are evening walks by the river, on days when the winds died and the land seemed to have metamorphosed into one great reflection:

> *1 June* [journal entry]:   The waters of the Thelon gurgle softly as they slide past the jagged floes, the river's surface a faintly distorted mirror. Reflections of crystalline ice assume a thousand patterns; Eagle Cliffs, spruce, and sand dunes, and swaths of brown tundra ripple across the water. The river is up several feet over yesterday, as meltwater swells its banks—yet the current is peaceful and I wonder how much longer until breakup. . . . Oldsquaw ducks yodel from across the way; pairs engage in their elaborate courtship dance, the male bobbing and weaving around the female. Suddenly they rise and surge upstream, their fast, low flight a black-and-white double image against sky and water. Geese flock overhead—Canadas and waveys—and the call of a yellow-billed loon drifts across the river; least sandpipers poke the sand and mud at the water's edge as they scold and chase one another.
>
> From the meadow comes the sound of Lapland longspurs proclaiming their right to territory; males ascend quickly from their perches atop tussocks or stunted spruce, then tumble groundwards with a cascade of trilled notes. The sun slides towards Home Hill in a long tangent as we walk through the mucky sedges, stopping to photograph, and discussing women, birds, and the prospective southern journey. It all seems so far away, part of a distant world:
>
> "It would be easy to assume a negative attitude." [This from Kurt.]
>
> "Yeah, it's the things that I worry about, more than the people—the

unnecessary possessions, the manifestations of our material culture."

There's no true sense of an impending return, and a different reality; the Barrens are before me, they exist only in the present, and I've lived with them in what might pass for a state of suspended animation for so long that it's difficult to look beyond Warden's Grove.

Summer awaits, and the land seems suffused with hope. The snow is almost gone, most of the migrants that I'd expect to breed here have arrived. Robins and redpolls are building nests, gathering mud and debris to shelter this year's broods. . . . On a beautiful, calm evening such as this it is difficult to think of Christian's last days of suffering; yet Robert has been alone all day, fasting and most likely thinking of death. I wonder if we seem callous to him, with our laughter, and meals as usual?

And it was difficult to concentrate on Christian in any meaningful way. I called my heart toward a halting passion, tried to imagine a young man's solitary death, not unlike that of the female musk-ox—just longer in coming. Hornby had died on April 16 and Adlard on May 3, while Christian had lasted for another month. The pain and terror of suffering alone; did these feelings ever dissolve into resignation, did hope ever evaporate? I recalled the ramshackle ruins thirty miles downstream and wondered what his end must have been like; even though I had lived along the Thelon and felt the Barrens winter, there was a barrier to my understanding, so I returned to camp and reread Christian's last journal entries:

> Now June 1st I have grub on hand, but am weaker than have Ever been in my Life and no Migration north of birds and Animals since 19th (Swan).
>
> Yesterday I was out Crawling having cut last piece of wood in house to cook me food I had which is a very fat piece of Caribou hide but while out I found fish and meat in plenty and greasy gut fat on in sides of foxes and 2 Wolverine containing Liver and hearts and Kidneys and Lights   1 fox Carcacass. All this I cooked up leaving the hide as a Cache. I ate all I could and got Rid of much fould food from my system, apparently been stopping me walking. At 2 a.m. went to bed feeling Content and bowl full of fish by me to Eat in Morning.
>
> 9 a.m. Weaker than Ever   have Eaten all I can   have food on hand but heart peatering? Sunshine is bright now   see if that does any good to me if I get out and bring in wood to make fire to night.
>
> Make preparations now.
>
> Got out   too weak and all in now. Left Things Late.

These words helped, but the murmuring of the heart was still faint, as if I had to work at generating feelings that conflicted with the wonder and clarity of the evening. . . .

And so the anniversary of our departure from the Macmillan arrived. June 13 was beautiful and insect-free, warm enough for shorts and shirtless backs as we attended to projects around camp, read, or explored the tundra. It was a rare day, one on which the Barrens seemed benign—when the warmth, the south-westerly breeze, and the mosquito-free air created an aura of gentle comfort. After a celebratory dinner of canned ham (saved since Christmas), rice, fresh bread, and pumpkin pie, I sat in the quiet cabin and considered the last year, and its components. They were like four contrasting movements of a sonata: the first summer's travels (definitely *presto*); building a home by the Thelon, and then sliding into winter (*moderato* becoming *adagio*); the insanity of Cosmos (*scherzo*); and, finally, the flowering of spring, which had to be *andante*. Only a postlude remained—the final six hundred miles of paddling, north and east to Hudson Bay. Had I changed in the last year? Had I benefited from the journey in any measurable ways? The sound of Robert's pennywhistle drifted down from the grove as he tried to harmonize with the high, whistled song of Harris's sparrows. Indefatigable singers, they raised their voices in fierce winds, when all the other birds were quiet, as well as on calm evenings. Robert's notes weren't quite as clear and thin as those of *Zonotrichia querula*, but they added to my relaxed and contemplative mood.

We had come full circle, from the beginning of one summer to the start of the next. My thoughts fled back to the willow-choked banks of the Macmillan, the final good-byes to Bruce and Owen, the cut and bashed shins of that first day, and all the miles that followed. I remembered the somber clouds and icy peaks of the Itsis, the infant journey swelling like the rivers that carried us along. I thought of my fears and excitement, the almost childlike innocence with which I faced the land and myself, how expectations had given way—first to the reality of the trail, then to the reality of the Barrens in winter. Had I been changed by my experiences, or was I just a year older, a bit stronger and heavier (too many biscuits last winter), and infinitely more disheveled? It would have been encouraging to look inside myself and find changes as vast as the land, to confront a person with greater confidence, a stronger sensitivity to fellow humans, a more selfless nature—someone who was ready to return to society and take on whatever project captured his imagination. But I knew that this wasn't the case, that I was much the same as I was before the trip. If the experiences had altered my personality and outlook, then they had done so in subtle ways; it might be years before I recognized the differences, and how they had arisen. For the most part, I was left with reminders of a wilderness year; try as hard as I might, I could not discern any changes that others would notice when I returned.

And yet there was a difference, one felt at the core of my being. In the last year I had developed a bond to the earth that transcended anything I had known previously. I had gone out for a year to look at the wilderness, and come away with a sense of place that filled me with joy. Coming to Warden's Grove was part of it: fifteen hundred miles, the exhausting portages and bone-weary days of paddling, the transition from taiga to tundra. But once at Warden's Grove, the process had truly begun—preparing for the winter, watching the land and heavens change, moving toward senescence with the animals and plants. I thought of all the days and hours spent watching and listening, the bitter cold, the solstice sun glowing huge and orange on the southern horizon. Now it was spring, a spring swelling into the hope and glory of summer. . . . We all want to belong to someone, or something, to find a place that the heart can nestle into, where our soul feels secure. I had found a deep connection for the first time, had gone beyond aesthetic appreciation of a landscape, the satisfaction of a good climb, or the thrill of an exciting rapid. I had been privileged to live a life open to a very few, and in the process I had discovered an abiding intimacy; the Barrens had created an interior landscape that rolled toward the boundaries of desire and experience. I had come looking for a home and had found it—one that I could carry with me into the future and a life thousands of miles from Warden's Grove.

The river went out the following evening, its waters cresting after three straight days of sun and pushing the final vestiges of winter seaward. It happened suddenly, with little warning: One minute the bottleneck of ice downstream from North Grove was intact; the next instant the entire mass collapsed and surged toward Eagle Cliffs. John, Kurt, and I raced from the cabin toward the river, hoping to catch the last of the spectacle. When we reached the bank, the river was choked with huge chunks of ice that bobbed and twirled in the flood. There were no loud explosions or groans like those described in books I'd read—only a subdued muttering as floes ground against one another and spun downstream. The current seemed to gather momentum, as though racing seaward in an effort to compensate for the long drought of winter. For an hour the waters built, sweeping with them a continuous mass of ice. Then the floes began to taper off; soon the main channel was clear, and all that remained of winter's mantle were two margins of ice stuck fast to each shore.

We scrambled down the bank to investigate the stranded floes. The reason for the weakness of the ice was obvious; it had become "candled"—transformed from a strong, rigid sheet into a collection of vertical slivers that disintegrated in the warm sun, or with a gentle kick. Like children, we were tempted to an orgy of destruction by the fragile ice; with each kick the slivers shattered, sounding like a delicate chandelier exploding on a stone floor. But we gave up the mayhem to turn back toward the river, and the massive cumulus rising into the southwestern sky above the Clarke River. The clouds gleamed pink in the evening light as vertical striations of rain fell against a backdrop of rich blue sky. The river was clear enough to mirror the magnificence of the sky, and we watched the reflections dance as we talked of the breakup. The river had completed its cycle. Last summer and fall we had paddled its waters and hauled out our canoes for the final time just before the freeze-up. Once the ice was firm, we had used the river as another kind of highway—snowshoeing, skiing, and running dogs over hundreds of miles of smooth water ice. Now the ice was going and we were again ready to think of paddling, of the slick wake of our canoes headed downstream.

After breakup, our stay at Warden's Grove began to wind down. We dismantled the winter entrance to the cabin, took down the dog shelters, and sorted the remaining supplies into what we would take and what we would leave behind. We packaged skis, snowshoes, down parkas, books, plant specimens, extra tents and sleeping bags, and myriad other items for shipment to Yellowknife and southward. We sent a radio message to Ron Catling informing him that the river had gone out and we were ready for a flight to transport our equipment out of the sanctuary. When most of our preparations were completed, all we had to do was wait—for the plane flight, and for the ice to melt off the huge lakes on the lower Thelon. Although the river was open, there was no sense in leaving Warden's Grove too early, only to be blocked by ice 150 miles downstream. The passing days brought a summer every bit as tentative as the spring that had preceded it. The cycle of sun and storm continued, even as the tundra became washed in green, wildflowers bloomed, and solstice arrived. Snow fell on the Fourth of July, snowbanks lingered on north-facing slopes, and the larger lakes around camp retained most of their ice. It was impossible to predict the weather, or when we would be able to leave—but at least the bad weather retarded the arrival of Our Winged Animal Pals. June passed into July without the mosquitoes building to what one biologist described as "levels of human intolerance." It was a fair trade, probably even an advantageous one: an extra layer of clothes and a few more days of waiting in exchange for freedom from insect persecution. Our motto became "Let the buggers freeze!"

When I wasn't helping to prepare for departure, Kurt and I were working on a bird census project in Warden's Grove and North Grove, and gathering information on the breeding chronology of birds in the area. Because Arctic-breeding birds are constrained by the short summer, breeding activities and maturation of the young must be compressed into a much shorter period than is usually the case in temperate environments. Some species spend less than ten weeks on their breeding grounds before flying south again; a case in point is the gray-cheeked thrush. Although not a true Arctic-breeding species, it nests to the tree line throughout the northernmost reaches of the boreal forest, and still must adapt to a short breeding season. The species arrived at Warden's Grove on June 1, and probably departed shortly after mid-August; although we were gone by then in 1978, there were no thrushes in the area when we arrived on August 20 the year before. In this ten-week "window," the thrushes have to establish territories, find mates, build nests, lay eggs, incubate them for two weeks, and spend another two weeks raising nestlings. Then the fledglings must gain sufficient size, strength, and nutrient reserves to begin the long flight toward Central and South America. Thus, there is little leeway in case of inclement weather; the adults cannot delay reproduction for too long because their offspring might then have to deal with harsh autumn weather. There is also evidence that many tundra-breeding birds, such as Lapland longspurs and snow buntings, have adjusted their breeding schedules so that young are produced at the time of long-term, "expected" July peaks in insect abundance; the result is that a tremendous amount of activity must be crowded into a short time period, and most species fledge young during the latter three weeks of July and the first week of August. This is true for plants as well as birds, so the tundra seems to explode into summer as its inhabitants rush to be done with the business of reproduction. Caught up in this surge as I tried to monitor what was occurring around me, I found myself sleeping less and less as our departure date approached; only on stormy days, when life retreated into its shelters, was there sufficient time to rest.

The results of our census work weren't going to capture the attention of the world's great ornithologists, but they did provide an idea of what was living where, and added to the sense of life's gathering force—and its fragility—as summer came on. As expected, we found few breeding species on the tundra—Lapland longspurs, horned larks, water pipits, and an occasional savannah sparrow. There were many more species and individuals crowded into the spruce islands that dotted the Barrens—perhaps as many as eleven species and fifty breeding pairs in the fifteen acres of Warden's Grove. But the three-day storm of mid-June, with its snow and seventy-mile-per-hour winds, affected breeding populations, particularly of those species which rely on insects during the summer. After the storm, the average number of census observations dropped by more than a third, and pairs of yellow-rumped warblers and blackpoll warblers disappeared from two plots.

My last trip away from Warden's Grove came on June 25 and 26, when Kurt and I traveled to Helen Falls to check an active gyrfalcon nest. Our return to camp was a wonderful exercise in machochism—into a wind-driven rain, and, by some perversity of our rational powers, through the marshiest and muddiest route across the tundra. Leaky raingear and soggy feet eventually led me to abandon any pretense of staying dry, and I plunged directly through each bog along the way. The idea of dry clothes, a comfortable bed, and a relaxed, warm meal entranced me— but alas, it was not to be. At four P.M., soon after we returned, a Twin Otter buzzed the cabin, set down on the river, and taxied to the opposite bank of the Thelon. Why? A hurried call to Yellowknife elicited groans and a sense of *déjà vu*: The plane was a charter, sent to collect our gear. No one had released the message of its impending arrival, and we were caught unprepared. Although we had packed much of our equipment, there were many loose ends to attend to before we were ready for the flight. Since air charter companies make money only when they are flying, there is usually a quiet, but insistent, pressure to keep ground time to a minimum. This, combined with the increasingly rotten weather, made us certain that the pilot's patience would be limited, and that we would have to hustle. The ensuing pandemonium was reminiscent of the previous fall's resupply flights, and the subsequent carries were an attenuated version of the tedious portages from Cache Lake. Boxes were taped, the barograph and weather data packed, the arctic tent collapsed and rolled into a bundle, a few mouthfuls of food inhaled, and a system for ferrying loads devised. John radioed the stations that had been our long-distance companions for the last ten months—Reliance, Contwoyto Lake, and Yellowknife. Final messages of good cheer were exchanged and then: "This is Warden's Grove going off the air." Down came the aerial, and our link with the Outside was severed—a link that we had accepted with initial reluctance, learned to enjoy, and that indirectly had caused us much grief.

Then came the carries to the riverbank, and some very wild canoe crossings. Why was it that planes with "official" business at Warden's Grove (i.e., Fish and Wildlife Service, Land Use, or Department of National Defence) managed to land conveniently close to camp, but the private charters found it best to plop down in difficult places? The winds had increased during the afternoon, and large whitecaps were rolling upstream. We made the crossing to the plane with the wind at our backs, surfing waves while paddling against the current, struggling to keep the canoe running parallel to the rollers. The return was worse—into the wind and rain as soaking waves splashed over the bow and gunwales. It took us almost five hours to pack and ferry our equipment and ten months' worth of unburnable garbage to the plane. Portaging heavy loads to the river, rushing through the packing, fighting the weather during the river crossing, and the walk from the Hanbury had sapped me of all energy; I was exhausted yet jubilant as the plane lifted into the wind. Somehow, we had created order out of chaos, and it was a relief to have ditched the radio and terminated business with the Outside. The treasured relaxation that follows frenzied activity washed over me as we sipped tea and discussed the afternoon's crazy adventures. All that remained was a week or so of birding work and tidying up around camp; then we would be on the trail and bound northeastward for Hudson Bay.

During the first few days of July, I rushed to finish my scientific work; with the help of John and Kurt, I ran the last vegetation transects and bird censuses. Robert and Mike collected trash from an old archaeological survey site across the river, packed it into two drums, and paddled them down to Cosmos Lake, where they could be picked up by the cleanup crew scheduled to return there in August. We packed for the journey, cramming five weeks' worth of supplies into four food packs that must have weighed more than a hundred pounds each. We burned garbage, tidied the cabin and cache, removed the plastic from John's hovel, and mended and washed clothes. We also entertained our first visitors of the summer, a party of seven canoeists on a trip from Hoare Lake to Beverly Lake. Clearly, their appearance meant we should take leave of Warden's Grove. They said that the lakes on the upper Hanbury were still frozen, but we figured that two weeks of paddling would give the downstream lakes time to break up.

Just as we were about to depart, another storm lashed Warden's Grove; for three days, clouds dragged their bellies against the hills, and the skies spat rain and snow. As we waited for better weather, I read nervously, fidgeted, and ate excessively. Enmeshed in an enforced lethargy, with the taste of stale beans and Jell-O in my mouth, I yearned for the storm's passage. I wasn't in the mood for a ceremonial leave-taking, or a final, contemplative walk; I just wanted to cut the cord and GO. And so when we awoke on July 8 to clear skies, the excitement of anticipated motion was with me.

What was it like to leave our home after 320 days, to step from the cabin one last time, to grasp the middle thwart of a canoe and heave it, in one rolling motion, onto my shoulders? Heading across the meadow, I was very conscious of leaving behind a precious world, one to which I might never return. How much energy, both physical and mental, had gone into Warden's Grove! How many swings of an axe, how many hours of wandering over the tundra and through the spruce, how many late-night sessions by the dim light of a kerosene lantern had gone into building and maintaining a sense of place in an environment that, if it wasn't trying to defeat us, certainly didn't go out of its way to make us welcome?

I hopped from tussock to tussock, supporting the unfamiliar weight of the canoe, listening to the creak of plastic and wood as I made for the river. The upturned bow pointed north, into the height of summer, toward the journey's end—yet my thoughts trailed into the past. I knew that I would be financially destitute when I returned to the South, yet life at Warden's Grove had made me immeasurably richer. Behind me was a string of memories that had been incorporated into my being: the first curious, expectant look at Warden's Grove; the weeks of wood-cutting and building to prepare for winter; the runs with the dogs through a luminous twilight world of snow and brittle cold; the first breath of spring blowing over the tundra; the death of the female musk-ox—and, yes, even the chaos of Cosmos 954.

I filed through a series of mental images, stills from an extended film, taken at monthly intervals from the same vantage point: looking eastward from near the arctic tent, over the cabin and the Thelon toward the Clarke River. In the first frame, the tundra was still green, with just a tinge of autumn in its foliage; the cabin had a long-abandoned look about it, with debris and lumber scattered around its exterior. In the second frame, the tundra was rich in reds, yellows, and browns; the river was much lower than in the first frame, and the cabin tidier. Piles of logs were gathered in a tumbled heap nearby, and a white Stevenson screen and outhouse had been added to the righthand edge of the scene. In the next frame, the river was choked with ice and the Barrens dusted with snow, although tussocks were still visible in the meadow. A wisp of smoke curled from the cabin chimney and neat stacks of cordwood extended around three sides of the dwelling. Frames four, five, six, seven, eight, and nine looked much the same—snow everywhere, the Thelon frozen solid, and the omnipresent plume of smoke. But a careful observer would notice differences. The woodpile gradually shrank until only a single row remained at the left of the cabin. At first the shadows lengthened and the light decreased, as though the world were sliding into dusk; the snow looked powdery and newly fallen. Then the movement toward night stopped, and the progression was reversed as the shadows retreated. The skies brightened and the snow became sculpted; even from a distance, it looked firmer than in earlier frames. Then frame ten showed a sudden, miraculous change: The tundra reappeared, with dull brown tussocks scattered among patches of snow. The river was still frozen, and heavy gray clouds helped paint the Barrens in subdued colors; a muddy path led from the foreground down to the cabin. In the eleventh frame, the tundra was a rich, vivid green. Scattered cumulus drifted through a brilliant sky, reflected in the waters of the curving river. Now the wood was almost gone; the cabin looked neat, as though it had been prepared for a special occasion. At the lefthand edge of the frame was an upturned red canoe, supported by two spindly legs poking out from underneath the shell. In the next frame, the first hints of autumn would begin to spread across the land once again—but I wouldn't see this frame, and Warden's Grove was already part of my past. . . .

My parting was like the realization that comes when you say good-bye to a high-school lover for what you both know will be the last time, or a group of friends after college graduation: It has been wonderful, this time together, but now it is over. And although I knew that there would be moments when I would yearn for a tiny cabin by the Thelon, for what someday might seem like an idyllic life, there was only one way for me to go, and I was ready for the journey. At the river we loaded the canoe and prepared to push off. I looked downstream toward Eagle Cliffs and imagined the Thelon as it flowed past Grassy Island and cut north and east toward Hornby Point, toward our journey's end and another life.

CHAPTER TWELVE
To the Bay

It was impossible to describe the feeling that was mine on coming out of the wilderness into the open space of the Bay. We sat in our canoes for a long time just looking at the open sea. The Bay was the only thought in my mind. No one spoke as we felt the first tidal swells; we had made it in spite of everything and my dream had been fulfilled.

—Sigurd Olson, *Reflections from the North Country*

WE BEGAN THE FINAL STAGE of our journey on July 8, 1978, by paddling north through familiar country, past Eagle Cliffs and Grassy Island. It was wonderful to move again, and to ride the crest of runoff rolling toward Hudson Bay. Alex Hall, who had guided parties on the Thelon for years, later told us that he had never seen the river so high. Along the way we counted waterfowl at Grassy Island, explored side canyons, and delighted in the brief taste of warm sun following the storm that had delayed our departure. Once again there was that familiar dance of the canoes, and the countless paddlestrokes. Although our boats were crammed with six weeks' worth of supplies and handled like sluggish scows, the river miles passed easily. Thus, the start of our second summer was far different from our first week in the Selwin Mountains when we faced tight rapids, lining, and exhausting portages. In all the 180 miles from Warden's Grove to Beverly Lake, seven days' travel downstream, there were no rapids or portages. The Thelon was quiet, and we were able to ease gently back into motion.

We stopped at Hornby Point on the morning of July 10. Despite the three weathered crosses, and the ruined logs where the cabin once stood, the place was much less somber than when Robert and I had visited in October. No longer part of an autumn landscape chilling into winter, it was alive with the sounds and colors of summer. Blackpoll warblers and robins sang in the forest; cloudberry, lousewort, and anemone flowered in clearings; and fresh moose and musk-ox sign lay scattered among the willows. There was too much light and too much life for me to connect with the place as I had in the fall; winter, and its season of dying, was behind us and we were immersed in summer's pulse.

That afternoon the weather turned progressively more stormy, and we were stopped thirteen miles below Hornby Point by winds gusting to well over twenty miles per hour. Thick streamers of stratocumulus raced across the sky, dumping rain and promising another protracted storm, but the winds died during the night and we were able to follow the Thelon the next day as it curved eastward and cut across the lay of the land. The current's velocity grew and we were carried past steep, spruce-lined banks and vertical, highly stratified cliffs of thin-bedded sedimentary rock, past willow-covered alluvial fans poking into the river wherever tributaries entered. Our world was restricted to the Thelon and its shores; we were reminded of what lay beyond our canoes only when we halted and scrambled up the banks to survey the vast plains of spruce-dotted muskeg and tundra. The miles slipped away, and I drifted in and out of a paddler's reverie, but I awoke soon after Kurt and I swung around a bend and spotted two herring gulls perched atop what appeared to be a large, dark rock near shore. A closer look established that the "rock" had horns and was a half-submerged bull musk-ox carcass. Twenty feet away was a large grizzly, frozen in midstride and staring intently at the river. He seemed uncertain about his next move, but when Robert and Mike's canoe joined us, he smashed through some willows and disappeared. We beached our canoe and poked around the remains, which were intact and fresh; the bear had consumed little besides some of the viscera. How had the bull died? There was no evidence of a struggle, nor did he have major wounds about the exposed portion of the head, neck, or shoulders. He may have succumbed to disease, although grizzlies are capable of killing a fully grown musk-ox; biologists Anne Gunn and Frank Miller found a dead bull that had been ambushed by a grizzly as it fed in dense willows along the Thelon. An eight-hundred-pound musk-ox may be a formidable opponent for a wolf, but it was easy to imagine a bear pouncing on a placidly feeding bull and dragging him to the ground. My trusty Swiss Army pocketknife suddenly seemed like inadequate protection. This was prime bear country—we would see as many as three in a single day during the downstream run—and the strength of those animals, with their crushing bite and deceptively fast gait, was an integral part of the power of the land; accepting their presence was necessary if we wanted to travel on the Barrens.

That evening I sat by the fire and mused over our first few days on the river. It was perfectly still; a narrow shaft of light cut through the clouds, bathing the ice-scoured gravel shore in gold, and an arctic loon whistled from across the river. We were camped at 64°24′ north latitude, the farthest north we'd been. Although we were still 150 miles shy of the Arctic Circle, I felt enveloped by the north country; it stretched away from the Thelon north toward the Arctic Ocean, icecaps, and polar deserts; south toward the boreal forest. We were already eighty miles from Warden's Grove; the cabin was relegated to the past, as if our movement had accelerated the drift of time and thrust us into a new world. We had slipped quickly back into the rhythm of the trail—as John said, "It seems that we're continuing last summer's travel without the interruption of winter." The details of our river days resurrected the structured pattern that had carried us from the Macmillan to the Thelon. Each facet of this life was suddenly familiar: loading canoe packs in the morning, rotating cooking chores on a two-days-on, four-days-off schedule, the slap of water against the bow, the first welcome sip of scalding tea after a long day, the evening's journal writing. After months of overindulgent eating, it was satisfying to be truly hungry, to regard every morsel as precious (but did we really gulp our meals like Krackedy?) and taste food spiced with the ache of tired muscles. And it was exciting to see new country, to transform cartographic symbols into experience. . . .

The next day brought us into more open country of ice-pushed gravel banks and large willow stands. A strong downriver breeze was blowing, and Mike and Robert rigged a lime-green tent fly as a sail—from a distance it looked like a billowing spinnaker—to take advantage of the tailwind. Their canoe soon bolted far into the lead, their customary position for most of the trip. To Gary, they had "two speeds, fast and idle." Whatever the reason—their combined strength or greater fixation on movement—Mike and Robert were often far ahead, and usually had to wait for us to catch up several times a day.

That evening we camped at the mouth of the Finnie River, opposite Lookout Point, where an abandoned Canadian Wildlife Service cabin had been partially destroyed by a bear. This would be the last area along the Thelon where thick spruce grew along protected drainages, and the land had a fertile air about it—an oasis of trees where I could imagine overwintering. There was sufficient wood for fuel and shelter, and enough wildlife to sustain my spirit. For the last two days we had traveled through country rich in fish (northern pike and lake trout, both caught easily with a trolling line) and wildlife: grizzlies, scattered caribou, moose, wolves, and musk-oxen. The latter were all adult bulls, mostly feeding alone in willows along the river. The bulls tolerated our presence; even if we canoed to within a few yards of one, its only response was to slowly raise its head, stare intently, and then resume feeding. Fresh willows are particularly rich in protein, and a preferred musk-ox food during the summer. Healthy musk-oxen gain weight rapidly on such forage, in contrast to their poorer-quality winter diet, and we weren't enough of a distraction to deter their feeding.

In addition to mammals, there were lots of waterfowl, including arctic loons, tundra swans with young, white-fronted and Canada geese, pintails, wigeons, scaup, white-winged scoters, and red-breasted mergansers. The Canada geese were molting their flight feathers; consequently, they were extremely paranoid about potential predators. If we paddled toward a large flotilla, most of the birds honked and flapped frantically across the water in their panic to escape. Others dove, or pressed themselves flat upon the water to reduce their silhouette, as if to say, "Stay low, be cool, and we'll get away." If we happened to trap geese in shallow water, they scurried ashore and dodged in and out of the willows before sneaking into thick cover. They were very vulnerable, rather like humans suddenly deprived of sight; John and Gary witnessed a lone wolf pursue and kill a flightless goose as it scrambled along the shore.

Raptors were also abundant—rough-legged hawks, short-eared owls, and gyrfalcons. In one gyrfalcon aerie was a pair of nearly fledged young, dark gray above and streaked below. As I clambered up to take a photograph, they sat motionless at the edge of the nest, with fresh meat on their bills; one clutched the remains of an arctic ground squirrel. They still were vulnerable, but the rough glint in their eyes, their savage regard, hinted of future flights and kills.

So much life! I wanted to record everything I saw, and pursue the descriptive side of field biology with all of my free time. In a world like that of the Thelon, which had been visited by relatively few biologists, I sensed what it must have been like for the pioneer naturalists who roamed the nineteenth-century American West, or those who first described the animals and plants of the Barren Grounds: Dr. John Richardson, who traveled with Franklin during his exploration of the Coppermine River in 1821; Richard King, George Back's surgeon-naturalist on the journey down the *Thlew-ee-choh-desseth*, or Great Fish River (later renamed the Back River); and later, A.E. Preble, C.H.D. Clarke, and A.E. Porsild. These men were privileged to travel in an undescribed, novel world, and to observe and catalog species new to science; they worked under conditions that were often very trying— Richardson almost starved to death on the Coppermine—and their perseverance was admirable. In this era of mainframe computers, complex mathematical models, and experimental manipulations, descriptive natural history is dismissed as trivial by some ecologists. Yet it is still the most fundamental aspect of field biology; without an accurate understanding of the distribution of species, and their basic life-history traits, we cannot begin to ask more detailed ecological questions. As I sat beside the Finnie River and wrote up the day's field notes, I could not imagine leaving behind the birds, plants, and mammals. I wasn't conscious of a desire to be done with the journey; I still was not prepared for the Outside, even though our goal was nearer, and I craved motion and new country. There were moments when I caught myself looking to Chesterfield Inlet and beyond, but the balance had not yet been tipped, and I was satisfied with the course of my days and the cadence of river life.

Two more days of travel brought us past the delta formed by the confluence of the Thelon, Kigarvi, and Tamarvi rivers to the Thelon Bluffs, situated near the extreme tree limit. The spruce growing near the bluffs were gnarled and weather-beaten, with branches trailing along the ground; few wind-flagged trunks extended above the protective contours of the land. In that harsh world, they clung to a tenuous life, yet dead trunks (or macrofossils, as they are known to paleobotanists) up to twenty-four inches in diameter were scattered among the living trees. Relicts from times more conducive to growth, the trunks were preserved from microbial decomposition by the dry, cold air. Palynological and peat studies, and evidence from radiocarbon dating, show that warmer conditions have occurred several times since the close of the Wisconsin glaciation, the last major ice advance of the Pleisto-cene Epoch: a shorter period a thousand years ago, and a period of maximum warming between three thousand and five thousand years ago. During the earlier warming, the tree line may have extended 150 miles to the north of its present loca-tion; as conditions cooled, the forest retreated, with spruce in the most northerly areas surviving only in favorable pockets.

As we moved through the forest-tundra ecotone (an area where two plant communities intermingle), the trees began to disappear, as did the birds depend-ent upon them—blackpoll warblers, robins, Harris's sparrows, and gray-cheeked thrushes. These were replaced by tundra-breeding species, such as water pipits, savannah sparrows, Lapland longspurs, and sandhill cranes—the latter were the first we had sighted since mid-June. We also began seeing more caribou and won-dered if we were brushing the edge of the Beverly Herd's postcalving aggregation, with its thousands upon thousands of milling animals.

Twenty miles below the Thelon Bluffs, the river spilled into Beverly Lake. We swung along the southern shore of the lake, past the mouth of the Dubawnt River, the next major drainage east of the Thelon, and paddled to within a few miles of Aberdeen Lake. The travel was generally easy, with only moderate winds and some intricate navigation in the channel east of Beverly Lake, and we covered the sixty-five miles in two full days. Our route was ice-free, although we had distant views of what looked to be extensive floes in the northeastern arm of Beverly Lake.

The long days brought us into a landscape that earned the name "Barren Grounds," a world that rekindled the feelings of vulnerability that I had encoun-tered on Ptarmigan Lake and in the midst of brutal winter storms—a sense that my presence on the Barrens was tenuous and could be overwhelmed easily by the forces of the land. Our first camp beyond the tree limit was idyllic—beside a small bay on Beverly Lake, with our tents ringed by garlands of bright yellow cinquefoil and cushion pink. Driftwood lined the shore, so there was ample fuel for cooking and warmth. The winds were calm, but no mosquitoes or blackflies harassed us. I lay by the fire and listened to the melody of savannah sparrows singing from nearby willows, finding it difficult to imagine that such a benign world could be transformed into a chaos of wind and waves. But when we were out on the lakes—especially when crossing a large bay—I felt very exposed. A glance down into the cobalt blue waters, liquid ice no warmer than 35°F, told me that a dunking would bring a quick, numbing death. Even when nothing more than a gentle swell rocked the canoe, there was always an air of brooding, barely restrained violence, and the threat of sudden fury. Things could change so very quickly. . . .

For mile after mile of paddling, the land remained the same—repeated variations on the theme of low, gray hills and rocky tundra. The evidence of recent glaciation was everywhere—in piles of morainal debris, scattered eskers, and even the alignment of lakes and streams. Most of the watercourses that flowed into the Thelon River and Beverly Lake followed the paths of ice and were oriented in a northwest-to-southeast direction, like parallel brushstrokes on a canvas. It was a world of thin soil, cold wind, and sparse vegetation; even shrubby willows and dwarf birch were scarce, and no plants grew tall enough to break the contours of the earth. Where vegetation was able to find a life-hold, it consisted mostly of matted, prostrate forms, beaten down by winds through countless seasons.

On the big lakes, water dominated the horizontal plane, and the land was peeled back toward the edge of the sky. Without distinctive landmarks or vertical development of the vegetation, distance became more and more of an abstraction, represented by units measured on a map (Just what did an inch mean in terms of space, or the energy required to traverse from point A to point B in the face of a hard wind?), but not registered by the senses and drawn into a sense of scale that included my body. Now I could better understand an incident from the spring, laughed off at the time as another Bozo phenomenon. John and I had stopped for a break near a broad summit. The day was overcast, without shadows; there were no nearby trees to impart a sense of scale, only the dull tundra falling away from our hill, and a breadth of gray sky. John looked up from our resting spot and pointed: "Look at those ravens."

I turned in the direction of the dark shapes gazing down on us, squinted through my binoculars, and replied, "Funniest-looking ravens I've ever seen!" We were looking at ten musk-oxen; they were several hundred yards away from us, not the twenty or so that would have been necessary if the scale had been right for ravens. I teased John mercilessly about his error—mistaking a six- or seven-hundred-pound mammal for a one-pound bird—but this wasn't quite fair. When reference points vanish, such seemingly foolish errors are possible. In the absence of familiar objects, spatial relationships can be distorted, in the same way that temporal boundaries may fade during the long continuum of a northern winter. Plop yourself down in the midst of thousands of square miles of treeless tundra, paddle along an endless horizontal plane, and what does a mile come to mean? One hundred yards? One hundred miles?

What did I think about during those long stretches on Aberdeen, Beverly, Schultz, and Baker lakes? When conditions were favorable, we usually traveled more than thirty miles per day; given an average pace of no more than three miles per hour, that translated into at least ten hours of sitting in the same position and pulling a paddle through the water for stroke after endless stroke. There were occasional route-finding problems to distract me, and later there would be winds and heavy ice, but there were also long periods when there was nothing to do but repeat an identical motion time and time again. Sometimes the endless cycle of lift, pull, lift, pull functioned like a mantra, and the miles slid by without conscious thought. Kurt and I also talked, although protracted conversations between us had become rare, and we passed hours absorbed in silence. It wasn't that we were feuding; we simply had talked through the "great issues" during the prior thirteen months and there was little new to discuss.

For the most part I concentrated on the Barrens, on its subtle textural variations and raw power. And if my imagination failed and the land metamorphosed into monotony, I could turn for relief to the vast panorama of the tundra sky. The very features that contributed to feelings of exposure and vulnerability, and imparted a sense of sameness to the land—the sudden changes in weather, the lack of tall vegetation and dramatic relief—in turn granted more power and beauty to the vault of space above the rock and water. The sky dominated the Barrens, much as it does the great prairies and steppes of North America and Central Asia. Most often, it possessed no single texture or uniform weather conditions. In the nearly 180-degree sweep of space, there may have been one quadrant of radiant blue; in another, a wispy trail of high cirrus; in a third, a mass of dark cumulus dumping walls of heavy, wind-driven rain. Would the hope of blue spread, or the clouds? Would the winds build to a frenzy and halt our progress? Or would there be a rare, halcyon afternoon of shirtless paddling and mirrored reflections? Since the weather was so unpredictable, I tried to avoid yearning for favorable traveling conditions. Yet it was difficult to live beyond desire, to accept with equanimity whatever the skies brought; so I hoped for blue, and more often than not was disappointed.

On July 16 we camped just west of Aberdeen Lake. The talk among us was that five more days of paddling would probably get us to Baker Lake, 170 miles to the east—if we didn't encounter ice or storm. Were we being foolish, or simply optimistic? Had the Bozos flunked Barren Grounds Psychology 101? Most definitely, because after leaving camp and paddling onto Aberdeen, we hit ice—an almost solid sheet, stretching as far east as we could see. From atop a small rise, it appeared that the ice also extended across the lake from north to south, completely blocking our path. A few near-shore leads and open bays were visible to the immediate north; since the prevailing winds were northerlies, and might eventually push the ice away from the shore, we decided to head around the north side of the lake. We wondered how long we might be held up, since C.H.D. Clarke had reported that miles of floe ice may linger on Aberdeen and Schultz lakes well into August of some years.

We began our traverse of Aberdeen by making a half-mile portage, threading through thick chunks of ice, paddling across an open bay, and then repeating the sequence twice more. The loads were heavy and awkward, the mosquitoes had made a belated appearance, and I could tell that certain muscles had remained dormant for too long. However, I comforted myself with thoughts of another probable Bozo first: Had anybody before us bothered to portage from Aberdeen Lake to Aberdeen Lake? We finally gave up on hauling loads and, urged on by Mike's and Robert's example, took to forcing our way through tiny leads and cracks in the candled ice. In many places, there was no open water to follow; progress was a matter of pushing and pulling the canoe along weaknesses in the floes. Although the ice was thoroughly rotten, it effectively resisted our advances, and sometimes I had to kneel in the bow and drag the canoe forward with bare hands, while Kurt pushed off the ice with his paddle. On a remarkably warm afternoon, with the glare of the sun reflected off a million facets of jagged ice, clawing our way forward in such a manner made for tiring sweaty work, but at least it was quicker than portaging.

When the ice appeared firm enough to support our weight, we played a version of Barren Grounds roulette. This involved running the bow onto a floe; I then gingerly stepped onto the ice to test its firmness. If the surface held, I dragged the canoe as far forward as possible, and Kurt eased onto the mushy ice. A nervous, light-footed dash then ensued, with both of us pushing the canoe along and clutching the gunwales for security. Our tiptoed prance across the ice probably did nothing to reduce the chances of falling through it into the lake, but when the ice had the consistency of cottage cheese, and water pooled in our footsteps, it made us feel more secure. Fortunately, there was only one partial dunking—near shore, John went through up to his waist—and we finally broke through into open water after a quarter-mile of grunting through and over the ice.

Soon afterward, we were halted by a solid mass of ice, so we decided to camp after having covered only fifteen miles. We went to sleep on a beautifully calm evening, fully expecting a protracted wait for the ice to break up. For once we wanted wind—to push the ice out from shore—and for once the quirky Barrens weather meshed with our hopes. When John awoke at two A.M., a freshening northwesterly breeze was rising and the ice was moving southward. By morning, a large lead had opened up and we were able to travel, first with the wind across our bow and then directly into the teeth of a twenty-mile-an-hour blow when we rounded the broad peninsula that divides Aberdeen Lake into east and west halves. We then began the long, curving paddle north and east toward the Thelon River and Schultz Lake. At one point, the lane of open water narrowed to just a few feet and we had to drag the canoes across a short section of ice, but otherwise the way was clear.

We were very fortunate, as it was probably the first day that season that travel was possible on the lake, but the shifting and building winds made the twenty-six miles that we covered tiresome and tedious. We paddled all day under dreary skies, with the dark, brooding outline of the Marjorie Hills an unbroken sweep to the south. We had to concentrate continuously to maintain a straight course, and strain at the paddles to force the canoes forward against the winds—a necessary price for the chance to travel, yet wearying all the same, and we made camp in a tired stupor.

The winds continued throughout the night; in the morning we debated whether to stay put or fight our way toward the end of Aberdeen Lake, twelve miles to the east. Kurt and I felt that it was best to wait, but the others argued that slackening winds could allow the ice to drift back in to shore and block our route. The latter viewpoint prevailed, so we pushed off into the gale. The traveling wasn't quite as bad as it appeared from shore, and we were able to make progress—cold, laborious, and frustrating at first, as the winds were either in our faces or off the beam, but much easier when we turned to the southeast and ran with a tailwind. During the winter, the Old Town Canoe Company had sent us newly designed spray covers and these provided an extra measure of security in the choppy waves. Each cover was a single piece of vinyl, attached to the canoe by a series of snaps along the sides of the boat; when in place, it allowed us to take water over the bow without fear of swamping, and it also kept legs and groins dry during storms. Thus, as long as our minds and muscles were willing, and the winds weren't too strong across our bow, we could travel. Yet there were times when the distance gained did not seem worth the effort, when I felt that it was taking all of our energy to keep the canoe stationary in the water. At one point, after struggling into the wind for several hours, Gary asked, "If we start going backward, will we stop?" The answer probably would have been yes, but there was no assurance of this; we were committed enough to motion to keep struggling against the Barrens in all but the most foolhardy conditions.

After reaching the end of the lake and downing a hurried, chilly lunch—I wore my life jacket because of the tiny bit of additional warmth that it provided—we turned into the channel leading toward Schultz Lake and began battling the wind again. Soon we encountered a mass of jumbled ice being blown southward by the wind, and we decided to stop while it drifted by us, which seemed likely to occur within the hour. Then came Gary's somewhat panicked question: "Has anyone seen my camera?" After five quick nos and a frenzied search, it became clear that he had left more than a thousand dollars' worth of camera equipment at the last campsite. And so, with an air of resigned disgust, John and Gary unloaded most of the equipment and food from their canoe and prepared for a quick dash back down the lake to retrieve the gear. I wasn't disappointed by the opportunity for an early camp, our first since leaving Warden's Grove, but the circumstances could have been better. It was a miserable afternoon for their trek; the only place that I thought seemed remotely interesting to explore was a dry sleeping bag inside a tent.

What we hoped would be only a twenty-four hour pause became a protracted residence, and a partial rerun of the Ptarmigan Lake Blues. John and Gary were back in camp by two P.M. the following day, tired and cold but with the forgotten camera gear in hand. The winds were strong enough to discourage further movement that day, so we sank into a wind-blown lethargy of eating, restless naps, reading, and card games that stretched over three and a half days. The gusts built to forty miles per hour, sending foaming whitecaps crashing into shore and making the nylon tent fly sound like the churning blades of a helicopter. Gary suggested banging on the tent poles in hopes that "the janitor would turn down the wind," but this had no noticeable effect. There were no periods of soothing calm, no escape from the incessant noise. I became conditioned to the mad flapping of the tent, and the sounds of waves and wind, but my acceptance was mostly a matter of sensory saturation. In the midst of a conversation, or after a nap, I suddenly would become aware of clenched teeth and tensed muscles. So I would escape from the tent and its frenzied racket, out into the less varied pitch of the gale—temporary relief at best, because the exposure soon drove me back to shelter. Hold onto your hat, and your mind, because this could go on for a long time. . . .

One afternoon I climbed to the top of a nearby hill, where three stone cairns stood guard over a great sweep of fractured gray rock. These cairns were *inukshuks*, built by Inuit, either to scare caribou toward an ambush or simply to serve as markers. From a distance, when backlit by the sun, they resembled human figures. How long had those markers endured the ravages of the Barrens winds? Lichens—symbiotic organisms that grow very slowly—had begun to cover some of the cracks between adjacent rocks, so the pillars must have been several hundred years old. I thought of the succession of years that those frozen men had witnessed, of the humans who had piled stone upon stone—people who most likely had never seen a European, people for whom this windy land was home.

The gale whipped at my anorak, and I squinted into its fury, north toward the plain of tundra and open water of the Thelon's channel. Take away the wind, and the lenticular clouds that hung in shreds across the blue sky, and the view was one of summer. But when I turned southward, all I could see was jumbled rock, and an ocean of ice that completely filled the eastern half of Aberdeen Lake: cold space, and an infinite flow of arctic air. I sought shelter in the lee of a large boulder near the summit of the hill, where the pale-green, urn-shaped blossoms of alpine bearberry and the delicate white flowers of a saxifrage grew in protected spots. Spiders scurried in and out of crevices, searching for prey; their resolute activity made the Barrens feel more hospitable, and in my huddled refuge I could think, could contemplate what it was that attracted me to this land.

Space. Power. True wilderness. Life near the end of its tether, with its wonderful adaptations for survival and reproduction. A harsh, spare world that forced a person to deal with the basic economy of survival, a world stripped bare, exposed to the wind and a probing eye—yet a world that retained an impenetrable air of mystery. For all my months of living in the wilderness, the Barrens remained something of an enigma, its spirit beyond the reach of my rational mind. Perhaps I was still too much of an outsider, unable to transcend the idea that the Barrens was ultimately inhospitable. Even if I were able to travel at minus 40°F and endure weeks of cold, rain-soaked paddling, I could never be completely comfortable, and I always would be tempted to look beyond the present. Or perhaps I had dwelt for too long in the realm of objective analysis. How could I, in spite of my scientific background, fail to view the North mystically, and search for methods of recognition outside the senses and reason? For this was the land of the shamans, where visions, solitude, and meditation enabled the Inuit to maintain contact with a mysterious spirit world. Those who were gifted in this special way could fly to the moon, subdue evil spirits, and swim under the ice; through their power, they helped the people whom they served find security in a world of cold, wind, and the long darkness of winter. If one believed, there was a bridge to understanding and acceptance of the harshness of the land. I could not believe, but I could still accept the need for recourse to vision and dreams. Crouched behind a block of ice-scoured granite, I understood that it was possible to see much farther than the bits of cloud that hung above Aberdeen Lake—deep into a world beyond humanity, into the soul of the Barrens. But this view was not without cost: It required time, far more than I had given, an openness that I had not gained, and perhaps a propensity that I did not possess. At the heart of the wind was an absolute silence, and an ultimate peace, but I heard only the roar of the gale as I rose from my resting place and started back down the hill.

The winds finally died on the evening of July 22. We were off by three o'clock the next morning to beat the ice, which had been released from the grip of the gale and was already drifting north toward Schultz Lake. It was a calm, chilly morning; our bows shattered delicate pans of ice that had formed overnight and sent long, sweeping waves rippling across the lake's surface. The wail of loons echoed across the water as we threaded through the ice-choked channel and paddled into the rising sun—on down a blinding corridor of light stretching from the east. It was a magical time, made all the more special by our release from five days of wind: the earth's canonical hour, when all of the Barrens' stillness was concentrated on our canoes, when the quiet was like a prayer. We paddled thirty-eight miles that day, more than halfway down the northern shore of Schultz Lake. The going was much easier and more pleasant than on Aberdeen, in part because the wind had died, but also because there was more relief for the eye and mind. Scarps of dark igneous rock tumbled several hundred feet to the water's edge, and we often were close enough to shore to spot scattered wildflower gardens, the first profusion of blossoms of the summer.

Schultz Lake has the rough shape of a fish arcing out of the water, with its head pointed westward and the Thelon's outlet flowing eastward from the northern tip of its tail fin. Our progress was fine until we approached the peninsula that formed the construction separating the "tail" from the main body of the lake, where we again encountered heavy ice. Shortly after breaking camp on the twenty-fourth, we ran out of open water entirely, and we took to the ice with the hope that, once past the peninsula, we would be able to paddle again. Mike and Robert led the charge as we pushed and dragged the canoes over the jagged surface of the candled floes. Below-freezing temperatures during the night had firmed up the ice, but it still had the dubious consistency of partially thawed orange juice concentrate. It was a creepy, vulnerable feeling to push the canoe across rotten ice a mile from shore, as the warm sun turned the undulating surface into an ice swamp. Occasionally, we encountered a lead five or ten yards wide. Rather than break stride, Kurt and I accelerated to a fast trot; just before reaching the water, he vaulted into the bow. I continued pushing as the bow plowed into the water, then hopped into the stern, shifting my weight forward so that the canoe slid completely free of the ice. We paddled furiously across the lead and ran the bow up on the opposite side; then Kurt stepped out and dragged the canoe as far onto the ice as possible, and I followed. Dicey work—Kurt went through the ice once and got soaked to his waist—and the needlelike points of the ice columns ripped long gashes in the outer layer of plastic laminate on the canoes, but we were able to cover four miles by traveling in a manner that would have been impossible in the days of canvas-covered canoes.

Toward noon, the ice became too weak for travel. We found a lead that ran in to shore and began a two-mile portage to a narrow, ice-choked channel with enough leads and rotten sections to allow paddling. After threading through the maze, which Robert compared to a shattered windshield, we crossed alternating sections of open water and solid ice, and finally reached the point of land that marked the last of Schultz Lake's ice. We celebrated our passage with a dinner of freeze-dried shrimp creole and swatted at the mosquitoes, which finally were out in full force and behaving as if they meant to compensate for every day that their emergence had been delayed by cold weather. Our efforts to avoid the tormentors while we ate—and they tried to—would have looked very odd to a distant observer who knew nothing of Barren Grounds insects: scattered figures walking in aimless circles, suddenly breaking into a run at randomly spaced intervals, like victims of a medieval dancing craze. Actually, we behaved more like caribou when they are harassed by insects—constantly in motion, drifting into every tiny breath of wind, their normal walk interrupted by bursts of frantic running. Occasionally, a devious trick might pass one's own winged companions to someone else. The most effective procedure was to sidle up innocently to the unsuspecting target, preferably someone who was sitting or standing in his personal cloud of the buggers. Most likely, he would be squinting to keep the tormentors out of his eyes, puffing and snorting to blow them away from his mouth and nostrils, and waving them away from his face with nervous wrist flicks. After moving quietly into his cloud, and halting for a brief moment, you then sprinted away from the victim, who became the happy owner of a cloud twice as dense as before. In the few seconds of mosquito-free peace that followed, it was possible to take several relaxed bites of food before the onslaught resumed.

Only Robert did not appear to be particularly annoyed by the mosquitoes. He eschewed insect repellent and went about his business as if they were benign creatures, stripping to the waist and shaving calmly as hordes swarmed about his unprotected flesh. As usual, Robert seemed impervious to physical discomfort, and completely at home in his surroundings—as though he were a Barren Grounds native and had lived there all of his life. He accepted the weather, insects, hard work, and physical discomfort with quiet composure, and he never displayed anger or frustration toward the environment. And although he was addicted to movement and strenuous labor, he could easily shift gears when the Barrens dictated a stop. I felt that he could have accepted being windbound for a two-week period better than the rest of us, although, conversely, a rest day not mandated by necessity could bring him to the edge of barely controlled impatience.

Whether playing his pennywhistle, paddling into a gale, or sitting in a downpour, Robert seemed the archetypal Natural Man. One evening, he captured a lake trout with his bare hands; it had been investigating a stringer of northern pike secured in an eddy, and Robert pounced. Perhaps the fish was distracted by the prospect of an easy meal, but Robert's feat was still illustrative of his abilities. He rarely washed himself or his clothes (shaving was the one "cosmetic" habit that he retained during the trip), and as the months passed, his wardrobe came to consist more and more of garments skillfully sewn from scavenged materials. Dressed in white canvas knickers tailored from one of the Queen's discarded mailbags (a relic of Cosmos 954), a leather loincloth, woolen helmet, black rugby shirt, tattered red knicker socks, and a multicolored woven belt, Robert looked like he belonged on the Barrens. Yet his apparent accommodation was not without its contradictions. Robert rarely remarked about the beauty and magnificence of the North. The sunsets, wildlife, panoramas of space, flowers, and details of the landscape never seemed to entrance him, although he was a skilled and accurate observer and must have noticed them. Perhaps his frustration with the rest of us, and his reticence, made him disguise his true feelings. Yet even during the first few weeks of the trip, before his dissatisfaction was nurtured by our call for a rest day on the Nahanni, he seemed disinclined to explore while on the trail. He rarely wandered far from camp or left the vicinity of the canoes during a rest break, unless we were at a place that had a particular connection to Hornby's story. Beyond moving, eating, and sleeping, there appeared to be little more to his days other than writing in his journal and playing music. I wondered if he had the mindset of a native, one who had been living with the land for so long that he accepted both its harshness and its beauty with equal equanimity. There is an obvious advantage in such an attitude—it allows one to accept even brutal conditions with surprising ease—but perhaps there is also a loss, for it seems that passion is sacrificed, and an appreciation for the unique aspects of one's environment.

Our ice dance continued the next morning. At 1:30 A.M., a light breeze sprung up out of the southwest, and the mass of ice that was jammed in a large bay to the south of us began to shift northward. By four, large blocks were drifting toward the outlet of the lake, so to avoid entrapment, we broke camp frantically and paddled toward the Thelon. We stopped for a quick breakfast amply spiced with mosquitoes goaded into action by the imminent rain, which started just as we pushed off onto the river and began some of the most exciting paddling of the trip.

Below the outlet of Schultz Lake, the Thelon flows northward for a short distance before making a right-angle bend to the east. Under normal circumstances, this would not have presented a problem. However, the winds had pushed the ice that had accumulated at the outlet of Schultz Lake into the river channel, which was filled with massive floes that jostled one another as they wheeled downstream and slammed into the large eddy at the northern angle of the river's dogleg. So the Barrens was in top form: a surging, ice-choked river, frenzied mosquitoes, and a gathering deluge. Since we were on the western bank of the river and wanted no part of the boiling eddy, we ferried across the Thelon, dodging large chunks of bobbing ice in the main current before turning downstream to run between some enormous floes. The trick was to gauge correctly the speed of the floes and maintain a safe distance between those at the front and rear of the canoe—a bit like riding a bicycle between two tractor-trailer rigs. It was very difficult to judge the velocity of the floes, for they were grinding into the shore and pivoting downstream. Annihilation seemed imminent, for if we rode up onto the ice in front of the canoe, or were hit from behind, we undoubtedly would have been dumped into the water. Rain fell in sheets, and the air was filled with the sound of swirling, grinding floes. Suddenly the world had contracted into a very small space, and all of my attention was focused on the canoe and the racing waters. The distance to the bend wasn't great—perhaps a quarter-mile—but I had no sense of time until we reached the safety of an ice-free channel. It undoubtedly took less than five minutes to negotiate that short stretch of river, but it could have taken an hour, or five seconds. When the run was over, I let out a deep breath, slumped back against the packs behind the canoe seat, and stopped paddling. Water trickled off my hood and into my eyes; as the rush of adrenalin subsided, I squinted through the downpour and saw that the others were safe. For a moment I felt a great physical release, a peaceful emptiness, and then we were paddling again.

As we moved toward Schultz Rapids, six miles downstream, the rain continued, and I contemplated the inadequate state of my raingear. It was constructed out of a "miracle fabric" supposed to be both waterproof and breathable—not unlike the properties of human skin. The introduction of this wonderful new material to the retail market was accompanied by much advertising fanfare and the presentation of impressive data on its waterproof/breathable properties, and we had been seduced by the propaganda. An equipment manufacturer had offered to make us rainsuits for the trip, and we enthusiastically accepted the offer—only to find out during the Nahanni "seventeen-day clearing trend" that the "miracle fabric" did not work and was almost as useful as fluency in Esperanto. Our negative tirades and the introduction of a "new, improved second-generation" fabric encouraged the manufacturer to try again, and we received another set of suits for the second summer. Since the fabric was not supposed to function properly when dirty (but how do you stay clean in the wilderness?), I packed away my new rain jacket until I encountered a deluge, and the opportunity to conduct a reasonable experiment. Well, here was the deluge; out came the "miracle fabric" and in came the rain. With the first sensation of creeping dampness, I began fulminating on advertising hyperbole, and my own gullibility. But how could I argue with hard data? Perhaps my senses were fooling me, and I was really dry. In the face of the fabric's impressive specifications, Robert suggested that "we should camp in the laboratory, cook our dinner over Bunsen burners, and use the sprinkler system for rain." I went back to coated nylon raingear.

At high water, the Schultz Rapids were impressive, with huge standing waves and homogenizing holes that extended completely across the river. The hydraulics —more like Colorado River whitewater than anything else I'd seen on the trip— discouraged any thoughts of a midchannel run. So we paddled partway down the rapid, then began our last portage, a three-quarter-mile carry along the right bank. At the end of the portage we encountered a biologist and his Inuit guide, who were trying to get a four-hundred-pound freight canoe and their outfit up the rapid. The cresting waters made the rapid unsafe to run, so we helped them carry motor, fuel, and canoe above the worst of the whitewater. The biologist was young, just out of college, and working on a caribou study for a company interested in developing uranium claims in the Schultz Lake area. There weren't many caribou around—

the Beverly Herd was far to the west, and the Kaminuriak Herd far to the south-east—so there was little for him to do, but he saw the job as "good experience."

The last part of the journey to the village of Baker Lake was a straightforward, southeasterly shot of eighty miles. We finished the day and camped near the Half-way Hills, then rode a racing, high-water flood to the lake. The Thelon dropped precipitously, or so it felt; we sped along at eight miles per hour, past stranded blocks of ice thick along the shore, and the morning's miles passed easily. Shortly before noon on July 26, we reached the settlement—360 miles out from Warden's Grove, with only two hundred to go. As we paddled across the bay that separated the mouth of the Thelon from the village, I considered the jumbled collection of buildings across the way, and what they represented. It was strange to confront an outpost of civilization, lost within the Barrens—but not as strange as a satellite having fallen from the sky and led us, like some aberrant Star of Bethlehem, to Yellowknife, Edmonton, and Camp Garland. . . .

Upon landing, we were greeted by a bevy of children, mostly Inuit, but with a few whites thrown in. All were attired in a similar uniform: knee-high black-rubber boots, blue jeans, nylon jackets, and ludicrously oversized baseball caps. Robert soon had a kid balanced on one knee, and we were all engaged in animated, if disjointed, conversations about names and where we had come from. ("That way," with a vague wave to the west, was all that seemed to make sense to them, or to me.) A few adult Inuit hung back at the edge of the throng; one man inquired whether we were interested in selling our canoes, but the rest were quiet and reserved, their demeanor the antithesis of the children's.

We established camp at the western end of town, behind an abandoned Anglican church, and spent the following three days exploring and trying to make arrangements to travel south; the expected funds to cover our final transportation expenses had not materialized, and we were scrambling to ensure that we would not have to continue paddling toward Churchill after reaching Chesterfield Inlet. Amid the phone calls and radio messages to the Outside, we wandered through Baker Lake, yet another group of visitors from the South (or perhaps temporary resident aliens?) trying to make sense of a northern community, and feeling much as we had in Fort Simpson.

Our center of activity was the Iglu Hotel, a large building in the Quonset hut tradition, and the only obvious representative of the private sector, aside from The Bay, in the village. Bill Davidson, the Scottish manager, was generous and hos-pitable, offering us free showers and coffee, a discount on meals, and a place to talk with the many visitors and locals who wandered in—DC-3 pilots, caribou biolo-gists, engineers conducting a hydrographic survey of Baker Lake, and the steady stream of kids who patronized the hotel's candy counter. In the previous month, the Iglu had sold more than nine thousand dollars' worth of candy and soda pop;

according to Bill, the community could consume almost an entire C-130-load of soft drinks in one month. Sugar comes to the Arctic: a World Health Organization study reports that Inuit and other Eskimo groups have the highest incidence of dental caries in the world, and the rotten teeth of the candy counter's patrons suggested that the people of Baker Lake were no exception.

At the time of our visit, Baker Lake's population was nearly a thousand, including some nine hundred Inuit. The village ran for a mile across low hills at the northwest corner of Baker Lake, the only inland settlement north of the tree line in the Canadian Arctic. It had the untidy, half-finished look of a haphazardly constructed frontier town, a result of its recent development, the lack of concealing vegetation, and the dominating influence of prefabricated architecture. The government-built homes were a collection of brightly colored, wood-and-metal rectangles—turquoise, pink, brown, yellow, red, and white blocks perched on concrete pilings to prevent thawing of the underlying permafrost. Intermingled with the homes were metal outbuildings; four silver fuel-storage tanks dominated the skyline, along with radio communication towers and a tangle of wires strung from telephone poles lining the unpaved streets. Other notable structures included the Anglican and Roman Catholic missions, the school, the omnipresent Hudson's Bay Company store (two and a half dollars for a head of lettuce, six dollars for a cabbage), the Iglu Hotel, a lone geodesic dome, and various government buildings. As in Fort Simpson, the territorial and federal governments were much in evidence; the Department of Transport, RCMP, Fish and Wildlife Service, Department of Indian and Northern Affairs, National Health and Welfare, Atmospheric Environment Service, and several other agencies all had personnel stationed in the village. Most of the white residents were government employees; exceptions included some staff of The Bay and the Iglu Hotel, the Anglican priest and his family, the manager of the village art cooperative, and a lone Baha'i missionary, who was having little luck converting the natives but was still strong with the optimism of faith.

For a town of Baker Lake's size, so far from the nearest highway system, there was an amazing number of motorized vehicles. Three-wheeled all-terrain vehicles, driven by young and old alike, raced along the village streets. Drivers were required to wear safety helmets, and the old men and women looked particularly incongruous with their weathered faces encased in fiberglass shells. Lots of motorcycles, too, plus a few trucks, Volkswagen Beetles, Detroit-styled bulgemobiles, and one orange van. In the winter these would be replaced by flex-track vehicles and snowmobiles; at least one of the latter rested by the side of every dwelling. Many were derelicts, long ago cannibalized for parts, and they provided the same decorative charm as do rusting autos in parts of the poorer, rural South. The gasoline-powered vehicles shared the dusty roads with a rattle-trap collection of bicycles, mostly of the "Stingray" variety, and an occasional pickup baseball game.

The modern history of Baker Lake began in 1916, when the Hudson's Bay Company opened a trading post in the area. The Anglican and Roman Catholic missions followed in the late 1920s, and the Royal Canadian Mounted Police established a post in 1931. The post–World War II period has been characterized by an increasing governmental presence and the concentration of Inuit in the permanent settlement that developed around the new facilities and services—which, by 1960, included a nursing station and a federal day school. The native population was drawn from people belonging to five cultural groups with different centers of activity: two from the Garry Lake and Back River areas, one from the south of Aberdeen and Schultz lakes, one from north of Chesterfield Inlet, and one from the lower Kazan River. All of these groups traditionally relied on caribou for their sustenance, and spent relatively little time hunting in marine waters, in contrast to other Inuit groups. Within the village, there were evidently social differences; political power was primarily in the hands of people from the Baker Lake and Chesterfield Inlet areas. The Back River people were the most prolific artists, but sometimes were viewed as generally less sophisticated by the others.

The town's postwar history—combined with the noise of two- and four-cycle engines, the prefab buildings, the TV shows that could be seen in the Iglu Hotel, and even the games of street baseball—made it seem like part of the modern world, even if only at the outermost fringes. Yet scattered about were conflicting images of an older way, and a deeper connection to the land: long rows of the brilliant red flesh of filleted arctic char on drying racks, two Inuit women cutting up a caribou carcass, and the weathered faces of the old people. It had not been very long since the adults of present-day Baker Lake and their immediate ancestors were seminomadic, dependent upon fish and caribou for their livelihood, and had only minimal contact with the Outside. The biologist G.R. Parker has estimated that, historically, an Inuit family would have required 150 caribou per year to feed itself and its dogs. When caribou were abundant, life was sustained; when the caribou failed, the people died. In the 1920s, more than a hundred are said to have died from starvation, and as late as 1958, fifty-three people out of a group of eighty-four starved to death at Garry Lake, 125 miles northwest of Baker Lake. The latter incident triggered an accelerated government-sponsored movement toward permanent settlements, where adequate food supplies and better social services could be provided.

In 1958 and 1959, some of the people who had congregated in Baker Lake were relocated by what was then the Department of Northern Affairs to the Rankin Inlet area, where it was hoped that some would find employment in the newly opened nickel mine, and to the newly established Whale Cove settlement on Hudson Bay. Whatever the benefits of such programs, the transition in lifestyles for the Inuit of the Barren Grounds had been extreme. In twenty years, they had left behind their almost-absolute dependence on caribou for food; they had abandoned snow homes and caribou tents, lighted by caribou-fat lamps, as well as their dog teams and caribou-skin kayaks. These cultural fixtures, part of their lives for many generations, had been replaced by prefab homes, snowmobiles, motorized skiffs, a diet high in sugar and prepared foods, and increased access to medical care, formal education, and wage-earning jobs. While some of these changes were obviously beneficial, and probably inevitable, it was easy to see the Inuit as suspended between two opposing cultural traditions, and to find in this conflict the cause of many of the social ills that afflict northern native groups, including poor health and high rates of violent crime, suicide, and alcoholism.

There was an impermanent feeling about Baker Lake: few buildings possessed the solid feeling of the old Anglican church that acted as our windbreak. It was as though the village, resting upon its concrete pilings and gravel pads, was *on* the land, but not *of* it. (But it is neither easy nor wise to sink foundations into the rocky permafrost, or even bury people; in many northern settlements, coffins are placed above ground and covered by large piles of rocks.)

The separateness that I imagined also might have been due to Baker Lake's location; lost in thousands of square miles of superficially featureless tundra, with one location seemingly as good as another for a settlement, why had the village developed where it had? Archaeological evidence indicates that the Inuit used the area long before Captain Christopher of the Hudson's Bay Company sailed up Chesterfield Inlet and reached the head of Baker Lake in 1761, but there was little about the topography of the place to suggest a rationale for its location—no great bay, no sheltering hills to block the northern winds, no lush meadows where game might congregate. Why had the first missionaries and merchants chosen the site? Historical inertia might explain later development, with more recent arrivals simply establishing themselves around the settlement's nucleus. But the logic of the site still escaped me.

As we wandered through the town, I sensed some of the same social problems that I had in Fort Simpson, particularly the division between the natives and whites, and I heard many comments about the same issues discussed in Simpson— hunting rights, native land claims, and economic development versus preservation of traditional lifestyles and values. The ambience of Baker Lake was different; it was cleaner, with no signs of alcohol abuse, fewer loitering bands of bored adolescents, no glaring evidence of despair or vocal antagonism, but the village still seemed split into two communities that existed side by side, with surprisingly little contact beyond that dictated by employment and commerce. It wasn't a matter of two physically discrete communities, but of attitudes that varied, quite naturally, with social and economic context.

One white, who was sympathetic to the situation of the Inuit, said, "My place in the community is unique; I work closely with the Inuit, so I'm shunned by the whites. But I'm also shunned by the Inuit, because I'm not native. There's a definite social discontent within the village, although it's difficult for an outsider [there was that word again] to detect, due to the natural courtesy of the Inuit."

Another white, connected with the private sector in Baker Lake, had been in the North for a year and "liked it very much." He was less sympathetic to native viewpoints and traditions; for him, it was a matter of the Inuit yielding to the inevitability of economic development—the frontier ethic once again. He felt that most of the conflict between whites and Inuit in the village was due to "a few troublemakers"; that many of the Inuit were on welfare; and, most important, that they no longer subsisted mainly on caribou and thus had little right to demand control over their management, or to oppose mining exploration and the possible routing of a natural-gas pipeline through the area.

A friend of his agreed: "The Inuit just don't want to give up control of this last vestige of their traditional life—even if it is no longer very important." For him, the data on the caribou harvest by Inuit families in Baker Lake, gathered by both an independent consulting firm and the territorial Fish and Wildlife Service, were "crap." I asked whether the caribou's status as a remnant of a traditional lifestyle didn't automatically endow it with a crucial value that went beyond arguments about statistics and dietary importance, but he could see the issue only in terms of pounds of meat used per person.

Two biologists studying the Kaminuriak Herd had a much different perspective on the caribou "problem." Although the Beverly Herd was in good condition, with a population of about one hundred twenty-five thousand animals, and about fifty-one thousand cows had calved that summer, the Kaminuriak Herd had declined from an estimated population of more than a hundred thousand in the 1950s to around forty thousand. They attributed the decline not to mining companies (whose activities were restricted primarily to areas not used heavily by the Kaminuriak Herd) but to a complex interaction of factors, including overhunting —both by Baker Lake residents while the caribou were on the calving grounds to the south of the village, and by Indians when the caribou moved into northern Manitoba and Saskatchewan during the winter. This suggested a need for a mandated limit on the annual kill from the herd. However, such an action would have been politically inexpedient, because it would have generated conflict over who owned, and had the right to manage, the caribou—the territorial government or the natives. The people of Baker Lake had been hunting caribou for hundreds of years, long before the Canadian government began to exert political control over the Northwest Territories. Even in the twentieth century, aboriginal hunting rights had been preserved, and there had never been a regulated hunt. Thus, the biologists saw widespread resistance to the idea that the government should, or needed to, regulate hunting by the Inuit.

So some of the whites in Baker Lake said that the Inuit were taking almost no caribou; the biologists said that they were taking too many, and at the wrong time of year. The Inuit refused to accept any responsibility for the decline. They maintained that they weren't hunting excessively, and that mining companies were mostly to blame for the decline, although even the aerial surveys and tagging programs of the biologists were suspect. My tendency was to accept the data and conclusions of the biologists; the herd was in decline, and there needed to be some control over the caribou harvest if the population was to recover. However, no regulation would probably ever be achieved unless the Inuit were included in the planning and regulatory process in some meaningful way.

Perhaps the most astute observer of the community with whom we spoke was the Reverend Chris Williams, the Anglican priest. A compact, pipe-smoking, energetic man, he spoke Inuktitut fluently and was sensitive to the issues that divided the community. Originally from Manchester, England, he had come to Baker Lake with his wife and two children in 1975, after a year in Coppermine and sixteen years at Sugluk on Hudson Strait in northern Quebec. In his early years, he traveled to outlying camps by dog team, sometimes in the harshest winter conditions; now the work was less demanding physically, and filled with different concerns. His years in the North had given him an appreciation for the land; he liked the expanse and didn't mind the cold, isolation, and absence of trees.

Reverend Williams felt that the caribou were an important part of the native diet, and that some whites exaggerated their dependence on welfare: "Most adults are on and off it in the course of a year, but reliance isn't chronic and most families have at least one wage earner."

Williams worried about the deteriorating relationships between whites and natives, although the situation might not be easily visible to a casual observer. He felt that some of the Inuit, especially the younger ones, were resentful of attempts by white "Them" from the South to interfere with their lives; this resentment was then transferred to whites in the village. (Interestingly, this criticism was not much different from that sounded by whites who accused misinformed southerners of meddling in the affairs of the North.) Williams was also concerned about the drop-off in interest in the church; he said that most of the Christians were third-generation converts and less fervent in their beliefs, and that the young were not embracing the faith as easily as their parents had—this in spite of his sense that the church was "doing a good job" and working to bring more Inuit into the priesthood.

It was, of course, difficult to understand much about the dynamics of Baker Lake or make reasonable judgments about the conflicting viewpoints, "facts," and government reports. So many of the disputes, and the proffered solutions to village problems, were obviously relativistic: Reality depended upon the observer's frame of reference. Even if the members of opposing factions could agree upon a statement (e.g., "The Kaminuriak Herd is in decline."), getting them to agree on a proximal or ultimate cause for the situation would be impossible. So we drifted through the village, more or less experienced in the northern wilderness, but still novices in its social environment. I was puzzled by how frequently the whites confided in us, how willing many were to comment upon life in Baker Lake—but not at all surprised that the Inuit were distant and reticent. Like the waters of two streams, one turbid and the other clear, joining at a confluence, we flowed side by side along the same path, but did not mix. Conversations were mostly limited to "Hi!" and smiling nods substituted for more involved interactions. I wondered how those quiet people saw the Barrens, and what remained of their life on the land. The village perspective was not enough; the strength of the people lay beyond the prefab homes and cases of soda, in the world of arctic char and caribou and winter winds. . . . And how did the Inuit perceive us? As Outsiders, I'm sure, if we were registered at all. And we *were* from the Outside; it would take years of living in such a community, years of patient listening and observing, rather than asking questions, to sort out the complexities of the situation. Still, I felt closer to the people of the village, both native and nonnative, than I did to the American tourists whom we met—guys from Wisconsin, chomping on stogies, dressed in polyester slacks and international-orange rain jackets, with "Miami Fishing Tournament" patches on their baseball caps—who were on their way to Chantrey Inlet for a week of char fishing. Friendly but loud, they were aliens from another world, a world that held my memories but was severed from my present reality. Whatever that reality might be—and I saw it in terms of my relationship to the land—I felt as though I shared a portion of it with the people of Baker Lake, lost as we all were in a sea of wind-scoured tundra.

We were away from Baker Lake on July 29, paddling eastward through intermittent, drenching rains. Soaked to the skin, with our raingear leaking badly, we moved through a world painted in shades of gray—ice, low clouds, rock, and dark water, all part of a symmetrical, achromatic scene. The capricious winds shifted from the north to the southwest, and after nine miles of progress and a shivering, mosquito-plagued lunch, we were stopped by ice drifting close into the north shore. So we threw up the tents, heated a brew, and gratefully crawled into our sleeping bags, temporarily free of both unwanted "Animal Pals" and the cold.

The ice also halted an Inuit family later in the afternoon—a mother, a father, and three children on their way to the Francis River to fish. We offered them tea and cocoa as they waited for the ice to clear before winds that had shifted northward again. There was a lot of smiling back and forth among us, but little conversation; even the children seemed shy. After half an hour of waiting, they declined a dinner invitation, clambered back into their launch, and disappeared to the east. We followed later and ran until eleven P.M., when we stopped at Ingilik Point, about nineteen miles out of Baker Lake. The evening was very peaceful: only gentle breezes, a fine misting rain falling at times, a brilliant orange ribbon of light to the north, and skies that darkened to the point of night as we made camp and rushed to erect the tents before the threatening deluge began.

The following morning was an exhausting struggle against unremitting headwinds gusting to more than twenty miles per hour. At one point we covered less than a mile in an hour. As my frustration grew and my arms weakened, there was little to do but grit my teeth and paddle as hard as I could. But the wind was the price we had to pay for being able to travel: A calm day would have meant miles of ice jammed thick against the shore. And once the shore curved to the southeast, we picked up a tailwind and were able to surf the crests of following waves. The spray covers were a blessing, since they shed water from waves that rose behind the canoes, bore us downwind, and then broke around the stern. (Unlike our "miracle fabric" rainsuits, the vinyl spray covers really *were* waterproof.) Still, it was an eerie, tension-filled experience to watch the icy waters, and hypothermia, rise to within inches of the gunwales, spill over the cover, and then recede.

We made camp at six, within sight of the soapstone quarry used by Baker Lake's artisans. The day's winds had worn me down. I was tired of fighting the Barrens; my back was tight and my legs were cramped from hour after hour of paddling. And despite the exertion and thick layers of clothes, I was chilled; lunchtime temperatures had been in the high thirties, and I hadn't been able to stay warm all day. I found myself thinking of warm deserts, and the end of the trip— suddenly I wanted to be done with all the effort, and Get South. To hell with the cold, the wind, and the ice: I didn't want to wear so many damned clothes that I looked like the Michelin Tire Man in the middle of the summer. And I felt like a slob, the ultimate Bozo; my ragged pants were coming apart at the patches, the material almost too weak to repair again. My socks were mostly holes, and my underwear the color of last night's used dishwater. I was filthy, in spite of a recent shower; my beard was a receptacle for numerous chemicals and bits of debris, including cheese, bread crumbs, the sticky residues of lemonade and cocoa, bug dope, the remains of squashed mosquitoes, and dried snot. In spite of its unaesthetic qualities, I was too tired to bother with washing, and surrendered to the dirt.

My mood was not helped by the fact that I had hardly said a word to my companions all day. We were talked out; I felt used up, as though I had little energy for anything but movement and necessary conversation. I didn't want to open up to anyone, because I didn't want to expend the effort. I craved distance from the others, the opportunity to rest for weeks and regain my patience. The trip was certainly ending at the right time; I was ready for a major change. So my heart focused on motion, and I felt my imagination drawn eastward by the magnet of Hudson Bay.

Yet we couldn't travel on the following day, in spite of favorable weather, for Mike was stricken with an intestinal ailment that displayed the symptoms of appendicitis: nausea, vomiting, fever, and tenderness in the lower right quadrant of his abdomen. His condition didn't improve during the morning, but a dash back to Baker Lake was impossible, for the ice had moved into shore again. So we began administering antibiotics, spread out our bright red spray covers and orange tarp on the tundra, prepared a signal fire, and readied a mirror and small flare gun in hopes of attracting a plane or helicopter. When a helicopter passed close to camp, we lit the fire, flashed the mirror, waved red, and fired off the flare—all to no avail, as the chopper continued along its westward path. The deflated silence that followed our unsuccessful attempt emphasized our predicament. Although we were only forty miles from a settlement, we were unable to travel, and we had a potential medical emergency on our hands. Mike lay swathed in sleeping bags—silent, miserable, and unmoving—and we could do little for him except plan a quick dash back to the village as soon as the ice moved out: Two people, traveling as light as possible, could cover the distance in less than twenty-four hours. But as we waited for the ice to disperse, Mike's condition gradually improved, and Robert began reporting some of the same symptoms. So we figured that a stomach virus had landed among us, and that we could continue traveling as soon as Mike felt better.

Eastward it was, then, past Jigging Point, James Point, and Chain Islet to a camp just short of the lake's outlet, on a day filled with bright skies, scattered cumulus, and warm sun. We had the customary shifting winds—sometimes off the beam, at other times off the bow—but our energy levels were high and conditions generally moderate. Twenty-five miles passed away, and the low tundra that dominated the western end of the lake gave way to outcrops of igneous rock that tumbled toward the shore. I enjoyed the increased relief but was distracted by the refuse that we found, both at the soapstone quarry and at an abandoned mining exploration camp farther down the lake. The quarry was bad, but the old T.M.T. boys, whoever they were, had really done a job on a small patch of the Barrens. Their former camp was a cluttered tangle of metal and wood: an ancient refrigerator and stove, a hundred empty fuel barrels, piles of cylindrical core samples, warped plywood sheets, survey markers, and spools of wire. There was even a small yellow John Deere bulldozer just offshore, partly submerged in the lake; I wondered whether the driver had deposited it there in a fit of rage, furious because the claim had not paid off.

The trash saddened me. The rusting piles of junk, abandoned by both Inuit and white, would scar the Barrens for generations, and I forgave neither group. I had heard it said, and had read, that the Inuit, so recently part of a culture that had produced only biodegradable garbage, have no prohibitions against dumping refuse wherever they wish. Yet I could accept the discarded snowmobiles and sleds, and the empty cans and shredded clothing scattered around the quarry, no more easily than the piles of fuel drums that dotted the lake's shores. No cultural relativity for me; no matter who was the source of the debris, it seemed like an unnecessary violation. But perhaps I was being overly righteous and smug in my fulminations against the trash. What did those isolated islands of garbage mean, swallowed as they were by the North? Didn't the immensity of the land absorb such nuisances? Move a mile in any direction, away from the locus of abuse, and the garbage disappeared. And there was also a perverse comfort in the rusted snow-mobiles and bulldozers, for they spoke eloquently of technological transience, of how machines would fail and the Barrens would ultimately endure. An anachro-nistic view perhaps, or an affectation borne out of my good fortune in not having to depend on the Barrens for my livelihood—I didn't need to be a utilitarian and worry about repairing a snowmobile in winter, or the unnecessary expense of removing my offal from a worthless claim. Yet the lack of any effort to concentrate the rubbish or ameliorate the impact testified to casual attitudes toward the Bar-rens. Like tiny flaws in an otherwise-perfect pane of stained glass, the pockets of ugliness disrupted the pattern of light that filled the North. And even though my perception of the Barrens transcended the blemishes, I didn't care for what they suggested about the attitudes of my fellow humans.

Kurt and I scrambled up the blocky cliffs, through gardens of Labrador tea, avens, cinquefoil, and heather, to the summit of the rocky islet. At the top we stood in a hemisphere of blue sky and water; behind us was North Channel Bay and the expanse of Baker Lake, spreading westward for seventy miles. To the east, the other canoes glided through sparkling light toward the Bowell Islands, at the lake's outlet, and Chesterfield Inlet, a narrow, fingerlike projection that sliced into the west shore of Hudson Bay for more than 110 miles. It was difficult to believe that August 2 had brought us to a point where we could gaze toward our final path, that an after-noon's paddle would lead us, on a gentle current, through intimate channels of rock into the brackish waters of the inlet. We were getting close; we covered twenty-six miles that day, to the mouth of the Quoich River, and we figured that four more days might see us through to the village of Chesterfield Inlet.

We followed the northern shore of the inlet for two and a half days, through fifty miles of low, rocky country full of sedge-ringed ponds and exposed granite knobs dotted with erratics and fields of brightly colored lichens—Canadian Shield country stripped bare by glaciers and kept that way by wind and cold. Marine animals became more common as we moved toward Hudson Bay—flocks of com-mon eiders; black guillemots, relatives of gulls, their bright red feet and mouthparts contrasting with black-and-white plumage; herring gulls; arctic terns; oldsquaw ducks; and ringed seals.

Traveling on salt water meant that we had to change the rhythm of our pad-dling and consider two factors that had not concerned us previously—the avail-ability of fresh water when we camped, and the tides. These had a vertical change of more than six feet in some parts of Chesterfield Inlet, which meant easy paddling as they ebbed and hard going when they switched directions and began flowing up the inlet. So we ran with the tides or paddled on slack water whenever possible, and adjusted our schedule accordingly. The mixture of wind and tide generated some tricky paddling conditions, particularly when incoming and outgoing tides met, including odd vortices of swirling waters and opposing series of irregular waves. On several occasions, wind-driven offshore waves broke across the beam while other, tide-generated ones crashed over the bow and stern; without the spray covers, we would have been awash.

My impatient desire to be done with the paddling had fled with the worst of the wind and rain, but I was still looking toward the end, as we all seemed to be. There was little enthusiasm for exploration, and when the tides and winds were cooperative, there were no disagreements among us about traveling. So on August 5 we were up early, roused by arctic terns screeching from atop our tents, and primed for a long push toward Hudson Bay. We were away from camp by seven, working furiously against a brisk wind and hugging the north shore for shelter on another gray and chilly day. The winds subsided for several hours, then shifted direction until they were out of the northwest; we bolted down a quick lunch and set off for Ekatuvik Point, on the south side of Chesterfield Inlet. The crossing was necessary, as our final destination was located just south of the inlet on Hudson Bay. We could have crossed easily at one of the many narrow points farther up the inlet, but we were reluctant to forsake the north shore and the meager shelter that it provided from the prevailing winds. Ekatuvik Point was our last opportunity for a relatively short crossing; from there, the inlet began to widen appreciably. So fortune was with us—following winds and a strong current pushed us across the channel, past an odd, churning vortex of powerful waves and eddies created by the opposing currents of the incoming and outgoing tides.

The afternoon turned warm and calm and we all stripped to the waist as we worked our way through a narrow passage separating Big Island from the mainland. It was odd to see the contrast between the pasty white skin of our backs, exposed to the sun only a few times in the last year, and our tanned and weathered faces. But what a delight the sun was, after the many weeks of wool shirts and long underwear—how wonderful to let my skin breathe! The paddling was pleasurable and we continued traveling even though the tide had shifted against us; it had little strength in the channel and we made steady progress before stopping for dinner and an extended conversation with the mosquitoes. We were off again a few hours later, through a channel lined with glacier-scoured rock, on water so still that I could trace quartz intrusions diving twenty feet or more below the surface. We paddled late into the evening and camped opposite Moore Island, long after the sun had set, when our canoes were no more than silhouettes against the western horizon—eighteen hours after starting the day and more than forty miles closer to our goal. The soft half-light and our tiredness made it difficult to pick out decent spots for the tents, so we erected them wherever the ground appeared at all forgiving, and crawled in for a rocky sleep on what we figured would be our last night on the trail.

Somehow, I awoke after only five hours of sleep; I was very groggy, but the thought of paddling with the outgoing tide was more enticing than a few more hours in the bag. We collapsed the tents and packed our gear in a rush, then downed a quick breakfast of biscuits and granola—cereal baked fifteen months earlier in Seattle and transported to Chesterfield Inlet via Hay River, Fort Reliance, Warden's Grove, and the Thelon River. . . . As we were eating, Gary gave a yell: "There's a whale!" A large dorsal fin sliced through the water like a black sail, disappeared, then rose once again. The great beast moved slowly, with an aura of powerful grace, its path a gliding undulation along the surface of the passage. For fifteen minutes we stood transfixed, silent, listening to the gentle waves rolling away from the whale's path, and the great pulses of air expelled from its blowhole.

On this, our last morning, the whale's appearance seemed like an omen of good fortune, an indication that all would go well. And so it did. We had come six hundred miles in thirty days, almost all of them windy, gray, wet, and cold—days that called for thick layers of clothing and a constant effort to move. But August 6 was different—a perfect day, without a breeze or cloud. We had to paddle out onto the waters of Hudson Bay, and around the exposed headlands marked by Jaeger and Finger points, and any northerly winds would have made traveling difficult, if not impossible. Yet there was only sun and absolute calm on what must have been the most perfect day of an otherwise stormy summer.

We were away by seven, chased by mosquitoes, drowsy with exertion and lack of sleep, slowly waking to the fact that we were on the verge of an ending. We passed to the inside of Ellis Island, then stopped at Observation Point and scrambled up the rocks to view the route ahead. The last points of land disappeared into a haze twenty miles to the east, as the waters of the inlet spread into the open sea: We had reached Hudson Bay. Mike was enthused; he extolled the beauty of the view and all it symbolized, and his joy at being so close to our goal. The rest of us were more laconic; to Mike we were "about as sentimental as a bowl of dog food."

Gary said nothing and swatted at mosquitoes; Kurt replied that he was "too tired to be sentimental." I sat down and opened a letter marked "Do not open until Hudson Bay," sent to me by a friend months earlier. Inside was a note of congratulations on having reached the endless blue waters that I had dreamed of for so long. I rose and looked out over the bay, then turned and faced up Chesterfield Inlet. I thought for a moment about Macmillan River crossing number 2, and contrasted it with the view from Observation Point: images separated by fourteen months and more than two thousand miles—the first looking eastward, the second westward. I felt that I was at the end of a long river; in its headwaters I'd been an innocent, filled with naive excitement, and with no clear idea about what lay ahead. Now that I'd reached the mouth of the great stream, my initial excitement had been replaced by a peace that reflected the morning's calm. The journey was almost over. . . .

And then we were moving again, paddling into an endless, halcyon sea. The inlet stretched before us, widening into the huge expanse of the bay. No breeze touched the mirrored surface; the tide, much weaker than it had been farther west, helped carry us into the warm sun, through vast kelp beds that rocked with the water's gentle flux. Female eiders and their broods of downy young fled before us with a panic of flapping wings. Ringed seals surfaced twenty yards away; regarded us with dark, luminous eyes; and disappeared if we stopped paddling and turned to watch them. They remained curious, though, and continued to follow us down the inlet at a respectable distance—sleek, silent watchers made wary by countless generations as prey for polar bears and Inuit.

On and on we paddled on that perfect morning, squinting into the sun and the blinding glare of its reflection. Ellis Island and Observation Point dropped slowly away from us; points of land lingered in the distance and seemed to grow no closer with our strokes. The low, rocky boundaries of the shore receded into thin, brown lines, and the waters of the bay blended with the sky. And finally there was no horizon, only a pale blue mingling of sky and sea: We were paddling into a void, into a world without spatial boundaries, where time was irrelevant. I imagined that the canoeing would go on and on, that we would remain forever suspended between two vertical planes, seeking an end that would never come as we ran eastward along a path of light and water. As close as we were to a village, it was hard to believe that we would ever stop paddling. We were 465 days out from the Canol Road, and the journey had long before transcended simple movement, had been transformed into a way of life—and an attitude.

But the end did come—after we passed Ptarmigan Island, Goose Point, Jaeger Point, and then Finger Point. We swung around a final promontory, into the small bay that sheltered the settlement of Chesterfield Inlet, and paddled toward the red-roofed buildings of the Hudson's Bay Company. As the last minutes of the journey disappeared, there was no great ecstasy in me, no spontaneous upwelling of emotion, not even a moment of silent contemplation. The end was, out of necessity, anticlimactic, for how could one moment ever match or summarize what had come before? The end was marked more by the absence of definitive emotion than by its presence; exaltation was replaced by the satisfaction of having attained my goal, and a quiet happiness.

The end: around a final point of land, and there was the settlement, a collection of buildings a half-mile distant. Fourteen months in the North, and twenty-two hundred miles, gone. . . . The end: the bow of our canoe ground against the shingled beach and I hopped ashore, wanting more from my heart than it could possibly deliver, knowing that there would never be more than a smile, and a simple acknowledgment that the paddling was finished. . . . The end: sitting in the

Hudson's Bay Company manager's home, devouring oranges and ice cream, while rock 'n' roll blared from his stereo. Still in the North, I recognized an obvious division that separated the preceding fourteen months from all that would follow, and one way of thinking and being from another. In a few days there would be plane rides, hassles with money, and final partings. There would be no more Barrens, no more canoeing: back to the South, and another life. Grateful to be done with the journey, and ready to move on to other things, I still confronted a future as empty and ghostlike as the morning's vague horizon, for I had stepped suddenly from a familiar world into one that had become alien to me. A creature of the North, metamorphosing into someone else: I took a bite of ice cream, felt its cool slide down my throat, and imagined the North slipping away from me, vanishing like a glistening whale diving dreamlike into silent arctic waters.

CHAPTER THIRTEEN
Aftermath

I imagine myself confronting a skeptic, and his obvious question: "Why bother?"
Why devote more than a year of my life to the wind, the cold, the isolation, the
insects? How could I justify this ridiculous endeavor, either by reference to some
vague interior significance, or fanciful benefits that might accrue to "society"?
I could not, and what I keep coming back to, in my search for justification, is
this: for every person, whether in New York City or on the Barrens, there exists
a personal Odyssey. And to whatever extent joy and satisfaction are possible
in this life, they are a result of this quest. There is only the journey, the love that
is poured into it, and that which is given out in return.
—Journal entry, August 17, 1977

THE TRIP SOUTH BEGAN on August 9, after a last-minute infusion of funds into
our exhausted account allowed the lot of us to board a Twin Otter for Rankin Inlet;
our canoes were to be barged to the railhead at Churchill in early September.
During the flight we had our final glimpses of graveled gray eskers running vector-
like across the Barrens, transparent blue lakes whitecapping in the wind, and
Hudson Bay off to the east—country that was already receding into my past. A
short flight—up and down, really—but also a rough one. My head swam, my
stomach rolled, and I marveled at our progress: sixty miles in less than thirty
minutes, a distance that would have required two full days of paddling in favorable
weather. We had passed into a different realm; the same calculus applied—change
in distance divided by change in time—but no personal energy expenditure was
involved, and movement was measured in miles per minute instead of miles per day.

We spent a day in Rankin, hopped a turboprop bound for Churchill, then
camped for two days by the airport—cooking our meals in the shelter of an

abandoned outhouse, waiting for the next empty seats on a southward flight, and worrying just a bit about marauding polar bears. (According to the locals, the bears were common and grouchy after months of being marooned ashore in a sealless world.) Finally, we were off for Winnipeg on August 12. The jet's rapid acceleration, with the slight sensation of g-forces and the blurring of runway markers, launched me across the boundaries of a final transition, a process that had begun six days earlier in Chesterfield Inlet. It had been a restless game of waiting, played out at the margins of northern airstrips, but the good people whom we met were compensation enough. The manager of the Hudson's Bay Company post in Chesterfield, who offered us lunches, a bottomless coffeepot, his stereo, and endless anecdotes about his previous job in the bush of northern Ontario; the Chesterfield postmistress, who sent our last bits of mail south to Rankin in a freight canoe, in the hopes that it might catch up with us. The manager of the Calm Air facility in Rankin, who supplied us with cold beer, showers, and sarcastic humor. The cab driver in Churchill, who offered us a ride, free of charge, because he was "going that ways anyhow." The woman who ran the fast-food stand in Churchill, who brought us hamburgers and fries as we were about to clamber onto the flight for Winnipeg—the best possible nourishment for the transition to a more southerly environment and frame of mind.

We scattered in Winnipeg. Robert, enigmatic to the end, broke first—in the terminal immediately after disembarking from the Churchill flight. There he offered a hurried round of handshakes and perfunctory good-byes before vanishing into the milling crowds. He was gone quickly, without prior notice or explanation, his motives and thoughts as private as they'd ever been. The nature of his parting left me puzzled and slightly saddened; it was as though the previous fourteen months could be shoved aside easily and dispensed with. The rest of us spent several days in the city, entertained and fed to the bursting point by friends of John's and subjected to eleven psychological tests administered by Frances Parks—tests for which I had even less patience than before the trip. Afterward, we went our separate ways, members of a tentative family no longer bound together by a common goal: Gary and John to Illinois and their families, Kurt to a job at the Minnesota Outward Bound School, Mike to Arizona and family, myself to visit friends in Montana. Soon we would embrace the patterns of our former lives; we would be among friends and family, enmeshed in jobs and perhaps involved in new romantic relationships. Civilization would claim us.

Several months later, I would find it difficult to believe how quickly and completely I had made the transition. My vision had been focused on the North for so long—and my heart turned toward latitudes of cold, windy space—that I expected the reentry into society to be a slow and very painful process. But the thoughts and experiences of the journey all too quickly became part of the receding murmur of personal history, and I had little trouble adapting to what I had very recently labeled the "Outside."

Yet I could not allow myself to believe that the journey would ever be reduced to mere nostalgia, to a narrative recorded on journal pages and cataloged transparencies. I believed, as I do now, that the spirit of the journey would endure—perhaps not in ways that could be quantified by psychological tests and noted as behavioral changes, but in differences in the way I viewed my connection to the land. There would always be a more intimate, heartfelt bond to the natural world, a deeper sense of belonging. And out of this relationship grew a corresponding concern for the fragility of the North and its wilderness; Cosmos alone had given me that much. There were also the lessons relating to the journey as a shared experience—the sometimes-painful reminders of the importance of personal honesty and integrity in decision and action, the absolute necessity of making expectations clear and talking about frustration and anger. Yet beyond these rather obvious caveats—demonstrable in almost all human interactions and without recourse to fourteen months in the wilderness—lay a more valuable dividend. For I had been bonded to the five others with whom I had shared the trip. Even though the six of us did not emerge from the Barrens as a harmonious collection of close friends, our common experience had nurtured connections that would endure. I strongly believed that the friendships that had developed during the journey would continue, perhaps despite years without contact, and I cherished this faith. But I saw something else—a recognition that comes from having lived through a unique and powerful time together. If I were to meet John, Kurt, Gary, Mike, or Robert for the first time in thirty years, I believe there would still be a mutual recognition—a feeling that, despite our differences, there was something about having come so far and seen so much together that bound us to one another and set us apart form others.

I have a photograph of the six of us at Finger Point on Hudson Bay, taken with a self-timer on the last day of the journey. Robert, Kurt, and John crouch in the foreground; Mike, Gary, and I stand to the rear. Behind us, partly concealed, are the three canoes and the great blue plane of Hudson Bay. It is a standard expedition photograph—assorted dirty and disheveled types, happy to have achieved their goal and united, at least temporarily, by the realization of "success." Thus, we are all smiling. But smiles are part of a human formula, and across the intervening years I search my own face, and those of my companions, to try to fathom the depth of our emotions, the feelings of that moment. It is easy to resurrect the physical sensations of the place—the smell of salt air; the gray, glacier-scoured rock underfoot; the gentle breeze just brushing the surface of the bay; the deliciously warm sun. The photograph is clear on much of this, and of course I've experienced similar conditions many times. But what to make of those smiles—grins that seem to express quiet joy rather than wild exaltation? So it was for me, although I never asked any of the others, "Just how does it feel to you, right now?" I wonder whether those smiles measure the worth of the journey, or simply register a relief at being done with all that bloody paddling. Were our eyes focused on the present or did they look beyond, either into the previous fourteen months or down the paths that rolled away from us, into the future? I don't know. I can't answer that question, except for myself, and there are times when I even question the accuracy of my own recall about the moment at Finger Point—distorted as it might be by time, a journal that is silent on the subject, and a slight nostalgic haze.

Yet one thing is very clear: What the photograph represents—fourteen months in the wilderness of the North, and the realization of a dream—is as precious to me as anything in my life, past or present. For hidden within the tangled strands of the journey and its more negative aspects—the conflicting desires, the frustrations, the lapses in judgment, and perhaps even the somewhat selfish nature of our quest—is a tiny grain of purity. This purity has little to do with the arrogant pride that can grow out of an ego-gratifying experience, the tendency to imagine some great significance attached to one's exploits in the wilder reaches of this planet. For me it's simply an acknowledgment of, and thanks for, having reached a deeply desired end and glimpsed a fragile, yet enduring, beauty along the way. In all that I have done since the journey, this purity has helped sustain me, and I trust that, in whatever may follow, I shall always remember.

Epilogue

THE BIOLOGIST C.H.D. CLARKE spent the summers of 1936 and 1937 exploring the Thelon Game Sanctuary, and he grew to love the Barren Grounds. He knew the country when it was still fresh and mostly empty, and near the end of his life he wrote, "To me the Sanctuary will always be what it was in my time." It is difficult not to be nostalgic about a special time and place, not to resent and fear change. It was true for Clarke, and it is true for me when I think about my stay at Warden's Grove. I have not returned to the Thelon since the end of my journey, and I wonder how the intervening ten years have affected the area. I imagine that the tundra looks and feels much the same as it did then, with an enigmatic beauty born out of harshness and isolation, a land of bitter winds and vast distances, where peace and fragility blossom in treasured pockets. Wildlife biologists report that musk-oxen are thriving, and that the Beverly caribou herd is healthy. Moose, which moved into the Thelon River Valley from forested areas to the south in the 1970s, are increasing. I would also guess that the scars left by Camp Garland are disappearing, as willows sprout from rootstalks and sedges reestablish themselves along the shores of Cosmos Lake. Today few people recall much about Cosmos 954 ("Hey, it sounds like a soccer team!"), and fewer yet would be able to locate the site without knowing exactly where to look.

A friend who paddled the Thelon River in 1979 told me that the cabin and cache at Warden's Grove had been destroyed by grizzly bears, their roofs torn off and contents scattered. The log book, with its record of passing canoe parties and detailed chronicle of our residence, had disappeared. What the bears did not ruin certainly has suffered from ten years of exposure to rain, thaw, and slushy autumn snows. Perhaps Warden's Grove will someday resemble Hornby Point without the graves; visitors will wonder about the history of the ruins, and imagine the ghosts of past residents.

There must be more air traffic in the area now—Twin Otters and Single Beavers ferrying mining geologists and canoeists across the Barrens. At least one canoeist's guide to the Hanbury and Thelon rivers has been published, and two commercial outfitters operate in the area. Whereas no more than a handful of canoeists paddled the Thelon River each season during the 1960s and 1970s, perhaps fifteen parties now do so during an average summer. More visitors will surely follow, reassured and attracted by advertisements and printed descriptions of the route, and by the stories of friends. Will the truly empty lands, those places where one can go months without seeing another human being, vanish? I pray that

240

they will not disappear entirely—that the Thelon Game Sanctuary from September until June, and the rivers that flow northward into Queen Maud Gulf from the height of land beyond the Back River, will remain free of all but a determined few.

More people. An inevitable change, and one that saddens me. Yet I can accept the change because it does not violate the integrity of the Barren Grounds. And the misanthrope in me can look elsewhere if need be. People should visit the Thelon Game Sanctuary if they are willing to do so in a manner that is compatible with the spirit of the place. They should learn to love the sanctuary and be willing to fight for its protection. For there are other changes in the works, changes that could affect how the sanctuary is managed and destroy much of what is special about it.

The Thelon Game Sanctuary currently is the only area within the tundra or boreal forest-tundra ecotone of the mainland Northwest Territories that protects an entire ecosystem—plants, animals, and the environment that supports them. As such, it is a valuable natural laboratory for studying ecological processes unaffected by human activity. The exceptional character of the area, particularly the vegetation of the Thelon River Valley, led Canadian biologists in 1975 to propose that a portion of the sanctuary be registered as an International Biological Program Ecological Site. The sanctuary is arguably the richest area for mammalian wildlife on the tundra. It protects the most commonly used spring migration corridor, post-calving range, and water crossings of the Beverly caribou herd. Although in recent years the Beverly Herd has used calving grounds outside of the sanctuary, calving areas within its boundaries used during the 1950s and 1960s could become important again. The sanctuary still harbors a large musk-ox population, believed to have stabilized at approximately six hundred animals. Important denning habitat for Barren Grounds grizzlies, wolves, and arctic foxes occurs along the Thelon, Clarke, and Back rivers and in the vicinity of Beverly Lake. The sanctuary also protects important nesting sites for three raptors—rough-legged hawks, gyrfalcons, and peregrine falcons—and supports one of the highest concentrations of moulting Canada geese in the Northwest Territories.

Hunting and trapping have been prohibited since 1927, when the sanctuary was established by Order in Council, and disposition of surface and subsurface mineral rights was withdrawn by a second Order in Council in 1930. In this latter aspect the Thelon Game Sanctuary is unique, because mineral and oil exploration are not specifically prohibited in other Northwest Territories wildlife sanctuaries. In 1948 responsibility for administering the Thelon Game Sanctuary passed from the federal government to the Northwest Territories government; all resource extraction remained prohibited, and only those licensed by the territorial government could enter. This requirement was rescinded by the 1978 N.W.T. Wildlife Ordinance, which revised territorial wildlife management policies. Access by recreational canoeists to the Thelon Game Sanctuary became easier, but the statute retained prohibitions against mining, hunting, and trapping. The management policies in effect since 1930 have also ensured that the Thelon Game Sanctuary has remained a wilderness, unspoiled by development and resource exploitation. No other areas in the Northwest Territories, aside from four national parks, are so well protected.

Even so, the area cannot be considered secure from future exploitation. In 1956, under pressure from mining companies, the territorial government deleted about 5,800 square miles from the southwestern portion of the sanctuary. Additional land to the north and southeast was added to the sanctuary in exchange, but the message is clear: The boundaries and management of the Thelon sanctuary can be influenced by mining and other special-interest groups. This is cause for great concern, because the status of the Thelon Game Sanctuary is currently under review by the federal and territorial governments, as a result of the release of the "Northern Mineral Policy" by the Minister of Indian Affairs and Northern Development in 1986. The intent of this policy is to maximize "the land area available for mineral exploration and development, while ensuring that unique and representative natural features of land, cultural and wildlife resources are protected." One directive of the policy mandates a review of the status of all game and bird sanctuaries and proposed International Biological Program Ecological Sites in the Northwest Territories with the goal of allowing the widest range of activities compatible with wildlife protection—multiple use, in other words. Multiple use is the doctrine that has guided the United States Forest Service for decades in its efforts to reconcile conflicting land-use activities, including mining, timber harvesting, grazing, wildlife and watershed conservation, recreation, and protection of scenic resources. In this difficult balancing act, more often than not, conservation loses out to purely economic interests in the National Forests. The 1956 changes in the boundaries of the Thelon Game Sanctuary leave no doubt that the same thing could happen in the Northwest Territories in the 1990s.

As I write this epilogue, it is unclear what the outcome of the review process will be for the Thelon Game Sanctuary. The final report *could* recommend no change in the status of the sanctuary. The "worst-case" scenario would open it to hunting, trapping, and unlimited mineral exploration, while protecting wildlife under existing territorial and federal statutes. None of these activities, if properly monitored, would *necessarily* cause excessive damage to wildlife populations. The number of hunters and trappers entering the sanctuary could be regulated and strict quotas enforced for species such as caribou, musk-ox, and grizzly bear. Development of mineral claims could be prohibited in or near critical wildlife habitat— the important denning sites for bears and wolves, the lush willow stands along the Thelon River where musk-oxen feed during the summer, or the calving grounds, migration routes, and water crossings used by the Beverly caribou herd. The animals would persevere. But as a biologist, I would prefer to see the sanctuary remain as it is—a unique natural area protecting a northern ecosystem from all economic development, including trapping and hunting. Although hunting and trapping are important to the economies and cultures of the Dene and Inuit, historical records suggest that most of what is now the Thelon Game Sanctuary, including the Thelon River Valley between the junction of the Thelon and Hanbury rivers and the western end of Beverly Lake, was little used by either Chipewyans or Caribou Inuit after the 1850s. Because for 130 years little hunting or trapping has occurred in much of the area currently within the sanctuary's boundaries, it seems reasonable to propose that wildlife in the Thelon Game Sanctuary could be protected from all harvesting without harming local economies.

Subsistence hunting and trapping could have some influence on the character of the Thelon Game Sanctuary, but opening the area to mining would have a much more profound effect, much as proposed petroleum exploration and development would irretrievably damage the coastal plain of the Arctic National Wildlife Refuge in northern Alaska. Because mining has been prohibited in the Thelon Game Sanctuary, there have been no thorough surveys of its mineral potential. However, significant uranium deposits do exist elsewhere in the Thelon Basin, and economically important ore bodies may also lie within the sanctuary. Prospecting permits have been issued to the southwest of the sanctuary near Beaverhill and Eyeberry lakes, to the southeast near Dubawnt Lake, and to the northeast from Schultz Lake to Garry Lake. Currently, 110 permits and twenty blocks of claims in good standing are on file with the Department of Indian Affairs and Northern Development for prospects within fifteen miles of the Thelon Game Sanctuary boundaries. The most promising deposits found to date are approximately twenty miles south of Schultz Lake and sixty miles east of the sanctuary boundary, at the site of the proposed Kiggavik mine. Urangesellschaft Canada Limited, developer of the mine, estimates total reserves at Kiggavik to be 48 million pounds of uranium, with an *in situ* value of over three billion dollars and a production life of at least ten years.

The impact of a similar development within the Thelon Game Sanctuary can be imagined by reading Urangesellschaft's summary report on Kiggavik, which proposes two open-pit mines, with a total of fifteen thousand metric tons of material being removed per day. Other planned facilities include a milling plant, a mile-long tailings pond, accommodations for a work force of 250, a 6500-foot-long airstrip, a marine terminal in Chesterfield Inlet capable of handling 400-foot-long barges or ocean-going tankers, and a 120-mile-long winter road over tundra and lake ice linking the mine and dock facilities. An estimated one thousand vehicle trips with tractor-trailers or fuel tankers would be made each winter. If approved, Kiggavik would be the world's first open-pit uranium mine to be dug in continuous permafrost. Lack of experience with open-pit mining in permafrost, and the numerous containment problems that have plagued other uranium mines, raise numerous environmental questions.

Residents of Baker Lake, forty-five miles downwind and downstream of Kiggavik, and Inuit communities along the coast of Hudson Bay are concerned about the mine's effects on their health and traditional livelihood. They fear air and water pollution by radioactive waste, contamination of tundra vegetation, and an adverse impact on caribou populations, although the proposed site currently is not used heavily by either the Beverly or Kaminuriak herd. They are also concerned because the developers premise federal ownership of the site and ignore Inuit land claims in the area. Whether to proceed with the Kiggavik project is a contentious issue, particularly in an area where the unemployment rate is officially estimated at over fifty percent. The matter will be argued about by governmental review panels and in community meetings in the North, and a final decision on Kiggavik by the federal government is not expected until at least the end of 1990.

Another mine or winter road; the opening of the only fully protected sanctuary in the Barrens to hunting, trapping, and mineral exploration—who cares? The northern economy needs the additional employment and business opportunities, even though many of the jobs and contracts related to the mining and petroleum industries go to southern companies and workers. And there will always be other wilderness areas, other godforsaken places protected by their isolation and harsh climate. There is so much "useless" land out there among the windswept lakes, rolling tundra, and wandering rivers. . . .

But the space is not limitless. Wide, high-bedded gravel roads push north to the Arctic Ocean at Prudhoe Bay and Inuvik on the Mackenzie River Delta. The lights of drill rigs shine out into the winter night on the Beaufort Sea, the North Slope of the Brooks Range, and the sea ice north of Melville Island in the Canadian Arctic Archipelago. There is a lead-zinc mine on Baffin Island and another on Little Cornwallis Island at 75 degrees north latitude. Seismic lines for petroleum exploration slash through the boreal forests of the Mackenzie Basin and run right to the boundaries of Nahanni National Park. A four-hundred-mile-long winter road snakes north from Yellowknife, across the Barren Grounds, to the Lupin gold mine on Contwoyto Lake. And I cannot forget that a nuclear-powered satellite once tumbled from the sky, scattering bits of its radioactive carcass from Great Slave Lake to Baker Lake. Technology, if not omnipotent, at least seems to be omnipresent.

In the conclusion of his report on the Thelon Game Sanctuary, C.H.D. Clarke wrote, "We should always be careful that in our search for new resources we do not destroy what we already have." Today northern industrial development has reached a level that Clarke could have scarcely imagined in 1940, when his report was published. Resource extraction is central to the northern economy, at least that portion of the economy beyond the hunting and fishing camps scattered across the bush. Given favorable economic conditions, sophisticated technologies permit development of oil, gas, and mineral reserves anywhere in the North. Isolation and a harsh climate no longer offer much protection to unique parts of the Arctic landscape. And so surely, somewhere in the 500,000 square miles of tundra and forest-tundra ecotone on the mainland of the Northwest Territories, there is room for *one* Thelon Game Sanctuary as presently managed—for one twenty-one-thousand-square-mile preserve kept free of all exploitation. Surely we possess enough foresight to protect something of the northern wilderness. Surely there is room in the hearts of those who will determine the fate of the Thelon Game Sanctuary for a place where humans are not ascendant over the earth, where they can embrace a relationship to the land that involves more than economic considerations alone.

May the spirit of the Barren Grounds endure.

Lawrence, Kansas
January, 1989

For further information on the status of the Thelon Game Sanctuary and how to help preserve it, contact:

Canadian Arctic Resources Committee, 111 Sparks Street, 4th Floor, Ottawa, Ontario, Canada K1P 5B5

Canadian Wildlife Federation, 1673 Carling Avenue, Ottawa, Ontario K2A 3Z1

For further information of the Kiggavik mine proposal, contact:

Keewatin Regional Uranium Intervention Coordinating Committee, P.O. Box 113, Rankin Inlet, NWT X0C 0G0

Pollution Probe Foundation, 12 Madison Avenue, Toronto, Ontario M5R 2S1

Bibliography

THE LITERATURE OF THE arctic and sub-arctic regions of Canada and Alaska is as vast as the land itself. The titles given here were useful in the preparation of this book, but do not represent an extensive bibliography even of the Barren Grounds. Most of the sources pertain to the exploration, ecology, or sociology of the Canadian mainland north of the sixtieth parallel. A few, such as Barry Lopez's *Arctic Dreams* and Richard Nelson's *Make Prayers to the Raven*, deal only indirectly with this region; however, they have helped refine the "sense of place" that grew out of my experiences during the Traverse of the Northwest, and are invaluable reading for anyone interested in northern peoples and landscapes.

Back, George. *Narrative of the Arctic Land Expedition to the Mouth of the Great Fish River.* London: John Murray, 1836.

Berger, Thomas. *Northern Frontier, Northern Homeland: The Report of the Mackenzie Valley Pipeline Inquiry*, vols. 1 and 2. Ottawa: Information Canada, 1977.

Calef, George. *Caribou and the Barren-lands.* Scarborough, Ontario: Firefly Books, 1981.

Christian, Edgar. *Unflinching.* London: John Murray, 1937.

Clarke, C.H.D. *A Biological Investigation of the Thelon Game Sanctuary.* Ottawa: National Museum of Canada, Bulletin no. 96, 1940.

de Coccola, Raymond, and Paul King. *The Incredible Eskimo: Life Among the Barren Land Eskimo.* Surrey, British Columbia: Hancock House, 1986.

Douglas, George. *Lands Forlorn.* New York: G.P. Putnam's Sons, 1914.

Downes, P.G. *Sleeping Island.* New York: Coward-McCann, 1943.

Eng, Marvin, *et al. Known Resource Values of the Thelon Game Sanctuary: A Preliminary Review.* Calgary: Delta Environmental Management Group Ltd., 1988.

Gordon, B.H.C. *Of Men and Herds in Barren-ground Prehistory.* Ottawa: National Museum of Man Mercury Series, no. 28, 1975.

Gray, David. "Social Organization and Behaviour of Muskoxen (*Ovibus moschatus*) on Bathurst Island, N.W.T." Ph.D. dissertation. Edmonton: University of Alberta, 1973.

Bibliography

Hanbury, David. *Sport and Travel in the Northland of Canada.* London: Edward Arnold, 1904.

Hearne, Samuel. "A Journey from Prince of Wales's Fort to the Northern Ocean." Edited by Farley Mowat in *Coppermine Journey.* Toronto: McClelland and Stewart, 1958. .

Hoare, W.H.B. *Conserving Canada's Musk-Oxen: Being an Account of an Investigation of the Thelon Game Sanctuary 1928–1929.* Ottawa: Department of the Interior, 1930.

Hodgins, Bruce, and Margaret Hobbs. *Nastawgan: The Canadian North by Canoe and Snowshoe.* Toronto: Betelgeuse Books, 1985.

Jenness, Diamond. *Indians of Canada,* 7th ed. Toronto: University of Toronto Press, 1977.

Kelsall, John. *The Migratory Barren-ground Caribou of Canada.* Ottawa: Queen's Printer, 1968.

Kuyt, Ernie. *Food Habits and Ecology of Wolves on Barren-ground Caribou Range in the Northwest Territories.* Canadian Wildlife Service Report Series, no. 21. Ottawa: Information Canada, 1972.

Kuyt, Ernie. "Distribution and Breeding Biology of Raptors in the Thelon River Area, Northwest Territories, 1957–1969." *Canadian Field-Naturalist* 94 (1980): 121–30.

Larsen, James. "Vegetation of Fort Reliance, Northwest Territories." *Canadian Field-Naturalist* 85 (1971): 147–78.

Lopez, Barry. *Arctic Dreams.* New York: Charles Scribner's Sons, 1986.

MacKinnon, C.S. "A history of the Thelon Game Sanctuary." *Musk-ox* 32 (1983): 44–61.

Miller, F.L., and E. Broughton. *Calf Mortality on the Calving Ground of Kaminuriak Caribou.* Canadian Wildlife Service Report Series, no. 26. Ottawa: Information Canada, 1974.

Mowat, Farley. *Tundra.* Toronto: McClelland and Stewart, 1973.

Nelson, Richard. *Make Prayers to the Raven: A Koyukon View of the Northern Forest.* Chicago: University of Chicago Press, 1983.

Parker, G.R. *Biology of the Kaminuriak Population of Barren-ground Caribou. Part 1: Total Numbers, Mortality, Recruitment, and Seasonal Distribution.* Canadian Wildlife Report Series, no. 20. Ottawa, Information Canada, 1972.

Patterson, R.M. *Dangerous River.* New York: William Sloan, 1954.

Pike, Warburton. *The Barren Ground of Northern Canada.* New York: MacMillan, 1892.

Project Concept Description of the Kiggavik (Lone Gull) Uranium Mine: Summary Report. Toronto: Beak Consultants Ltd. and Urangesellschaft Ltd., 1988.

Sage, Bryan. *The Arctic and Its Wildlife.* New York: Facts on File, 1986.

Smith, James, and Ernest Burch, Jr. "Chipewyan and Inuit in the Central Canadian Subarctic, 1613–1977." *Arctic Anthropology* 16, no. 2 (1979): 76–101.

Tener, J.S. *Muskoxen in Canada.* Ottawa: Queen's Printer, 1965.

Tyrrell, James. *Across the Sub-arctic of Canada.* Toronto: William Briggs, 1897.

United States Department of Energy. *Operation Morning Light: A Non-technical Summary of U.S. Participation.* Washington, D.C.: U.S. Government Printing Office, 1978.

Whalley, George. *The Legend of John Hornby.* London: John Murray, 1962.